The Unread Vision

The Liturgical Movement
in the United States of America:
1926–1955

Keith F. Pecklers, S.J.

A Liturgical Press Book

THE LITURGICAL PRESS
Collegeville, Minnesota

Cover design by David Manahan, O.S.B. Illustration by Clemens Schmidt.

1   2   3   4   5   6   7   8   9

Library of Congress Cataloging-in-Publication Data

Pecklers, Keith F., 1958–
    The unread vision : the liturgical movement in the United States
of America, 1926–1955 / Keith F. Pecklers.
        p.   cm.
    Includes bibliographical references and index.
    ISBN 0-8146-2450-2 (alk. paper)
    1. Liturgical movement—Catholic Church—History—20th century.
    2. Catholic Church—United States—Liturgy—History—20th century.
    I. Title.
    BX1977.U6P43   1998
    282'.73'0904—dc21   97-41220
                                                                          CIP

The Unread Vision

*To my mother, my brother, Michael,
and the memory of my father*

Contents

Abbreviations

CA	Catholic Action
CFM	Christian Family Movement
CW	The Catholic Worker
ER	*Ecclesiastical Review*
FH	Friendship House
HPR	*Homiletic and Pastoral Review*
LA	*Liturgical Arts*
NCRLC	National Catholic Rural Life Conference
NCWC	National Catholic Welfare Council
OF	*Orate Fratres*
SJAA	St. John's Abbey Archives
YCW	Young Christian Workers

Foreword

In his *Apostolic Constitution "Missale Romanum"* Pope Paul VI writes: "No one should think that this revision of the Roman Missal has come out of nowhere. The progress in liturgical studies during the last four centuries has certainly prepared the way." Something similar can be said of the liturgical agenda defined by Vatican II and implemented by the postconciliar reform. Both vision and implementation have not come out of nowhere, but had been prepared for over fifty years by scholars, pastors, and lay leaders.

After more than thirty years of postconciliar liturgy there is an ever growing interest in the liturgical movement that happily concluded with the promulgation of the Constitution on the Liturgy. Who were the people and what were the factors responsible for the liturgical movement that swept across the globe? We can understand and evaluate more objectively the present state of the postconciliar reform when we examine more closely its historical background.

Books and articles have appeared tracing the history of the movement in general or as it evolved in some countries. In the United States a number of authors have written on the different aspects of the movement, including the work of notable pioneers like Virgil Michel and Godfrey Diekmann. The present volume by Keith Pecklers is one that studies the liturgical movement in the country in an integral and synthetic way. Pecklers examines the history of the movement not only from the perspective of the people who were behind it but also from its socio-cultural context. In many respects this work may fittingly be described as a social history of the liturgical movement in the United States. Although Pecklers studies the theological foundation of the movement, which is a call to full and active participation, he significantly contributes to history in those pages where he discusses the alliance between the liturgical movement and the socially-oriented movements such as the Catholic Worker, Friendship House, and the Grail.

An important finding of the author is that liturgical participation and social justice were intertwined during the early stages of the liturgical movement in the United States. He explains this by recalling the profound impact the doctrine of the Mystical Body had on the pioneers at a time when the social conditions in the country were at a deplorable state. Liturgical participation by the socially and economically afflicted became an expression of being part of the Mystical Body and a sure hope of finding community and justice in an oppressive world.

While the initial pioneers of the liturgical movement in the United States were clergy, lay leaders quickly joined them with amazing dedication. Pecklers names these lay pioneers: Justine Ward, John Ross Duggan, Sara Benedicta O'Neill, Dorothy Day, Nina Polcyn, Catherine De Hueck Doherty, Ed Marciniak, and Elizabeth Sullivan. It is interesting to note that unlike in other countries, especially in Europe (Germany excepted), many of the pioneers were women.

The liturgical movement in the United States raised the hope of many for the advent of Christian cooperation based on social justice and respect for each person's human dignity. Liturgy and community are an inseparable reality. Pecklers hopes that the community spirit of the liturgical movement will continue to inspire the Church in the United States as it works for Christian community among its multicultural members. Much has been achieved in matters pertaining to social justice, but the call for unity in cultural diversity remains a challenge. Perhaps a postconciliar liturgical movement is needed.

Anscar J. Chupungco, O.S.B.
Third Sunday of Advent, 1996

Preface

"Redeem the unread vision in the higher dream."
T. S. Eliot, "Ash Wednesday"

The vision of the liturgical pioneers—of Virgil Michel and his colleagues in the reformation of American Catholic liturgy—carried with it the hope and promise that a renewed liturgical participation would demand social responsibility, uniting the table of the Eucharist with the table of daily life.

This book is an attempt to introduce the reader to the liturgical movement, to the socially-minded vision of its pioneers and promoters, and to the major themes and issues that emerged. Acknowledging that their vision has yet to be fully realized, the text concludes with a call for a refounding of the liturgical movement in our time. The historical period of this study extends from 1926, when the liturgical movement in the United States was founded, to 1955, when under the leadership of Pope Pius XII, the Sacred Congregation of Rites restored the Easter Triduum culminating in the Great Vigil on Easter night. Those reforms, only several years after the publication of Pius XII's encyclical on the liturgy, *Mediator Dei*, were the culmination of years of liturgical pioneering on both sides of the Atlantic, and gave clear indication that the liturgical movement's call for full and active participation was being heeded and authenticated by official Church leadership.

The first chapter explores the European roots of the liturgical movement in the United States, focusing on developments in France, Germany, Belgium, and Austria. The chapter concludes by examining the European influences upon Virgil Michel, Benedictine monk of St. John's Abbey, Collegeville, and founder of the American movement.

Chapters Two through Five are divided thematically, and the material in each is treated chronologically, beginning with a consideration of the topic in its broader socio-cultural context. Chapter Two treats the fundamental goal of the liturgical pioneers: full and active liturgical participation. Liturgy was the celebration of the whole Mystical Body of Christ—women and men, ordained and lay members together. Cultural differences in liturgical participation among immigrant groups are explored, with special attention given to the liturgy of the hours, the *missa recitata*, and the debate over use of the vernacular in the liturgy.

Chapter Three explores the strong relationship between the liturgical and social movements during the 1930s and 1940s. From an examination of the Church's response to the Great Depression, we look more closely at the response of liturgical leaders and their efforts at helping American Catholics recognize that liturgical participation and social activism were intimately connected. Liturgical pioneers and social activists shared a common foundation in the Mystical Body theology and supported one another's projects. Several interesting points surface in this chapter: (1) it was Germans and German-Americans who first recognized and fostered the intimate relationship between liturgy and social activism; (2) Chicago was the center of such activism; (3) the social outreach that took place was often done without any governmental or institutional support.

The fourth chapter deals with liturgical education in all spheres of American church life, from elementary school through adult education. American Catholics were educated liturgically in such unlikely places as the Boston Common, and through lectures organized by women in religious bookstores. The final chapter studies the relationship of the liturgical movement to the arts: art, architecture, and music.

The United States is a young country compared with countries in Europe or other parts of the world, and so, too, the American church. Our youth, however, can lead some with an impoverished sense of history, to the impression that all liturgical renewal in the United States began with Vatican II. It is the hope of the author that this book will prove otherwise.

I wish to express my gratitude to a number of people and institutions whose support assisted me greatly in the research and writing of this book: to Vincent Tegeder, O.S.B., archivist of St. John's Abbey, for his kindness to me during my research at Collegeville; Philip Runkel and Mark Theil, archivists at Marquette University, Milwaukee; William J. Leonard, S.J., Boston College; Virginia Sloyan of the Liturgical Conference, Silver Spring, Maryland; Gabe Huck of Liturgy Training Publications, Chicago; Aidan McSorley, O.S.B., librarian of Conception Abbey, Missouri. Thanks especially to the University of Notre Dame where the greater part of the research was done: to Theodore M. Hesburgh, C.S.C., president emeritus of the university, for his support and interest in this project; to Lawrence Cunningham, former chair of the department of theology; to Richard P. McBrien, Crowley-O'Brien-Walter Professor of Theology, for inviting me to come to Notre Dame as a visiting scholar in the fall semester of 1994; Anne Fearing, administrative assistant in the department of theology; Charlotte Ames, University librarian in American Church History; and Kevin Cawley, assistant university archivist.

Thanks to my colleagues on the faculty of the Pontifical Liturgical Institute for their support and friendship, especially to Anscar J. Chupungco, O.S.B., who first suggested this topic to me, directed the original project as a doctoral dissertation, and graciously agreed to write the foreword. I am also indebted to Robert F. Taft, S.J., Pontifical Oriental Institute, and Michael Witczak, professor of liturgy at St. Francis Seminary, Milwaukee, and the Pontifical Liturgical Institute, for carefully reading the manuscript and offering many helpful suggestions. I also want to express my thanks to Daniel Merz and to Jesuits Joseph Carola, Philip Judge, and Andrew Krivak for their assistance in editing the original text. I am grateful to Michael J. Buckley, S.J., director of The Jesuit Institute at Boston College, and Marcel Rooney, O.S.B., abbot-primate, for their friendship and for encouraging me to come to Rome in the first place.

To those who graciously agreed to be interviewed my heartfelt gratitude: Steven M. Avella, professor of history, Marquette University; Jaime Bellalta, retired professor of architecture, University of Notre Dame; Patty Crowley, co-founder of the Christian Family Movement, social activist, Chicago; John A. Coleman, S.J., professor of sociology and religion, Loyola-Marymount University, Los Angeles; Jay P. Dolan, professor of history, University of Notre Dame; John J. Egan, Chicago priest, assistant to the president for community affairs, De Paul University, Chicago, formerly assistant to the president and director of the Center for Pastoral and Social Ministry at the University of Notre Dame; R. William Franklin, Episcopal priest, professor of church history, The General Theological Seminary, New York City; Philip Gleason, retired professor of education, University of Notre Dame; Theodore M. Hesburgh, C.S.C., president emeritus, University of Notre Dame; Kathleen Hughes, R.S.C.J., professor of Word and Worship, The Catholic Theological Union, Chicago; Frank Kacmarcik, O.S.B., Obl., liturgical pioneer, artist, consultant in liturgical design, St. John's Abbey, Collegeville, Minnesota; William J. Leonard, S.J., liturgical pioneer, retired professor of theology, founder and curator of the "Liturgy and Life Collection," Burns Library, Boston College; Ed Marciniak, liturgical promoter and social activist, director, The Center for Urban Life, Loyola University, Chicago; Richard A. McCormick,

S.J., eminent moral theologian, The John A. O'Brien Professor of Christian Ethics, University of Notre Dame; Frederick R. McManus, founder of the NCCB Secretariat for the Liturgy, liturgical *peritus* at the Second Vatican Council, professor emeritus of canon law, The Catholic University of America; Blair Meeks, The Liturgical Conference, Silver Spring, Maryland; Henry Nolan, S.J., retired, Florence, Italy; Burkhard Neunheuser, O.S.B., monk of Maria Laach, Germany, retired professor of liturgy, author; Paul Philibert, O.P., director, the Institute for Church Life, University of Notre Dame; Nina Polcyn Moore, social pioneer and liturgical promoter, Evanston, Illinois; Robert Rambusch, consultant in liturgical design, New York; Peggy Roach, administrative assistant, Office of Community Affairs, De Paul University, Chicago; John R. Quinn, retired archbishop of San Francisco; R. Kevin Seasoltz, O.S.B., St. John's Abbey, editor of *Worship;* Gerard Sloyan, liturgical and catechetical pioneer, professor, School of Religious Studies, The Catholic University of America; Ralph Van Loon, Lutheran pastor, executive director, The Liturgical Conference, Silver Spring, Maryland; Christopher Vescey, professor of humanities, Colgate University, Hamilton, New York; Rembert G. Weakland, O.S.B., St. Vincent's Archabbey, Latrobe, Pennsylvania, archbishop of Milwaukee; James F. White, Methodist minister, professor of liturgy, University of Notre Dame;

And to those who corresponded: Ade Bethune, liturgical and social pioneer, Catholic Worker artist, founder of the St. Leo Shop, Newport, Rhode Island, writer for *Orate Fratres;* Joseph P. Cardone, doctoral student in moral theology, St. Louis University; Godfrey Diekmann, O.S.B., St. John's Abbey, liturgical pioneer, successor to Virgil Michel, O.S.B. as editor of *Orate Fratres;* Alan F. Detscher, pastor of St. Catherine of Siena Parish, Riverside, Connecticut, formerly director, Secretariat for the Liturgy, National Conference of Catholic Bishops, Washington, D.C.; Regis Duffy, O.F.M., professor of theology, St. Bonaventure University, Olean, New York; Gerald P. Fogarty, S.J., professor of religious studies and history, University of Virginia, Charlottesville; Peter E. Fink, S.J., professor of sacramental theology and liturgy, Weston School of Theology, Cambridge, Massachusetts; Virgil C. Funk, president, National Association of Pastoral Musicians, Washington, D.C.; Andrew J. Greeley, director of the National Opinion Research Center and professor of social science, University of Chicago; Wilton D. Gregory, liturgist, bishop of Belleville, Illinois; Jeffrey M. Kemper, professor of liturgy, Mt. St. Mary's Seminary Athenaeum of Ohio, Cincinnati; Lawrence J. Madden, S.J., founder of The Georgetown Center for Liturgy, Spirituality, and the Arts, pastor, Holy Trinity Parish, Washington, D.C.; Aidan McSorley, O.S.B., librarian, Conception Abbey, Conception, Missouri; John R. Page, executive secretary, International Commission on English in the Liturgy, Washington, D.C.; H. Richard Rutherford, C.S.C., professor of theology, University of Portland, Portland, Oregon; Robert L. Tuzik, pastor, St. Emily Parish, professor of liturgy, University of Saint Mary of the Lake, Mundelein, Illinois.

Thanks to Michael Naughton, O.S.B., director of The Liturgical Press, and to Mark Twomey, managing editor, for their interest in publishing this work and for their generous collaboration.

Finally, I wish to thank my brother Michael, and my parents for their love and support over the years, to Jesuit brothers in New York and Rome, Chicago and California, and to the late Robert W. Hovda, liturgical pioneer, mentor, and friend.

CHAPTER ONE

❈

The European Roots: 1833–1925

The nineteenth century was a time of great intellectual activity throughout Europe. This was the age of Darwin, Hegel, Hume, Marx, and Engels. Theologically, it was the era of Möhler, Scheeben, Passaglia, Franzelin, and Schrader, who campaigned for a return to the Pauline concept of the Church as the Mystical Body of Christ. It was within such a milieu that the liturgical movement in Europe was born.

The early twentieth-century pioneers of the European liturgical movement were, for the most part, Benedictine monks, and it was their monasteries—Beuron and Maria Laach in Germany, Maredsous and Mont César in Belgium—that became the great liturgical centers of Europe. Each of those monasteries, however, ultimately traces its roots and liturgical inspiration back to nineteenth-century France, to the Benedictine monastery of Solesmes and its founder, Dom Prosper Guéranger (1805–1875).[1] Consequently, this study begins with a look at Solesmes and its founder. In order to understand the nature of this peculiar monastic foundation, however, we must see it in the ecclesial and liturgical context in France, leading up to the founding of Solesmes in 1833.

The French Liturgical Movement

The seventeenth through the nineteenth centuries in France was a period of tremendous liturgical creativity.[2] These innovations began as minor additions to the already existing Roman liturgical structure, but

---

[1] Two other nineteenth-century liturgical scholars should be noted: Louis Duchesne (1843–1922) who wrote a critical edition and commentary on the *Liber Pontificalis* in 1877, and Pierre Battifol (1861–1929) who wrote the *History of the Roman Breviary* in 1893.

[2] See Cuthbert Johnson, *Prosper Guéranger (1805–1875): A Liturgical Theologian* (Rome: Pontificio Ateneo S. Anselmo, 1984) 147–89.

gradually became more independent to the extent that each diocese in France eventually had its own liturgy. The Roman liturgical books at that time were badly in need of reform. Meanwhile, there was a patristic and biblical revival taking place in France and in other parts of Europe. Such renewal brought with it a genuine desire to return to the sources, both in terms of doctrine as well as practice.

Pastoral concerns contributed to liturgical changes. French bishops approved these early modifications with the genuine desire of contributing to the spiritual upbuilding of their churches. These bishops viewed their own situations as similar to that of their episcopal predecessors who had exercised the same power in approving the study and revision of earlier liturgical texts. While such innovations were well-intentioned, they were not completely without Jansenist influence.[3] Prosper Guéranger, who re-founded the Benedictine Abbey of Solesmes in 1833, saw all the liturgical innovations in France as the corruption of Jansenism, made without the permission of the Holy See as a way of restating the independence of the French Church. The first generation of French Jansenists were disciples of St. Cyran, a friend and collaborator of Jansen. This group of intellectuals was already in existence by 1638 and known for their rigorism in religious practice. Rigoristic as their piety was, however, it was nationalistic and anti-Roman. It is, however, inaccurate to generalize the Jansenist movement, or to claim that all Jansenist supporters shared equal enthusiasm for its propositions.

Following the French Revolution, the French church was in a state of tremendous disarray. Prosper Guéranger, a presbyter of Le Mans, desired to reopen the ancient monastery of Solesmes which had been suppressed during the French Revolution. Solesmes was to be a Benedictine house of prayer and study offered as a service to the Church within France. In his letter to Pope Gregory XVI in January 1832, Guéranger stated his concern about the poor standards of seminary education in France. He noted the tradition of the great European monasteries as centers for spiritual, cultural, and educational renewal. He mentioned, as well, that several of his contemporaries shared his sentiments and were interested in contributing constructively to such a renewal within the French church.

Guéranger saw in the French church and its liturgical innovations a lack of fidelity to tradition, attributing the state of the French church to Jansenism and Gallicanism.[4] Concretely, Guéranger desired to found

[3] See Louis Bouyer, *Liturgical Piety* (Notre Dame: University of Notre Dame Press, 1954) 54–5.

[4] For a survey of the neo-Gallican liturgies, see F. Ellen Weaver, "The Neo-Gallican Liturgies Revisited," *Studia Liturgica* 16 (1986–87) 62–5.

Solesmes as a response to the needs of the contemporary Church and the world, while always remaining faithful to the monastic rule and the teaching of the Church. Rather than continuing the liturgical experimentation found elsewhere in France, the Eucharist and the Divine Office at Solesmes were celebrated strictly according to the Roman Rite. The Choral Office and the Eucharist were to be the heart of Solesmes' monastic life, and Guéranger saw to it that Roman rubrics were carefully observed.

Monastic life at Solesmes was to be centered on the liturgical year and its important feasts and seasons.[5] More particularly, it was Guéranger's intention to help his monks, along with the rest of the Church, to "grasp the intention of the Holy Spirit in the diverse seasons of the Christian year."[6] To this end, he developed his famous work: *L'Année Liturgique* (begun in Advent of 1841). His plan was to write a commentary on the entire liturgical year, but he died after completing only nine of the projected twelve volumes. While his other major work, *Institutions liturgiques* (begun in 1841), was a more scholarly, detailed study of the liturgy, *L'Année liturgique* was a more pastoral series, aimed at helping parish priests and parishioners in their understanding of the liturgical year as expressed in the liturgical life of the Church.

Guéranger advocated a return to Gregorian chant as the official liturgical music of the Roman church. He encouraged chant in place of the contemporary or popularized liturgical music which had found its way into French churches during this period. It is in this area of chant revival where Solesmes made one of its most significant contributions to the Church, especially in the work done on chant manuscripts in the 1870s. To this day, the monastery is known not only for its fine execution of Gregorian chant during the monastic liturgy, but also as the major creator of publications on the development and study of Gregorian chant.

It is ironic that Guéranger is considered by some to be the founder of the European liturgical movement. His approach was highly subjective, often leading him to inaccurate liturgical conclusions. While Guéranger was quick to critique French liturgical innovations and dismiss them as lacking in substance, some of those innovations were later incorporated into the liturgical reforms of Pius X and ultimately

[5] See Michael Kwatera, "Marian Feasts in the Roman, Troyes and Paris Missals and Breviaries and the Critique of Dom Prosper Guéranger" (Ph.D. diss., University of Notre Dame, 1993).

[6] "Toute notre application sera de saisir l'intention de l'Esprit Saint dans les diverses phases de l'Année Chrétienne." *Année Liturgique*, Avent XX, my translation.

into the Roman liturgy itself.[7] Nonetheless, despite Guéranger's limited vision, his contribution to European liturgical renewal was significant. His aim was to restore and revive the liturgy focused on the
Eucharist, making it more central to the monastic life. Moreover, the
liturgical year was emphasized as essential for giving shape to life in
the monastery. Guéranger's passion for the liturgy and for a Christian
life with liturgy as its source had a charismatic quality about it which
instilled that same passion in others. In the words of Louis Bouyer, one
of Guéranger's greatest critics: "there is no achievement whatever in
the contemporary liturgical movement which did not originate in
some way with Dom Guéranger."

Although the liturgical movement in France did not grow until
years later, Guéranger's influence held sway throughout the nineteenth century, not only in France, but also in Germany and Belgium,
especially in monasteries founded by Solesmes. It is to those monasteries that we now turn.

The German Liturgical Movement[8]

The German liturgical movement traces its origins to the Benedictine monastery of Beuron, founded in 1863 by the brothers Maurus and
Placidus Wolter, both Benedictine monks. They desired to offer to the
Church in Germany that same spirit of monastic and liturgical reform
that Solesmes had offered to the Church in France. Consequently, a
study of the early years at Beuron reveals concerns and interests similar to those found at Solesmes. There was, for example, a great admiration and respect for the classic Roman liturgy. Both its monastic
liturgy and overall governance were strictly controlled by Solesmes, at
least in the early years of the monastery.

In 1856, Maurus Wolter followed in the footsteps of his brother,
Placidus, and entered the novitiate of the Benedictine monastery of St.
Paul's "Outside the Walls" in Rome. Here the Wolter brothers came to
know the princess and widow, Catherine of Hohenzollern-Sigmaringen,

---

[7] Bouyer, *Liturgical Piety*, 55.

[8] For treatments of the German liturgical movement in the wider context of in-
tellectual, cultural, and political thought, see Thomas O'Meara, "The Origins of the
Liturgical Movement and German Romanticism," and R. W. Franklin, "Response:
Humanism and Transcendence In the Nineteenth Century Liturgical Movement,"
Worship 59 (1985) 326–53; Arno Schilson, "Restauration und Erneuerung. Ein Blick
auf den Ursprung und die erste Etappe der Liturgischen Bewegung," and "Kul-
terelle Dimensionen Kirchlichen Liturgie. Liturgische Bewegung und Öffnung der
Kirche zur Welt," in *Erneuerung der Kirche aus dem Geist der Liturgie* (Maria Laach,
1992) 4–14, and 27–8, respectively.

who was a great admirer of Benedictine monasticism. The princess was interested in the founding of such a monastery on German soil and she had the financial resources to see that such a dream became a reality. In 1862, Maurus Wolter spent three months at Solesmes observing its monastic life, and was deeply influenced by the enthusiasm for the liturgical and monastic reform he witnessed during that sojourn. With the help of Princess Catherine, Beuron was re-founded one year later, giving birth to the liturgical movement in Germany. Its fruits were not long in coming. In 1884, Dom Anselm Schott published the first German-Latin Missal, *Das Messbuch der Hl. Kirche*. In 1893, the *Vesperbuch* followed. Each volume contained numerous explanations taken from Guéranger's *L'Année Liturgique*.[9] Aside from the Beuronese contribution of texts on the liturgy, a famous art school was founded by another of its monks, Desiderius Lenz, who was influenced by the art of Giotto, El Greco, and others.[10] He worked at establishing artistic unity within one liturgical space and thereby fostered the harmonic relationship between art and liturgy and encouraged others to do the same.

The daughter house of Beuron, Maria Laach, also became a stronghold of liturgical developments in Germany. Founded in 1093, the monastery had been suppressed by Napoleon in 1803. In 1892 William II offered what was his imperial church in the Rhineland to the Beuronese monks for their use. One year later, in 1893, with William's help and the pope's blessing, the monks of Beuron re-founded Maria Laach. During the suppression of the monastery, the property had belonged to the Jesuits for a brief period of time.

Under the leadership of Abbot Ildefons Herwegen (1874–1946) and two of his monks, Kunibert Mohlberg and Odo Casel (1886–1948), in collaboration with the young diocesan priest, Romano Guardini (1885–1968), and with the aid of two professors, Fr. J. Dölger and Anton Baumstark, the German liturgical movement was given shape and direction. They organized a three-fold series of publications which were begun in 1918: *Ecclesia Orans, Liturgiegeschichtliche Quellen,* and *Liturgiegeschichtliche Forschungen*. Aside from these significant serials, the well-known periodical, *Jarbuch für Liturgiewissenschaft* began at Maria Laach in 1921.

[9] Burkhard Neunheuser, "Il movimento liturgico: panorama storico e lineamenti teologici," in *Anamnesis*, vol. 1 (Genova: Marietti, 1991) 19.

[10] In place of the contemporary principle of "art pour l'art" Lenz's goal was to emphasize the principle of "l'art pour Dieu." D. Lenz, *Zur Ästhetik der Beuroner Schule* (Vienna, 1912). A thorough treatment on the style and symbolism of Beuronese art is given in J. Kreitmaier, *Beuroner Kunst. Eine Ausdrucksform der christlichen Mystik* (Fribourg, 1923).

The influence of Odo Casel cannot be underestimated. Born in Koblenz-Lützel, Germany, Casel came into contact with Ildefons Herwegen as a student at the University of Bonn. Under Herwegen's influence, Casel entered the monastery at Maria Laach in 1905. A theoretician, Casel wrote hundreds of articles and a number of books in the next thirty years, and in the tradition of many other great thinkers, his work was initially considered highly controversial. The controversy was not limited to Casel alone. Strong criticism against the entire German liturgical movement led to a number of published articles and pamphlets calling into question the work that the monks of Maria Laach and others had been promoting.[11] Casel's major contribution was the classic text, *Das christliche Kultmysterium*. In this work, he spoke of the sacraments as mysteries, believing that pagan mystery cults were a preparation for the Christian mysteries.[12] While this theory is no longer held by sacramental theologians, his interpretation of the sacraments gave way to a very positive and rich view of the Church as the Mystical Body of Christ which expresses itself relationally and symbolically through sacramental participation. This concept of the Church as the Mystical Body of Christ would become an important element in the European liturgical movement and one of the founding principles of the liturgical movement in the United States.[13]

When one hears of the German liturgical movement, it is almost always the names of Odo Casel or Romano Guardini that are associated with it. Although Ildefons Herwegen is mentioned less frequently, he was equally influential in the process of German liturgical renewal. Indeed, it was under his direction as abbot that Casel was encouraged to pursue his own explorations, that the *Missa recitata* began and developed as an experiment at the monastery, and that Maria Laach became a center for the liturgical movement.

German liturgical scholar Burkhard Neunheuser recalls the event of the first *Missa recitata* at Maria Laach quite vividly. The date was 6 August 1921, and Neunheuser was a young monk at the time. Though the Mass was celebrated with the permission of Abbot Herwegen, it was Prior Albert Hammenstede who presided. The Mass, celebrated early in the morning in the crypt of the abbey church, included the

---

[11] One of the more famous pamphlets was the two-part series written by M. Kassiepe, O.M.I., "Irrwege und Umwege im Frömmigkeitsleben der Gegenwart," vol. 1 (1939) and vol. 2 (1940).

[12] *Das christliche Kultmysterium* (Regensburg: Verlag Friedrich Pustet, 1960). See also "Die Liturgie als Mysterienfeier," *Ecclesia Orans* 9 (1923) 3–5.

[13] See Jeremy Hall, *The Full Stature of Christ: The Ecclesiology of Virgil Michel, O.S.B.* (Collegeville: The Liturgical Press, 1976).

praying of the Gloria, Credo, Sanctus, and Agnus Dei, in common. Those who took part in the Mass also participated in the offertory procession, reviving the ancient practice of bringing their own altar bread to the altar rail. Neunheuser recalls his enthusiasm at that event but laughs as he hears more recent descriptions of that first *Missa recitata*. That crypt-Mass in 1921 was not celebrated in German, but in Latin, he insists, although it did include responses and common prayers on the part of the assembly.[14] Despite episcopal approbation for the liturgical experiments at the monastery, rumors quickly spread throughout Germany that the monks of Maria Laach had created a new liturgy, disregarding Church tradition, and advocating a lay priesthood which would, of course, destroy respect for the clerical priesthood. For those concerned members of the German clergy, this liturgical experimentation sounded just a little too Lutheran. The Cardinal Archbishop of Cologne came to investigate, but the next morning at Mass, upon witnessing the event, he was apparently moved to tears. One year later, he stood behind a portable altar in his own cathedral celebrating the *Missa recitata* with the whole congregation. From then on, at all the annual Catholic congresses in Germany, often with thousands of participants, the papal nuncios celebrated Mass facing the people, and members of the assembly joined in the appropriate prayers.

Those were times of great hope and experimentation. Monastic centers like Beuron and Maria Laach advanced the German liturgical movement primarily through academic liturgical renewal. The scholarly research of such figures as Casel, Guardini, Baumstark, and Mohlberg, had a tremendous influence far beyond the confines of Germany.[15] At the same time, the German youth movement and related groups assisted the pastoral dimension of that renewal. Romano Guardini, for example, was pastorally involved at places such as Burg Rothenfels, organizing various liturgical celebrations, especially for the more significant feasts and solemnities.

It must be noted, however, that Germany was not the first country to witness the force and effect of an organized liturgical movement. Prior to the founding of Maria Laach, Beuron had already been planting seeds of change elsewhere in Europe: Maredsous in Belgium,

---

[14] Burkhard Neunheuser, O.S.B. Interview by author, 26 September 1994, Abtei Maria Laach, Germany. See Neunheuser, "Die 'Krypta-Messe' in Maria Laach. Ein Beitrag zur Frühgeschichte der Gemeinschaftmesse," in *Beten und Arbeiten: Aus Geschichte und Gegenwart benediktinischen Lebens*, Ed. Theodor Bolger (Maria Laach, 1961) 70–82.

[15] For a fuller treatment of the liturgical movement in Germany, see W. Trapp, *Vorgeschichte und Ursprung der liturgischen Bewegung* (Regensburg, 1940) 14–189.

Emmaus-Prague in Czechoslovakia, and Seckau in Austria, always with a view toward the renewal of the liturgy. The most liturgically significant of these new monastic foundations was what developed at Maredsous, then at Mont César; these monasteries paved the way for the Belgian liturgical movement.

The Belgian Liturgical Movement

While the movement in Belgium officially began in 1909, one can trace its roots back to 1872. In that year, Maurus Wolter, then abbot of Beuron, founded a Benedictine monastery at Maredsous, Belgium, with the help of the Desclée family of Tournai. It soon became famous for its liturgical publications. It was Maredsous' liturgical publishing that would inspire the young American Benedictine student, Virgil Michel, some years later, to initiate a similar project in the United States.

One of its early publications was the first French-Latin Missal, *Missel des fidèles,* published in 1882 by Dom Gérard van Caloen, rector of the abbey school. The following year in an address to a French eucharistic congress, van Caloen spoke in favor of lay participation in the Mass. He went on to suggest that those present at the Mass should likewise receive Communion. Van Caloen's comments were considered so outrageous that he was removed as school rector. He did not cease publishing, however. In 1884, he founded the review *Messager des fidèles* (from 1890, *Revue bénédictine*). *Messager des fidèles* is significant as the first publication founded to assist the promotion of the liturgical movement.[16] In collaboration with the newer monastic community of Mont César at Louvain, Maredsous remained a moving force in the Belgian liturgical movement.

Founded by Robert Kerchove (1846–1942) and several other monks from Maredsous in 1899,[17] the Benedictine monastery of Mont César was indirectly an outgrowth of the romanticism of the nineteenth century and the monastic liturgical renewal initiated by Guéranger at Solesmes. The influence of Solesmes was indirect, filtered through the monastic experience of Beuron. Like Maredsous, Mont César was also known for its publications and for the periodical *Les Questions liturgiques,* founded in 1910, but especially for its *sémaines liturgiques,* held each summer from 1912. These liturgical conferences began with

[16] See André Haquin, *Recherches et Syntheses: Dom Lambert Beauduin et le Renoveau Liturgique* (Grembloux, 1970) 63–4.

[17] For a detailed history of Mont César, see *Le Mont César 1899–1949* (Louvain: Editions de l'Abbaye du Mont César, 1949).

small numbers and were initially aimed at clergy, especially parish priests, as a way of offering them an enthusiasm for the liturgy and for the liturgical apostolate as the fundamental and most important element of parochial ministry. The pastoral liturgical movement, in fact, grew out of this monastery, thanks to the prophetic vision and leadership of one of its monks, Dom Lambert Beauduin (1873–1960).[18] To understand Beauduin's vision, something must first be said about his background as a labor chaplain, for this had a tremendous influence upon his liturgical interest.

Lambert Beauduin was ordained a presbyter of the Diocese of Liége on 25 April 1897. His early years as a priest were spent teaching at the minor seminary in Saint-Trond. Some years earlier, when Beauduin was beginning his theological studies, Leo XIII's encyclical letter *Rerum Novarum* (15 May 1891) was issued as the Church's response to the conditions created by the Industrial Revolution. It was a strong call for social justice, especially with regard to labor and the right to a just wage.

Three years later, on 21 November 1894, the *Congrégation des Aumôniers du Travail* was proposed by Reverend Théophile Reyn (1860–1941) as a localized Belgian response to the pope's mandate. Permission was granted for its formation and the congregation began on 25 March 1895.[19] This was to be an official organization of labor chaplains, as a way of expressing the Church's solidarity with workers, particularly in their struggle for a just wage. The local bishop, Victor Doutreloux, was supportive of the plan. In fact, under his leadership, there were congresses on social issues sponsored by the Diocese of Liége in 1887, 1888, and 1890, which received international attention. All sectors of the Belgian church were not equally encouraged by the strong stand which the Church had been taking on issues of labor. Nonetheless, the Aumôniers continued their work, and Bishop Doutreloux remained equally supportive and enthusiastic. The priests who became labor chaplains formed a type of clergy association with regular meetings and occasional conferences. In 1899, less than five years after they were founded, the Aumôniers du Travail had eight houses in four dioceses.

---

[18] Bernard Botte, *Le mouvement liturgique: Témoignage et souvenirs* (Paris: Desclée, 1973); Louis Bouyer, *Dom Lambert Beauduin, un homme d'Eglise* (Tournai, 1964); Sonya Quitslund, *Beauduin: A Prophet Vindicated* (New York: Newman, 1973).

[19] See Abbé Pire, *Histoire de la Congrégation des Aumôniers du Travail* (Charleroi, 1942); G. Fallon, "Les Aumôniers du Travail" *Revue Sociale Catholique* 2 (1897–1898) 372–7.

Lambert Beauduin was known for a strong social consciousness along with a genuine compassion for the oppressed, so his membership in the *Aumôniers du Travail* was to be expected. He presented himself as a candidate and was accepted in 1899, two years after his presbyteral ordination. Under his leadership, a number of buildings were constructed at Montegnée, near the group's headquarters at Seraing, to provide housing for workers. The Aumôniers had their difficulties, however. There were twenty-three members on the roster in 1901. Of that group, thirteen eventually left the community. In addition, the political stand of the Aumôniers brought them into conflict with many of their most important patrons. This was combined with the loss of a solid financial grounding. Nevertheless, Beauduin remained with the Aumôniers until he left the Diocese of Liége in 1906 to enter the monastery of Mont César.

Beauduin recognized within himself the gifts of a preacher. In the monastery he would be able to better devote his energies to deepening his relationship with Christ, through personal and communal prayer, out of which would then flow the ministry of preaching. His compassion for the oppressed and his strong social convictions did not diminish when he left the diocese. He looked toward entrance into a religious community that would provide him with the atmosphere of prayer and support he was seeking, as a means of becoming an effective preacher.

He first considered entering the Dominican order, but one of his professors at Louvain advised against this. That same professor, Canon Jacques Kaminne, had recently come into contact with the new monastic foundation at Mont César. Knowing Beauduin, and convinced that he would thrive in such a Benedictine atmosphere, he recommended the monastery. Beauduin entered the monastery on 1 July 1906 and became a novice in the fall.

The prior at the time was none other than the well-known spiritual master, Columba Marmion (1858–1923). Marmion was an Irish diocesan priest who had entered the monastery at Maredsous in 1886. There is no doubt that Marmion's own spiritual and especially liturgical convictions had great influence upon Beauduin. What is not clear is just how extensive such influence was. Beauduin often criticized Marmion, suggesting that he was more a spiritual than a liturgical theologian, albeit a spiritual theologian captivated by Christian worship. Both monks shared a deep love and devotion for the Liturgy of the Hours, and saw such liturgical prayer as foundational to their monastic life.[20]

---

[20] Quitslund, 9–10.

It was not long before Beauduin came to the conclusion that monasticism could have a potentially powerful effect on the secularized world through liturgical prayer, especially the monastic celebration of the Eucharist. In other words, it was the liturgy and only the liturgy that was capable of giving the necessary grounding to Christian social activism. With the resources of the monastery in his favor, Beauduin's potential for communicating this message was greatly increased. He soon began to stir up his confrères with his ideas. Early on at Mont César, he remarked:

> What a shame that the liturgy remains the endowment of an elite; we are aristocrats of the liturgy; everyone should be able to nourish himself from it, even the simplest people: we must democratize the liturgy.[21]

Beauduin's biographer recalls his enthusiasm at the realization that it is in the Eucharist that the Church takes on flesh. Beauduin once rushed into class immediately after Mass and proclaimed enthusiastically to his students: "I've just realized that the liturgy is the center of the piety of the Church!"[22]

Among other things, Beauduin was bothered by the fact that Pius X's decree on frequent Communion in 1905 failed to stress the reality that Communion was an integral part of the Mass itself. As a result, Beauduin did not tire of promoting the fact that Communion with one another and with Christ was to be the summit of the Church's eucharistic celebration. He wondered, for example, why it was that more solemnity and attention was given to eucharistic adoration and benediction than to community Mass.[23]

As his monastic vocation deepened, so too did his vision—the vision of a Church which lived as the Mystical Body of Christ; the vision of such a mystical body which overflowed with a passion for justice; the vision of a mystical body united, where Anglicans, Orthodox, and Roman Catholics might dwell together in mutual respect, open to dialogue. It was this same vision that would capture the enthusiasm of Virgil Michel (1890–1938), who incorporated those same concerns into his promotion of the liturgical movement within the United States.[24]

The first concrete evidence we have of Beauduin's liturgical interests can be traced back to 2 February 1909, when he invited a number of students to an informal discussion on the liturgy. The basis of their

[21] Ibid., 16.

[22] Ibid.

[23] Ibid., 17–8.

[24] Paul Marx, *Virgil Michel and the Liturgical Movement* (Collegeville: The Liturgical Press, 1957) 27–8.

discussion was a small pamphlet which another student, F. Mercenier, O.S.B. (1885–1965), had shown to Beauduin in January. Mercenier suggested that something comparable be produced for the laity which would include Mass texts as a way of encouraging better liturgical understanding and participation.[25]

The official beginning of the liturgical movement in Belgium, however, is usually dated to September 1909, when the National Congress of Catholic Works *(Congrés national des Oeuvres catholiques)* took place. Indeed, many liturgical historians prefer this event, rather than Guéranger and Solesmes, to mark the beginning of the European liturgical movement. Beauduin delivered an address entitled: *"La vraie prière de l'Eglisé,"* in which he called for full and active participation of all people in the Church's life and ministry, particularly in the liturgy. He took as his mandate one of the statements from the *Motu proprio* of Pius X, *Tra le sollecitudini* of 22 November 1903. The statement described the liturgy as the Church's most important and indispensable source:

> Since we have very much at heart that the true Christian spirit be revived in all possible ways and that it be maintained among all the faithful, it is above all necessary to provide for the holiness and dignity of the sacred places where precisely the faithful gather to draw this spirit at its primary and indispensable source, that is, active participation in the sacred mysteries and in the public and solemn prayer of the Church.[26]

Beauduin exhorted those present to foster such active participation in the sacred mysteries, as the grounding for an apostolic life of social action.

During the Malines Conference, Beauduin met with Godefroid Kurth, an historian and prominent Catholic layman at the time who shared hope for the restoration of the assembly to active liturgical participation. It was Beauduin's analysis that too often pastors and pastoral assistants put their efforts into spiritual and social outreach while giving much less attention to liturgical concerns. According to Beauduin, such confused pastoral priorities needed to be reversed. The liturgy was far more fundamental than spiritual or social outreach. As such, it deserved a corresponding degree of care and attention. Together with Godefroid Kurth, they devised a practical plan, with the full support of Cardinal Désiré Joseph Mercier, archbishop of

---

[25] Quitslund, 20.

[26] *Acta Sanctae Sedis (ASS)* 36:28 (1904) 331, as given in eds. J. Neuner, and J. Dupuis, *The Christian Faith in the Doctrinal Documents of the Catholic Church* (New York: Alba House, 1982) 340. In 1909, the name of the *ASS* was changed to the *Acta Apostolicae Sedis (AAS)*.

Brussels, to launch the liturgical movement. Their goals were: 1) to work on liturgical texts: to translate *The Roman Missal* and to encourage its use as a devotional as well as liturgical book; to adapt the liturgical texts (at least for the Sunday Eucharist and Vespers) so that they were more pastorally accessible; 2) to develop a liturgical spirituality where the Christian life is lived out of the font of the liturgy. More concretely, Beauduin's plan was to encourage greater use of the Liturgy of the Hours by parishioners and greater participation in all parish-wide liturgical events. Further, he stated that the best preparation for the reception of Communion was strong liturgical participation during the Mass; 3) to cultivate the use of Gregorian chant within the liturgy, according to the wishes of Pius X, which the pope had expressed in the *Motu Proprio*; 4) to propose that those entrusted with the ministry of music in parishes, i.e., music directors and their choirs, should set aside time each year for a retreat in monasteries or other liturgical centers.[27]

In November of that same year, 1909, Mont César initiated the monthly publication in both French and Flemish editions, of a periodical entitled *Liturgical Life*. The number of subscriptions to *Liturgical Life* soon exceeded seventy thousand, so Mont César was forced to announce that no more subscriptions could be accepted as they were simply unable to handle the workload. This led to the founding of a new publication in 1910, designed for the clergy: *Les Questions Liturgigues* (later *Questions Liturgiques et Paroisssales*). In June of 1910, the first liturgical day was held at the monastery, drawing over two hundred and fifty participants. Cardinal Mercier was the featured speaker.

Two years later, in 1912, Beauduin, in collaboration with the other monks at Mont César, initiated the annual *sémaines liturgiques*. Along with publications, these liturgical weeks were the primary means of communicating the message of the liturgical movement, and of implementing the principles established at the Malines Conference. Beginning in 1913, the proceedings of these liturgical weeks were published under the title *Cours et Conférences des Sémaines Liturgiques*.

In 1914, Beauduin published his *La piété de l'Eglise* (Louvain, 1914), which was a public declaration of the liturgical movement, offering the movement solid theological and ecclesiological grounding.[28] Beauduin

---

[27] Bouyer, 60–1.

[28] The previous year, Maurice Festugière had published *La Liturgie catholique. Essai de synthèse suivi de quelques développements* (ed. Maredsous, 1913), which originally appeared as a lengthy article in *Revue de Philosophie* (1913) 692–886. Festugière's work was violently opposed by those who were against liturgical change. The controversy provoked Beauduin to write his *La piété de l'Eglise*, both to support

was a dreamer but he was also a realist. His program of renewal was a great success precisely because he was able to communicate both the dream and the reality in a practical, pragmatic way. He always tailored the program to the particular group. His approach was concrete and pastoral, consistently drawing out the connections and implications between the liturgy and the lived reality of the people. He made such connections, not only to show how the liturgy could respond to the needs of the people, but also to demonstrate that liturgy is morally formative, challenging the worshipping community concretely to live as the body of Christ.

Further, Beauduin's program of renewal demonstrated that, far from being a museum piece, the liturgy needed to be contextualized and even reformed to adapt to the concrete age and culture in which it was celebrated. He was clear, however, always to make the distinction between a reform and a movement. According to Beauduin and others in the movement, the term "reform" signified liturgical changes officially sanctioned by the Church. In his *motu proprio* of 1903, for example, it was the desire of Pius X to reform the liturgy through the restoration of Gregorian chant, the reform of the Breviary, etc. A movement, on the other hand, laid the groundwork for such officially sanctioned changes. Beauduin's desire in founding the liturgical movement, was, to put it simply, to assist the people in living out their baptism through worship and social action.[29]

Unlike the emerging liturgical movement in Germany, which was primarily the work of an intellectual, monastic elite, the Belgian movement was thoroughly pastoral, aimed at the grassroots level: parish communities. Beauduin was convinced that the way to attract parishioners to the liturgical movement was through their priests. So his plan began with a renewal of the clergy. He explained that the two questions a presbyter should have for studying the liturgy are: 1) How will the liturgy enable me to live as God calls me to live? 2) How will the liturgy enable me to assist my parishioners in living that same life, as demanded by virtue of their baptism? For Beauduin, these two questions were ultimately one: both were a call to see the liturgy as source of moral formation, as having the power to shape ethical behavior and thus, ultimately, a call to the whole Church to discover in the liturgy the source of its apostolic life.[30]

Festugière and to carefully explain why the liturgical movement was a legitimate and necessary movement within the Belgian Church. See Beauduin, "Grief contre le movement," *Questions Liturgiques* 2 (1912) 529–36.

[29] Botte, *Le Mouvement*, 32.

[30] Ibid., 64.

With an integrated vision, Beauduin's passion for ecclesial renewal included a strong concern for ecumenical issues, particularly regarding Anglican and Orthodox Christians. He was convinced that the Anglican Church should be invited to return to communion with the bishop of Rome without having to be completely absorbed by the Roman Catholic Church. He suggested that Anglicans might continue to maintain their liturgical and disciplinary autonomy in much the way Eastern Catholics preserved that same autonomy while remaining in communion with the Roman pontiff.[31]

As for liturgical differences among churches of east and west, Beauduin believed that since the eastern liturgical tradition was far older, the west should give greater consideration to the major differences, i.e., concelebration, use of the vernacular, an audible consecration, the reception of Communion under both forms and while standing rather than kneeling, and the practice of full Christian initiation for those baptized in infancy. He wondered why such ancient practices were so common in the east and yet considered unacceptable in the west.[32]

In 1925, Beauduin's ecumenical concerns led him to found a monastery at Amay sur Meuse. The community was later moved to an abandoned Carmelite monastery in Chevetogne. He saw this as a monastic contribution to the unity of the churches. Many of the efforts of that monastery, first at Amay and later at Chevetogne, have been directed to the relationship between eastern and western Christianity.[33]

Through Beauduin's efforts, the liturgy in Belgium was returned to the assembly rather than remaining only in the hands of the specialists. He attempted to popularize complicated theological concepts so that average Catholics had greater access to the traditions of the Church. In 1910–1911 he called for a return to the celebration of the temporal cycle, at least on Sundays. The Belgian bishops failed to honor his request, however. He opposed Eucharistic exposition during the Mass precisely because it conflicted with the Eucharist being celebrated. He called for a shorter eucharistic fast, so that more could participate in the principal sung Mass on Sunday, and as a pastoral response to workers and those who had to travel some distance. He encouraged pastors to introduce the dialogue Mass even though it was quite controversial. He was impressed by the three-year cycle of readings in the

---

[31] Quitslund, 66.

[32] Ibid., 137. Despite his good intentions, Beauduin's view of Byzantine liturgy was overly simplistic, and in some cases, demonstrably inaccurate. See Robert Taft, *The Byzantine Rite: A Short History* (Collegeville: The Liturgical Press, 1992).

[33] See Quitslund, 125–45.

Jewish liturgy, although he made no move to have such a cycle introduced into the liturgy.[34]

While the Belgian liturgical movement gained many sympathizers,
the numbers attending the liturgical weeks were small. According to
Bernard Botte (1893–1980),[35] those first years of the movement were
absolutely crucial. It was a challenge even to have the topic of liturgy
included in the Malines Conference. In 1959, in a message to the fifti-
eth anniversary of the Conference, Beauduin confirmed this:

> Its [the liturgical movement's] first steps in life were hesitant; we first
> had to win a spot in the sun. I made several attempts in vain: I first tried
> to get the paper on the liturgy listed in the doctrinal section . . . a cate-
> goric refusal from the president of this section who regarded the paper
> like a Cinderella of the fairy tale. A second move—the section on moral-
> ity—underwent the same fate. The third, at the section on piety, was
> even more badly received: they considered the liturgy as a whimsical
> kind of piety that could not have any place in spirituality! Finally, on the
> advice of an architect, I was able to find a spot in the section on art where
> it [the liturgy] cut a strange figure.[36]

The strong direction which Beauduin offered set the stage and gave
firm grounding, not just for the renewal of liturgical celebration, but to
the overall renewal of Church life, as well. A look at the liturgical
movement in Austria reveals a similar pastoral, pragmatic approach.

The Austrian Liturgical Movement

As the seeds of a predominantly intellectual movement were growing in the monasteries of neighboring Germany, something new in the
German-speaking world was emerging at the Augustinian monastery
of Klosterneuburg in Austria, thanks to the imagination and efforts of

---

[34] Ibid., 30, 34–5.

[35] Botte, himself a monk of Mt. César, played a very significant role in the Belgian
liturgical movement, was one of the founders of the Institut Supérieur de Liturgie
in Paris, and was a member of the Second Vatican Council's Commission for the
Implementation of the "Constitution on the Sacred Liturgy." See Bernard Botte,
From Silence to Participation: An Insider's View of Liturgical Renewal (Washington: The
Pastoral Press, 1988); Pierre-Marie Gy, "Dom Bernard Botte (1893–1980)," *La Maison
Dieu* 141 (1980) 167–9; and A. Verheul, "Hommage à Dom Bernard Botte, O.S.B.,
1893–1980," *Les Questions liturgiques et paroissiales* 61 (1980) 83–92. The last article
also contains an extensive bibliography of Botte's writings.

[36] "Message de dom Lambert Beauduin," *Les Questions liturgiques et paroissiales* 40
(1959) 200.

one of its canons, Pius Parsch (1884–1954).[37] Parsch was aware of what was developing at Maria Laach and was deeply influenced by it. He promoted the liturgical movement in Austria by taking the strong scholarly foundations offered by his colleagues in Germany and giving those foundations a pastoral scope and expression. In 1919, Parsch accepted responsibility for the small Church of St. Gertrude, not far from the monastery, which became a testing ground for his liturgical ideas. He emphasized that the Eucharist is a sacrificial meal, offered and shared by the entire parish community in union with the rest of the Church. Consequently, like Beauduin in Belgium, Parsch called for liturgical participation which was full and active, and sought to make connections between liturgy and daily life. What began to emerge at Klosterneuburg was a movement with a common goal of biblical and liturgical renewal. These efforts at widening the liturgical movement to encourage biblical renewal helped to unite liturgical renewal with Church renewal in a unique way: to serve the renewal of the Church at its very core, rather than to treat the liturgical issue in isolation.[38]

Such renewal was promoted through two important publications. The first was *Das Jahr des Heiles,* a commentary on the Missal and Breviary for the entire liturgical year, begun in 1923. A second and perhaps even more significant publication was *Bibel und Liturgie,* founded in 1926. This journal promoted the relationship between liturgy and Scripture, encouraging a wider knowledge of the Bible among Catholics. A renewed interest in patristic studies also emerged during this time, making its own significant contribution to liturgical renewal. In general, what was developing at Klosterneuburg and elsewhere was a more integrated movement which fostered the union of Word and worship.[39]

The Liturgical Movement Elsewhere in Europe [40]

In Italy, the monks of Finalpia, Savona, fostered the liturgical apostolate through their important review, *Rivista Liturgica,* in which most of the Italian liturgical pioneers communicated their ideas on the renewal

[37] For a good treatment on the work of Pius Parsch, particularly in the areas of liturgical participation and Parsch's view of the relationship of the liturgy to the lay apostolate, see Boleslaw Krawczyk, *Liturgia e laici nell'attivita e negli scritti di Pius Parsch* (Rome: Pontificio Ateneo S. Anselmo, 1990). Of particular value is the useful bibliography of Parsch's published works (11–21).

[38] Bouyer, 65–6.

[39] Ibid., 66.

[40] For a survey of the movement within Europe, see R. K. Fenwick and Brian D. Spinks, *Worship in Transition: Highlights of the Liturgical Movement* (Edinburgh: T. and T. Clark, 1995).

of the liturgy. The journal, founded in 1914, continues to be published today. A leading figure in the Italian liturgical movement was Abbot Emmanuele Caronti, O.S.B., who sought to ground ecclesiastical piety in a solid liturgical spirituality. His text *La pietà liturgica* (Turin, 1921) contributed significantly to such efforts. His greatest contribution, however, was the widely acclaimed *Messale festivo per i fedeli* (Turin, 1921). This Missal helped a large number of Italian Catholics encounter the richness of the Church's worship by assisting their understanding of the liturgical texts and thereby enhancing their appreciation of the liturgy itself.[41]

In other countries as well, the liturgical movement began to take shape emerging differently from country to country according to the cultural and ecclesial situation at the time. In particular, there were significant developments in the Netherlands,[42] Spain and Portugal, Switzerland, Holland, England,[43] Czechoslovakia, and Poland. The movement was also beginning to take hold in Brazil and other South American countries.[44] It was, however, the movements within Belgium, France, Germany, and Austria that had the greatest influence upon Europe and ultimately upon Virgil Michel and the liturgical movement in the United States. To be more precise, it was the guidance of Michel's mentor Lambert Beauduin that had the most significant effect on his life and mission within the liturgical apostolate.

In Belgium, while the *Questions liturgiques et paroissiales* resumed immediately after World War I, the national "Semaines Liturgiques" did not resume until 1924. With the beginning of the academic year 1921, Beauduin's abbot assigned him to Sant'Anselmo in Rome as a professor, enabling him to give birth to yet another liturgical movement—this time in the United States—thanks to his mentoring the young Virgil Michel, an American Benedictine monk from Saint John's Abbey, Collegeville, Minnesota.

The Passage of the Liturgical Movement from Europe to the United States

While Virgil Michel's abbot, Alcuin Deutsch (1877–1951), had officially sent him to Rome to study philosophy, it seems likely that the

---

[41] Franco Brovelli, *Ritorno alla liturgia: Saggi di studio sul movimento liturgico* (Rome: Edizioni Liturgiche, 1989) 231–2.

[42] The first Netherlands Congress on Liturgy was held at Breda on 16–17 August 1911. In response to the low attendance at that first congress, the Diocese of Haarlem instituted a liturgical commission the following year, and soon after in Utrecht.

[43] For a history of the liturgical movement in England, see Donald Gray, *Earth and Altar* (Norwich: Alcuin Club Collections, No. 68, 1986).

[44] José Ariovaldo Da Silva, *O Movimento Litúrgico No Brasil Estudo Histórico* (Petrópolis, 1983) 40.

abbot wanted him to be exposed to European liturgical developments as well. The abbot himself had studied in Europe from 1897 until 1903, and had visited and been deeply impressed by such places as Maredsous and other monasteries influenced by Guéranger.

Elected abbot in 1921, Deutsch worked at trying to instill a passion for the liturgy in the minds and hearts of his novices. Further, he was very much impressed by Romano Guardini's *Vom Geist der Liturgie*, which he ultimately passed along to Michel. This text was the beginning of Virgil Michel's interest in the liturgy. Prior to Michel's departure for Europe, there is some evidence that the two had discussed the possibility of Michel's working in the liturgical apostolate upon his return to the United States. The exact content of such discussions and possibilities for his future apostolic service, however, are rather sketchy.[45]

Upon arrival in Rome, Michel devoted himself entirely to the study of philosophy, reading extensively the great philosophical works, especially the different schools of social, industrial, and economic ethics. While Michel was studying philosophy at Sant'Anselmo, Lambert Beauduin was teaching apologetics, ecclesiology, and liturgy at the same institution. Michel found Beauduin's courses to be stimulating, particularly his development and interpretation of the doctrine of the Mystical Body of Christ. There was a mutual admiration and the two had many private discussions on the liturgy, especially as it related to what Michel was reading in social ethics. Beauduin writes:

> I knew him well at Rome, and when he discovered that I was concerned with the liturgical movement at Louvain, we became quite friendly, and he often came to talk to me in private; but liturgy was not for him just a matter of study; it was above all a powerful means of doing apostolic work, by increasing the faith and devotion of the faithful. His vocation for such work seemed part of himself. He asked me to arrange for him to spend the holidays in our monastery at Louvain, in order to become familiar with all the details of the organization of liturgical work . . . .[46]

It became increasingly clear to Michel that he was exhausting the academic resources available in Rome. The Catholic University at Louvain had far more to offer, particularly in the area of philosophy. He requested the abbot's permission to spend the following year at Louvain, travelling throughout Europe and visiting the great monasteries and liturgical centers on his way.

---

[45] Marx, 24–8.
[46] Letter to Paul Marx, 27 September 1952. Quoted in Marx, 28.

With the abbot's consent, Michel departed for what he called a three-month "journey of study." In a letter written to Deutsch on 20 April 1924, Michel wrote: "I'm after Benedictine life, churches and shrines, and the ordinary people and their life."[47] He travelled through Italy, France, Spain, and Germany, with Benedictine confrère, Roger Schoenbechler, living close to the people, observing daily life in monasteries and churches, in urban as well as rural settings. In the words of his biographer, Paul Marx, O.S.B.: "He discussed philosophy with philosophers, farming with farmers, and liturgy with liturgists."

His impression of the clergy in France and Spain was that they were apathetic, living far removed from the people they were called to serve. He was impressed by a visit to the Benedictine monastery of Montserrat. Throughout Spain he was deeply impressed by both the strong sense of family and the equally strong sense of Christian womanhood exhibited by the Spanish women with whom he came into contact. His travels had a lasting effect upon him, influencing him to encourage a Christian social order and always to remain close to ordinary people.[48] In Germany, at Maria Laach and Beuron, he spent tremendous amounts of time in the library, reading all he could find on the liturgy and enjoying the rich liturgical prayer of both monastic churches.

He wrote his abbot from Maria Laach:

> I had eyes and ears open here and at Beuron and was very much impressed by everything. I wonder if we will ever have public Office, etc., unto universal edification and the unified serious purpose of our life evident in the actions of individual and community alike. . . . I have been talking liturgical projects and pamphlets here with good results. . . . The project itself is developing in the realm of ideas, at least; it would be aided greatly later, if our life were an open living example of the liturgical life. But there our church has a great handicap. By the way, don't approve any new church plan before reading *Christozentrische Kirchenkunst.*[49]

Michel's studies at Louvain were significant. He was influenced by what Jacques Maritain would later call "practical" philosophy. Such "practical" philosophy attempted to deal with the critical problems of contemporary society.[50] At the same time, Michel continued to be intrigued by the liturgy. Beauduin had returned to his Louvain monas-

---

[47] Ibid., 29.
[48] Ibid., 29–32.
[49] Letter of 29 September 1924. Marx, 33.
[50] Marx, 36.

tery of Mont César and Michel would go there every ten days for long talks with Beauduin. He likewise continued visiting the great monasteries—Maria Laach, Maredsous, and Solesmes. The contacts made in these monasteries were invaluable and served him well in his future work at Collegeville.

One of Michel's greatest discoveries in Europe, through his talks with Beauduin and the time spent in those monasteries, was the doctrine of the Mystical Body of Christ. Such a doctrine was virtually unheard of in the United States at the time. He began to recognize that a community transformed by its worship could ultimately be instrumental in the transformation of society. Thus, as early as 1925, Michel saw the liturgical movement as a means of countering the secularism and individualism of the modern age.

There is no question that Michel's main interest at the time was philosophy.[51] Convinced that he would spend the rest of his life in that discipline, he offered himself only on a short-term basis to assist in launching the liturgical apostolate in the United States, as initiator and editor of what he called the "Popular Liturgical Library." He had suggested this to the abbot soon after arriving in Europe.[52] He envisioned this work consisting primarily in the publishing of books and pamphlets on the liturgy. Michel had witnessed the effect of active liturgical participation in the lives of the people whom he met at the great European liturgical centers. At that time, the liturgical movement was not yet known in the United States.

To further assist the promotion of such a movement in the United States, he became convinced that a popular liturgical periodical should

---

[51] "I am daily becoming more convinced that philosophy is like liturgy a great means of apostolic work in the U.S., and for that reason I must expect to be doing continually less at the liturgical project after the first years. Others can jump into that work, while it takes all the preparation I have had in the last nine years, and more, even to commence the other work." Letter of Michel to Abbot Alcuin Deutsch, written at Louvain, 14 March 1925. Marx, 35.

[52] While awaiting the abbot's response, he wrote another letter on 18 January 1925: "The liturgical project got a good boost at Solesmes and has otherwise developed without a loss of time. I am enclosing a tentative program of our Liturgical Library. Of course, these are the merest suggestions, but I am keeping my eyes open for all possibilities. The thing is growing in magnitude, but the grace of the Lord may be behind it. I (this is all suppositional) should do no more translating myself (the first two are almost done) but direct the whole matter, and make selections. I really anticipate no difficulty in getting men to do translations. . . . Just think how it would help to transform the mentality towards the liturgy at home, not to think of the possible providential work that lies before us in the whole English-speaking world." Marx, 37.

be founded in addition to the "Popular Liturgical Library."[53] The abbot responded favorably to Michel's request, even suggesting that the periodical begin publication in the near future. Michel responded immediately with the news that he already had a layout design for the magazine as well as six month's worth of columns written for the "Editor's Corner." He then wrote: "I have been bashful about suggesting the title, here it is: 'Orate Fratres'—a review that aims at fostering a deeper understanding and wider participation in the official prayer of the Church."[54] In the meantime, he encouraged the abbot to send other monks to study in Europe, "so that they too could gradually imbibe the liturgical spirit."

Michel's association with Lambert Beauduin was clearly formative. Beauduin's concerns became Michel's, and therefore, ultimately became the concerns of the liturgical movement in the United States. Aside from Beauduin's influence, Michel's sojourn in Europe planted seeds in his thinking, which would, years later, grow into major topics of interest once he returned to Collegeville: the role of women in the world; a series of texts for religious education which were rooted in the liturgy; liturgy and social justice; the full and active participation of the laity in the liturgy. A chronicle of Michel's publications reflects all these themes, from one aspect or another. Several years after Michel's death, H. A. Reinhold spoke of Michel's formative European experience:

> It is almost beyond human comprehension to grasp the completeness with which he absorbed everything that Austria, Belgium, and Germany had to offer. But greater yet was what he did with it. Instead of dragging his find across the border as an exotic museum piece, he made it as American as only an American mind can make it. He had seen the high

---

[53] Michel wrote to his abbot: "And our Popular Liturgical Library has kept pace with time, except that it still awaits your approval (in its general lines). But before that comes I must frankly warn you. While the whole thing may get to be one of the biggest events that struck the Catholic U.S. since the NCWC (I believe that very sincerely), it also may mean what every big thing means—*work* and manpower. The prospects for its growth as a movement of liturgical restoration are so big that I sometimes feel like backing out of the whole matter. And still there is the urge to go on, which apparently can only be checked by your word. Which way will your decision fall? There are many indications that a liturgical movement will be well received in the U.S. in many quarters—and that means going ahead once the start is made. That again means on our part the giving over of a few men to that work, the founding of a popular publication (not immediately, of course), further books in the series (the *offer* has even been made by Mrs. Ward to get the series out in school children caliber) if that is at all feasible." Letter of 14 March 1925. Marx, 38.

[54] Marx, 39.

sweep of German ecclesiology and sacramentalism; he had admired the Belgians for their clear grasp of a new spirituality and their critical awareness of all that stood in the way of liturgical, ecclesiastical piety from traditional carry-overs; he had learned in Austria what the common people could gather from the Church's treasure without fright, but he did not come back to force these foreign and incoherent moulds on the American church. Besides, his clear realism and his burning apostle's heart had one urge none of the great masters in Europe seemed to see: the connection of social justice with a new social spirituality. For Virgil Michel the labor encyclicals of Leo XIII and the liturgical reforms of Pius X did not just by accident happen within one generation, but were responses to cries of the masses for Christ, who had power and gave the good tidings. They belonged together.[55]

It was such an integrated vision, formed by Michel's studies and observations in Europe, which marked the founding of the liturgical movement in the United States.

Before returning home to Collegeville, Michel again travelled extensively through Europe, then on to the Holy Land and Egypt. This time his father was his travelling companion. On 28 August 1925, the two sailed for home from Bremerhaven, Germany. Michel returned to his monastery of St. John's, Collegeville and the liturgical movement in the United States was initiated. In the words of his biographer, "Virgil Michel was the bridge over which the liturgical apostolate of Europe came to America."[56]

[55] *National Liturgical Week: Proceedings* (Ferdinand, Ind.: The Liturgical Conference, 1947) 11.
[56] Marx, 41-2.

CHAPTER TWO

The Beginnings of a Movement: Toward Full and Active Participation in the Liturgy

INTRODUCTION

The liturgical movement within the United States, like its European counterpart, was founded on the principle of participation where the Church recognizes itself as the living body of Christ, which best expresses and symbolizes this organic relationship in worship. The ideal of full and active participation was fundamental in every aspect of the liturgical movement in the United States, whether the topic was the relationship of liturgy to justice, liturgical education, art and architecture, or liturgical music. Participation in the liturgy was the point of departure for all these issues. While such a high ideal was the moving force in the lives of the liturgical pioneers, the pastoral reality in the 1920s and 1930s presented quite a different situation.

During the 1920s, religious individualism dominated much of Catholic life and piety in the United States.[1] In retrospect, it is not surprising that there was little recognition of the Eucharist as a common act of worship (that is, as fundamentally social in nature) because a good number of Catholics failed to recognize their own relationship to

---

[1] See James Hennesey, "Catholicism Unbound: The Church of the Twenties," in *American Catholics: A History of the Roman Catholic Community in the United States* (New York: Oxford University Press, 1981) 234–53; and also William. M. Halsey, *The Survival of American Innocence: Catholicism in an Era of Disillusionment, 1920–1940* (Notre Dame: University of Notre Dame Press, 1980).

one another as brothers and sisters—as members of that same living body of Christ.[2]

Virgil Michel is commonly accepted as the founder of the liturgical movement in the United States. There is no question as to his influence in shaping the direction of the movement, and even more importantly, in laying the foundations for the liturgical renewal that would only be realized years after his death. But it is also true that there were others, even before Michel, who endeavored to bring about the same change, albeit with varying degrees of success.

In the late eighteenth century, John Carroll, the first American bishop, argued for reforms that would bring about a more participative liturgy. Besides advocating the use of the vernacular in the liturgy, Carroll also wrote his own "Explanation of the Mass." This text provided background on the theology and meaning of the liturgy itself. His aim was to assist congregants to understand better and appreciate that which they were celebrating.

In this century, several of Virgil Michel's contemporaries had a similar vision of an American liturgical revival. William Busch, a diocesan priest who was professor of Church history at the St. Paul Seminary in Minnesota, had an interest in the liturgical movement as far back as 1919.[3] He had been in communication with Abbot Alcuin Deutsch of Collegeville, and in 1925 the two began seriously discussing the possibility of starting a liturgical publishing venture that would help to popularize and make available some of the literature being produced in Europe. In a letter to Virgil Michel, dated 28 September 1925, Busch wrote:

> During the past months while you were in Europe I had taken up with Abbot Alcuin both by letter and conversation the subject of the presentation to priests and people in this country of some of the excellent European literature on the liturgical movement. . . . The abbot told me that my first suggestion to him in this regard came to him just at the time when a similar one was made to him by yourself.[4]

Busch also made a liturgical study tour through Europe and was impressed by what he witnessed. It is no surprise, then, that soon after his return from Europe, Virgil Michel and William Busch became close

[2] J. Leo Klein, "The Role of Gerald Ellard (1894–1963) in the Development of the Contemporary American Catholic Liturgical Movement" (Ph.D. diss., Fordham University, 1971) 113–4.

[3] Marx, 47, note 44. See W. Busch, "An Apostle of Liturgical Life," *Orate Fratres (OF)* 13 (1939) 102–3.

[4] Quoted in Marx, 38.

collaborators, not only because of the close geographical proximity of Collegeville and St. Paul, but more fundamentally, because together they shared the vision of a liturgical movement which, they were convinced, would renew Church life and particularly liturgical life across the United States of America.

Alcuin Deutsch is frequently overlooked when church history considers the liturgical pioneers of the 1920s and 1930s, but his contribution was quite significant. Like Michel, Deutsch had also studied in Rome and observed the liturgical practice of the great European monasteries. At Maredsous, for example, he was greatly influenced by Dom Columba Marmion. It was Deutsch who gave Michel a copy of Guardini's *The Spirit of the Liturgy* in 1920, after he himself had been so impressed with that text. According to Michel's biographer, it was this book that incited Michel's interest in the liturgy.[5] The liturgical journal *Orate Fratres* was initiated in 1926, thanks to the support and encouragement of Deutsch, who soon became a frequent contributor with articles on the liturgical renewal. Godfrey Diekmann, O.S.B., Virgil Michel's successor as editor of *OF* and another of the great pioneers of the movement, spoke of Deutsch's leadership in this way:

> He had a vision of the Church, a vision of the greatness of the Church and the needs of the Church, and they always took precedence over our own needs. And he gave us a sense of that greatness, that vision. And he had a great sense of faith. After the Second World War, we gave ten percent of our total income to European relief . . . At a time when no Catholic institution in the United States dared to send anybody for higher education except to Catholic University, Notre Dame, or Rome, we had all sorts at universities all over the United States and Europe . . . Now that gives you a sense of his vision.[6]

Another collaborator with Michel and Busch in the early days of the movement was the German born Martin Hellriegel (1891–1981). In 1925, he was already pastorally active in O'Fallon, Missouri, as chaplain of the Sisters of the Most Precious Blood. He too had been steeped in the liturgical renewal of Europe and sought to introduce, slowly but surely, elements of that renewal on American soil. As a result, O'Fallon became known for its innovative liturgies. Many would travel great distances to witness the liturgy as it was celebrated in the convent there. While some were threatened by Hellriegel's innovations, many

---

[5] Marx, 24–5.

[6] Interview by Kathleen Hughes (April 1987), in Hughes, *The Monk's Tale: A Biography of Godfrey Diekmann, O.S.B.* (Collegeville: The Liturgical Press, 1991) 22.

were greatly impressed by his efforts and carried back that same enthusiasm for the liturgy to their own parishes and communities.[7]

Hellriegel was familiar with the name of Virgil Michel and with Michel's desire to launch the liturgical apostolate in the United States, so he wrote to Michel on 23 September 1925. He informed him of his own work and invited the young Benedictine to come to O'Fallon that Christmas to witness the work being done there and to discuss plans for a possible liturgical journal. Michel accepted the invitation. Meanwhile the two continued to correspond and exchange ideas about how best to promote such a movement in an American context.

In April of that year, a Jesuit scholastic by the name of Gerald Ellard had written a letter published in *America* magazine, entitled: "Open Up the Liturgy." He wrote:

> Open up the liturgy in sermons and instructions. College men, tomorrow's leaders, ask for such sermons. . . . Why not such a series of sermons and classroom lectures? Why not a liturgical column in every Catholic paper? Why not an *American Journal of Liturgical Studies?*[8]

The letter caught the eye of Martin Hellriegel and Virgil Michel. Ellard was studying in St. Louis, Missouri, at the time, and had heard much about the liturgies at O'Fallon and about Hellriegel. On 1 November 1925, he travelled to O'Fallon to see firsthand the work being done there and was impressed by what he witnessed.[9] Within a short period of time, Ellard and Hellriegel became very good friends. In fact, Hellriegel soon became something of a mentor to Ellard, encouraging him in his liturgical interests and including him in his own plans and projects.

Having already invited Michel to O'Fallon for Christmas, Hellriegel issued the same invitation to Ellard. That meeting was historic because, in many respects, it was the first of many gatherings among those who would give shape and direction to the liturgical movement in the United States. As it was the first meeting of the promoters of the movement in the United States, it was, in effect, the inception of the liturgical movement itself. Each of the three brought diverse gifts to their corporate project: Michel was pragmatic and a great organizer; Hellriegel was gifted with a keen pastoral sense and a wealth of pas-

---

[7] See Noel H. Barrett, "The Contribution of Martin B. Hellriegel to the American Catholic Liturgical Movement" (Ph.D. diss., St. Louis University, 1976) 87–121.

[8] Gerald Ellard, "Open Up the Liturgy," *America* 33 (1925) 37.

[9] In an article published in *America*, in December of that year, Ellard described his experiences at the All Saints' Day liturgy at O'Fallon in which he participated. See Ellard, "A Pilgrimage and a Vision," *America* 34 (1925) 201–3.

toral experience; Ellard was able to translate and popularize the liturgical scholarship that was taking place at that time.[10]

Apart from the professional relationship among these three and the other pioneers in the movement, a very close human rapport existed. This might well be a phenomenon common to leaders of all types of social movements, but it was certainly operative within the liturgical movement. It was as if they were symbolizing, whether consciously or unconsciously, the very image of the Mystical Body of Christ which they were attempting to promote.

In a 1925 article that he co-authored with Anthony Jasper,[11] Hellriegel made the helpful distinction between an organism and an organization. He described the Church as a living organism that reveals its true nature as the Mystical Body of Christ through the liturgy.[12] The reality in the 1920s was that most Catholics in the United States saw their role in the Church more as individual members of an organization than as integral members of the living body of Christ. The pioneers of the liturgical movement recognized that at the root of the problem regarding liturgical participation, there was the far more fundamental issue of an individualistic baptismal and ecclesial consciousness. Thus, the work of the liturgical movement would need to begin by providing a solid theological and ecclesiological grounding of what it means to be members of the Church.

Theological Foundations for Liturgical Participation

While the image of the Church as the body of Christ is as ancient as the Church itself, it was gradually replaced by a more hierarchically structured ecclesiology, beginning in the medieval period, reaching its height at the time of the reformation, and continuing to the present century.[13] Consistent with such an approach, liturgy became the work of the priest while those in the assembly became passive spectators.

It was not until the nineteenth century that the image of the Church as the Mystical Body of Christ was significantly recovered, thanks to the work of the German scholar, Johann Adam Möhler (1798–1838). Möhler's two major works *Die Einheit in der Kirche* (Tübingen, 1825),

[10] Klein, 78–9.

[11] Martin B. Hellriegel and A. J. Jasper, "Der Schluessel zur Loesung der sozial Frage" in *Central Blatt* (July/August 1925), later developed into a pamphlet: *The True Basis of Christian Solidarity,* (trans.) W. Busch (St. Louis: Central Bureau of the Central Verein, 1947).

[12] Barrett, 108–10.

[13] See Bernard Cooke, *The Distancing of God: The Ambiguity of Symbol in History and Theology* (Minneapolis: Fortress Press, 1990) 125–257.

and *Symbolik* (Mainz, 1832), emphasized the organic unity of the Church. He based his research on patristic sources of the first three centuries, and argued for a vision of the Church as a community of the faithful rather than a juridically structured institution. Möhler was convinced that the divine life was communicated by the apostles not to individuals, but to brothers and sisters who were incorporated into the same body of Christ.[14] He was not alone in his approach.

There were other nineteenth-century theologians—Matthias Scheeben (1835–1888), Carlo Passaglia (1816–1886), Johannes Baptist Franzelin (1816–1886), and Klemens Schräder (1820–1875)—who promoted such an ecclesiological view in their teaching and research. Together, these theologians paved the way for the First Vatican Council's *Dogmatic Constitution on the Church of Christ*, where the proposed draft begins: "The Church is the Mystical Body of Christ."[15]

Despite the work done by nineteenth-century theologians to promote the Mystical Body, such an ecclesiology was yet to be popularized. Scholarly works were being written almost exclusively by German theologians, but there was precious little periodical literature available on the topic until this century. In the United States, for example, in the period from 1890 to 1906, only one periodical article appeared on the theme of the Mystical Body.[16] Even in seminaries, the topic was hardly presented or discussed.[17]

---

[14] Ernest B. Koenker, *The Liturgical Renaissance In the Roman Catholic Church* (Chicago: The University of Chicago Press, 1954) 34. For a more extensive treatment of Möhler's thought, see R. William Franklin, "Johann Adam Möhler and Worship in a Totalitarian Society," *Worship* 67 (1993) 2–17. In this excellent article, Franklin develops and analyzes Möhler's theory of the Church as an organic unity.

[15] *Sacrorum Conciliorum nova et amplissima collectio*, J. D. Mansi, ed. (Arnheim, 1926) 539, my translation. In "The True Christian Spirit," *The Ecclesiastical Review* (hereafter *ER*) 82 (1930) 134f., Virgil Michel notes that had the Council not been disrupted, this definition of the Church as the Mystical Body of Christ might well have made a significant difference in what aspects of the Church were emphasized. In "The True Christian Spirit," Michel develops his understanding of the doctrine of the Mystical Body, stating that "the inspirational idea of Catholic life as it should be" could be found in the example of the early Church and in the living out of their membership in the Mystical Body (132).

[16] J. McSorley, "The Mystical Body" *Catholic World* 81 (1905) 307–14. See Joseph Bluette, "The Mystical Body of Christ: 1890–1940, A Bibliography," *Theological Studies* 3 (1942) 261–89.

[17] In 1952, one priest who had been ordained fifty years was asked what he had heard about the Mystical Body when he was a seminary student. He responded: "Mystical Body? Why, not even the Pope then knew there was a Mystical Body." Quoted in Marx, 100, note 48.

Part of the agenda of the liturgical movement was to help popularize such a rich notion of the Church universal, since the liturgical pioneers saw it clearly as the key to liturgical renewal. Building on these nineteenth-century foundations and inspired by the *Motu Proprio* of Pius X, liturgical leaders in the early years of this century—people like Herwegen,[18] Casel, Guardini, and Beauduin—initiated the liturgical movement in Europe. The promoters and pioneers of the liturgical movement in the United States were likewise convinced of the importance of those same theological foundations for the growth of a baptismal consciousness which would foster full and active participation in the Church and its worship.[19] In the words of Virgil Michel:

> The doctrine of the mystical body emphasizes the true position of the "new creature" that is born of water and the Holy Ghost. Baptism is a birth into the Christ-life through which we become engrafted on the vine Christ, incorporated in the mystical body of which Christ is the Head and we are the members. Thenceforth we are "other Christs," adopted children of our divine Father . . ."[20]

And just what did such Christian initiation imply? Michel answered this question in an article entitled "The True Christian Spirit":

> Thus membership in the Church is not confined to the minimum discharging of a debt, but implies an active participation in the life of the Church. To be a member of the mystic body of Christ means always to be a living member, and to cooperate actively in the life of the whole. To nothing less than that is the true son of the Church called.[21]

---

[18] Koenker, 35. Möhler's influence is clearly seen, for example, in Herwegen's "Kirche und Mysterium," *Mysterium, Gesammelte Arbeiten Laacher Monche* (Münster, 1926), where he emphasizes many things the Church is not: a legal institution, the authority in morals, etc. Herwegen then goes on to stress a corporate view of the Church where members live out their baptism through shared participation in its life.

[19] For additional European writers on the subject see Friedrich Jurgensmeier, *The Mystical Body of Christ As the Basic Principle of Spiritual Life,* (trans.) Harriet G. Strauss (New York: Sheed and Ward, 1954); E. Mersch, *The Whole Christ, the Historical Development of the Doctrine of the Mystical Body in Scripture and Tradition,* (trans.) John R. Kelly (Milwaukee: Bruce Publishing Co., 1938). For American treatments of the Mystical Body, see D. Day, *The Mystical Body of Christ* (East Orange, N.J.: Thomas Barry, 1936); Martin B. Hellriegel, *Vine and Branches* (St. Louis: Pio Decimo Press, 1948); Daniel Lord, *Our Part in the Mystical Body* (St. Louis: The Queen's Work, 1935); Fulton J. Sheen, *The Mystical Body of Christ* (New York: Sheed and Ward, 1935).

[20] "The Philosophical and Theological Bases of the Liturgical Movement" (unpublished manuscript, n.d.). St. John's Abbey Archives (hereafter SJAA) Z-32.

[21] Michel, "The True Christian Spirit," 140.

Relying on 1 Corinthians 10, and then on Augustine's development of the theological notion of the Mystical Body, Basil Stegmann, O.S.B., made an even more direct connection between the Mystical Body and the Eucharist, describing the Eucharist as "the mainspring of the Christ-life and the bond of union between the members."[22]

It should also be noted that speaking of the Church as the Mystical Body of Christ was not always an image unanimously embraced. There were many, particularly some members of the hierarchy, who felt that the doctrine of the Mystical Body of Christ was an attempt to undermine the hierarchical structure of the Church. As late as 1942 the doctrine was being attacked as a "new conception of the Church."[23] Only one year later, in 1943, Pius XII issued the encyclical *Mystici Corporis Christi,* which affirmed the doctrine of the Church as the Mystical Body of Christ, albeit a hierarchically structured body. Even following the promulgation of the encyclical there continued to be uneasiness with themes which the doctrine of the Mystical Body was promoting.[24] Some of this criticism also found its way into the work of the liturgical movement. Chicago liturgical pioneer Reynold Hillenbrand told the story of a retreat director in 1951 who preached that too much was being said about the Mystical Body of Christ and not enough was being said about the Church.[25]

Despite the controversial nature of the doctrine of the Mystical Body, the liturgical pioneers did not tire of promoting it, convinced as they were of its intrinsic relationship to the liturgy. Through the sacraments of Christian initiation, men and women are incorporated into Jesus Christ.[26] Such incorporation unites them not only to Christ, but also to

[22] Stegmann, "Christ In His Church," *OF* 7 (1933) 112–3.

[23] Koenker, 37. The attack was launched in France by a Monsignor Groeber in his ninth thesis against "une conception nouvelle de l'Eglise."

[24] Theodore M. Hesburgh, C.S.C., in a conversation with the author, spoke of his own doctoral dissertation, "The Relation of the Sacramental Characters of Baptism and Confirmation to the Lay Apostolate," submitted in 1946 to the Theology Faculty of The Catholic University of America, Washington, D.C. In the dissertation, Hesburgh argued that rather than the lay apostolate being a sharing in the work of the hierarchy (a view commonly held at the time), it was baptism which gave the call to service of the whole Church—the mandate to participate, not in the work of the hierarchy, but in the overall mission of the Church which lay members were entitled to share. As a result of the proposed thesis, Hesburgh's dissertation was considered controversial at the time. Interview by author, 18 January 1994, University of Notre Dame, Notre Dame, Indiana.

[25] Reynold Hillenbrand, "The Priesthood and the World," *National Liturgical Week: Proceedings* (Ferdinand: The Liturgical Conference, 1951) 163.

[26] See Ellard, "The Dignity of a Christian," *The Catholic Digest* 1 (November 1936) 41–2.

one another through shared membership in that same body. This incorporation gives all members a share in Christ's life and in his priesthood. Baptism, then, is the beginning of their dwelling with Christ living in and through those who have been claimed by him. So it is through the liturgy that the Mystical Body continues the work and mission of Christ from age to age. Michel wrote:

> It is the exercise of this power that constitutes the essential life of the Church on earth. . . . The liturgy can truly be called the life of the Church. Without the liturgy there would be no Church such as Christ has instituted. Without the liturgy there would be no Mystical Body of Christ, in which the divine mission of Christ continues. It is above all in the official liturgical acts of the Church that Christ himself lives and acts. In them He continues His active mediatorship between God and man, there He continues to offer to God His own all-sufficient Sacrifice of praise and atonement. It is through the liturgy that the redemption of Christ is extended over all time for the constant glory of God and the salvation of souls.[27]

Pragmatically, life in the Mystical Body of Christ was concretely experienced in the local church, particularly within the parish:

> Every parish thus presents a miniature of the mystical body of Christ. Christ is its Head, Lord and King. . . . For as a miniature of the body of Christ, the parish is to be animated, dominated, and transformed in all its departments of life by the spirit of Christ. Its associational process is to realize in its territory the idea that all the faithful are the members of the family of God, and constitute a people, a spiritual edifice.[28]

The call to renewal was to be a return to the sources, "to active contact with the living sources of life in Christ," to full and active participation in the body of Christ which expresses itself and rediscovers its mission in the liturgy. The liturgical movement contributed to overall ecclesial renewal by leading people back to the liturgy as the "primary and indispensable source of the true Christian spirit."[29] Such a return to the sources, then, was a return to full and active participation:

> Participation in the liturgy naturally produces in us the consciousness of our union with Christ and of our dignity as sharers in the divine nature.

[27] Michel, *Our Life in Christ* (Collegeville: The Liturgical Press, 1939) 50–1.

[28] John Harbrecht, *The Lay Apostolate* (St. Louis: B. Herder Book Company, 1929) 42.

[29] Michel, "The Significance of the Liturgical Movement," *National Catholic Welfare Council Bulletin* (hereafter NCWC) 10 (1929) 26.

It brings us into contact with the many- sided aspects of the life of Christ, with the rich inexhaustible content of His life, and thus manifests the rich possibilities of our life in Him. It elevates our minds above the things of this earth and of self, broadens our spiritual outlook while deepening it, gives us a better sense of the truly beautiful and truly valuable, a better sense of unity with a sympathy for our fellow members of the body of Christ, a human family feeling for all mankind, and, being rooted in the wonderful condescension of God, a firmly founded optimism in regard to all things that count in life.[30]

For Virgil Michel and his colleagues in the movement, this participation was intimately linked with the notion of sacrifice. Basing his own thesis on the work of Thomas Aquinas, Michel argued that the purpose of sacrifice was not simply the destruction of the one being sacrificed, but also the forgiveness of sin, the preservation of grace, and the union between God and humankind. Thus, the eucharistic sacrifice embodied was not to be viewed from a minimalistic perspective, simply the discharging of a debt, but as the active participation of all Christians in the priestly act of Christ.

Liturgical Participation: The Pastoral Challenges

With the growth in immigration to the United States at the beginning of this century, the Church had to deal not with just one culture but with many. Rather than appreciating the diversity of each culture, the United States prided itself on being "the great melting pot," blending many different cultures into one.

Monsignor Martin Hellriegel, himself an immigrant, had the foresight and vision to challenge the "melting pot" theory. He disliked the theory precisely because one can throw anything into a melting pot and the uniqueness and individuality of such a thing is lost. All is blended into sameness. Hellriegel preferred the image of a mosaic, where every individual tessera is precious, diverse, and valuable, and needs to retain its unique character and dimension in order to complete the piece.[31] Hellriegel was, of course, ahead of his time. In proposing his own view of a multi-cultural situation, he was articulating a vision that would become normative forty or fifty years later.

To preserve their cultural heritage and find support among those who spoke the same language, many immigrants tended to settle in the same neighborhood. These cultural groups often had their own national churches, German, Polish, or Italian national parishes where the

---

[30] Michel, *The Liturgy of the Church* (New York: Macmillan Publishers, 1937) 60–1.
[31] Barrett, 64.

liturgical, musical, and cultural traditions (e.g., festivals, the honoring of particular saints) of those countries were continued.[32] Bonds within such ethnic neighborhoods were strong and there was very little inter-action with those from a different neighborhood. Those strong, ethnic and religious bonds had sharp lines of demarcation which tended to divide one cultural group from another. Divisions also existed be-tween Catholics and other Christians, where those seen as different were viewed with suspicion.

Of all those tensions, none were as fierce as the prejudice often lodged against black Americans. When blacks moved into a neigh-borhood, whites usually moved out. For instance, by 1925, the black center of New York City had moved uptown to Harlem, but with the population increase of 87,417 new blacks came the departure from Harlem of 118,792 whites.[33] Sadly, resistance to African-American ex-pansion was greatest in areas settled by Catholic immigrants. This is demonstrated by the famous Chicago riots of 1919. The riots occurred in one of the most Catholic cities in the country, in a neighborhood seventy percent Catholic.[34] While Church leaders deplored such racial violence, they were not opposed to segregation. Luigi Giambastiani, the Sicilian pastor of St. Philip Benzini parish in Chicago, wrote in a 1922 parish bulletin: "It is true that some *idealists* dream of an Ameri-can millennium when all races will be found fused into one new American race—but in the meantime it is good that each one think of his own . . . ."[35] Like other immigrant groups, and particularly in the face of such oppression, black Catholics wanted their own parishes. One Omaha pastor argued pragmatically that black Catholics needed their own parishes where they could sense their equality with each other and avoid oppression.[36] The reality remained, however, that

---

[32] See Jay Dolan, *The American Catholic Parish* (New York: Paulist Press, 1987) vol. 1, 177–85; vol. 2, 333–48.

[33] Dolan, *The American Catholic Parish,* vol. 1, 47.

[34] John McGreevy, "American Catholics and the African-American Migration: 1919–1970" (Ph.D. diss., Stanford University, 1992) 7. Thirty-eight died and five hundred and thirty seven were injured as a result of the riots. The report issued after the riot claimed that "a mob of 300 or 400 white people, all ages, ripped a streetcar carrying African-Americans off the tracks and chased the Negro passen-gers, stunning one man with a brick and then killing him with a piece of wood." Ibid., 1.

[35] Ibid., 31.

[36] The pastor wrote: "I do not say they are inferior—from man to man all are equal before God—but they feel oppressed, and so they prefer to have a church of their own . . . where they feel themselves an equality with their fellow worship-pers . . . Have they not the same right to this privilege as the Poles, Italians, and

African-Americans knew oppression within the Church as well as without.[37]

Gradually, at least among European immigrants, perhaps as inter-marriage among immigrants became more acceptable, these diverse cultural groups found their way into the same parish community. Each of these cultures brought its own tradition of liturgical participation, and its own understanding of worship, and church membership.

Until 1890, the two major immigrant groups in the United States were the Germans and the Irish. Each group brought distinct traditions and pastoral challenges. Having suffered under English persecution for almost four hundred years, the Irish had been stripped of their liturgical and musical traditions. Landowners in Ireland were Protestant, thus the Irish Catholic church was closely identified with the oppressed.[38] Forbidden to have churches or schools, Irish Catholics had to celebrate the Eucharist in secret, frequently in barns and other hidden places. The ultimate result of this privation was such a lack of liturgical understanding that some Irish thought singing during the liturgy was a Protestant custom.[39] This was further confirmed by a 1929 letter to Virgil Michel:

---

others?" A member of the Board of Indian and Negro missions was far more blunt in his rationale: "Most of our people do not care to go to resorts notably frequented by the Jews or even in a less pronounced way such a place would not be frequented [sic] by the Poles if it were known that Italians largely predominated there . . ." Both quoted in McGreevy, 34.

[37] Jay Dolan writes: "Southern white Catholics pushed black Catholics into basement chapels, escorted them to galleries, forced them to sit in back pews of side coves, segregated them into separate parishes and schools and discouraged them from seeking the priesthood"(*The American Catholic Parish,* 185). In general, blacks were often made to feel that their religious experience and tradition were inferior. This was another reason for the emergence of black Catholic parishes—so that believers in the black community could pray freely and without having to apologize for who they were or how they prayed.

[38] On this topic, see David W. Miller, "Irish Catholicism and the Great Famine," *Journal of Social History* 9 (1975) 81–98.

[39] Marx, 86. Lambert Beauduin made the following observation about Dom Columba Marmion's (1858–1923) youth in Ireland: "During the 1914 war Dom Marmion collected together in a country house of his native land some monks who had been expelled from Belgium. We can still remember the wonder caused by the solemn celebration of the liturgy: an aged priest had never attended the singing of Vespers, and told us how amazed he was; the office which he had been reciting every day for forty years was then intended to be chanted solemnly in choir! . . . Such were the religious surroundings at the end of the nineteenth century, at the time of the youth and formation of Dom Marmion. If Benedictine life [in Belgium]

The Church in the USA has been started and organized by the Irish quota of immigrants. Now in Ireland religion was reduced to its elements and essentials due to the Penal Times when Mass was said stealthily and in caves and barns. The consequence is that we in the USA have the Dublin Rite, as I saw it called in the German Quartalschrift. And if you ask me what is the Dublin Rite, I answer it consists in eliminating the trimmings, so called.[40]

German immigrants, whose liturgical traditions were not as impoverished as those of the Irish, found themselves better prepared for the liturgical revival in the United States. They had brought with them from Germany a strong tradition of congregational participation, particularly in terms of liturgical music. Likewise, they had a strong sense of community, and with that, an active social consciousness.

While it is inaccurate to claim that the liturgical movement in the United States was fundamentally a German movement, there is little question that the immigrants most receptive to the movement were German. Furthermore, the pioneers of the movement—Michel, Hellriegel, Ellard, Reinhold, Hillenbrand—were almost exclusively German, whether of the first or second generation. It is reported that there were some clergy on the east coast of the United States who were convinced that all this concern about the liturgy was merely "a midwestern fad." This same group was said to refer to one of the national liturgical weeks as "a meeting of a bunch of Germans out in the midwest."[41] Nonetheless, it was due to the German leadership that the liturgical movement was launched. And it was the German Catholic Central Verein, the first social action group in the United States (founded in Baltimore in 1855) that gave corporate endorsement as an organization to the liturgical movement.

The Poles are not often mentioned in connection with the liturgical movement in the United States, but their own contribution should not be overlooked. In big cities like Chicago and Detroit, there were a number of large Polish parishes. In those communities, congregational singing and use of the vernacular were already well in place by the late 1930s and early 1940s. In 1934, a vernacular Missal was already in use

---

later revealed to him all the riches of the liturgy, there was nothing in the memories of his childhood to awaken in him the desire for a liturgical apostolate in the parishes, or to make him foresee the effectiveness of such an apostolate among the general populace." *More About Dom Marmion,* ed. Monks of Glenstal Abbey (Westminster: Newman Press, 1948) 67.

[40] Henry Borgmann, C.S.S.R., Letter to Virgil Michel, 25 June 1929, SJAA: Z-22.

[41] J. J. Murphy, "A Call for Irish-American Honest Self-Appraisal," *Homiletic and Pastoral Review* (hereafter *HPR*) 54 (1954) 512.

in Polish communities like St. Stanislaus Kostka Parish in Chicago.[42] Despite papal decrees in 1903 and 1928 prohibiting vernacular hymns during Mass, congregational singing in Polish was normative in many of those parishes. Like the Germans, the Poles too sang the Mass back in the late 1930s and 1940s. By 1948, for example, Polish hymns were sung at the principal Mass of St. Francis Parish in Detroit, the pastor reported, "and the church is packed to capacity."[43] In 1947, one newcomer to SS. Peter and Paul Parish in Detroit, a non-Pole, complained that "every high Mass . . . is sung in Polish. When the priest intones the Gloria, the choir responds with a Polish hymn."[44] Poles in Detroit were admired for carols that they sang at the Pasterka (Shepherd's Mass) early on Christmas morning, as well as for the haunting tones of the "Gorzkie Zale" (Bitter Lamentations) sung by a number of Polish congregations during Holy Week.[45]

While liturgical developments within the African-American community developed much later and more in connection with the civil rights struggle, there were some early voices addressing issues of liturgical participation among black Catholics,[46] along with the relationship of liturgical participation and social justice:

> Where the Mass is keenly appreciated the mist of racial prejudice is dissipated like the snow under the rays of the sun . . . Nothing shows more the universality of the Church than the sight of a congregation of all

---

[42] Ed Marciniak, Interview by author, 21 November 1994, Institute of Urban Life, Loyola University, Chicago.

[43] Leslie Woodcock Tentler, *Seasons of Grace: A History of the Catholic Archdiocese of Detroit* (Detroit: Wayne State University Press, 1990) 350.

[44] Ibid., 423.

[45] Ibid., 181.

[46] In a 1940 article which appeared in the *Interracial Review,* a young black seminarian affirmed the fundamental equality of black Catholics as co-sharers in the Mystical Body, possessing the same inherent right to liturgical participation as white Catholics. He wrote: "Holy Mass is a national act of worship for the cross of Christ has created a new nation of men . . . It is a race created not by blood but by grace. It is a nation whose boundaries are not determined by geographical lines or linguistic affinities but by a common profession of faith . . . Some thirteen million American Negroes are seeking their share in these treasures of God's bounty. They know the bitterness of human sacrifices on the demands of human greed and inhuman indifference. They dread a sacrifice that brings death not life. They know of the divine democracy of Christ. They should belong to the new race; to the people of God . . . Christ is our Brother. He is their Brother. God is our Father. He is their Father. They are legitimate heirs *de jure* to Heaven. They need the Mass. They must have the Mass." Gladstone Wilson, "The Mass and Interracial Justice," *Interracial Justice* 13 (1940) 29.

races kneeling together before the common altar. Holy Mass promotes the attainment of social justice for the whole racial group.[47]

John La Farge, S.J., promoted the *Missa recitata* among black communities in the USA. One editorial noted that by 1933, the black Catholic parish in Newark, New Jersey, had already been celebrating the dialogue Mass for some time.[48] Despite those early voices, it was not until the 1960s that black Catholics would retrieve their own African-American cultural heritage in worship.

During the 1920s and 1930s, talk of a liturgical movement or liturgical renewal was as foreign to most Catholic parishes in the United States as was talk of the Mystical Body of Christ. The liturgy was not taught, nor was it discussed or evaluated. It was something to be done strictly according to the rubrics, without feeling or expression. For most, liturgy was a passive experience. William J. Leonard, S.J., one of the pioneers in the movement, described it this way:

> Liturgically, it was an era of subsistence rations. Mass was offered (solemnly on great occasions, without splendor most of the time), and Sundays were observed as days of rest, respectable dress, and sober conduct, often climaxed by attendance at parish devotions in the evening. Holy Communion was becoming gradually more common, but was still thought of as something extra, added to the Mass on certain significant days. There was no participation by the congregation; silence, in fact, was generally imposed and observed as the only fitting response to the sacred mysteries being enacted on the distant altar. If hymns were sung, they had little relevance to the eucharistic action, and were for the most part rendered by the choir rather than sung by the assembly. The rosary or other devotional prayers were recited during the greater part of the service, sometimes aloud and communally, more often silently. Missals were so rare as to be virtually unknown; a few people used prayer books but occupied themselves as a rule rather with the devotions they continued ("acts" of faith, hope, love, contrition, etc.) than with the text of the Mass itself. The liturgical year brought round its fasts and its solemnities, and these attracted the people in large numbers, especially during Lent; but the emphasis was moral rather than doctrinal, and looked chiefly toward "a good confession." The Bible, except for the fragments read as "the Gospel" on Sundays, was a closed book. Vespers as an evening service on Sundays and great feasts lingered on in cathedrals and in a few churches, but it was of course sung in Latin, and attendance dropped off steadily until the practice virtually disappeared. Mass on week-days was offered at a very early hour, so that only a handful of the

[47] Ibid.
[48] *OF* 7 (1933) 179.

people could be present. The prevailing attitude of the clergy, concurred in by the laity, was that the liturgy *was* celebrated, the sacraments *were* conferred; God was objectively honored and the means of sanctification were made available. It did not matter very much that the people could not comprehend all that was done, or that they had almost no active share in it.[49]

Many lived with a certain tension in their religious practice between a bodily presence at liturgies which they hardly understood, and the practice of reciting their private prayers which had no connection at all with the public prayer of the Church except that the two were taking place at the same time.[50] Virgil Michel called such a phenomenon a type of "disassociated personality."[51] Even as the work of the liturgical movement began to take shape in areas located geographically around liturgical centers like St. John's Abbey in Collegeville, Minnesota, there remained many parts of the United States whose liturgical and overall parochial life would remain unchanged for many years to come. This, at least in part, can be explained by the different cultural traditions of American Catholics at that time.[52]

[49] William J. Leonard, "The Liturgical Movement in the United States," in *The Liturgy of Vatican II: A Symposium in Two Volumes,* ed. William Baraúna, (Chicago: Franciscan Herald Press, 1966) 294–5. See also: *The Letter Carrier: The Autobiography of William J. Leonard, S.J.* (Kansas City: Sheed and Ward, 1993) 145ff.

[50] An amusing description of the pre-Conciliar Mass is given in Garry Wills, *Bare Ruined Choirs: Doubt, Prophecy, and Radical Religion* (Garden City: Doubleday and Co. Inc., 1972) 65–75.

[51] Michel, "The Liturgical Apostolate," *The Catholic Educational Review* 25 (1927) 4.

[52] American Catholic historian Jay P. Dolan, in a conversation with the author, noted that on the east coast of the United States, for example, the liturgical renewal in the parishes did not arrive with any force until the early 1950s. There were organizations like the Liturgical Arts Society and the Pius X School of Liturgical Music, both based in New York. There was the Catholic Worker and publications like *America* or *The Commonweal,* but the reality in the local parish was quite different in places like New York and Boston. (Interview of 18 January 1994, University of Notre Dame, Notre Dame, Indiana.) Of course, one cannot ignore the significant contribution of Boston priests like Thomas Carroll, William Leonard, and Shawn Sheehan. In addition, the pages of *OF* make frequent mention of the Archdiocese of Newark as a center of liturgical activity in the 1930s and 1940s, headquartered at Saint Mary's Abbey, Newark, and Saint Joseph's Priory, Keyport, New Jersey, with individuals like Damasus Winzen, O.S.B., and Bishop Thomas Walsh leading the way. Nonetheless, in speaking of average east coast parishes, Dolan's theory remains convincing, and his appraisal is substantiated by the ethnic demographics of this period. German immigrants tended to settle in the middle west, in places like

One such cultural issue that impeded full and active participation was the topic of popular religiosity.[53] These popular devotions were religious exercises often enacted in common, but separate from the Church's official liturgy. Over the centuries, as the liturgy was increasingly removed from the laity, these devotions grew in number and variety. Since they were often celebrated in the vernacular, they had an appeal which was lacking in a Mass celebrated in a language no one could understand. Further, in a Church whose public rituals had become increasingly clericalized, popular devotions offered the possibility of an experience of prayer that was authentically of the people.[54]

As immigrants brought with them a history of varying levels of liturgical participation, so too did they bring various traditions of popular devotions.[55] Since Great Britain and Ireland had a substantial

---

Minnesota and Illinois. German parishes, in general, had a strong tradition of liturgical singing and participation. Irish immigrants tended to settle in the larger cities on the east coast. Having worshipped in secret for several hundred years due to their oppression by the English, there tended to be much less participation in Irish parishes. See Marx, 85–7.

[53] On the origins and development of popular devotions in the United States, see Ann Taves, *The Household of Faith: Roman Catholic Devotions in Mid-Nineteenth Century America* (Notre Dame: University of Notre Dame Press, 1986). On the relationship between popular religiosity and liturgy, see Anscar J. Chupungco, *Liturgical Inculturation: Sacramentals, Religiosity, and Catechesis* (Collegeville: The Liturgical Press, 1992) 95–133.

[54] Louis Bouyer writes: "Taken in their historical setting, these devotions are certainly not to be condemned. If the people of that time had not been given these devotions, they would have had nothing at all, and they would have lost all Christianity. Since the liturgy had become inaccessible to them, something else had to be substituted for it, something which was able to lead them to some Christian religion, if only because it took them as, and from where they were." *Liturgical Piety*, 249; see also: 243–56.

[55] One excellent example of such popular religiosity is found in Robert A. Orsi, *The Madonna of 115th Street* (New Haven: Yale University Press, 1985). Orsi demonstrates the very close connection between home and parish in the annual *festa* of la Madonna del Carmine, as celebrated by Italian immigrants in Harlem, New York City, in the 1920s and 1930s. This summer festival included street processions, music, the crowning of the Madonna in Jefferson Park (the church could not accommodate the size of the crowd) and, of course, plenty of good food. The neighboring Irish clergy were "against" these Mount Carmel devotions, viewing them as pagan superstitions. In addition to the Mount Carmel festival, baptisms, weddings, and funerals, lead us further into the significance of Italian popular religion. Orsi asks: "Why be so faithful about baptisms and not about Catholic schools? Why weddings and not Sunday Mass? . . . My informants in Harlem continually made a distinction between religion and church" (xvi–xvii; 56).

hold on Church practice in the United States in this century, devotions usually centered on the reserved sacrament or Marian devotion. Following the Marian apparition at Fatima, Portugal, in 1917, devotions to Mary reached a record high. Many of these devotions—whether a holy hour, a procession, or the celebration of forty-hours devotion before the exposed sacrament—almost always concluded with eucharistic benediction. In many American parishes, it was normative to hold some type of devotional service on a Sunday afternoon, and perhaps also on one night during the week. Parish missions, usually preached by clergy of different religious orders, the Redemptorists or the Jesuits, for example, often included similar devotional elements. There were devotions to the Virgin Mary in May and October, to St. Joseph in March, and to the Sacred Heart of Jesus in June. There was little reference to or connection with the liturgical feasts and seasons of the Church year. In fact, popular devotions often overshadowed the liturgical calendar, giving greater attention to dedicating the month of May to the Blessed Virgin, for example, than to the celebration of the Easter season which normally fell at the same time. The only possibility for some form of corporate prayer outside the context of the Mass was the rosary or another form of popular devotion. It was within such an environment that the liturgical promoters and pioneers would labor and strategize to instill an enthusiasm for the liturgy across the United States, and thereby encourage liturgical participation which was informed and active and a lay spirituality grounded in the liturgy.

These devotions, even when they were practiced in common, usually focused more on individual spirituality and needs, rather than on the community. One made a novena (nine consecutive days of prayer usually directed to a particular saint) to ask for something in particular. Votive candles were lighted in church with a particular intention in mind.[56] Although there was an awareness of praying with the group when these devotions were made in common, the sense that the community was being formed and united into the one body of Christ was lacking. The well-known writer, Flannery O'Connor, gave her opinion about novenas:

> Having grown up with them, I think of novenas the same way I think of the hideous Catholic churches you all too frequently find yourself in, that is, after a time I cease to see them even though I'm in them. The

---

[56] A Chicago pastor, Bernard Laukemper, wrote: "It is difficult to kill the superstition which clusters around the word 'novena.' It is horrid that the people always wonder, if the dog will get well, or the cows have twin calves, if they miss one day of the novena." Letter to Godfrey Diekmann, 13 June 1938, SJAA: #1165.

virtue of novenas is that they keep you at it for nine consecutive days and the human attention being what it is, this is a long time. I hate to say most of these prayers written by saints-in-an-emotional-state. You feel you are wearing somebody else's finery and I can never describe my heart as "burning" to the Lord (who knows better) without snickering.[57]

Many came to the Sunday liturgical assembly with rosary in hand, praying the rosary while the priest prayed the Mass. Thus, the agenda of the liturgical pioneers and promoters was challenging some very deep-rooted styles and traditions that were ingrained in the hearts and minds of many American Catholics.

Louis Bouyer addressed the issue directly:

It is when people are no longer in touch with the authentic spirit of the liturgy that such devotions are developed; but once these are in posses-sion, return to the liturgy is almost impossible. You cannot at the same time hail Christ as if He were still a little Baby in His cradle, and adore Him as the risen Lord, the *Christos-Pneuma*. You cannot weep for His passion as if you did not know that it has already ended in victory, and also exult in the resurrection. You cannot combine a mysticism centered on Jesus considered as the "Prisoner of the tabernacle," with celebrating the Eucharist as the saving Mystery by which Christ sets us free from all created limitations to bring us into the divine life. The more you are at-tached to one set of these alternatives, the more you must accept the loss of the other . . . You cannot eat your cake and treasure it for tomorrow: you must choose . . . We cannot hope to return to a living liturgy while we concentrate on these devotions and even add to them.[58]

Toward Full and Active Liturgical Participation

As in Europe, the American movement was fostered by Bene-dictines, but unlike its European counterpart, it was not overly aca-demic or theological in nature. Rather, it was fundamentally a pastoral, grassroots development within the Church. The promoters were con-vinced that liturgy possessed a transformative power for social change. The movement reached the very heart of American Catholic society. There were public discourses on the liturgy held on the Boston Common in the summertime. There were radio broadcasts in New York City every Tuesday evening, explaining the work of the move-ment towards a fuller, more active liturgical participation on the part of the whole church. Parents wrote letters to magazines like *Orate Fratres* inquiring about the feasibility of praying Compline at home

[57] Quoted in Dolan, 388.
[58] Bouyer, *Liturgical Piety*, 248–9.

with their young children. Guilds of Catholic lawyers and Catholic nurses were forming liturgy study clubs. The American promoters and pioneers of the liturgical movement popularized the best of European theology at the time, moving their hearers to a grassroots participation as full and equal members of the body of Christ.

For the movement's promoters, the key to such grassroots participation was the connection between liturgy and the rest of life. In an interesting article entitled "Baptismal Consciousness," Virgil Michel suggested that the liturgy is the awareness of one's baptism and its ongoing renewal, which offered the foundation and rationale for all Christian participation, liturgical and otherwise. To this end, the article encouraged a regularly scheduled communal ritual where baptismal promises were renewed, and offered practical suggestions about how such a ritual might be executed.[59]

In an article published shortly before his death, Michel spoke of the priesthood of Christ lived through married and family life by virtue of that same baptismal foundation. He noted that in the sacrament of marriage it is the husband and wife rather than the priest who are the ministers of that sacrament. The Christian family grows and develops by Christ's power acting through these two members of his Mystical Body. The family constitutes, as a unit, a segment of that Mystical Body of Christ.

This segment of the Mystical Body was then expanded to incorporate groups of families and individuals who made up the local parish. Michel understood the parish to be the very "cell of Christian life," with the eucharistic table focal in the life of that local community. It is focal precisely because it is there that the parishioners are drawn to participate in the sacrament of Christ, and from that same table those same parishioners are sent forth to care for the poor and the needy.[60]

Fundamentally, then, the founders of the movement were not attempting to introduce anything new, but to encourage the Church in the United States to return to its roots in the early Church where the lives of Christians, both individually and corporately, were formed and shaped by the worship in which they participated, living their

---

[59] Michel, "Baptismal Consciousness" *OF* 1 (1927) 309–13. See also "Announcing Baptisms," *OF* 2 (1928) 404–7.

[60] See: Michel, "The Parish, Cell of Christian Life," *OF* 11 (1937) 433-40; Joseph Schlarman, "The Liturgy and the Parish," *OF* 9 (1935) 10–3. Schlarman was bishop of Peoria at the time the article was written. His name figures prominently in this period, as one who was very supportive of the efforts of those in the liturgical movement. See also John P. Murphy, "Parishioners and Liturgy," *The Clergy Review* 24 (1944) 481–6.

baptismal dignity as partners in Christ's Mystical Body. Gerald Ellard delineated four elements that needed to be restored:

1. The concept of Christian worship in general.
2. The concept of Christian sacrificial worship in particular.
3. The notion of the general priesthood of the faithful.
4. The sacraments as channels of Christ-life.[61]

In other words, for the early Christians, the *lex orandi* was not only the *lex credendi*, but also the *lex vivendi*. The liturgical pioneers sought to revive that same consciousness within the American church. In responding to the critics of the movement, Virgil Michel had this to say:

> . . . the Liturgical Movement is not primarily a movement to restore more artistic vestments and church utensils, or to promote better-looking church buildings, or even a more artistic rendering of melody at church services. . . . Keen observers see in the Liturgical Movement of today the most hopeful sign for that renewal of Catholic Christian spirit and influence . . .[62]

Michel's abbot, Alcuin Deutsch, offered this realistic appraisal of the work of its promoters:

> Many are not gauging correctly the importance of the Liturgical Movement. It is not the work of a few enthusiasts or faddists, though there may be some such among its promoters; nor of a single religious Order. It is a movement inaugurated by the head of the Church—bound to be fruitful because the creative power of the Holy Ghost impregnates it. Its promoters have made and will make mistakes, but it will go on until it has produced the fruit desired by God—provided we consent to be tools in God's hands.[63]

Participation in the Eucharist

The promoters of the liturgical movement were convinced that integration between liturgy and life would only come about through increased liturgical participation. Thus, participation in general, and participation in the Eucharist in particular, became the primary aim of the movement. For it is in the eucharistic assembly that Christians

---

[61] Ellard, "The Liturgical Movement: in and for America," *The Catholic Mind* 31 (22 February 1933) 61–76.

[62] Michel, "The Liturgical Movement," *ER* 78 (1928) 139, 141.

[63] Ibid., 396–7. See also Dom Albert Hammenstede, O.S.B., "The Liturgy and the Liturgical Movement: Some Corrections and Suggestions," *ER* 4 (1936) 225–36.

most fully recognize themselves as members of the body of Christ and there, again and again, rediscover their mission as his disciples. The first volume of *Orate Fratres* states:

> There is no choice in regard to the first project of the liturgical life to be taken up by this department. The center of religious worship of the Church is the Mass, both as sacrifice and sacrament. And participation of the faithful in the liturgy of the Church must mean primarily participation in the Mass. The idea of this participation was never better expressed than by Pius X, when he gave his oft-quoted exhortation: "Do not pray in the Mass, but pray the Mass."[64]

The liturgical pioneers and promoters were a microcosm of the Church; they were women and men, young and old representing a wide variety of professions. They were pragmatic and well aware of the gap between the goals which they established and the reality of the situation.[65] They also remained aware that there were many well-intentioned communities that desired to enter into a more participative liturgical life but hesitated, either due to a lack of information or simply because the task of such a project seemed too daunting.[66] For this reason, they encouraged communities to take small steps and to experiment. They noted that the degree of participation would differ from place to place, and that given resources and ability, each commu-

---

[64] "Editor's Corner," *OF* 1 (1927) 32. This quotation from Pius X was recalled again and again throughout the early years of the American movement. It is quoted numerous times in articles and books, as well as in conferences and lectures given around the United States in the late 1920s and 1930s.

[65] One parishioner wrote to *OF*: "We are delighted with *Orate Fratres*. It inspires us to become Lay Apostles, but just where to begin and what to do is the question. Every morning at Mass while I was enjoying my Missal, the priest when speaking of the Rosary, urged the people to say their Rosary during Mass 'as it is one of the best ways of attending Mass.' He also added that of course the prayers in the prayer book were also very appropriate. It made me feel that there was need of much work to make the people appreciate the Liturgical Movement. We are in a rural parish, the people coming from miles around, quite plain farmers, most of them. How fine it would be if we could have congregational singing and say the Mass prayers according to the Missal." Parishioner, "What to Do?" *OF* 4 (1930) 45–6.

[66] Ibid., 31. Liturgical participation was greatly aided by the transmission of information about the work of the movement. One brief letter, written by L. J. H., of St. Leo, Florida, and sent to the editor of *OF* is very much to the point: "Before receiving *Orate Fratres*, I acted like a good many other Catholics reciting rosaries, litanies, etc. But this is different now. I am beginning to understand the Mass." "Begins to Understand the Mass" *OF* 7 (1933) 475.

nity would have to determine for itself to what degree such participation was possible. Further, the editors of *Orate Fratres* encouraged its readership to use those pages as a clearinghouse for shared information and experiences, writing about those experiments that failed and those that were successful.[67] There was an underlying sense in the movement of partnership—together, all were learners and there were no experts.

This partnership was also reflected in how the theme of participation was presented. In the 1920s, most Catholics in the United States went to church to "hear Mass," while promoters of the liturgical movement consistently stressed that the entire assembly celebrated or offered the Eucharist together with the priest:

> It is obvious that if a Mass were merely "said," "read," or "sung," it would be invalid, since certain actions are essential to its integrity. Inasmuch as the Mass is a real Sacrifice, the proper verb to be used in describing it is, clearly, "offer." One offers a sacrifice; it is impossible to "say" or "read" or "sing" it. "Celebrate" is tolerable, as it has been sanctioned by usage, and connotes reenactment of the entire prescribed ritual; but "offer" is unquestionably the more meaningful, and accurate, word.[68]

The idea of "hearing" Mass suggested passivity, whereas those who "offered" or "celebrated" the Mass were not spectators at that event, but active participants:

> . . . It is not good Catholic terminology (except by way of reproach) to have the congregation "hearing Mass" or "attending Mass." The faithful

---

[67] "It is one of the hopes of the editors of *OF* that a real impetus can be given to the liturgical apostolate by taking note of the attempts that have been made towards greater active participation of the people in the Mass and in other forms of the Church's public worship. For that purpose, a cordial invitation is hereby again extended to all who have had some experience in this regard. Let the slogan be: Give your fellow Catholics the benefit of your experiences! Many questions naturally arise in the matter of inaugurating any practical form of liturgical life. What were the difficulties encountered in trying to promote participation, personal or corporate, in the Mass? What means have been successfully used to overcome these difficulties? How was the problem approached or 'tackled'? What was the result?" "Editor's Corner," *OF* 1 (1927) 63.

[68] Editorial, "Can't Say Mass," *The Catholic Mind* 42 (1944) 100–1. Twenty years earlier, Patrick Cummins, O.S.B., of Conception Abbey, spoke even more directly of "concelebration by the people which we have as the very soul of our program, under the name of active participation." Letter to Virgil Michel, 17 June 1927, SJAA: Z-24.

are supposed to participate in the offering of the Sacrifice and therefore they "assist at Mass," at least they should. To be merely present while Mass is being offered is not enough; some measure of cooperation with the officiating priest is required . . . To be satisfied with the expression "say Mass" and "attend Mass" is to dull appreciation of the sublime meaning of the central act of Christian worship.[69]

The concept of the assembly as celebrants of the Eucharist was not readily accepted by all. Terminology was debated extensively in the 1930s and 1940s in Catholic periodicals like *Orate Fratres, America,* and *The Commonweal.*[70] Those who resisted such inclusive terminology for liturgical participation tended to see the efforts of the liturgical movement as unrealistic or even misguided. While the majority of the correspondence published in *Orate Fratres,* for example, reveals a very receptive audience to the liturgical ideals being advocated, there were frequent references to friends or colleagues who resisted the movement or who considered it suspicious.[71] There were references to clergy who were responsible for impeding liturgical participation.[72]

---

[69] Ibid. Paul Bussard made a similar point in an article entitled: "Merely Spectators," *OF* 8 (1934) 449–52. See also: The Editor, "Participation in the Mass," *The Ave Maria* 56 (1942) 678, which addresses the difference in terminology and significance between "hearing" and "participation in" the Mass. In a less than enthusiastic endorsement of the latter, we read: "There are those who stress group participation by the entire congregation in a recitative exchange with the celebrant. Even if some celebrants, it is reasoned, do not like this method, they will get to like it. You can grow to like anything if you keep at it long enough."

[70] See, for examples, Letters to the Editor, F. J. Mutch, *America* 65 (1941) 130; and Kathleen Schmitt, *America* 65 (1941) 186.

[71] Many continued to prefer their devotional practices to the call of the liturgical movement to active participation, as exemplified by R. Kelly, R.N., of Springfield, California: "Editor: I would like to express my opinion on how I feel about the Holy Sacrifice of the Mass and novenas. . . . I have always been led to believe that the highest form of worship is adoration, and anyone who meditates on the passion of Christ, which *is* the Mass, does not need to labor over a missal. I have met many converts and people who have changed their lives during a novena. The thousands of people who rush to a daily Mass do not all have brand new homes and husbands. They often have to make their thanksgiving on their way to a long, hard day's work. During a novena we can relax and hear a good sermon and receive God's blessing at Benediction. . . . God bless the priests who say Mass quickly." Letter to the Editor, *America* 64 (1941) 437.

[72] One Canadian priest, N.B., wrote in response to such hesitation: "I never found any real difficulty among the people beyond a certain laziness and spirit of routine; on the contrary, I have found that they take to things liturgical like ducks to water. It always seems to me that the great handicap of the liturgical apostolate is to be

Others claimed that the renewal being encouraged was simply not practical. It would take too much time to explain to the congregation the rationale for greater participation. Moreover, celebrating such a participative Mass would take too long. Some suggested that Mass should not be shorter than twenty minutes in length and not much longer than thirty.[73] Virgil Michel and his colleagues at *Orate Fratres* consistently responded that good liturgy takes time. Sunday Mass could not be well-celebrated in less than forty-five minutes.[74]

Given their ideals, the pioneers remained grounded in the pastoral reality. On the issue of time, for example, Michel, Hellriegel, Ellard, and others recognized that it was difficult for many people to attend Mass, given the pressures of work, particularly in light of the economic crisis brought on by the Great Depression. They began calling for the possibility of an evening Mass, which accordingly implied altering the rules for fasting.[75] Church members responded with great appreciation upon hearing of such a potential change.[76] Those who desired to participate in a daily Eucharist were often deprived of doing so as they had to leave their homes for work prior to the first scheduled Mass in the parish church. An evening Mass would make such participation more feasible.

As another tool for increasing liturgical participation, the use of the Missal by the congregation was encouraged.[77] This was a new option

---

found among the clergy, e.g., the haste with which so many priests say Mass—no one can possibly follow intelligently." Letter to the Editor, *OF* 8 (1934) 43.

[73] J.I.S. from Maryland wrote: "Editor: Regarding the amount of time which should be devoted to Mass, while opinions of private individuals are interesting, it might be useful to cite the opinions of moral theologians, who are supposed to be experts in such matters. They say that Mass should take no less than twenty minutes and not much more than half an hour." Letter to the Editor, *America* 64 (1941) 494.

[74] "Editor's Corner," *OF* 2 (1928) 125.

[75] See Ellard, "Evening Mass," *The Commonweal* 32 (1940) 37–9.

[76] Responding enthusiastically to Ellard's article, one woman wrote: "Why could we not at 8 p.m. have Mass instead of night prayers or novena prayers to some-for-the-time-being-popular saint? I was thinking of the Last Supper, at night, with Christ and the apostles presumably not fasting . . ." M. McLaughlin, Letter to the Editor, *The Commonweal* 32 (1940) 127.

[77] Statistics on the sale of missals are interesting. The Lohmann Company of St. Paul, Minnesota, published the *St. Andrew Daily Missal*, which was promoted by the pioneers and considered the most accurate edition of the Missal available at the time. While 4,826 of these missals were sold in 1926, in only the first nine months of 1927, the number of sales jumped to 10,600. Of those sales, it was estimated that 75 percent of those missals were shipped to the eastern part of the United States,

in the 1930s, since it only became permissible to translate the Missal at the turn of the century. Like other liturgical items being proposed there were those who criticized the Missal project, as well. Some critics suggested that it was unrealistic to expect the average Catholic to purchase a Missal of his or her own and then to use it regularly. Others expressed concern that following the Missal offered too many challenges for the average layperson.[78] At least initially, members of some congregations did, in fact, express difficulty in using the Missal during Mass.[79] A solution came quickly.

Of the assortment of missals which began being published in the 1930s, the most popular by far was *My Sunday Missal,* which Joseph F. Stedman (1896–1946), a presbyter of the Diocese of Brooklyn, first published in 1932. Known as the "Stedman-you-can't-get-lost-missal," the text was clearly laid out with large print and simple but tasteful art by Adé Bethune, the *Catholic Worker* artist. His edition of the Missal gave reasons for "praying with the Church," and included liturgical reflections on each Sunday's gospel, which congregants were urged to read before but not during the Mass. In addition, Stedman also published *Daily Readings from the New Testament.*

Stedman's Missal soon made its way around the world, largely due to its use among the armed forces during the Second World War. It was eventually translated into Polish, Italian, French, Spanish, Chinese, one of the native American languages, Dutch, German, Japanese, and Portuguese. Stedman was the primary pioneer of the Missal project within

---

while only 25 percent went to Chicago and the west. Further, it was noted that a good number of secondary schools and colleges began using that edition of the Missal as a textbook in conjunction with the *Guide for the Roman Missal* by Dom Cuthbert Goeb. "Editor's Corner," *OF* 3 (1929) 62.

[78] In defense of the Missal, David A. Elms wrote the following: ". . . I believe that there remains a large body of intelligent laymen who would use the Missal, if only they knew more about it. I understand that in several of our large city parishes the meaning and appreciation of the Missal are being expounded to children of Sunday-school age, while the priest is saying Mass. There should obviously be a great deal more of this sort of instruction." Letter to the Editor, *The Commonweal* 12 (1930) 164.

[79] In response to the letter of a woman who expressed difficulty using the Missal, *America* magazine received the following letter from A. E. H. of Newburgh, N.Y.: "Editor: May I suggest to the lady who has difficulty using her missal (*America*, December 14) to follow the *Ordo* and arrange her missal before attending Mass? Light has just dawned on my efforts following a year of much confusion in learning to use my missal, but following the priest during Divine Service is so much more interesting now that I wish to pass this information along to others." Letter to the Editor, *America* 64 (1941) 437.

the American liturgical movement, and helped millions of people become familiar with the contents of a book they had not previously known or understood. Dorothy Day wrote in the *Catholic Worker:*

> During a trip to our Seattle House, I saw a Pullman car porter reading the day's Mass in Fr. Stedman's little Sunday Missal. In our backyard at Mott Street I saw a man on the breadline reading one of his new testaments.[80]

The Missal surely assisted the work of groups like the Vernacular Society which were arguing for a liturgical experience that would be intelligible to the large majority of those who were participating.

As the reforms have taken hold in the United States, we now recognize that it is problematic when participants (including the one presiding) are overly dependent upon a text, whether it be *The Sacramentary,* a hymnal, or some other service book used by the assembly. In 1944, Donald Attwater, one of the founders of the liturgical movement in England and a frequent contributor to *Orate Fratres,* recognized the potential for such problems; the service book can become an obstacle rather than an aid to participation.[81] Attwater went on to raise some questions about the issue of illiteracy vis-à-vis the liturgy. He drew on his knowledge of the armed forces during World War II when many soldiers were unable to read or write. In those situations Missals were of no help at all. How then, he asked, was the Church to encourage a fuller, more active participation among those who were illiterate?[82]

Another early pioneer, Hans A. Reinhold, suggested that while Missals served a very important function prior to the arrival of the vernacular in the liturgy, they should be viewed as a step toward full and active participation, rather than a permanent fixture in liturgical assemblies. In a letter published in *Amen,* the journal of the Vernacular Society, he wrote:

> As long as we need translations, missals are good, necessary, and to be multiplied. But when the blessed day arrives on which the gospel is

---

[80] *The Catholic Worker* 13 (5 April 1946) 2, quoted in F. Krumpelman, "Joseph Stedman, *My Sunday Missal,*" in *Leaders of the Liturgical Movement,* ed. R. Tuzik (Chicago: Liturgy Training Publications, 1990) 221.

[81] ". . . 'using a missal' may easily become a private devotion like any other, with all the fussiness over small matters that is so often associated with such—the colour of the day, rank of the feast, 'commemoration chasing,' and so forth. But at best the English missal can only be a partial solution." D. Attwater, "In the Beginning Was The Word," *The Dublin Review* 214 (1944) 135.

[82] Ibid.

chanted in English distinctly, worthily, and with solemnity, or when for an Introit we sing a hymn, then the people are welded together in a common experience which would be destroyed by reading of books. This day may be far off, much farther than we expect, but it seems closer than I hoped to see it when with the courage of despair I made my first pleas for the mother tongue in the liturgy in America.[83]

J. A. Winnen, a catechist who promoted the liturgical movement, cautioned against over-emphasizing the Missal, lest the impression be given that one cannot participate fully in the Mass without a printed text:

There lurks already in the offing a liturgical heresy, that might be called "Missalitis," the error of those who think that the Liturgical Movement begins and ends with the printing press, that the more Missals in circulation, the stronger the Liturgical Movement, that a Missal is as essential to Holy Mass as a car, a radio, a telephone or a refrigerator to that mythical "American standard of living." Today it seems: "No Missal, no Mass."[84]

Another important theme in the effort at increased liturgical participation was that of frequent Communion and the reception of Communion within the Mass itself. While we now take for granted that the liturgical assembly receives the consecrated bread and wine within the context of that Eucharist, it was not always so. It was normative, prior to the liturgical reforms, for the assembly to be communicated by the priest before the beginning of Mass. In this way, the priest would not need to "interrupt" the Mass for Communion. Moreover, despite the 1905 decree of Pius X promoting frequent Communion, there were still many Catholics around the country who only received Communion several times each year, usually on special feasts. As always, much depended on the particular parish. Where catechesis was done well, there was greater eucharistic participation on all levels. Nonetheless, it cannot be denied that Pius X's decree on frequent Communion had a profound effect in many places across the United States. One interesting example comes from St. Ignatius Parish in Portland, Oregon. Although the number of parishioners remained constant, parish records recorded only 330 Communions in 1919, while only four years later, in 1923, that number jumped to 14,400.[85]

---

[83] H. A. Reinhold, "More Confidence Needed," *Amen* 6 (15 May 1951) 2.

[84] J. Winnen, "Teachers and the Liturgical Movement," *Journal of Religious Instruction* 11 (1940–41) 797.

[85] Dolan, *The American Catholic Experience,* 386.

Virgil Michel argued that the division between the reception of Communion and the Mass heightened the fracture between sacrament and sacrifice. He described the growing understanding of the relationship of Communion to the Mass as one of the greatest fruits of the liturgical revival.[86] Patrick Cummins, O.S.B. of Conception Abbey, Missouri, was another strong advocate of the reception of Communion during Mass. "The non-Communion Mass," wrote Cummins, is "always as absurd as a family dinner with nobody eating."[87] Even Communion ministered to the ill and homebound, or in the context of viaticum, always finds its relationship in the context of the eucharistic table, where the sick or dying brother or sister is united, not only to Christ, but also to the eucharistic assembly from which he or she has been forced by ill health to be absent.[88]

In 1938, Reynold Hillenbrand, while rector of the seminary at Mundelein, Illinois, insisted that the tabernacle not be relied upon as a dispensary for the distribution of Communion during Mass. Rather, each presider was to consecrate a sufficient amount of eucharistic bread for each Mass. The reserved sacrament existed primarily for the sharing of Communion with those who were ill and as viaticum for the dying. The largely Jesuit faculty found this and other liturgical innovations introduced by Hillenbrand difficult to understand and accept, since Jesuit spirituality, in general, centered more on a privatistic piety of meditation, popular devotions, and the Spiritual Exercises, and less on the corporate, communal nature of the Eucharist or other forms of liturgical prayer.[89] Bernard Laukemper shared Hillenbrand's position. He wrote:

---

[86] Michel, "Communion at Mass: V. The Effect of Communion," *OF* 4 (1930) 311–5.

[87] Letter to Editors of *OF*, Holy Saturday 1927, SJAA: Z-24. The letter continues: "It makes me sad (sometimes mad). At St. Anselm's, after the non-Communion Easter Mass, followed a community congratulation to the Abbot (the only man who had dined, i.e., received Communion). Then only could these, (and there were a goodly number), for whom Easter without Communion was inconceivable, slink back into the Church and receive privately. But everybody does it. So they did, the more's the pity, with First Communion, till Pius X came. Was everybody right?"

[88] Roger Schoenbechler noted that although Pius X had issued a plea for frequent and daily Communion in 1905, thirty-one years later, in 1936, that ideal had yet to be realized. He further describes the practice of the early Church, where the sense of participation in the eucharistic assembly was intimately linked with the sharing of Communion. In those days, one would not think of coming to the eucharistic liturgy without the intention of eating the eucharistic bread and drinking the eucharistic wine. "Pius X and Frequent Communion," *OF* 10 (1936) 59–63.

[89] Ed Marciniak, interview by author, 21 November 1994, Center for Urban Life, Loyola University of Chicago. See Robert Tuzik, "The Contribution of Msgr.

At present, I am trying to get the sisters at the Josephinum away from canned Communion. I hope the term is not irreverent. There is no reason in the world why the nuns should not participate in the sacrifice hic et nunc. I think that we shall devise some way of having at least the server or a delegation of the sisters bring the container with the hosts to the altar at the proper time. I told them last Sunday that what counts is not that we adore the blessed sacrament, but that we offer ourselves with Christ, that we become absorbed in Christ the victim, of which the offering of the host is the visible sign. It begins with this offering, it becomes real in the consecration of *that* host, it is consummated in communion, it is lived daily. The priest consecrates a new host daily, why should not the same thing be right for the people? Think about it.[90]

In 1950, Joseph Payne, C.S.C., pastor of Little Flower Parish in South Bend, Indiana, challenged another type of fragmentation that existed in the reception of Communion. In writing about First Communion celebrations, Payne criticized the concept of children receiving the Eucharist for the first time with their peers, while their parents and family members remained in the background. Instead, Payne introduced family first Communion, where the parents approached the table with the child and together shared in the sacrament. He prepared the assembly for the change on the preceding Sunday, and initiated a practice that would gradually become normative throughout much of the American church.[91]

The topic of liturgical participation at weddings and funerals was also discussed, particularly in ecumenical situations when other Christians were present. This concern was not expressed in terms of the later issue of eucharistic hospitality, but more with the extension of an overall liturgical hospitality where visitors were sufficiently informed and at home in what they were witnessing, inviting their participation. Some writers recommended the availability of service books to assist guests in their understanding of what was being celebrated.[92]

The editors of *Orate Fratres* noted three distinct types of liturgical participation. The first was entitled "The silent praying and offering of the Mass with the priest." This was described as the literal observance of the words of Pius X to "pray the Mass," that is, to pray the prayers

---

Reynold Hillenbrand (1905–1979) To The Liturgical Movement In The United States: Influences and Development." (Ph.D. diss., University of Notre Dame, 1989) 44–6.

[90] Letter to Godfrey Diekmann, 9 August 1938, SJAA: #1165.

[91] Sandra Yocum Mize, "Lay Participation in Parish Life: Little Flower Parish, South Bend, Indiana," US *Catholic Historian* 9 (1990) 423.

[92] See Caroline M. Bouwhuis, Letter to the Editor, *America* 62 (1939) 46.

of the Mass along with the priest who was presiding. This method was described as complicated, normally requiring some instruction beforehand. In general, this mode of participation was "remote." For those who participated at this first level, along with the use of a Missal, an introduction to the prayers of the Mass and the eucharistic rite was also recommended, especially for Masses with children. Several specific examples of available texts, both Missals and study texts were offered.[93]

The second type of participation was called the *Missa recitata*, or "dialog Mass." In this form, the Mass prayers were said aloud alternately by a leader and the whole congregation. It was also possible to do the same, alternating with the congregation divided into two groups. The ideal dialog Mass was described as an alternation between the one presiding and the assembly, with everyone answering together as a group and, perhaps, reciting some prayers together with the priest. Permission of the local bishop was required. The editors recommended the dialog Mass for smaller group situations or in a pastoral environment where the assembly was more liturgically aware (e.g., in convents, colleges, and seminaries). Ernest Koenker wrote in 1954 that the dialog Mass was either infrequent or non-existent in most American parishes. In Germany, however, it had become normative in as many as seventy-five percent of the parishes.[94] In proposing this second mode of participation, the feasibility of such a model was questioned. Parishes were encouraged to experiment with this second model and then to share their results with others contemplating the same experiment. Like the first model, some instruction or the use of a study text was recommended prior to the celebration of a dialog Mass.

The third method of participation involved congregational singing of the choir or server parts of the Mass. This particular mode of participation was described as most resembling celebrations of the early Church, where musical parts now sung by the choir were originally sung by the entire assembly and *not* recited by the priest.

Prior to the Second Vatican Council, it was required that the priest recite all the parts of the Mass, including those sung by the choir. Apparently, the promoters of the liturgical movement did not have much hope of ending this practice:

> It seems probable that the older custom, according to which the priest did not in person recite the whole of the Mass prayers, will never return. But it is certain that the movement towards a participation of the people

---

[93] "Editor's Corner," *OF* 2 (1928) 94.
[94] Koenker, 158.

in the Mass by means of chanting the parts assigned for that purpose will grow steadily.[95]

Several years later, John La Farge, S.J., spoke more generally of three diverse modes of liturgical participation, each of which would contribute to a sharing in Christ's priestly action. According to La Farge, the first mode was where the assembly united interiorly to the sacrifice. The lack of such interior union leaves the liturgy as nothing more than a mere formality. The second mode described was that of an external or outward participation, where the diverse liturgical ministries were employed. The third mode he described as closely related to the second: the total participation of the entire community, where one worships not as an individual, but as one body, as in the parish Eucharist. This third mode is, in fact, a summation of both the first and second modes suggested by La Farge. The capacity of the Church to live its priestly dignity was dependent upon its ability to participate fully and actively when it gathered liturgically as the body of Christ.[96]

Early on in the publication of *Orate Fratres*, the editors began chronicling concrete instances and examples of liturgical experimentation on the pastoral level. The information provided is extremely helpful, offering good insight into how the liturgical theory was being carried out in practice.[97] Prior to his tenure with *America* magazine, John La

---

[95] "Editor's Corner," *OF* 1 (1927) 63.

[96] J. La Farge, "With Scrip and Staff: The Layman's Great Action," *America* 58 (1937) 275.

[97] One such example comes from a letter written in 1927, and sent to the editors of the magazine. The Reverend H. F. Flock, who served, at the time, as pastor of St. Patrick's Church, Sparta, Wisconsin, wrote: "About fifteen years ago I began with the children to say the whole Ordinary of the Mass in English. I bought a supply of cheap prayer books, and marked as many of the prayers as could conveniently be said aloud while keeping the priest at the altar—omitting the words of Consecration from the *Hanc igitur*, etc. A few boys with good voices were trained to watch the priest at the altar and announce the various parts and prayers and start them. These boys would also read the Epistle and the Gospel of the day from the English missal. A few years ago, when the children were quite well practiced, I had them say the Mass in this manner for the congregation at early Mass on a Sunday. The people were very attentive and by this visual and practical illustration learned more about the Mass and how to 'pray the Mass' than by many theoretical instructions. We had these congregational Mass prayers with the children at least once a week until about three years ago, when I found an item in the *American Ecclesiastical Review* stating that Rome, in answer to an inquiry, had forbidden the loud congregational prayers that the priest said in secret. We then gave up the practice and have not taken it up since. I understand now that these congregational prayers in the vernacular are allowed, all except the Canon. I have been waiting for your little

Farge wrote to *Orate Fratres* describing his experimentation with liturgical participation in an African-American parish in Ridge, Maryland, where he was working at the time. It was the custom at that particular parish to have congregational singing (hymnody or litanies from a printed card) on the first Sunday of the month. The choir sang on the second Sunday. The third week included children's hymns, while the fourth Sunday was always a "high Mass." La Farge goes on to note that unlike many white congregations where there was a certain critical resistance to such participation, parishioners in his congregation were always positive and spirited in their worship and eager to contribute to its upbuilding.

One hallmark event in the early years of the American liturgical movement was the *Missa recitata* celebrated in St. Louis at the opening of a national gathering of The Students' Spiritual Leadership Convention. The group existed under the auspices of The Sodality of Our Lady. One thousand delegates gathered together on Friday, 17 August 1928 at St. Francis Xavier Church in St. Louis, to celebrate the dialogue Mass together. Upon entering the church, each member of the assembly was given an order of service, with the printed text of the Mass, including the responses to be made by the assembly. The text began with an introduction to the *Missa recitata:*

> The Missa Recitata is very much in accord with the mind of the Church and the spirit of the Liturgical Movement. Such a Mass supposes that the priest and the people are really offering the Holy Sacrifice together; that the priest, when he turns from the altar to the congregation, addresses the people directly, and that they answer him with one voice . . . When a congregation thus assists at Mass, they feel the fullness of the significance of the priest's words when at the "Orate Fratres" he begs them to pray with him and refers to the Mass as "Our Sacrifice."[98]

The sermon was preached by Daniel Lord, S.J. While there was no rehearsal with the delegates before the Mass, Daniel Lord primed the group on the previous day, telling them that they were expected to "use the pamphlet, follow the leader, and pronounce the words clearly, and pause at the asterisks." Finally, he insisted on this idea: "We will celebrate the Sacrifice together with the priest." On Sunday morning, 19 August 1928, at eight o'clock, participants celebrated the *Missa recitata* again, this time with Martin Hellriegel as presider. Most of the thousand delegates received Communion during the Mass. Hellriegel

book *Offeramus,* and intend to try to introduce the *Missa recitata.* . . ." "Editor's Corner," *OF* 1 (1927) 93–4.

[98] William Puetter, S.J., *Missa Recitata* (St. Louis: The Queen's Work, 1928).

had brought his acolytes with him from O'Fallon, who were already well acquainted with his liturgical innovations and style. Puetter noted: "He wore his green bell vestment and you may be sure the impression was even better than that at the Solemn Mass on the previous day."[99] Following the convention, there were immediate requests for six thousand copies of Puetter's text of the dialog Mass.

Liturgical experimentation continued to expand in the 1930s and 1940s, and one of the places known for its serious efforts at liturgical participation was Holy Cross Parish in St. Louis, Missouri, where Martin Hellriegel had become pastor. Hellriegel had already experimented liturgically at O'Fallon, Missouri, during his tenure as chaplain to the Sisters of the Most Precious Blood. While many who visited O'Fallon were impressed by Hellriegel's efforts, his critics were convinced that his liturgical ideas were successful only because they were being executed in a convent setting. Such ideas, they thought, would be unsuccessful if they were tried in a parish.[100]

In taking on the pastorate at Holy Cross Parish, Hellriegel proved his critics wrong. When he arrived as pastor in 1940, there was no congregational singing, nor were Missals being used by the assembly. A gifted teacher, Hellriegel gradually catechized his parishioners, presenting a solid rationale for liturgical participation and convincing his hearers that the liturgical changes being introduced into the parish were not maverick, but had solid grounding in the tradition of the Church. Hellriegel described liturgical participation as a sacred thing that needed to be carried out with reverence and great care, whether in terms of gesture or speech, whether on the part of the assembly or the one presiding. Further, he described the Sunday Eucharist as the primary parish activity. He used the Sunday homily as an opportunity for such catechizing, calling for intelligent use of the Missal and frequent reception of Communion. But perhaps his greatest means of convincing the parishioners of what he was advocating was that he modelled what he was teaching and preaching. One parishioner said of him later: "He did things around the altar like they were the most important things in the world."[101]

Soon after his arrival, Hellriegel introduced the dialog Mass to the grade school children on a daily basis, including a homily of about eight minutes. The children were taught to speak normally when they prayed aloud and to avoid a type of artificial or forced speech. Out of that experience grew the ministry of lector, which members of the stu-

[99] William H. Puetter, S.J., Letter to Virgil Michel, 19 September 1928, SJAA: Z-24.
[100] Barrett, 166.
[101] Ibid., 180–4.

dent body were trained to carry out within the Sunday assembly. A sung Mass was also introduced, and a boys' schola and adult choir formed. The dialog Mass soon found its way into the Sunday schedule of Masses. Congregational singing grew quickly, along with the use of the Missal. Within the first year of his pastorate, three hundred Missals had been purchased by parishioners, and a Missal study club had been formed.[102]

Likewise, the liturgical seasons were treated with great care.[103] Parishioners came to see Advent not only in terms of the historical coming of Jesus, but also in the wider context of Christ's final coming. Hellriegel introduced Advent wreaths to the parish and included a blessing of the wreath during the liturgy of the first Sunday of Advent.[104] He likewise presented Lent in a more informed manner, explaining to the congregation something of the history of the stational liturgy, for example. During Lent, a map of the stational churches was provided in the vestibule of the church and in each classroom of the grade school.

Parishioners also came to appreciate Holy Week in a new way.[105] Tenebrae was introduced on Wednesday, Thursday, and Friday evenings. The assembly joined the choir in chanting the psalms and lamentations in English. Each evening, between seven hundred and nine hundred people took part. Easter was celebrated with a solemn Mass at 6:00 a.m., which included a procession with the children who were to receive first Communion carrying candles that had been lighted from the paschal candle. As a way of highlighting the centrality of Easter in the calendar, a solemn sung Eucharist was celebrated every day of the Easter octave, which drew large numbers of people.

Compline, sung by the whole assembly, was regularly scheduled on Sunday evenings. The Liturgy of the Hours came to be celebrated normatively at other times as well. The offertory collection came to be seen as symbolic of the connection of Eucharist to justice. The offertory

---

[102] Ibid., 188–91.

[103] See Hellriegel, *How to Make the Church Year a Living Reality* (Notre Dame: University of Notre Dame Press, 1955).

[104] Today this practice is now recognized as a devotion, the proper place for which is in the home. Nonetheless, it was Hellriegel's idea to use the Advent wreath as a means of focusing the season for his parishioners, even in the liturgical assembly. While the practice may be primarily devotional, it remains common today to find the presence of some form of an Advent wreath in contemporary worship spaces during the Advent season.

[105] See Anne Huneke, "Monsignor Hellriegel and the Church Year: lent, holy week and easter," *The Priest* 39 (1983) 20–33.

procession was seen as another important means of the assembly's liturgical participation. [106]

There were other American parishes where liturgical experimentation was taking place. Hillenbrand's influence at Mundelein had at least some effect on a number of Chicago parishes, and there are several that should be mentioned here. Our Lady of Sorrows Basilica on Jackson Boulevard in Chicago was also well-known for its liturgical music. In addition, the Servites at the Basilica introduced their congregation to the *Missa recitata*. The practice was sustained and grew in popularity among those who worshipped there. St. Aloysius Parish in Chicago offers another example. While not as well-known as Reynold Hillenbrand, the pastor of St. Aloysius, Bernard Laukemper, was deeply influenced by Hellriegel and Hillenbrand, and also quite involved in the liturgical movement. Like many of the other liturgical pioneers, Laukemper was born in Germany. Word of his innovations quickly spread in the 1930s, and before long, St. Aloysius had become a liturgical model for other Chicago parishes. Laukemper hosted a liturgical conference for the Chicago area in 1936. He replaced the elaborate high altar with a more modest one, introduced the offertory procession,[107] and instituted the *Missa recitata* as a regular part of the Sunday schedule.

Laukemper, like his colleagues in the liturgical movement, was often misunderstood by those who saw him as tampering with sacred traditions. Nonetheless, he remained faithful to his convictions:

> I received an unsigned letter just last week, which was full of insults to the pastor, who is presumably too lazy to have devotion to our blessed mother, or has no love for her. I was referred to Father Kean of the Servite Order to get the spirit. The writer also asked me to state my case the following Sunday. In doing so, I stated only that it is very bad to move the center from its place; the center of worship is the Eucharist, the center of the week is Sunday, the center of Christianity is Christ and not the Blessed Virgin, who is greatest next to Christ. I said that if they value the mass properly and keep the whole Sunday holy, they can also think of other days, but as long as they look for the shortest mass on Sunday, to have it over with and have no more interest in the Sunday and the

---

[106] Ibid., 208, 213–7.

[107] Laukemper wrote to Godfrey Diekmann: "We shall try the offertory-procession at the graduation-mass next Sunday, however only with the graduates, who will also form a special group in the Corpus Christi procession. We have discarded all plays and commencement exercises and what have you, that the children of God may start their way into the world, as they say at this occasion, from the steps of the altar and not from the stage. The impression should be more lasting" (Letter of 13 June 1938, SJAA: #1165).

> Eucharist, they remind me of the man who is very generous with presents but neglects to pay his debts.[108]

By 1939, sixty-five of the two hundred and fifty city parishes in Chicago had introduced the *Missa recitata*. The practice was also common in Chicago educational institutions like De Paul University and Rosary College, as well as in seventeen of the sixty-six Catholic high schools.[109]

As always, the level of experimentation depended on the openness of the local bishop. In Detroit, where Cardinal Mooney was notoriously cautious when it came to liturgical innovations, only two or three parishes were known to have had the *Missa recitata* in the 1930s. In the 1940s, the Detroit Archdiocese limited the celebration of the *Missa recitata* to weekdays in those places where it was in use. It was not until 1951 that Mooney allowed a Sunday celebration of the dialogue Mass in response to a request from the Young Ladies' Sodality at Sacred Heart Parish in Dearborn, Michigan. In granting their request, Mooney insisted that the Mass be celebrated at 6:00 a.m. In a letter to the pastor, the cardinal wrote: "If you find that there is any complaint from others attending the Mass, then the practice should be discontinued."[110] As a result of Mooney's liturgical caution, the Detroit presbyterate was largely indifferent to the efforts of the liturgical movement in the 1930s and 1940s. There were exceptions, but one does not find the same kind of enthusiasm for liturgical renewal as in Chicago. There was no Hellriegel or Hillenbrand in Detroit.

On the west coast, there was an exchange of letters in the spring of 1940 between H. A. Reinhold and the archbishop of Seattle, Gerald Shaughnessy, S.M. Apparently, Reinhold had introduced the *Missa recitata* during a retreat at Everett, Washington, without the permission of the local ordinary. In addition, Reinhold made use of the text by William H. Puetter, S.J. of St. Louis, which, unbeknownst to Reinhold, had been banned in Seattle. The bishop wrote:

> While you are free in any future missions that you may happen to preach, to discuss with the relative pastor the matter of a *Missa recitata*

---

[108] Letter to Godfrey Diekmann, 15 July 1938, SJAA: #1165.

[109] Steven Avella, *This Confident Church: Catholic Leadership and Life in Chicago 1940–1965* (Notre Dame: University of Notre Dame Press, 1992) 153. In other parts of the country, examples would include Sacred Heart Parish, Hubbard Woods, Illinois, where Reynold Hillenbrand served as pastor from 1944 until 1974, St. Joseph's Parish in Sunnyside, Washington, where H. A. Reinhold was pastor from 1944 until 1956, and Corpus Christi Parish in New York City.

[110] Tentler, 414.

and to recommend it from a liturgical point of view, the law still remains as laid down by the Holy See that the custom may not be actually introduced anywhere in this Diocese without specific written permission from this office.[111]

Despite Shaughnessy's apprehensions, the *Missa recitata* continued to be popularized, not only in the state of Washington, but throughout the United States.

Participation and the Vernacular

As early as 1787, John Carroll, S.J., was arguing in favor of changing the liturgy from Latin to English. In that year, while still an apostolic prefect prior to being named the first bishop of Baltimore, he discussed the problem of the use of Latin in the liturgy in a letter to Father Joseph Berrington:

> With respect to the latter point, I cannot help thinking that the alteration of Church discipline ought not only to be solicited, but insisted upon as essential to the service of God and the benefit of mankind. Can there be anything more preposterous than an unknown tongue; and in this country either for want of books or inability to read, the great part of our congregations must be utterly ignorant of the meaning and sense of the public office of the Church.[112]

Some time later, Carroll wrote to Fr. Arthur O'Leary, an Irish Capuchin, urging once more the use of the vernacular:

> . . . I do indeed conceive that one of the most popular prejudices against us is that our public prayers are unintelligible to our hearers. Many of the poor people, and the negroes generally, not being able to read, have no technical help to confine their attitude.[113]

There is some evidence that the vernacular was, in fact, used experimentally in some places during that period.[114] In 1822, Bishop John England edited the first American edition of an English Missal,[115] taking much of the text from a Missal already being used in England.

---

[111] Letter to H. A. Reinhold, 5 April 1940, SJAA: #1166.

[112] Peter Guilday, *The Life and Times of John Carroll,* 2 vols. (New York: Encyclopedia Press, 1922), quoted in C. J. Nuesse, "English In The Liturgy," *The Commonweal* 41 (1945) 648.

[113] Ibid.

[114] Guilday, vol. 1, 131.

[115] John England, ed., *The Roman Missal Translated into the English Language for the Use of the Laity* (New York: William H. Creagh, 1822) iii. See Peter Guilday, *The Life*

In the present century, during the 1930s and 1940s, there was no liturgical issue more discussed in pastoral circles in the United States than that of the vernacular. Following every article published on the subject, and there were many, there was a series of letters to the editor, either in favor of the change or demanding that Latin be kept as the only language employed in the liturgy. The reasons given on both sides were varied.[116] For the liturgical pioneers of the United States, reasons for the use of English in the liturgy were quite simple. The entire thrust of the liturgical movement was toward greater participation, and such participation was impossible without a clear understanding not only of the meaning behind the texts, but of the texts themselves. Thus, the shift to the vernacular became an aim of the movement. With the founding of the Vernacular Society to promote such a linguistic shift, the division around this controversy grew even stronger.

The 1946 Liturgical Conference, held in Denver, Colorado, on 14–17 October, decided that the vernacular issue did not come directly within the scope of the Conference, and recommended that another organization be established for that purpose. As a result, the St. Jerome Society was founded in that same year, under the leadership of H. A. Reinhold and several other Conference members. In 1948, a group of seventeen met at the St. Benet's Bookshop in Chicago to organize the Vernacular Society, successor to the St. Jerome Society, with Monsignor Joseph Morrison of Chicago as president and Colonel John K. Ross-Duggan as secretary. The Society held annual meetings, often in conjunction with the Liturgical Weeks, published the journal *Amen*, and lobbied for the vernacular among the American hierarchy and also in Rome. Membership continued to increase around the country, reaching a total of 10,000, although some members were more committed than others.

The name always associated with the Vernacular Society is that of Colonel Ross-Duggan (1888–1967). Like many others in the liturgical movement, Ross-Duggan became involved as a side interest. And like many others in the liturgical movement, the colonel's commitment grew to the extent that in 1949, he left his full-time position publishing

---

and Times of John England, 2 vols. (New York: America Press, 1927); John K. Ryan, "Bishop England and the Missal in English," *ER* 95 (1936) 28–36.

[116] One of the more interesting reasons for continuing the use of Latin was offered in an unsigned "Letter to the Editor," telling the story of an English pilot who was forced to land in Holland during the war. "Ignorant of Dutch, the pilot recited the *Pater Noster* (Our Father) and *Ave Maria* (Hail Mary) to a Dutch farmer. The farmer, a Catholic, gave the pilot refuge and then, at great personal risk, helped him across the frontier." Editor, "Comment," *America* 68 (1943) 368.

a periodical in Chicago entitled *Quick Frozen Foods* to devote all his energies to the cause of the vernacular.[117] Though he was tireless in promoting the cause,[118] the colonel lacked diplomacy, and those who met him never forgot him.[119]

Amen, begun in 1950 as a mimeographed bulletin, was issued three times each year, informing Vernacular Society members of information on the Society's progress throughout the English-speaking world.[120] The byline of the magazine read: "How can one who holds the place of the layman say the 'Amen' to thy thanksgiving, since he does not know what thou art saying. 1 Cor 14:16." With the Society's rapid expansion, *Amen* soon took on a more professional format, including (along with

[117] "Lieut. Col. John Ross-Duggan, Liturgical Reformer Dies," *The New York Times,* 4 February 1967, 27. The date of death was 1 February 1967. Under Ross-Duggan's direction, the Vernacular Society opened chapters in most of the English-speaking countries represented in the International Commission on English in the Liturgy (ICEL).

[118] When Ross-Duggan visited Rome, he always made a point of meeting with American seminarians. When news of his arrival reached the North American College, some seminarians inevitably went to Ross-Duggan's hotel near the Vatican to hear him talk about the strategy and projects of the Vernacular Society. (The author is indebted to Archbishop John R. Quinn for this information.) Ross-Duggan was shrewd. Seminarians sent to Rome were considered among the brightest from their dioceses. As such, they would potentially have significant influence back in their dioceses in the future. Thus, if he could convince these young seminarians about the vernacular while they were in studies, this would be beneficial in gaining greater support in the future.

[119] In his autobiography, William J. Leonard, S.J., describes the audience with Pius XII in the Sistine Chapel at the conclusion of the 1956 Assisi Liturgical Congress. Rumors had been circulating that the pope was going to announce major concessions regarding the vernacular. Pius XII was carried in solemnly and spoke to the congress delegates for forty-five minutes, but said nothing about any changes in liturgical language. On the contrary, he reaffirmed the permanent place of Latin in the liturgy. Leonard writes in his autobiography: "When he was being carried out the Colonel cried in a loud voice, 'Take him away!' I was sitting beside him, and I said, 'Sh-h-h, Colonel!' 'No, no' he shouted, 'He'll never do us any good. Take him away!'" Leonard, *The Letter Carrier,* 150. For the full text of that papal address, see Pius XII, *Christ the Center of the Church's Liturgy. Address by His Holiness, Pope Pius XII to the Delegates of the First International Congress of Pastoral Liturgy, Assembled in Vatican City, 22 September 1956* (trans.) Vatican Press Office (Clyde, Missouri: Benedictine Convent of Perpetual Adoration, 1957).

[120] The magazine continued until 1961 when it was suppressed by the Apostolic Delegate, Egidio Vagnozzi. W. E. Wiethoff, "Popular Rhetorical Strategy in the American Catholic Debate Over Vernacular Reform" (Ph.D. diss., University of Michigan, 1974) 36.

information of interest to the membership) articles on various facets of the liturgical movement with a primary focus on the vernacular.

In 1950, a number of bishop-members of the Vernacular Society prepared to make an intervention at the annual November meeting of the American bishops, asking that they approve the use of some English in the Ritual.[121] For whatever the reasons, the opportunity to address the plenary assembly of bishops did not present itself. The bishops involved with the Vernacular Society remained persistent, however, and tried again at the 1951 meeting. This time they were successful in making their presentation, and their request was forwarded to the Bishops' Committee on the Confraternity of Christian Doctrine (CCD), under the direction of Edwin V. O'Hara, bishop of Kansas City at the time. A commission of liturgical and literary specialists was established with an additional sixty-four consultants, including five from England, and representatives from France, Germany, Italy, Canada, Africa, and Australia, in addition to other countries. For the next twelve months the commission studied the initial request of the Vernacular Society, drafted English texts, and in 1952, presented a proposed revised Ritual with some portions in English. The bishops discussed the text at their November meeting, then sent it back to the CCD Committee for further revisions. The commission went back to work and presented the new draft at the 1953 plenary meeting of the American bishops where it was unanimously approved. The Ritual was then sent to Rome for papal approbation and was approved by the Sacred Congregation of Rites on 3 June 1954; it was announced in the United States by Archbishop Meyer on 17 August 1954 at the Milwaukee Liturgical Week.[122] This was a great victory for the Vernacular Society and for the liturgical movement in the United States as a whole.

The work of the Vernacular Society did not cease with the publication of the new Ritual. One month after the papal approbation, Ross-Duggan wrote the membership of the Society from Paris:

> Now that the English Ritual has been approved for the United States, it is the duty of the Vernacular Society to do its part in activating this splendid concession and reform. It is up to each and every member of the Society to play a part in *popularizing* the new Ritual, to reveal its beautiful meaning and sentiments, to lead parish priests to *use* this apostolic and catechetical instrument and to get our fellow laity to desire it and to love it.[123]

---

[121] The proposal had been prepared by Msgr. Joseph Morrison, president of the Vernacular Society.

[122] Editor, "A Bit of Vernacular History: 1946–1955," *Amen* 9 (1 July 1955) 3.

[123] Ross-Duggan, Letter to the Vernacular Society, Paris, 31 July 1954. *Amen* 9 (1 July 1955) 4.

The debate on English in the liturgy was not limited to the Vernacular Society. Rather, it fueled much discussion within the American church in the 1940s and 50s. It was clearly a controversial issue and there were many different opinions, even among liturgists themselves. In an article entitled: "A Vernacular Liturgy?" Ernest Graf, O.S.B., argued for a compromise. While arguing that Latin should be maintained for the celebration of the Eucharist, he suggested that the vernacular might gradually be utilized in other sacramental celebrations, such as the anointing of the sick. In defending the continuation of Latin in the eucharistic liturgies, he spoke analogously of Hebrew as the traditional liturgical language in synagogue worship. Graf suggested that if pious Jews were capable of learning a sufficient amount of liturgical Hebrew for participation in their worship, then pious Catholics should be capable of learning Latin. He based his own position, however, primarily on the arguments given at the Council of Trent. Graf noted that one of the first projects of Martin Luther and the sixteenth-century reformers was to adopt the use of the vernacular in their liturgies, thus, making the question of liturgical language one of orthodoxy and loyalty to the Church.[124]

In addition, he argued that even though the Council of Trent acknowledged the fact that the faithful attending Mass were not grasping the richness of the liturgical texts, the council chose nonetheless to keep Latin as the only permissable liturgical language. In that council, use of the vernacular had been opposed for three primary reasons. First, it would be difficult to find accurate translations of texts, which would necessitate endless supervision, correction, and retranslation. Second, priests would not be able to celebrate the Eucharist outside of their own countries. Third, the use of the vernacular would mean the risk of possible error and heresy.

Graf argued that the Mass stands apart from the other sacraments, but that, regarding the sacraments, those celebrations would be greatly enhanced if the participants could understand at baptism or marriage, for example, just what was being expressed and celebrated. In pastoral situations such as the anointing of the sick or the rite of Christian burial, much more comfort would be gained if those involved were able to understand the words being spoken by the presiding minister.[125]

---

[124] Ernest Graf, "A Vernacular Liturgy?" *HPR* 45 (1945) 584.

[125] Ibid. Mary Perkins Ryan elaborated on this point in an article entitled: "I'm Going to Like More Vernacular," *Amen* 9 (1954) 5–7, 12. She wrote: "No, experience certainly shows us that the greater and more personal the crisis, the less most of us are capable of using the books that would enable us to understand the sacramental answers of Christ and the Church to our needs. Weariness, weakness, concern for

Permission for the use of a Latin-French edition of the Ritual was approved for the dioceses of France on 28 November 1947 by the Sacred Congregation of Rites. In the United States, inquiry about the possibility of celebrating baptism in the vernacular had already surfaced in 1928.[126]

Monsignor Ronald Knox adopted a position similar to that of Graf's, but for pragmatic reasons.[127] He argued that the issue of liturgical participation was beyond language, suggesting that those who entered the liturgical assembly and began fidgeting were not doing so because the Mass was in Latin. According to Knox, they would do the same thing if the Mass were celebrated in English. They were disengaged liturgically precisely because they lacked a more fundamental commitment at the level of faith.

On the other side of the issue, H. A. Reinhold suggested that while many Americans might argue for the beauty of Latin when used in the liturgy, they meant it sounded beautiful, even if they had little understanding of what was being communicated. He writes:

---

others, the emotions that inevitably attend the great moments of Christian life— make the use even of the best booklet almost impossible . . . As for the other sacraments, there is no need to tell anyone who has received Holy Communion when sick either in a hospital or at home, what a difference it will make to hear the prayers in English," 6–7. Another woman wrote: "I have attended Episcopalian friends' funerals and the rites are so beautiful and comforting because the consoling words of the Scriptures are brought to the ears of the mourning ones. I shudder to think how my family will feel at the 'foreign' funeral of mine. I am the only Catholic in my family." Mrs. E. C. S., "A Convert's Plea," *Amen* 6 (15 May 1951) 2.

[126] See "Substitution of Vernacular for Latin at Baptism," *ER* 79 (1928) 197–8.

[127] Speaking of the possibility of chanting the Liturgy of the Hours in English, Knox stated the following: "I cannot help feeling that the movement would do well to drop this item on its agenda. In the first place, because English is on the whole such a bad language to sing in; and in particular, such a bad language to sing plainchant in. Only those who have listened to the Cowley Fathers singing a gradual which included the words 'Our be-e-e-e-elly cleaveth u-unto-o-o the-e-e-e-e ground' can appreciate its limitations. In the second place, because phrases like 'With thee is the principality in the day of thy strength, in the brightness of thy saints', or 'Of the business that walketh in dark, of invasion, or of the noon-day devil,' are hardly more informative in English than in Latin. No, the Divine Office is designed for clerics and nuns; it is their *job;* if the laity like to make a hobby of reciting or singing it, let them by all means—in whatever language they prefer. But there is no call for fresh legislation here." Ronald A. Knox, "Understanded of the People," *The Clergy Review* 23 (1947) 535. Of course, Knox was inaccurate in his understanding of the Divine Office, as demonstrated by Robert Taft, S.J., who has

The Mass is not an opera of Verdi or Bizet. You can enjoy *Carmen* perfectly well if you don't understand French (although you will enjoy it more if you do, given an equal amount of musical capital to go on), but liturgy is "Logos," mystery, not drama and music.[128]

In another article published in *The Commonweal*, Reinhold made a strong case for the move to the vernacular.[129] In calling for such a change, he stressed the importance of employing poets and other writers to develop a translation worthy of T. S. Eliot or W. H. Auden. While many were calling for use of the vernacular, Reinhold was one of the first in the movement to emphasize the importance of quality texts. The savor of these texts, he suggested, should resemble, on a religious plane, Winston Churchill's "power of formulation" and needs to have the earthiness and force which was typical of Churchill's political language.[130] Reinhold's own approach exemplified such earthiness and force. His words were strong and direct and often provoked strong reactions on both sides, regardless of the issue.[131]

Reinhold was concerned about language because he was convinced that words possess power to move the heart to greater conversion, to action, to service. Such power is lost when the hearers are unable to comprehend that which is communicated. To that end, he suggested translating only those parts of the Mass which directly involved the assembly. The private prayers the priest said silently could well be left in Latin. Such prayers were not spoken aloud and it was not worth wast-

---

proven the exact opposite of Knox's thesis. In his excellent history of the Divine Office, Taft shows clearly that the Liturgy of the Hours is fundamentally the prayer of all Christians. See Taft, *The Liturgy of the Hours in East and West* (Collegeville: The Liturgical Press, 1986).

[128] H. A. Reinhold, "The Vernacular Problem in 1909," *The Clergy Review* 27 (1947) 366.

[129] See Francis B. Donnelly, "Our Catholic Liturgy in a Catholic Language: A rejoinder to 'English in Our Liturgy,'" *The Commonweal* 42 (1945) 89–92. In this article, Donnelly takes the side of Knox and challenges the position of H. A. Reinhold and other promoters of the use of the vernacular in the liturgy.

[130] H. A. Reinhold, "About English in Our Liturgy: What its advocates ask for and why," *The Commonweal* 41 (1945) 537. Reinhold's views are all the more remarkable from one who, after all, was not a native English speaker.

[131] One reader of *OF* wrote to Godfrey Diekmann, in his capacity as editor of the magazine: "The article of this month—The Vernacular by H.A.R.—is just another sample of stupidity. He longs for the flesh pots of Protestantism, and their liberal mindedness in Church authority, and their heretical translation of the Scriptures. Let him join them if he finds them so much to his liking." Letter from V.C.T. (1943) SJAA: #1166.

ing endless hours and energy attempting to find the proper translation of private texts. It was more important to devote energy to the texts that engaged the assembly.

In response to those who defended the continuation of Latin on the grounds that it was the language of the Church, Reinhold contended that Greek, Coptic, and Slavonic were also languages of the Church. Latin was good for Canon Law and Thomistic Theology, for concise collects, for certain prefaces, for the more majestic hymns like the "Vexilla Regis." But what was the significance of all this to the majority of those who worship in our churches? Participants in the liturgical assembly were there "to pray, to sing, to listen, to sacrifice." So the liturgy needed to be simplified to help worshippers do those things. The vernacular was one step in the right direction, as far as Reinhold was concerned.[132]

Echoing Reinhold's words, John Cort, associate editor of *The Commonweal*, wrote an article in *Amen*, arguing that the vernacular issue brought to the fore the credibility of the American church. Cort began his article: "The great scandal of the 19th century was that the Church lost the working class." As the article proceeds, Cort asked whether the same would be said of the twentieth century. In writing on behalf of union workers, he criticized liturgy which he said had become overly feminized.[133] He went on to suggest that for many men, union workers, for example, the liturgy suffered from a lack of credibility. He contended that a liturgy whose language was understandable and which invited participation by the whole assembly—men and women—had the potential for alleviating such a problem.[134]

In a strong letter sent to the editor of *The Catholic Herald* in London, Clifford Howell, S.J., one of the pioneers in the liturgical movement in England, made the distinction between a "Vernacular Liturgy" and "Vernacular in the Liturgy." He argued that no one wanted a vernacular liturgy, since such had already been condemned by the Council of Trent. What people were asking for, according to Howell,

---

[132] Reinhold, "About English in Our Liturgy," 538–9. Reinhold's article was highly controversial and caused quite a stir for several months afterwards. There were numerous letters sent in to *The Commonweal* and other periodicals, either in support of Reinhold or challenging various points in his thesis.

[133] "Today one of the most frightening things about the Church is the absence of an appeal to men. The art is feminine; the hymns are not only feminine but girlish; the Communion rail is so crowded with women that a man feels de-sexed if he is seen there." J. Cort, "O Come, All Ye Faithful," *Amen* 6 (15 May 1951) 10.

[134] Cort used the example of Holy Cross Parish in St. Louis, under Hellriegel's leadership. The liturgy at Holy Cross had tremendous credibility, in Cort's estimation, precisely because the liturgy had a way of drawing in all sectors of that parish, and uniting them in their common liturgical participation.

was vernacular in the liturgy. In the Eucharist, for example, this would mean that the collects, epistle, and gospel would be in English while the rest of the Mass would remain in Latin. He concluded his letter:

> Therefore, Sir, let us have no more letters about "Vernacular Liturgy." The subject is dead, and may not be discussed. Instead let us discuss "Vernacular *in* the Liturgy." This subject is very live . . .[135]

While the debate continued for a number of years, there were some parish and religious communities that experimented with the vernacular in the eucharistic celebration and in other sacramental events. The vernacular discussions along with the experimentation helped to focus the issue for the American church, and laid the foundations for the move to a vernacular liturgy in the Conciliar reforms.

Excursus: Liturgical Abuses In the Celebration of the Eucharist

The early promoters of the liturgical movement attempted to address some of the liturgical abuses which were brought to their attention.[136] While some listed experimentation with the vernacular in the category of such liturgical abuses, others criticized those advocating greater liturgical participation because such an approach was not sufficiently strong in enforcing the doctrinal and legal aspects of Church teaching.[137] Those who were overly zealous in liturgical efforts pointed to the behavior of others who allowed their devotional practices to

---

[135] Clifford Howell, S.J., "Language in the Liturgy," *The Commonweal* 52 (1950) 606.

[136] It is interesting to compare the letters to the Editor and the published responses in both *OF* and *ER* during this period. *ER* reveals a very cautious, even scrupulous concern about rubrics and elements of liturgical practice. A random sample of questions and answers in assorted issues of *ER* in the late 1920s and 1930s finds the following titles: "The Indulgenced October Devotions," "At the 'Lavabo' In Requiem Mass," "Boys Camping Over Week-End Without Mass," "White Veil Over Ostensorium Before Benediction." On the other hand, *OF* reveals a concern for far more substantive liturgical and pastoral issues—issues like liturgical participation and the vernacular; raising liturgical consciousness through education, etc. The diverse issues raised in these two magazines suggests something both about the type of readership and also about the tone and agenda of the particular periodical.

[137] In responding to a letter signed, "Not an Intentional Liturgical Fadist," inquiring whether or not it was permissable to allow children to say aloud the words of the eucharistic prayer, so as to better appreciate the Mass, the writer for *HPR* who responded to the question, argued that children and adults will only learn to appreciate the liturgy by being taught "the dogma of the mass." The response con-

override a full and active participation in liturgical prayer. Still others took a more pessimistic view, seeing the entire liturgical situation of the time as hopelessly chaotic and desperately in need of help.[138]

---

tinued: "Preoccupation with externals is seemingly leading some priests into wild statements and wild actions." The lengthy response warns against liturgical diversity, and encourages a strict adherence to liturgical rubrics rather than being influenced by enthusiasts in the liturgical movement: "Recently I heard of an old lady who was disturbed, not by war and the rumors of war, but by her pastor saying Mass in the aisle of the church—a *Missa ad populum,* no doubt. Then some years ago I was told of a priest who at a meeting of some Catholic activity set up a portable altar in the sanctuary of the convent chapel and said Mass on it facing the congregation—. . . I know of no faculty whereby local Ordinaries can allow the use of a portable altar under such conditions, right in front of a marble altar. Disordered liturgical zeal no doubt excused the official *liturgist* from the objective guilt of violating an important precept of the Church's laws." "Liturgical Enthusiasts and Violations of Rubrics," *HPR* 41 (1941) 1218–9. See also "A Papal Warning about Liturgical Excesses," *HPR* 48 (1948) 289–91.

[138] One amusing letter was written by the Reverend Vitus Stoll of Des Moines, Iowa, and was entitled "Our Present Situation?": "Dear O.F.:—Well, well, so you have sufficient courage to print the following: 'The writer recalls the monotonous drawling of the rosary during Mass in many localities,' and 'the writer confesses frankly that much opposition to the introduction of liturgical Mass prayers is raised by narrow educators, who, because of hide-bound custom, would rather drone the rosary or sing some popular hymn than pray the Mass.' Congratulations! The above expressed the vortex of the whole liturgical problem. It is my conviction that nothing has done and is doing more harm to and causes greater disintegration of the liturgy than the enforced recitations of the rosary at Mass. It has come to be and is still almost universally advocated by 'narrow educators.' Until this situation can be rectified, there is little progress in store for the liturgy. Your correspondent, who had to listen to the advocacy of the rosary for the Mass, is just one in millions; just a sample of the state into which things can come in the kingdom of God. As to attendance at Sunday afternoon services, the best that can be said is that they are universally a total failure. The reasons are, distance from church in the country, and the movies and pleasure in the cities. But besides that is the fact that the Vesper service is for the average layman the deadest and most unattractive thing he comes across in a dreary world. The singing of psalms in Latin, which the learned scarcely understand, and which are full of expressions (even if they read them in English) that are utterly foreign to their mentality, is simply hopeless. And the usual custom of other services, which are nearly altogether devotions to the Blessed Virgin, or now to the Little Flower, have so little connection with the Eucharist that one wonders why the Blessed Sacrament is exposed at all. Anyhow there is not enough devotional spirit in the people to want to go to the Sunday afternoon devotion, and not enough inspiration in the devotions to make them want to go, so that the whole thing constitutes a vicious circle out of which we are curiously waiting for some one to lead us." *OF* 4 (1930) 141–2.

One example given of an abuse of the overly zealous was that of a congregation praying the eucharistic prayer so loudly that it upstaged the one presiding. Apparently, the congregation recited aloud the eucharistic prayer in the vernacular while the one presiding recited it in Latin, presumably *sotto voce*. The response on the part of *Orate Fratres* is interesting. The assembly's behavior was not considered problematic for reasons that might be given today, say, in terms of a concelebrated Eucharist where, rather than praying the eucharistic prayer *sotto voce* as the rubrics demand, the concelebrants speak so loudly that the presider's voice becomes inaudible. Nor was the reason given that the assembly might be distracted, thus fracturing the unity of the prayer. Rather, the arguments advanced against this abuse are the following:

> The decree of the Sacred Congregation of Rites (August 4, 1922) states that what is forbidden to the celebrant (i.e., reading Secret, Canon and words of a consecration in a loud tone) "cannot be permitted to the faithful, and must be reprobated as an abuse, and must be removed wherever it has been introduced." . . . And the priest will be disturbed by *any* loud recitation of the Canon, regardless of language. The Ceremonial of Bishops . . . insists on silence during the elevation.[139]

Orate Fratres readers were then reminded that saying aloud the ejaculation "My Lord and my God" during the elevation was likewise not permitted.

Another abuse mentioned is related to the dialog Mass. The concern was that some were celebrating the dialog Mass without proper instruction beforehand. Without adequate preparation the only possible result would be a mechanical recitation which goes against the whole purpose of increased participation in the liturgy. The editors noted:

> Participation means primarily participation as to mind and body—an intelligent participation. The first requisite, the most essential one, is therefore an understanding of what is going on in the liturgy. Without that there can be no real participation, no entering into the holy action with mind and heart.[140]

A further abuse involved a hasty, mechanical presiding style. *Orate Fratres* editors had received numerous letters from persons frustrated in their attempts to participate better in the liturgy. Their complaint was consistently that the priest would rush through the prayers of the Mass without waiting for the assembly to find its own place and thus

---

[139] *OF* 1 (1926) 253.
[140] Ibid.

be able to participate from the pews. This problem, addressed in the very first volume of *Orate Fratres*,[141] continued to surface in subsequent volumes well into the 1930s.

The liturgical pioneers addressed another challenging issue early in the American movement—a problem which has continued to exist from the Middle Ages to the present, even despite the reforms of Vatican II—namely, the tension between eucharistic celebration and the cult of the eucharistic presence outside of Mass. Alcuin Deutsch wrote:

> . . . there is one thing that he who loves Christ in the tabernacle in the spirit of the Liturgical Movement will never do—he will never let his love for Christ in His sacramental presence in the reserved species induce him to forget that the Mass—the Sacrifice—is by far the more important thing . . . [The] reservation, therefore, also has for its primary purpose consumption by those unable to assist at the Mass . . . Should there be the danger that the faithful attach more importance to benediction of the Blessed Sacrament after Mass than to the Mass itself, they should be instructed, and the benediction rather be omitted than that it should give rise to a misunderstanding of relative values.[142]

The pioneers were clearly ahead of their time in challenging a eucharistic piety which placed a greater emphasis on the reserved sacrament than on participation by the whole assembly in the eucharistic action.

Participation in the Liturgy of the Hours

At the beginning of the liturgical movement in the United States, the main emphasis of the founders was on eucharistic participation, consequently, great attention was paid to the Missal. Lay participation in the Liturgy of the Hours was also an issue in those early days, but it was not a priority.[143] The pioneers were convinced the day would come when the laity would be praying the Liturgy of the Hours, at least in part. But they were also convinced that Church members would first need to get acquainted with the Missal before familiarizing themselves with the Breviary.

That day did come. Within a few years, organized lay groups were regularly praying the Office, frequently in private but sometimes in common. When the Office was prayed in common, it was often done as part of a group meeting of one or another Catholic group. There were two groups, in particular, that incorporated the Liturgy of the Hours into their regular program of events. The first was the Society of

---

[141] "The Apostolate," Ibid., 254.
[142] Deutsch, "The Liturgical Movement," 395–6.
[143] William Busch, "The Breviary and the Laity," *OF* 10 (1936) 103.

Approved Workmen, in Brooklyn, New York. The Approved Workmen was a fraternity organized to instruct its members in theology and Church history, Scripture and liturgy. The upper level of this organization recited a part of the daily Office privately and occasionally parts of the Office in common, either in English or in a combination of Latin and English. The group began praying the Divine Office in 1932, only six years after the founding of the liturgical movement in the United States. The second lay organization, the Campion Propaganda Committee, was based in New York City. This group, connected to the Catholic Worker, was composed of students, young women and men committed to the reconstruction of a genuinely Christian social order. Their program included a study of liturgy and social justice, focusing especially on the Church's social teaching and on the pastoral care of the needy and oppressed. Members were pledged to the daily praying of Prime and Compline in private, or in common at the student hostel. On Sundays and the more important feasts, they also prayed Lauds, Terce, and Vespers in common in Latin, and participated in a recited or chanted Mass. William Busch, in his article, previously cited, used these two examples as proof that lay participation in the Office was possible. Busch suggested that American Catholics might begin praying parts of the Office in private as a first step toward the goal of praying the Office in common. It was not uncommon, on occasion, to find the Hours prayed by families at home.[144]

As a means of promoting the Hours among all members of the Church, *Orate Fratres,* at the initiative of William Busch, established the League of the Divine Office.[145] This league spread throughout the United States in just a few years.[146] Their aim was to communicate the message that

---

[144] B.A.B. of San Francisco wrote: "To the Editor:—As a subscriber to *Orate Fratres* and the father of children eight and a half years and seven years of age, I would like to have your opinion in regard to the use of Compline as a night prayer by such young children. The older child is in the forth grade and uses Dom Lefebvre's *Child's Missal,* while the other is in the third grade and uses *Offeramus* at Mass. In recent weeks they have been taught to read Compline from the booklet *Into Thy Hands,* by D. Attwater. In this I join them, when possible, reading from Stanbrook Abbey's *Day Hours;* otherwise I interpret the rubrics for them, as regards the use of the ferial and dominical psalms, the *preces,* doxology, etc. They take to the practice like the proverbial duck to water and show no indications of weariness because of the length of Compline." *OF* 7 (1933) 377–8.

[145] William Busch, "The Divine Office For All," *OF* 10 (1936) 527.

[146] In New York City, for example, the St. Joseph Center of the League was established at St. Joseph Church on 125th Street and Morningside Drive. Chapters consisting of seven members each were formed. Each chapter member pledged to pray daily one of the seven hours of the Breviary. Each member was assigned a particu-

the Liturgy of the Hours belongs to the whole Church, not only to religious communities and the ordained. It was their desire, then, to encourage and persuade others to take part in this liturgical prayer of the Church, though they recognized that there would be varying degrees of participation.[147] Love of the Missal began taking root in the United States, providing members of the league sufficient proof that with the proper instruction and encouragement, an appreciation of the Breviary would take root as well.[148] They were also realistic. They knew that their enthusiasm had to be tempered with patience, for they could not force people into believing that such prayer was liturgy, nor that such liturgy was meant for all. Reports gradually began coming into the League's office of attempts being made at the common praying of various parts of the Office throughout the United States.

As with the other projects of the liturgical pioneers, the task of introducing the Breviary to the laity presented its own problems. Some clergy were concerned that the length of the Office would interfere with the ordinary lives of average parishioners.[149] Others argued that

---

lar hour to be prayed for a week, at the end of which each of the seven moved to the next hour of the cycle. In this way each chapter, through its individual members, prayed the full compliment of the Office every day, with each chapter member reciting all the hours in a seven-week cycle. The writer noted that people would travel from all parts of the New York metropolitan area including New Jersey, to pray Vespers and Compline in common. Eugene P. McSweeney, "Laypraises," *America* 55 (1936) 378.

[147] Their project was also supported by a growing number of the American hierarchy. In addressing a provisional conference of Franciscan tertiaries in 1935, for example, Bishop Schlarman of Peoria, Illinois, urged members to participate, not only in the Eucharist, but also in the fuller liturgical life of the Church—the Liturgy of the Hours. Eugene P. McSweeney, "Liturgical Life," *America* 55 (1936) 117.

[148] Such encouragement was increasingly found in the major Catholic periodicals of the time. One amusing article was entitled: "Laymen May Read the Breviary: If matrons sang matins and chauffeurs chanted." The writer concluded: "This present interest in the inspired prayer is a movement that should be blessed, advertised, and encouraged. When policemen chant prime, when nurses say nones, when veterinarians and cooks recite vespers and compline, ours will be a lovelier and a holier world." Gerard Donnelly, *America* 55 (1936) 318.

[149] In response to this objection, William Busch quoted President Roosevelt, who had just given a speech regarding the Boulder Dam enterprise. In speaking about the modern application of energy and looking toward the future, he urged his hearers to consider their leisure, their culture, and their way of life. Such things, he suggested, could not be left solely in the hands of bankers, government officials, and demagogues. Busch suggested that taking the time for common liturgical prayer be considered in this context. Busch,"The Divine Office," 531.

the Office was too complicated for the average layperson.[150] Progress was slow. William Busch asked why, in 1936, with so many more college and university-educated Church members than in the previous century, there was such difficulty in convincing people of the value of the Office as liturgical prayer when it had been so easily prayed by native Americans in the middle of the nineteenth century.[151]

Problems in promoting the Liturgy of the Hours were not limited to the laity in parishes, but were also an issue in monastic circles. Abbot Alcuin Deutsch appointed a liturgical board at St. John's Abbey, chaired by Virgil Michel, to oversee the monastery's liturgical practice. On 5 June 1936, the board offered the abbot an evaluation of celebration of the Liturgy of the Hours at St. John's:

> St. John's is known all over the country as a liturgical center, which for many persons naturally means a *model* center of the liturgical life. Some of these persons visit us only to be shocked at the manner in which we fall short of reciting the divine office *digne, attente, ac devote*. There are not a few of the monks here at St. John's who are quite disgusted with the way in which the office is being recited. It has been a matter of complete discouragement even to many of the clerics. The main untoward features of our choir recitation are the speed, the jumbling speed, of our recitation and the gross disharmonies that constantly mar the unison of tone.[152]

St. Vincent's Archabbey, in Latrobe, Pennsylvania, had its own tensions between those monks who were involved in the liturgical movement and those who were not. Some of these tensions revealed themselves when the monastic community gathered for the Hours. Archbishop Rembert G. Weakland, O.S.B., of Milwaukee, entered the monastery at St. Vincent's in the late 1940s:

---

[150] *OF* reported that some priests objected to Vespers because people were unable to appreciate the services since they were sung in Latin. Rather than celebrating Vespers in English, these priests replaced the common celebration of Vespers with devotional services in the vernacular. *OF* noted that such a change was not permissible since, as a liturgical office of the Church, the Office of Vespers was official, and therefore always took precedence over a private devotion. "The Apostolate," *OF* 9 (1935) 332.

[151] Busch refers to a chronicle of the missionary activities of Father Skolla in the Lake Superior region around the year 1850, which tells how the native American congregations there were accustomed to chanting Vespers on Sunday afternoons. In 1866, Father Kauder published a manual of prayers for the Micmac Indians of Nova Scotia. That text, printed in their own language, contained not only the text of the ordinary of the Mass but also the hours of Prime, Vespers, and Compline. Busch, "The Divine Office," 529.

[152] SJAA: F-20.

I remember old Father Felix who would say: "These young monks sit up until midnight talking about the liturgical movement, and then they all oversleep for morning prayer. The liturgical movement begins here every morning at 4:00 a.m.!"[153]

The promotion of an authentic celebration of the Liturgy of the Hours, then, was an issue for the whole Church. But was it worth all the effort? Why pray the Office? Why encourage the whole Church to pray the daily Office? Three reasons were cited. The first was that praying the Office in common would return the Church to a true sense of community prayer, along with a restored consciousness of the social character of Christianity. It would be a bold, prophetic statement in the face of an individualistic culture which had its effect upon Catholic piety and worship and had weakened Christian solidarity. Second, it would return Church members to a clearer understanding of the vital character of Christianity, leading those who participated into the regular current of the Church's own life. Regular participation in the common liturgical prayer of the Office would lead the assembly to see in the liturgy a pattern of life. The third reason given was that participation in the Hours would restore a deeper consciousness of the objective character of Christianity. It would move the Church to a greater recognition of where God was at work and would challenge the subjective attitude of those who viewed piety and prayer as their own personal matter. The focus, instead, would be on the common good, on one's participation as contributing to the unified, corporate worship of the body of Christ. As a school of prayer, the liturgical assembly would learn what it means to be incorporated into Jesus Christ.[154]

Writing in *America*, Gerald Donnelly, S.J., offered six reasons for lay participation in the Liturgy of the Hours.[155] In the first place, the Office is the prayer of the Mystical Body. When one prays as a member of that body, one unites his or her voice with the chorus of the whole Church. Second, the Office is chiefly a prayer of praise. It is theocentric rather than egocentric. It aims at giving glory to God rather than focusing upon one's personal agenda. "Its theme is 'we adore'—a nobler theme than 'please give.'" Third, participation in the Office moves one away from selfish and rugged individualism in worship. Like the Eucharist, the Office is essentially social and corporate worship. Fourth, "nearly

[153] Rembert G. Weakland, O.S.B., Interview by author, 10 December 1994, Milwaukee, Wisconsin.

[154] Busch, 529–31.

[155] Gerard Donnelly, "Let Us Glorify Him With Psalms: Reasons and a plan are added to exhortation," *America* 56 (1936) 269.

all prayer-book prayers are written by some pious clergyman. Admirable as they are, they exemplify his personal idea of prayer." The psalms, on the other hand, as the backbone of the Breviary, move one away from pious subjectivism and closer to a normative style of worship. The fifth point deals with the relationship of the Office to the Eucharist. To stress such a relationship, Donnelly emphasized the connection between Missal and Breviary texts, suggesting that the Office "enshrines the day's Sacrifice, echoes its prayers, extends and continues the Mass." Finally, Donnelly contends that all of one's favorite devotional prayers are subsumed in the morning and evening prayers of the Office. Mary and the saints are honored. All intentions are included—praying for the dead, for the missions, for sinners, for benefactors, for friends: "It [the Breviary] is all manuals of piety rolled into one—and is more efficacious than them all."

Lancelot Sheppard went so far as to speak of "the right of the laity to the divine Office" by virtue of their membership in the Mystical Body of Christ, which began at baptism.[156] Such a right continued to be emphasized in diverse ways, with growing enthusiasm, for years to come.[157]

In general, the call to participation in the Hours was less controversial than the call for greater participation in the Mass. Certainly, there was resistance to the Office as a prayer for all Church members, but such resistance pales in comparison to the arguments over the dialogue Mass, a Eucharist where the assembly moved, slowly but surely, from their passive presence as spectators to active participants.[158] Even

---

[156] Lancelot C. Sheppard, "The Divine Office and the Laity: The Right of the Laity to the Divine Office," *OF* 11 (1937) 169–73.

[157] The Archdiocese of New York's office of the Society for the Propagation of the Faith, for example, chose to utilize sung Vespers to bring about a greater realization of the importance of prayer as the greatest help to the missions. With the encouragement of New York's Cardinal Hayes, the Society sponsored a "mission vespers" in each of the five deaneries of the archdiocese on the Sundays from 9 December through 13 January, 1934–35. The choir was composed of twenty-four students from the Pius X School of Liturgical Music. The proper Sunday Vespers were sung in Gregorian chant. Churches were packed for each event, signaling, according to the editors of *The Catholic News*, a "sympathetic interest aroused by this important—though all too frequently neglected—liturgical function." *The Catholic News*, as reported in *OF* 9 (1935) 132.

[158] In 1940, *The Chicago Catholic Worker* noted that some people were praying morning prayer on the way to work each morning, and Compline on the way home each evening. The article continued: "It would be good if Catholic meetings closed with Compline, a demonstration of corporate prayer and worship, a striking example of praying as one Body. It was once the practice of families to have common

though William Busch argued that Catholics of the 1930s were less engaged and appreciative of the Hours than their native American fore-
bears of the 1850s, one can at least maintain today that the American
Catholics of the 1930s made far greater use of the Office as a vibrant
form of liturgical prayer than is the case in the American church today.

CONCLUSION

In this chapter, we have seen that full and active participation was
the fundamental goal of the liturgical movement in the United States,
and this was grounded in the doctrine of the Mystical Body of Christ.
Through baptism, Christians are initiated into that body and take their
rightful place at the Lord's table. Acceptance of this and other goals of
the liturgical pioneers varied greatly, however, depending on socio-
cultural factors. German Catholics in the United States were clearly the
most receptive, thus it follows logically that the movement first took
hold in those parts of the country where German immigrants had
settled. In calling for liturgical renewal in a variety of American Catholic communities, the pioneers presented their goals in varied ways.
Moreover, the issue of liturgical participation had serious implications
for the spirituality of American Catholics. One could not speak about
liturgical participation without considering how such participation
influenced everyday life: the relationship between liturgy and a just
society; liturgy and the assembly's responsibility to the poor and mar-
ginalized; liturgy as shaping moral behavior. Likewise, as education
was one of the primary emphases of the movement, this theme was
also intrinsically linked to liturgy—both to enhance and to inform such
participation and ritual enactment. The themes of liturgical art, architecture, and music, also found their home in the area of participation.
The pioneers and promoters called for art, architecture, and music that
would assist rather than detract from the assembly's participation in
the liturgical act. Liturgical participation, then, was full and active only
when it extended beyond the confines of the church building into the
daily life of the community.

---

prayers in the home. Reciting Compline every evening the family would pray not
only as *a family,* but even *with* and *for* and *as* the whole church prays." Such liturgical prayers were strong, "not the wishy-washy affected language of many devotional prayers." Editor,"Prime and Compline," *The Chicago Catholic Worker*
(November, 1940) 3.

CHAPTER THREE

❖

The Liturgical Movement
and Social Justice

INTRODUCTION

The doctrine of the Mystical Body of Christ was foundational for an organic understanding of the Church symbolically expressed in the liturgy, grounding a view of liturgical participation which flowed into service, into social activism.[1] Virgil Michel and his colleagues did not tire of promoting this fundamental principle: liturgy and social action are inseparable. Historian Ernest Koenker has observed:

> The Roman Catholic Liturgical Movement deserves the strongest praise for its social awareness. It has demonstrated the spiritual meaning of man's life in society as most Protestant churches in America have not done. It has instilled meaning into daily life and activity by rendering meaningful . . . the ancient symbols arising from work.[2]

In the 1930s, as today, the term "social justice" was used in many different contexts, sometimes glibly. From the outset, it is important to establish a working definition of social justice in order to better understand just what the liturgical pioneers and promoters were advocating. In an article which appeared in *The Commonweal*, Virgil Michel relied upon the definition given by social activist John A. Ryan:

[1] Liturgically-based social activism became a common theme in the 1930s. Catherine De Hueck wrote in 1938: "Participation in the Mass will teach us the full understanding of the mystical body of Christ, leading us to a Christian sociology, which is the corner-stone of the Christian social order and which alone can save our mad world from destruction." Catherine De Hueck, "I Saw Christ Today," *OF* 12 (1938) 309.
[2] Koenker, 136.

Just treatment for every class in the community, particularly the working classes. Pius XI uses and applies the expression in many places; for example, in discussing just wages, just interest, the rights and duties of property and in describing the nature of the new social order which he sets forth. Social justice, he says, must permeate all institutions of public and social life, and must build up juridical and social order capable of pervading all economic activity.[3]

Michel argued, however, that Ryan's definition did not go far enough. The "social question," as it was called, was not simply a matter of economics and a just wage, but encompassed all of human life. The response to the social question was "social reconstruction," which would involve an organic reconstruction of the whole society. Basing his own definition of social justice on Thomistic principles which viewed the individual in relationship to the whole, Michel offered this alternative to Ryan's definition:

. . . we can then define social justice as that virtue by which individuals and groups contribute their positive share to the maintenance of the common good and moreover regulate all their actions in proper relation to the common good.[4]

The early years of the liturgical movement were challenging years for American society, particularly for American Catholics. These were the years of the Great Depression. A brief look at the social history of this period is important for the establishment of the cultural context in which the liturgical movement developed, and to better understand the link between liturgical and social action.

This chapter is then divided into two major parts. *Part One* is entitled *Catholic Social Teaching and the American Church's Response,* and *Part Two: The Liturgical Pioneers and Social Justice.* Following a brief exposition of the two major social encyclicals which served as the basis for the Church's social programs in the 1920s and beyond, Part One studies the organizations which emerged as a response to social needs within the American church. It is interesting to note that the response to social injustice on the part of organizations of the 1920s was generally founded on a privatistic piety and morality. These organizations, which pre-dated the rediscovery of the doctrine of the Mystical Body, functioned with the conviction that social justice was unrelated to liturgy.

---

[3] J. Ryan, "New Deal and Social Justice," *The Commonweal* 19 (1934) 657–9, quoted by Michel, "Defining Social Justice," *The Commonweal* 23 (1936) 425.
[4] Ibid., 426.

The social movements of the 1930s, on the other hand, show significant contact with the liturgical movement and represent a more socially-conscious spirituality and morality, grounded in the liturgical life of the Church.[5] Not surprisingly, the reader finds frequent references to the Mystical Body of Christ in these writings. One notices, then, a paradigmatic shift in Part One, from social justice grounded in a private, personal piety to a liturgically-based social justice that calls for a new Christian social order with mutual concern and responsibility among its members.

Although the liturgical pioneers are referred to and are occasionally discussed in the first part of this chapter, Part Two addresses more directly their contribution to social justice and their vision of how liturgy and justice were integrally linked. As one who was both founder of the liturgical movement in the United States and social reformer, Virgil Michel gave the movement in this country its impetus for the emphasis on justice. The chapter concludes by examining the contributions of two other liturgical pioneers and promoters: Hans A. Reinhold and Reynold Hillenbrand.

With that introduction, we begin with a look at the socio-economic background of American cultural life of the 1920s and 1930s.

The Roaring Twenties

In the 1920s, the United States became increasingly industrialized and urbanized. With such industrialization came a type of laissez-faire capitalism. The "roaring twenties" were a time of great prosperity for those who were fortunate enough to have been successful in business ventures. Such competition brought with it an unfair distribution of wealth along with an acute sense of individualism, the repercussions of which were felt throughout all segments of American society.[6]

---

[5] Edwin Ryan noted a connection between the indifference to social welfare and the disproportionate pursuit of devotions, calling both "evils," and "a manifestation of individualism." Both social indifference and the pursuit of personal piety, in Ryan's estimation, isolate the individual and ignore the reality that we are brothers and sisters, one to another, and must worship accordingly: He continued: ". . . it is wrong for an individual Catholic to follow too much his own bent in prayer while participating too little in that corporate worship which the Church as a society owes to God. A visible church without visible organized worship would be impossible; consequently, when liturgical worship is relegated to the background all Catholic activities suffer." "Social Action and the Liturgy," *Liturgy and Sociology* 1 (Summer, 1936) 6.

[6] For surveys of this period, see Sean D. Cashman, *America in the Twenties and Thirties: the Olympian Age of Franklin Delano Roosevelt* (New York: New York University

The Church was not immune to such individualism. Catholic clergy contended that their responsibility was to care for the spiritual needs of people, but considered it inappropriate to enter into public life or to criticize unjust social conditions. In fact, clergy were suspicious of labor unions, since such groups competed with the Church for time and commitment on the part of parishioners.[7] Catholic devotional life was likewise privatistic, seeking to give solace and comfort through novenas or benediction, but in such a way that there was little or no connection to the rest of life.

A growing sense of Catholic identity emerged in the 1920s. Catholics were increasingly seen by their non-Catholic neighbors as exclusive participants in a separatist culture. They joined newly-founded Catholic organizations like the Catholic Library Association (1921), American Catholic Philosophical Association (1926), and the Catholic Anthropological Association (1928).[8] Ecclesiologically, the Church of the 1920s was generally understood to be "an organized society constituted by the exercise of powers with which pope, bishops and priests were invested." While there were "some interesting hints of renaissance," ecclesiology in those days meant "almost entirely . . . a treatise of public law."[9]

The growing sense of a Catholic culture in the United States along with varied and sundry demonstrations of Catholic pride were not well-received by the wider American society. In fact, anti-Catholicism increased substantially during the 1920s. There were some political officials who spoke in public about the threat of the Catholic Church in the United States, while others attacked the Church's "immorality." The Ku Klux Klan increased in membership, as a 35,000-member march on Washington in 1925 clearly demonstrated. The governor of Florida spoke of a papal plot to invade the state and move the Vatican there. It was not a popular time to be Catholic.

In 1926, one year after the Klan parade, Cardinal George Mundelein of Chicago sought to respond to anti-Catholic sentiments with a demonstration of Catholic strength at the first international eucharistic congress held in the United States. Mundelein arranged with the Pullman Company for a special train reserved solely for the visiting cardinals, the other bishops, and their entourage. Each cardinal was given his own car,

---

Press, 1988); James Henry Gray and Loren Baritz, *The Culture of the Twenties* (Indianapolis: Bobbs-Merrill, 1970).

[7] David O'Brien, *Public Catholicism* (New York: Macmillan Publishers, 1989) 93.

[8] Halsey, 55–7.

[9] Yves Congar, "My Path-findings in the Theology of the Laity and Ministries," *The Jurist* 32 (1972) 170.

which was painted red with his name painted in gold. The "Red Special" had the right of way as it moved from New York to the specially constructed station in Chicago and must have been quite a spectacle with ten cardinals, two apostolic delegates, four archbishops, seven bishops, and their entourage on board. It may well have been a "unique demonstration of Catholic faith," as Cardinal Mundelein suggested, but it was also viewed as opulent and a scandalous display of wealth, particularly by those who were already suspicious of Catholicism.[10]

The industrialization and urbanization of the 1920s also began to threaten the family and to challenge traditional family values, oftentimes separating workers from their families. Workers complained that they were nothing more than a number, serving the already wealthy while they were living without human dignity and respect.[11] Despite such problems, however, there was nothing in that period more disastrous than the stock market crash of 1929 and the Great Depression that followed.

The Great Depression

The stock market crash occurred on Wall Street on Thursday 24 October 1929. The collapse of the market was initially downplayed. The *New York Times*, for example, chose to run as its top story an article on Richard Byrd's South Pole expedition rather than the market crash. Even the most pessimistic of forecasters predicted nothing more than an economic recession of several months.[12] They were wrong. From 1930–1932, about 5,000, or twenty percent of commercial banks in the United States had closed. By March of 1933, unemployment reached a high of sixteen million people or one third of the available work force, and held steady at about ten million throughout the 1930s.[13] The

---

[10] Gerald Fogarty, "Public Patriotism and Private Politics: The Tradition of American Catholicism" in *U.S. Catholic Historian* 4 (1984–85) 31–2.

[11] In a 1936 pamphlet, Virgil Michel quoted from the memoirs of one such anonymous worker: "When I entered industry I found it a nightmare of time—recording clocks . . . which impressed upon me that my place in the universe was C702 . . . The machine took hold of me with its iron fingers and worked me into the shape required . . . attention was lavished on the stresses and strains of machinery and metal, but the more delicate mechanism of human nerves and sinews—not to speak of human souls—was ignored." *Critique of Capitalism* (St. Paul: Wanderer Publishing Co., 1936) 42–3.

[12] Linda Marie Delloff, *A Century of* The Century (Grand Rapids: Eerdmans Publishing Company, 1984) 45.

[13] A good summary of the Depression is given in Robert McElvaine, *Down & Out In The Great Depression* (Chapel Hill: The University of North Carolina Press, 1983)

Depression widened the already existing gap between rich and poor, black and white, educated and uneducated. Thousands lined the streets on breadlines in big cities like New York and Chicago and were fed in soup kitchens. The birthrate dropped to a record low.[14]

The international scene proved to be problematic, as well. In 1933 an estimated thirty million people were unemployed throughout the world. Hitler took over Germany in that same year. Two years later Mussolini invaded Ethiopia; in 1936, Japan walked out of the League of Nations; the Spanish Civil War also began that same year. Whether at home or abroad, the decadence and security of the twenties gave way to tremendous poverty and hopelessness.

Throughout the Depression, believers found warmth and a sense of community in their churches and synagogues. In a more recent and interesting article, Stephen Recken suggests that success in the 1930s was measured, not by financial wealth or a high position in society, but by a sense of belonging. The anxiety brought on by the Depression gave rise to this desire, since with the loss of everything else, the biggest fear haunting Americans was the loss of supportive relationships or the loss of a place in the community. Recken contends that such belonging not only offered security, but also provided grounding in a time when many were searching for roots. He argues convincingly that the fundamental goal of Americans in the 1930s was "an assured status in a familiar community."[15]

The Church, then, provided roots and a sense of continuity. It likewise served as a center for the kind of relationships and shared loyalties which, according to Recken, American citizens of the thirties were seeking. But to what extent did the Church directly address the social issues brought on by the Depression? To what extent did worship address these concerns? And did the Church witness a new thrust of membership and energy because of the Depression?

An interesting study done in 1937 explored such questions, not simply in terms of the Catholic Church, but including the other mainline Christian churches as well, and concluded that while the churches, unlike the banks, survived and endured the Depression, they were not thriving and teeming with new energy. In fact, in many cases, it was business as usual. The average parish did not reflect a significant

---

3–32. A collection of letters written by the poor and unemployed of that period, addressed primarily to President and Mrs. Roosevelt, is found in the same volume, 38–229.

[14] Lester Chandler, *Economics of Money and Banking* (New York: Harper, 1953) 145.

[15] Stephen Recken, "Fitting-In: The Redefinition of Success in the 1930s," *Journal of Popular Culture* 27 (1993) 206. See also Susman, *Culture and Commitment*, 60–74.

change from the years prior to the Depression.[16] The Diocese of Toledo ran a major building campaign for a new cathedral all through the Depression. At a time when so many people were unemployed, the content of the Sunday sermon week after week was that of fundraising for Holy Rosary Cathedral. Such situations were probably not limited to Toledo.[17] The Vatican, for its part, had issued two major encyclicals, in 1891 and in 1931, calling Catholics to social awareness and to action.

PART ONE:
CATHOLIC SOCIAL TEACHING AND THE
AMERICAN CHURCH'S RESPONSE IN THE 1920s

Part One explores the Church's response to the socio-economic environment of the 1920s under three distinct headings: (1) Catholic social teaching, (2) Church-sponsored service organizations, and (3) Catholic social movements. After treating those two key social encyclicals: *Rerum novarum* and *Quadragesimo anno*, this first part of the chapter looks at how the American church attempted to implement Catholic social teaching in the 1920s and 1930s. This is followed by a consideration of the work of the National Catholic Welfare Council (NCWC); the National Catholic Rural Life Conference (NCRLC); the contribution of Reverend Charles Coughlin, the "Radio Priest"; the Laymen's League for Retreats and Social Studies; and, finally, the German Catholic Verein. Representing the paradigmatic shift already discussed, Part One then continues with a study of social movements such as Catholic Action (CA), The Catholic Worker (CW), Friendship House (FH), and the Grail. These were social movements closely associated with the liturgical movement, founded on the doctrine of the Mystical Body of Christ. They were organic movements that exemplified the integral relationship between liturgy and justice.

The Social Encyclicals

In his encyclical *Rerum Novarum* issued on 15 May 1891, Pope Leo XIII proposed to outline a program of Catholic social reform, in light of the new conditions created by the Industrial Revolution. Considered one of the most important modern pronouncements on social justice, the encyclical demanded a just wage and called the Church to responsibility in the moral aspects of employment. While calling for

---

[16] Samuel Kincheloe, *Research Memorandum on Religion in the Depression* 33 (New York: Social Science Research Council, 1937) 93–6.

[17] Richard A. McCormick, S.J., Interview by author, 3 November 1994, University of Notre Dame.

social reform, the encyclical condemned socialism as infringing upon the right to private property. *Quadragesimo anno,* the encyclical of Pius XI, issued on 5 May 1931 to mark the fortieth anniversary of *Rerum novarum,* took the Church's social agenda even further, calling for a more unified, organic view of society as a means of confronting the social and economic problems of the world. It stressed the common good and noted that in labor as well as in ownership, the social aspect must always be considered along with the personal or private. Despite these two great encyclicals, however, there was little awareness of the Church's social teaching in this period. There were a number of groups which tried to remedy that—The National Catholic Welfare Council, for example.

The Response of the American Church in the 1920s

The National Catholic Welfare Council (NCWC) was established after World War I as the American church's program for coordinated social action. Headquartered in Washington, the NCWC kept close contact with national affairs, keeping Church leaders, organizations, and the Catholic press informed, and lobbying before congress for Church interests. Of the different departments represented in the NCWC, the Social Action Department was the most noteworthy, led by the most prominent Catholic cleric involved in social activism, John A. Ryan.

Monsignor Ryan of The Catholic University of America was so influenced by his reading of *Rerum novarum* that he dedicated the rest of his professional life to encouraging Catholics to support social and economic reforms, to offering a systematic and constant critique of the American economy, and to rejecting laissez-faire capitalism.[18] His system, however, was dualistic in that it created a distinction between being American and being Catholic. In asking the question of how liturgy and the spiritual life could be related to the work of justice, he turned to authority and Church law as solutions. His famous work, published in 1916, was entitled *Distributive Justice: The Right and Wrong of Our Present Distribution of Wealth,* in which he studied and critiqued the national economy in light of Catholic social teaching.[19] He was not only an academic but also an activist.

---

[18] See Frederick Broderick, *The Right Reverend New Dealer* (New York: Sheed and Ward, 1963).

[19] John Ryan, *Distributive Justice: The Right and Wrong Of Our Present Distribution of Wealth* (New York: The Paulist Press, 1916). See also Ryan, *Organized Social Justice: An Economic Program for the United States Applying Pius XI's Great Encyclical on Social Life* (New York: Paulist Press, n.d.).

Ryan's activism also worked against him. He was preoccupied with immediate national concerns and misunderstood the fundamental import of the encyclicals he was promoting. He also failed to attend to the need for a true religious revival within the country as foundational for social change. His activism lacked the spiritual and liturgical grounding which was found in other social reformers like Virgil Michel, Dorothy Day, and Catherine De Hueck. Likewise, his view of the Catholic social movement was rather self-centered, believing that the only effective leadership in American social reform came from himself. Virgil Michel was critical of Ryan's stress on material rather than spiritual reform, and saw Ryan's approach as being too shallow and superficial. Michel believed that in attending to social and economic reform as the only immediate need, Ryan clearly had little time for moral reform. Ryan did admit to a friend that while he respected the need for moral reform, it was not a high priority on his agenda. What he did offer to those involved in the social and liturgical movements was a detailed, systematic understanding of American economics. This was something which participants in both movements had been lacking.[20]

Working intensely with the NCWC[21] in his capacity as an early leader of its social action department, Ryan encouraged American bishops to speak out more forcefully on behalf of social justice. A major breakthrough came in 1919 with "The Bishops' Program of Social Reconstruction." Authored by Ryan, this was the first document of the American episcopate to call for social and economic reform.[22]

In the 1920s and 1930s, the NCWC expanded its scope to collaborate with other movements and organizations of American church life. From 1–4 May 1938, for example, the NCWC sponsored a "National Catholic Social Action Conference" in Milwaukee on the theme of "A Christian Social Order and the Church." By the time of that conference, facilitated by Francis Haas who had been rector of St. Francis Seminary, Milwaukee, and was working at The Catholic University at the time, the NCWC had sponsored seventy such conferences in cities around the country. It was publicized in the pages of *Orate Fratres,*

---

[20] David O'Brien, *American Catholics and Social Reform* (New York: Oxford University Press, 1968) 142, 147–8.

[21] For a thorough treatment of the NCWC, see Douglas Slawson, *The Foundation and First Decade of the National Catholic Welfare Council* (Washington: Catholic University of America Press, 1992).

[22] See Joseph McShane, *"Sufficiently Radical," Catholicism, Progressivism, and the Bishops' Program of 1919* (Washington, D.C.: Catholic University of America Press, 1986).

urging "all liturgical apostles to attend who can possibly do so, and in attending to do their part towards bringing the fundamental truths of the Christian spiritual revival to bear upon all matters of theory and practice."[23]

The National Catholic Rural Life Conference (NCRLC) was an agrarian movement founded in St. Louis in 1923 by Edwin Vincent O'Hara. It grew out of the rural life bureau of the NCWC. When O'Hara organized the first national conference on Catholic rural life, his efforts met with such success that the conference became a permanent organization. O'Hara lamented the fact that rural parishes were frequently a dumping ground for problematic, sometimes alcoholic clergy. He believed that a religious center out in the country would hold very positive implications for the future, not only in rural areas but for the cities as well.[24]

Population growth in the cities was constant, often with people moving in from rural areas. Thus, the rural population of one day would become the urban population of the future. The Conference challenged such things as corporate farming and national policy with regard to agriculture, and fostered cooperative farming, subsistence households, and a return to rural life. As with the other attempts at implementing Catholic social teaching, the fundamental goal of the Conference was the fostering of something which had a distinctly Catholic character: Catholic agrarianism.

W. Howard Bishop, president of the Conference from 1928 until 1934, noted three dimensions of Catholic agrarianism. First, it offered a popular theology of rural life as a place of religious encounter, as sacred space. This position was also held by Virgil Michel. Second, it offered a critique of capitalism[25] and promoted and called for a renewal of farming with the cooperative principles of Catholicism. Third, in calling for a return to the land, to rural living, it offered the

---

[23] Editor, "The Apostolate," *OF* 12 (1938) 273–4.

[24] Slawson, 233–4.

[25] Bishop addressed a 1935 convention in Rochester, New York: "Individuals, groups and nations bow down to the power of greed. Unbridled capitalism, ruthless individualism holds the scepter. Money is the acknowledged ruler of the world . . . It (Capitalism) makes a direct assault when it reduces the human individual to the status of a work-horse,—when with a paramount concern for dividends it subjects him to all the cruel indignities and handicaps that modern industrialism knows, to the point, alas, that it is no longer easy for him, and the world about him, to remember that he is a child of God and an heir of Heaven." W. Howard Bishop, "Agrarianism, The Basis of a New Order," quoted in Christopher Kauffman, "W. Howard Bishop, President of the National Catholic Rural Life Conference," *US Catholic Historian* 8 (1989) 139.

best religious response to the Depression. Bishop saw the Conference's task as evangelical—to make Catholic an area that had largely been Protestant.[26] Bishop believed that in helping people to solve their economic and social problems on the farm, they would then be led to the Church. He rejected a dichotomy between religion and culture, suggesting that "the environment and life of the farm furnish a *perfect* setting for an ideal Christian life."[27] Bishop's efforts gave impetus to Catholic agrarianism through the 1930s and well into the 1940s.

Virgil Michel was involved in the NCRLC, as well.[28] At a 1936 Rural Life convention in Fargo, North Dakota, Michel argued that the liturgical and cooperative movements were both reactions to selfishness and narrow individualism: the cooperative with regard to the economic system; the liturgical with regard to the spiritual.[29] Michel had been invited to lecture on the liturgical apostolate to members of the Antigonish cooperative movement in Nova Scotia. Those three weeks were a time of tremendous learning for him. In the principles of the cooperative movement, he recognized great complimentarity with the principles of the liturgical movement. In that brief time, he was a kind of apprentice with the pioneer of cooperatives, Reverend James Tomkins, keeping a diary of that visit. He was deeply impressed by what he witnessed there because he saw the principles of social reform at work on the grassroots level.[30] While participants in cooperative

---

[26] Bishop ultimately founded the Glenmary Home Missioners to promote a corporate evangelization of rural life. Kauffman, 131.

[27] Ibid., 133.

[28] Michel wrote in 1938: "I know that it is indeed very often a misfortune to be born in a larger city; and subsequent experience and contacts have convinced me that it may become almost an irreparable spiritual calamity to be born in some of our largest metropolitan areas." "City or Farm," *OF* 12 (1938) 367.

[29] He said: "For us Catholics, this means in particular that the cooperative movement needs the help and inspiration of the liturgical movement, and it necessarily means that the liturgical movement, under pain of remaining sterile, needs to flower out into ever-increasing Christian cooperation in all things of life . . . For the Catholic then, the liturgical movement . . . must be both the inspiration and the model of the cooperative movement in economic life. Not only is the Mystical Body the model at which the organization and functioning of the economic body must aim, but the proper restoration of the latter is possible only under the inspiration of the former." Michel, "The Cooperative Movement and the Liturgical Movement," *Catholic Rural Life Objectives,* quoted in Marx, 370. This lecture was reprinted in *OF* 14 (1940) 152–60.

[30] In the words of Michel's biographer: "Here he witnessed the downtrodden, drunkards, and paupers learn to read, study, work together under cultivated lay leadership and clerical direction and to become 'human' beings and fervent Chris-

movements such as the NCRLC were challenging the American system of capitalism through their common life out in the country, the cities did not remain idle. Individuals like Reverend Charles Coughlin carried the same message through a different medium.

For Catholic Americans of this century, Bishop Fulton J. Sheen popularized the medium of church-sponsored broadcasting. But years before Sheen began his ministry over the airwaves, Americans were familiar with another Catholic communicator, a controversial figure who addressed American issues of social injustice in light of Catholic social teaching, Father Charles E. Coughlin (1891–1979).

Charles Coughlin was a priest of the Archdiocese of Detroit. Early on, he was known for his powerful homilies and his combative diatribes on social justice. His reputation as a preacher led him, in 1926, to preach those same social justice themes on a Detroit radio station, WRJ, with a series entitled: "Want in the Midst of Plenty." In one of his first sermons, he said:

> In our country, with its lakes and rivers teeming with fish; its mines heavy with minerals; its banks teeming with money, there are approximately five million unemployed men walking aimlessly through the streets of our cities and the by-paths of our country sides, seeking not doles but labor.[31]

Three years later, the radio program was expanded to include Cincinnati and Chicago, and Coughlin's fame spread. In that pre-ecumenical age, Lutheran Church historian Martin Marty notes that Coughlin was the first American Catholic priest to have a serious following among non-Catholics.[32] In 1930, he dramatically changed the style and content of his broadcasts. He expressed serious concern that American economic and political policy was fundamentally un-Christian. He attacked bankers and politicians, the Republican party, and the Hoover administration. As controversial a figure as he was, he had great support in the Catholic community and reflected the sentiments of many who felt shunned in American society. In 1936, he began a weekly journal, *Social Justice,* which gave Coughlin another medium for communicating his message, often quoting from papal encyclicals as a way of

---

tians again; non-Catholics cooperating with Catholics . . . a movement of, by, and for the people, from the bottom up." Marx, 371.

[31] *Father Coughlin's Radio Sermons, October 1930–April 1931* (Baltimore, 1931) 16, quoted in O'Brien, *American Catholics and Social Reform,* 152.

[32] Martin Marty, *Modern American Religion, Vol. 2: The Noise of Conflict 1919–1941* (Chicago: University of Chicago Press, 1991) 273. See also Donald Warren, *Radio Priest: Charles Coughlin, the Father of Hate Radio* (New York: The Free Press, 1996).

giving credibility to his controversial positions. Coughlin's bishop disapproved, arguing that Coughlin distorted the meaning of those Church documents because he used them as proof-texts. His message, often anti-Semitic, did more to create paranoia and fear than to bring healing.[33]

With the move to a national radio network, he had an estimated ten million listeners. Although he supported the election of Franklin Roosevelt to the presidency, he soon attacked Roosevelt as well, which failed to please his colleague in social activism, Monsignor Ryan.[34] Ryan was a great supporter of Roosevelt's New Deal policies and had been named to several national commissions by the President. Ryan claimed that while Coughlin was accurate in his critique of American policy, he offered no solutions, no program of reform. If Ryan's approach lacked the integration between spirituality and activism, Coughlin's agenda lacked the spiritual component completely.[35] Coughlin's outspoken behavior finally caught up with him and in 1942, full ecclesiastical sanctions were brought against him by the archbishop of Detroit, Edward Mooney. He continued his preaching, but that was limited to the pulpit of Little Flower Parish in Royal Oak, Michigan, where he remained pastor until his retirement in 1966.[36]

A much less controversial figure in Catholic broadcasting was Fulton J. Sheen. His radio program, "The Catholic Hour," was inaugurated in 1930 as a nationally aired program. Sheen was born in Illinois and ordained a priest in 1919. Following ordination he did graduate studies in philosophy at The Catholic University at Louvain, Belgium, and, upon completion of the doctorate, joined the faculty at The Catholic University in Washington, D.C. He later became bishop of Rochester, New York. While not a social activist like Coughlin, Sheen was an extremely effective radio preacher whose themes often touched upon issues of Christian responsibility within secular society. Sheen was convinced, like many of his contemporaries, that the Mystical Body of Christ was the integrative key to the Church's desire to evangelize the American culture. While "The Catholic Hour" was heard on twenty-two radio stations of the National Broadcasting Company in

---

[33] Marty, 276.

[34] In a press interview on 4 October 1938, Coughlin referred to the "personal stupidity" of President Roosevelt regarding his position on the presence of Catholics as members of affiliated unions of the Congress of Industrial Organizations (CIO). Coughlin held that the CIO was incompatible with Catholicism. Tentler, 333. At another point, he called the president "anti-God and a radical." Marty, 279.

[35] O'Brien, *American Catholics and Social Reform*, 173–5.

[36] Tentler, 332, 342.

1930, that number increased to seventy-one in only ten years. Gradually, Sheen's listening audience numbered more than seven million people and he received more than six thousand letters daily from listeners throughout the United States.[37]

Terence Shealy, an Irish Jesuit based in New York, and several prominent business professionals founded The Laymen's League for Retreats and Social Studies in 1911. This was the beginning of the lay retreat movement in the United States. The league obtained an estate on Staten Island, New York City, renamed it Mount Manresa, and held the first retreat there on 8 September 1911. Several months later that same group opened a school of social studies at the Fordham University Law School. Whether preaching at the retreat house or lecturing at Fordham, Shealy remained consistent in calling the laity to a profound recognition of their own priesthood:

> You are all priests . . . and responsible to Him as I am for the spread of His Kingdom . . . A layman today can preach more effectively the gospel than the priest; for the world is asking for the gospel of character . . . of work . . . of service, and they will not listen to the gospel of creed and dogma: they want the gospel of deeds.[38]

Shealy adapted *The Spiritual Exercises of Saint Ignatius* to the style of a weekend retreat, convinced that such an experience could help to instill and nurture the Christian character in Catholic laity as they struggled to live the gospel in daily life. The school, on the other hand, trained lay leaders to apply Catholic social teaching to social and economic problems. Ryan was one of the lecturers in that program. When Shealy died in 1922, so too did the social dimension of the retreat movement. What remained was the program of Pius XI.

The retreat movement as envisaged by the pope led activists out to the wilderness of contemplation as it were, but did not participate in the activity of social reform which Shealy and his colleagues had been advocating. For Pius XI, all social activism on the part of the laity had to be mediated through priests and bishops. Some in the more conservative sectors of the Church feared that the liturgical pioneers and promoters were opposed to such clerical or hierarchical mediation. These critics believed that the Mystical Body theory might imply a demo-

---

[37] Dolan, *The American Catholic Experience*, 392.

[38] Terence Shealy, "Points for Meditation at Retreat: Preparedness" (13–16 October 1916) 19–20; "Retreat Talk #8," 5–8 April 1918, 8, Retreat File, Archives of Mount Manresa, quoted in Joseph McShane, "'The Church Is Not For The Cells And The Caves,' The Working Class Spirituality of the Jesuit Labor Priests," *U.S. Catholic Historian* 9 (1990) 300–1.

cratic or an egalitarian view of the Church which, as far as they were concerned, was inaccurate. Michel and his associates, in fact, never suggested such a democracy.

In the March 8, 1930 issue of *America,* there was a comment in its regular column, "The Pilgrim," referring to Virgil Michel and suggesting that there was some tension between the liturgical and retreat movements. Michel was concerned that readers might draw inaccurate conclusions on the issue, so he wrote the editor of *America:*

> All of the promoters of the liturgical movement known to me have never thought of any real opposition between the two movements . . . But I do think, in fact, that the liturgical movement may make a difference in the spirit of some retreats (or retreat masters?). If the movement helps to bring us back to a better understanding and living of the true Christian spirit, the latter will also act as a leaven in all Catholic activities. As to retreats, my personal hope is, that this will give the death-blow to the Methodist-revival sort of retreat we have occasionally had (or the kind that leaves scrupulosity in its wake), and will lead retreatants permanently closer to the heart of the true Christian spirit, the Church's own life.[39]

In 1928, the first national conference of the Laymen's Retreat League was held. At that gathering one speaker did suggest a link between the retreat and liturgical movements, along with the eucharistic movement.[40] However, promoters of the Eucharistic movement viewed the liturgical movement with suspicion, fearing that its agenda included a de-emphasizing of eucharistic devotion while favoring a more horizontal, communitarian model focusing on the assembly.

Since the 1920s were years of economic success and fortune, there was not a significant amount of attention paid to raising the national social consciousness concerns, even on the part of the Church. Certainly, Ryan and the work of the social action department of the NCWC moved the issue of social justice forward in those years, but this was less the case on the local level. Parishes often had St. Vincent de Paul and Holy Name Societies, or the Knights of Columbus, but the degree of social activism and conviction differed greatly from place to

---

[39] Michel, Letter to the Editor of *America,* "The Liturgical Movement and the Retreat Movement" (1930) SJAA: Z-22.

[40] Father Weyland, S.V.D., "The Value of Retreats to Home Life, to Social, Business and Personal Contact," in *Proceedings of the First National Conference of the Laymen's Retreat Movement in the United States of America* (Philadelphia: Laymen's Weekend Retreat League, 1928) 77–81, quoted in Joseph Chinnici, "Virgil Michel and the Tradition of Affective Prayer," *Worship* 62 (1988) 226.

place. In some cases, these societies were mere parish-based social clubs.

While there were some isolated efforts at social activism around the country, there was little recognition that such action needed to be grounded in that sense of the Church which defined itself as the Mystical Body, and which expressed such a relationship liturgically. This was the case with organizations like Catholic Action which, in those early years, tended to keep liturgical practice and social action divided. Ryan's own work received the same critique, namely that in calling for a more just society, he advocated a privatistic spirituality which was unrelated to social reform.

German Catholics possessed a strong sense of community, reflected not only in their strong liturgical participation but also in their social concern, so it is not surprising that the first organization for Church-based social outreach was the German Catholic Central Verein, founded in Baltimore in April 1855.[41] When the society was restructured in 1908, its social mission became even more focused, calling for a restructuring of American society. Their publication, *Central Blatt and Social Justice* (renamed *The Social Justice Review* in the 1930s) assisted in the promotion of their plan for societal reform. They also published pamphlets and books and offered lectures given by prominent Americans who had a strong agenda of social reform. Such concern for social justice was not limited to German Catholics of the Central Verein, but was a characteristic of German Americans in general.

There were other organizations of social outreach in which members of the Central Verein collaborated. These included the Catholic American Federation of Labor, the American Federation of Catholic Societies, and the Catholic Colonialization Society of the Church Extension Society, all of whose goal was to reach out beyond the confines of the Church to both immigrants and migrants alike.[42] While the social activism of the Central Verein and related organizations was Church-related or even Church-sponsored, there was little connection made between liturgy and social action in those early years, even though German Catholics were active participants in both areas. These were two distinct worlds that simply did not intersect.

Virgil Michel recognized the potential of the Central Verein. With the agenda of the restoration of an organic Christian society, the Central

---

[41] For further discussion of the significant role which German Catholics played in the social apostolate, see Colman J. Barry, *The Catholic Church and German Americans* (Milwaukee: The Bruce Publishing Co., 1953); and Dolores Liptak, *Immigrants and Their Church* (New York: Macmillan Publishing Co., 1989) 92–113.

[42] Liptak, 108–12.

Verein held great promise. Given the already impressive commitment to social justice which the Central Verein exhibited, Michel added the dimension of worship. This was consistent with Michel's own approach, making liturgy the fundamental core of every activity with which he was involved. Under Michel's leadership in the 1930s, the Central Verein showed greater attention to the doctrine of the Mystical Body and to the role of liturgy in the work of social justice. It was, however, not until the emergence of the larger social movements in the American church that the integration of liturgy and justice would begin to become a reality on the local level. Our study proceeds with an exploration of those movements.

Catholic Social Movements and Worship

A number of social movements emerged in the American church during the 1930s. In some cases, movements like Catholic Action (CA), were merely branches of an organization that existed throughout the whole Church, worldwide. In other cases, movements like the Catholic Worker (CW) were founded in the United States and were peculiarly American in their scope. What united all these movements was the vision of a new social order which was distinctly Christian. And in all these movements, albeit to varying degrees, it was the doctrine of the Mystical Body of Christ that grounded the agenda and goals of each. Further, these movements promoted the liturgy as the source, the fountain for true Christian social action. This section considers several of the more prominent movements of the 1930s and 1940s—Catholic Action, the Catholic Worker, Friendship House, and The Grail.

Catholic Action

Lest reform Catholicism be left solely on the level of theory or simply as a matter for discussion at conferences and symposia, Catholic Action was established in the United States as the organ of the NCWC to mobilize Catholic laity in working cooperatively with Church leadership in social justice. The ultimate goal of the American CA was to renew the culture by a return to a more organic view of American society. This task would be accomplished through the apostolic, social activism of CA members, in collaboration with the hierarchy. While Pius XI accomplished a great deal in the promotion of CA, his predecessor, Pius X, had laid the groundwork for a vibrant lay apostolate throughout the whole Church, using the motto: "to restore all things in Christ." With an obvious correlation to the doctrine of the Mystical Body, local chapters of CA were called "cells." The local parish constituted a CA cell, since parishes were described as the Mystical Body in miniature. The emphasis was on quality rather than quantity, so, small cells were recommended. The Catholic Action movement occasionally came under fire by some conservative groups within the American church because of their "cell technique," as it was called. Critics claimed that such imagery too closely resembled communism, which was an increasing threat to American interests. The CA call for an organic society, along with its critique of materialism and individualism, did not help matters. CA leaders responded to the critique by stating that their efforts and interests were fundamentally Christian in nature and that members were not under the influence of the communists.

In an attempt to expand the spiritual grounding of CA, Pius XI chose the retreat movement as a means of helping members to grow in personal sanctification. In the encyclical *Mens nostra* (20 December 1929), the pope articulated his plan. Albeit foundational, the connection between CA retreats and the social apostolate was indirect. The retreat was to concern itself with the spiritual life and personal sanctification, strengthening lay apostles to return to the world, as it were.[43] The direct apostolate of CA, on the other hand, took place outside and independent of the retreat. Thus, the link between the retreat and the apostolate, while present, was not organic, and so the division between spirituality and the social apostolate continued.[44] The reality was that in the early years, CA had not yet recognized the intrinsic link between liturgical action and social action.[45]

---

[43] In responding to a lecture given by Dr. Charles Bruehl where the fundamental base of CA was described as "personal sanctification," echoing the words of Pius XI, William Busch, one of the pioneers of the liturgical movement, said: "I wish that in his (Dr. Bruehl's) passing from the basic theme of personal sanctification to that of the apostolate of social action he had paused for a moment to make mention of social sanctification. Personal piety is preliminary to personal action; and similarly the antecedent to social action is social piety . . . Modern individualism and subjectivism have almost undermined our very conception of social piety and corporate sanctity, so that we hardly understand the words of St. Peter: 'You are a chosen generation, a kingly priesthood, a holy nation.'" William Busch, "The Liturgy: A School of Catholic Action," *OF* 7 (1933) 9.

[44] Typical of the mentality of the time, a 1928 article entitled "The Spiritual Quality of Social Work," makes no reference to the liturgy or the doctrine of the Mystical Body of Christ as the foundation for social action. Rather, the author addresses the issue in scholastic terms: "The works of mercy are the spontaneous product of supernatural charity . . ." William Kerby, "The Spiritual Quality of Social Work," *ER* (1928) 376.

[45] Busch made reference to the work of Dom Boeser of Beuron, Germany, who argued that it was the action of the Mass which prompted and oriented social action. Busch, "The Liturgy: A School . . .," 11.

William Busch made yet another important observation. The lack of a liturgically-based spirituality for CA, which would suggest that the Church is sanctified through its personal piety, led potentially to a Pelagian view that Christians through personal piety and good works sanctified the Church and built the reign of God. Busch wrote:

> We imagine ourselves as so many individuals, each bringing the contribution of his own personal piety to make up the holiness of the Church, whereas in truth we do not make the Church holy, but it is the Church that makes us holy; we are all embraced in the sanctity of Christ without whom we can do nothing; it is by our incorporation into one Body in Him that we are made the *plebs sancta Dei*, the holy people of God . . . It should be plain, therefore, that the apostolate of Catholic social action must have as its antecedent the domestic work of Catholic social sanctification, which, in turn, is something more than the cultivation of private devotions . . . Why, then, amid all our talk of Catholic Action, do we not give more attention to Catholic Liturgy?[46]

In the mind of the pope, the goal of CA was to renew secular society through Christian apostolic service. This vision of a renewed Christian society was symbolized in his presentation and promotion of Christ the King: the one to whom all must be accountable.[47] In the pope's view, Christ the King was the answer to all the social and economic problems that plagued the world in the 1920s and 1930s. And what better way to express this obedience to Christ the King than through obedience to the hierarchy of Christ's Church. Americans, democratic by nature, accustomed to a sharp division between Church and state, found it difficult to accept an apostolic program which attempted to Christianize secular society under the authority of the Church.[48] One

---

[46] Ibid., 9–10.

[47] There is a reference in the personal notes of Reynold Hillenbrand to an article published in *America* (28 September 1935), referring to Pius XI's encyclical on the Feast of Christ the King. Pius XI ends the encyclical calling for "a *course* of sermons to be preached *every year* on fixed days *in every parish* for the celebration of this feast, so that the faithful be instructed fully in the nature, meaning, and importance of the feast." The *America* article concluded, "We offer no comment, except that implied by our (underlining) of several words. Ver sap. sat." Hillenbrand, "One is Your Leader: A Conference on Devotion to the Pope" (Notes, 1935) Hillenbrand Papers (8/2), University of Notre Dame Archives.

[48] On the contrary, the idea-feast of Christ the King gave a more political, revolutionary impetus to CA in countries like France and Italy. Thus, the movement held greater force in those countries. Historian Ernest Koenker suggested that this was because of the politicized, communistic and sometimes anti-clerical nature of the European branch of the movement which was less the case in the United States.

link, forged by the pioneers of the liturgical movement in the United States, was the "baptizing" of non-Christian American festivals such as New Year's Day, Memorial Day, Independence Day, Labor Day, and acceptance of the originally Protestant Thanksgiving Day, with the composition of liturgical texts for those occasions.

An early article on the subject of Catholic Action in the United States used the model of the kind of Christian commitment exhibited in the early Church. Conscious of their identity and relationship as members of the one body of Christ, those early Christians challenged and came into conflict with the secular culture of their day, even to the point of death. That was the "Catholic Action" of the early Church. The article challenged American Catholics of the twentieth century to respond to the CA initiative with a similar level of conviction and commitment.[49]

As CA expanded in the 1930s, its agenda became more integrative. The doctrine of the Mystical Body of Christ became the unifying factor, thanks to the efforts of the liturgical movement.[50] Further, liturgy, not the retreat movement, became the foundation for true Catholic Action. A talk given at a 1935 CA week held in Dubuque, Iowa, substantiates this shift:

> . . . true Catholic Action must spring from the social, official, and universal worship of the Church, and particularly from the Eucharistic Sacrifice which forms its climax. Catholic Action must emanate from the altar and must lead back to the altar.[51]

As late as 1954, thirty years after the encyclical of Pius XI, Koenker wrote: "Leaders admit that, in the United States, Catholic Action is still embryonic; it has not been born yet." Koenker pointed to American labor unions which held more of the revolutionary character, albeit secular, found in Catholic Action in Europe. Koenker, 127.

[49] J. Kreuter, "Catholic Action And The Liturgy," *OF* 3 (1929) 165–70.

[50] "The liturgy and Catholic Action are thus respectively the mystical body at prayer and sacrifice and the mystical body in action upon the world. *Each of these functions requires the other.*" W. Boyd, 113. See also Boyd, "Militants of Christ," *OF* 16 (1941) 338–47. Thus, liturgical participation of cell members led them to direct involvement in issues of justice. For example: "Basing its appeal on the doctrine of the Mystical Body of Christ, the Brooklyn CA Council in conjunction with a committee of Catholic college graduates and undergraduates, sent a circular to all Catholic colleges in the United States, in which they asked the cooperation of Catholic college men and women in the cause of justice for the Negro." Editor, *OF* 8 (1934) 420.

[51] Jaeger, 15. The article goes on to make the link even more explicit: "Catholic Action demands a true Christian spirit for its execution. Now the 'primary and indispensable source of the Christian spirit' is found in an active participation of the Liturgy of the Church."

One leader in Catholic Action, John Griffin, addressed the pneumatic character of CA in relationship to the liturgy and the goals of the liturgical movement:

> Is not the purpose of Catholic Action the renaissance of the primal spirit in Catholicism and a fuller unfolding of the active life of the Church? The Liturgical Movement is a return to virginal Christian spirituality vivified by Paracletic charity, and Catholic Action is a remanifestation of the zeal of Pentecostal apostolicity.[52]

Such "Pentecostal apostolicity" promoted the idea that all members of the Church were worthy of bearing Christ through the exercising of their baptismal priesthood. In a time when it was still normative to speak only of a priest or bishop as an "other Christ" ('alter Christus'), the liturgical movement and CA held the common conviction that all Christians were called to represent Christ through their participation in Christ's priesthood. Such participation meant living a life of radical commitment, using Christ's own kenotic witness as a model.[53] This vision had obvious implications for the work of justice and for the integral link between liturgy and social activism.

Passive liturgical participation which emphasized personal piety and neglected the corporate dimension of liturgy was also challenged. Writing in scholastic terms about grace motivating social activism through liturgical participation, Griffin preferred to speak of grace "ex opere operantis," rather than "ex opere operato," which remained too passive a process, making liturgy the servant of personal devotion. When one speaks of "ex opere operantis," one is speaking of more active collaboration with God's grace on the part of the recipient or recipients, thus emphasizing the social, corporate nature of the Mystical Body as it acts liturgically.[54]

This link between liturgy and Catholic Action became even closer in the 1930s and 1940s, when the summer schools of CA and similar courses became one of the testing grounds for ideas and experiments being advocated by the liturgical movement.[55] In those years, liturgical

---

[52] John Griffin, "Catholic Action And The Liturgical Life," *OF* 9 (1935) 366.

[53] Gradually the term "lay apostolate" came to replace the term "Catholic Action." In October 1957, with Pius XII's address to the Second World Congress of the Lay Apostolate, the term gained official recognition, replacing the old term, "Catholic Action." The Conciliar documents on the laity employed the new terminology.

[54] Griffin, "The Spiritual Foundation of Catholic Action," *OF* 9 (1935) 455–64.

[55] See the Editorial, "The Mystical Body At Prayer And Work In Summer Schools Of Catholic Action, 1938," *OF* 12 (1938) 513–15.

leaders were often employed as members of the faculty.[56] The reactions to liturgically-based CA programs in the United States were positive. Participants in one CA course at the Catholic Junior College, Grand Rapids, Michigan, recorded their responses through course evaluations, several of which appeared in a 1933 article in *OF*.[57]

Almost from its inception, Virgil Michel and the associate editors of *OF* recognized the importance of CA, along with the Catholic Worker, as a means of promoting the goals of the liturgical movement. With the relationship of liturgy and justice so fundamental to the liturgical

[56] During the 1933 Summer School of Catholic Action held at Saint Francis Xavier College, West Sixteenth Street, New York City (28 August to 2 September), Gerald Ellard, S.J., taught a course on the liturgy. Editor, *OF* 7 (1933) 520. An even fuller account on the teaching of liturgy in the summer schools of Catholic Action is given in an article which described the program in St. Louis. William Puetter, S.J., lectured on "Christ in the Liturgy" in which the sacraments of baptism, confirmation, and Eucharist were discussed, as well as penance and marriage. Puetter taught an additional course on the liturgical year. Gerald Ellard lectured on "the Mystical Body of Christ, the Priesthood of Christ, and on the Papal Mass in the eighth century." In addition, Ellard led the students on a pilgrimage out to O'Fallon, Missouri, "a renowned center of liturgical life," where Martin Hellriegel, chaplain to the sisters at O'Fallon, had been experimenting with liturgical reforms. There the seventy-two students participated in Compline and Benediction of the Blessed Sacrament. *OF* 7 (1933) 85. In 1934, well over seven hundred participated in the program, which was based on the doctrine of the Mystical Body of Christ, "the well-spring of Catholic Action." This was the description given by Daniel Lord, S.J., who was director of the school. *OF* 8 (1934) 569. Three years later, Virgil Michel and Gerard Donnelly, S.J., associate editor of *America*, lectured for a program at Manhattan College. Their topics included: "The Laity and the Loss of the Liturgy," "The True Significance of the Mass," "The Mystical Body and the Mass," "Catholic Action and the Mass." John Sheehan, "Catholic Action at Manhattan College," *OF* 11 (1937) 512–4.

[57] One student wrote: "The first month this course had me 'standing on my head.' It was different from anything I had heretofore taken . . . Other than teaching me how to cope with a new situation, this course has accomplished many things for me. The most important is, I think, the fact that now I look for the coming editions of such magazines as *America, The Commonweal, Orate Fratres* and the *Catholic World*." In the response of another student: "How I managed to go through twelve years of Catholic school training, repeating yearly 'The Mass is the unbloody sacrifice of the Body and Blood of Christ' and still be able to dream and be stupid in church, I do not know. Such, however, was the case up to perhaps a month ago when my skull cracked and knowledge seeped in. How the Mass joined Christians in Christ's Mystical Body was of about as much importance to me as the theory of relativity. I have just recently come to realize a little of the significance of the holy Sacrifice." Burton Confrey, "Reactions to Basing Catholic Action On The Liturgy," *OF* 7 (1933) 66, 67, 68, respectively.

movement, the pioneers recognized that these movements within the American church needed to work together. Thus, we find a plethora of articles on CA throughout the different volumes of *OF*.[58] CA, according to Michel, was prolonged worship, a continuation in daily life of the sacrifice offered to God at the liturgy:

> CA is but the further development of the liturgical life . . . Not only are the liturgical life and Catholic Action inseparable, but the two go to the very heart of the Christian dispensation . . . The true significance of the liturgical movement, therefore, lies just in this: that it tries to lead men back to the "primary and indispensable source of the true Christian spirit"; it tries to restore that of which Catholic Action is the further flowering and fruitage.[59]

CA grew in leaps and bounds. By 1936, for example, the Chicago Student CA (CISCA), forerunner to the Young Christian Workers, included sixty high schools, colleges, and universities in the Chicago metropolitan area with over thirty thousand students participating.[60] In addition to a liturgy committee, other committees included a social action committee with subcommittees on relief, community centers, hospitals, and braille, in addition to committees on international and interracial relations, industry, and Christian family.

The Young Christian Workers (YCW) took up the CA call in 1938 under the leadership of liturgical leaders and social activists like Reynold Hillenbrand and John J. Egan, although the Young Christian Workers did not begin in earnest until 1947 due largely to the interruption of

---

[58] Editorials and articles such as "Using *Orate Fratres* To Motivate Catholic Action" were not uncommon. Confrey, *OF* 6 (1932) 226–7.

[59] Michel, "Significance of the Liturgical Movement," NCWC Bulletin 10 (1929) 8, 26.

[60] These groups possessed a high level of commitment: "We have in Chicago—besides railroads, stockyards, and gangsters—a student organization with the avowed intent of training youth to become revolutionists. These young 'radicals,' five hundred strong, meet every Saturday morning in a downtown auditorium to discuss ways and means of overthrowing the present materialistic moral order and of setting up a world-wide Supernational, the mystical body of Christ. Their weapons? Not bombs and tanks. For this revolution must be fought out in the depths of each individual soul against the natural man with all his undivine nature—his hates, his lust for power and pleasure. For this purpose youth must be so oriented in that world-state that they, once recognizing their organic relationship to Christ, may put themselves more fully in contact with the heart-beat of His mystical body—that is, the liturgy." M. Cecilia, "School For Revolution in Chicago," *OF* 15 (1941) 352.

World War II.[61] In many respects, the YCW functioned as the youth and young adult branch of CA. Paul McGuire addressed a YCW meeting of several hundred young adults in May of 1939:

> You must be a new youth for a new world! If the faith is to survive, it must be preached by lay people like you who are living and working among the people in the factories and the stores and the offices where the priests cannot go.[62]

Like the CA structure, the YCW met in small groups which they called "cells," normally limited to twelve. When a cell exceeded twelve members, a new cell was formed. The doctrine of the Mystical Body of Christ expressed liturgically and socially was the guiding principle. Together with other participants in the CA movement, the YCW breathed new life into the American church in those years.

The Catholic Worker

The Catholic Worker movement was co-founded by Dorothy Day and Peter Maurin. Before discussing the movement, however, a brief look at the founders is in order.

Dorothy Day embodied the kind of integration that Virgil Michel and others were advocating in the time of the Depression. Steeped in the Church's liturgy, Day had a great passion for justice that she was able to instill in others. Her life prior to her conversion and baptism in 1927 was difficult, full of struggles and challenges. She had one abortion following an unwanted pregnancy and had another child out of wedlock, and this was in the 1920s. Yet it was her desire to have her baby baptized against the wishes of the father, which led to her own desire for baptism only several months later.

From her youth, even in the midst of her own problems, Day had a unique compassion for others and was able to understand the plight of those who suffered because of the American socio-economic system. She looked for ways to help. Convinced that capitalism was not the answer, she tried communism but still remained unsatisfied. At the age of twenty she was writing for a socialist newspaper in New York. She gradually recognized that her search for fulfillment and her search for God were one and the same, so, she sought membership in the Church. Her search continued following her baptism. Day saw

---

[61] On the history of the YCW, see Mary I. Zotti, *A Time of Awakening: The Young Christian Worker Story in the United States 1938–1970* (Chicago: Loyola University Press, 1991).

[62] Zotti, 5.

people's religious practice and liturgical experience as divorced from daily life, particularly from the poor. While in Washington for the march of World War I veterans, Day was impressed by the communist support of workers which she witnessed there and wondered why the Church was absent from such a struggle. She had been an activist before her conversion, giving much attention to the injustice suffered by workers and associating with the more progressive segment of society in Chicago and then New York. Following her baptism, those associations and friendships continued and the circle was ever-widened.

One of those friends was Peter Maurin, an itinerant French peasant and social visionary. Through their conversations, Day began to imagine a way of combining her new-found faith with socialism and, more specifically, with social activism.[63] They envisioned a life of decidedly Christian radicalism, based on the gospel and rooted in the liturgy. Maurin, although very intelligent, was often dismissed by the more sophisticated crowd because he looked unrespectable by American societal standards, resembling those who lived on the streets. Day, however, was able to see in him what others had missed. An appreciation of the Church's liturgical life grew within her and she could not help but see the relationship between the eucharistic banquet and the hungers of those who lived on the streets.

Together with Maurin, Day found hope in the social documents of the Church. She was convinced, like Virgil Michel and the liturgical pioneers, like Pius XI and the leaders of CA, that the key to the restoration of a Christian social order in the United States was the doctrine of the Mystical Body. Day and Maurin set out on a radical path of Christian activism, opting for a life of voluntary poverty and inviting others to join them.

According to Day, the heart of such radicalism was commitment. She was infused with a sense of Christian responsibility. Robert Coles reports a conversation which she had with her spiritual director:

> I told him I feel like crying sometimes, or I flush with anger: to be in Church isn't to be calmed down, as some people say they get when they are at Mass. I'm worked up. I'm excited by being close to Jesus, but the closer I get, the more I worry about what he wants of us, what he would have us do before we die.[64]

---

[63] Maurin wrote that the time had come to "blow the lid off so the Catholic Church may again become the dominant social dynamic force." Peter Maurin, "The Dynamite of the Church," in *Easy Essays* (New York: Sheed and Ward, 1936) 15.

[64] Robert Coles, *Dorothy Day: A Radical Devotion* (Reading, Mass.: Addison-Wesley Publishers, 1987) 77.

Attracted by such a life of Christian simplicity, Day and Maurin soon had a following, and on 1 May 1933 the Catholic Worker was founded, originally just as a newspaper, and soon including houses of hospitality which became the hallmark of the movement. The CW attracted those who were tired of capitalism and yet found communism with its inherent atheism unacceptable.[65] The movement's major goals were to provide hospitality to those who had been forced into the streets because of the financial depression, and to teach the social doctrine of the Church to workers through their journal of the same name.[66] The houses of hospitality hosted regular round-table discussions on topics of social thought and reform in the Christian context. This was Maurin's idea, as he was always interested in promoting discussion between workers and the intellectual community. A further development was the establishment of farming cooperatives, both to provide work for the unemployed and to provide food for the different houses of hospitality.

---

[65] In the words of Martin Marty: "The approach of Christian openness meant that the movement attracted all kinds of radicals, reformers, drifters, and fanatics. Day sometimes grew depressed about these." M. Marty, *Modern American Religion*, Vol. 2, 338. For a good description of The Catholic Worker Movement and its constituency see Marty, 331–40.

[66] The first edition of *The Catholic Worker* in May, 1933, was addressed to "those who are sitting on benches, huddling in shelters, walking the streets." The paper began with a circulation of 2,500 copies and had reached a circulation of 140,000 only seven years later in 1940. The editors of *OF* welcomed the new publication: "It is with genuine satisfaction that we greeted the appearance of *The Catholic Worker*. This monthly paper, published at 436 East Fifteenth Street, New York City, has a mission of far-reaching scope. It appears a veritable godsend in our time of social disintegration and unrest. As the title indicates, it appeals to the worker, particularly the down-and-out worker, whose number is legion in our industrial centers. Its appeal for social justice and charity on behalf of the poor and neglected members of society rings as true and sincere as was ever made since the industrial revolution began to create social problems of a most serious nature . . . What strikes one particularly is the solid Christian basis on which the work has been placed and the thoroughly Catholic spirit that breathes through its pages. The friend of the Liturgical Movement will be agreeably surprised to note that the editors of the paper have caught the spirit of the Church's liturgy and admirably link up their restatement of the Church's social doctrines with the inner life of the Church. They have come to realize that the doctrine of the Mystical Body of Christ is the focal point for all efforts at curing the ills of human society. *The Catholic Worker* is an excellent apology for the Liturgical Revival . . . 'The liturgy of the Church is the prayer of the Church. The religious life of the people and the economic life of the people ought to be one.' *The Catholic Worker* (1 February 1934)." "The Apostolate," *OF* 8 (1934) 277.

If Christians were indeed members of the same body, then they had a serious obligation to one another, especially to the weaker members.[67] Thus, the needs of one member were necessarily the responsibility of all.[68] While the Catholic Worker was a Church-based movement, it functioned independently, unlike Catholic Action, which defined its own mission in relationship to the hierarchy. The Catholic Worker found no room for such distinctions between clergy and laity.[69] Such a separation was viewed as problematic, contributing to the division between spirituality and social activism.[70]

This was a social movement founded on the doctrine of the Mystical Body of Christ, a doctrine which the CW took from the liturgical movement. These same themes were carried out in the CW newspaper,

[67] Adé Bethune, a liturgical artist who was an active member of both the Catholic Worker and the liturgical movements, offered the following reflections: ". . . If we are each (in our soul) part of Christ individually, then we are also all part of Christ, and all part of one another. We are all brothers. We should be as good and kind to every single human being, because he is a part of Christ, as we would be to Christ himself or to ourselves. When we are disrespectful and mean to poor people, to Negroes, to Jews and Gentiles, to foreigners, to Communists, to bankers and capitalists, we are mean to ourselves and to Christ. This is just common sense, but it had never occurred to me." Bethune, "Common Sense," *The Catholic Digest* 1 (1937) 2.

[68] The CW was founded precisely as a Christian response to social problems which, in the opinion of Dorothy Day, were not being addressed by the Church: "I was very upset by what I saw—the Church's apparent indifference to so much suffering. In (the early years of the Depression) people walked the streets, hundreds and hundreds of them, looking dazed and bewildered. They had no work. They had no place to go. Some groups tried to help them, but neither the state nor the Church seemed as alarmed as my 'radical friends.'" Quoted in Coles, 11.

[69] There were those within the Church who wanted to keep those distinctions between clergy and laity, and thus the CW was a threat to some. Several years before the founding of the Catholic Worker, Virgil Michel wrote a letter to George Schuster, editor of *The Commonweal*: ". . . Some day an 'official teacher' will have to [restate] the age-old Catholic doctrine that the lay folk are not merely trained dogs but true living members of the Church & in their own way true Apostles of Christ." Letter of 13 February 1929, SJAA: Z-27.

[70] Day did not tire of speaking out against such divisions: "When I see the Church taking the side of the powerful and forgetting the weak, and when I see bishops living in luxury and the poor being ignored or thrown crumbs, I know that Jesus is being insulted, as He once was, and sent to his death, as He once was. The church doesn't only belong to officials and bureaucrats; it belongs to all its people, and especially its most humble men and women and children, the ones He would have wanted to go and help, Jesus Christ. I am embarrassed—I am sickened—when I see Catholics using their religion as a social ornament." Quoted in Coles, 58.

which included regular articles by Virgil Michel. Day believed that Virgil Michel's work offered the best religious foundation for the CW. She wrote in 1933: "We feel that it is very necessary to connect the liturgical movement with the social justice movement. Each one gives vitality to the other."[71] Day insisted that each aspect of the CW movement gave attention to the liturgy.

As an independent movement within the Church, there were some who held it in suspicion, convinced that the Catholic workers were really communists in disguise.[72] Upon returning from a visit to several states and shortly before his death, Virgil Michel noted that such misconceptions were still in existence, at least in certain areas.[73] For his part, Michel continued to promote the CW movement, encouraging *OF* readers to subscribe to the various journals of the movement.[74] In so doing, he assured Dorothy Day, Peter Maurin, and the other leaders, that the liturgical movement valued the unique contribution made by the Catholic Worker:

> Catholic Workers and apostles! You have your faults and your shortcomings. But who among us on earth is not burdened with them? . . . You are indeed an eyesore and a scandal even to Catholics, but usually only to such as revel in their self-complacency, whose religion is one of

---

[71] Mel Piehl, *Breaking Bread: The Catholic Worker and the Origin of Catholic Radicalism in America* (Philadelphia: Temple University Press, 1982) 84–5.

[72] Paul Marx writes: "Ever since Dorothy Day carried the first of 2,500 copies of the initial *Catholic Worker* into Union Square, where 200,000 communists and their sympathizers held a rally on May 1, 1933, the paper has either edified or angered its readers. The communists, who claimed to profess the ideal of social justice and human brotherhood, called the Catholic Workers fascists, while many Catholics called them communists, fellow-travelers, revolutionaries, idealists, crackpots— and other names." Marx, 375.

[73] ". . . believe-it-or-not, the old slanders are still believed, even by some priests. Isn't the Catholic Worker group 'a bunch of communists' boring from within? And what about worse things, such as should not be mentioned by word?—So all the old dirt is still going the rounds." Michel, "Catholic Workers and Apostles," *OF* 13 (1938) 30.

[74] In promoting the *Chicago Catholic Worker,* Michel wrote: "In the casual way in which it takes the doctrine of the mystical body of Christ for granted and mentions it frequently to build upon it the motivation for an apostolic Christian life, it reminds us of the homilies of the Church Fathers, who likewise drew constantly for their admonitions and exhortations on this most ancient and vital conception of the Christ-life. Why not save on lip-stick (women) or cigars (men) or cigarettes (both) and try a year's subscription?—And always remember the parent *Catholic Worker* of New York." Ibid., 29–30.

asking from God and knows not the blessedness of giving. If you are a stone of scandal to the self-righteous, so was Christ.[75]

As Day and Maurin were convinced of the image of the Church as Christ's body, they were equally convinced that liturgy was the heart of such a body and the fountain of social activism. When the CW was founded, therefore, it was not simply concerned about feeding the poor and giving shelter to the homeless, noble as those tasks were. Nor was its primary concern the social education of workers. It was to be an organic community, grounded in the liturgy. Day delighted in the common elements of the Eucharist—bread and wine. Such physical elements were earthy, real, connecting the material with the spiritual. Reflecting on Christian baptism, she noted: ". . . all water had become holy since Christ was baptized in the Jordan."[76]

Following Virgil Michel's visit to New York in 1934, the singing of Prime and Compline mornings and evenings at CW houses became a regular, albeit optional part of the daily order. Liturgy at the Catholic Worker was a rather earthy experience, because it was the prayer of those who lived on the streets. In her book *Loaves and Fishes*, Dorothy Day recounts a typical celebration of Compline:

> Joe Maurer, a late recruit who does just about everything around the place, starts handing out Compline books. In a good strong voice, the product of Dominican vocal training, he leads us. Soon we will drown out the talkers who have grown louder with the advancing hours. . . . There is a hymn then, and the little chapter, and responsories and prayers. Smokey Joe knows all these by heart—though he is not very tuneful. But then neither are the others. Some sing *basso profundo* and some sing *recto tono*, and if there is an Irish tenor he complicates the sound still more. It does not help matters that two or three older women, who are tone deaf delight in singing too. But they enjoy themselves and it is the night prayer of the church, and God hears. The agnostic sings with the Catholic, because it is a communal act and he loves his brother. Our singing prepares us for another day. Early tomorrow morning the work will start again, and so our life, which St. Theresa described as a night spent in an uncomfortable inn, resumes. It will continue. The surroundings may be harsh, but where love is, God is.[77]

Michel sent them copies of The Liturgical Press edition of Compline, which was printed in both Latin and English, side by side. Tom Coddington, who later founded the Campion Propaganda Movement,

[75] Ibid., 30.
[76] Piehl, 84.
[77] Day, *Loaves and Fishes* (New York: Harper and Row, 1963) 214–5.

gave lessons in liturgical Latin, which enabled participants to sing the Salve Regina. He also instructed them in the proper rubrics. One participant wrote: "I believe that outside of a monastery, one never saw such profound bowing, as we did, at the proper places."[78]

Dorothy Day encouraged the singing of hymns and the chanting of the psalms, often quoting Augustine's words: "He who sings prays twice." She encouraged everyone to sing: "Don't be afraid of singing, even if you have a weak voice."[79] Nonetheless, the praying of Compline was not universally accepted by all CW members, which probably explains why it always remained an optional element in the CW daily house order. During Compline some rattled their rosaries in protest. Mary Sheehan was skeptical of the whole idea of Compline, suggesting that Tom Coddington was trying to manipulate the group.[80] "Who ever heard of lay people saying these prayers?" she asked. "If they want to be monks then they should go into monasteries."[81]

As in *Orate Fratres*, where the 1930s brought a significant increase in articles and editorials on issues of economic and racial justice,[82] so likewise in *The Catholic Worker*, one finds a tremendous amount of material regarding liturgical renewal, the call to full and active participation, and a desire to wed liturgy and social action. Different terms were used to describe the relationship of such social activism to the wider

[78] Stanley Vishnewski, *Wings of the Dawn* (New York: Catholic Worker Books, 1984) 58.

[79] Ibid., 59.

[80] "You can't trust these Englishmen." Ibid. Coddington later responded in an article in *Liturgy and Sociology:* "Some may condemn it [the liturgical movement] as a 'novelty,' . . . or others, with less wit, may label the liturgy as 'British propaganda!' When the wolves of 'Wall Street' begin to recite Prime together in the morning before the Missa Recitata, and come together again in the evening for the singing of Compline, the social result will be breathtaking! We seriously recommend this to 'Big Business.'" Editorial, "The Divine Office," *Liturgy and Sociology* 1 (March, 1936) 3.

[81] Vishnewski, *Wings of the Dawn*, 59. Vishnewski continues: "Someone told us of a community of nuns who had introduced the saying of the Divine Office. They were in choir reciting Compline when an electrical storm broke. The Sisters were frightened by the violence of the storm whereupon the Mother Superior announced that it would be prudent to put aside their Compline books and say a few prayers instead."

[82] In 1933, *OF* was reorganized to attend more directly to such a social reconstruction—to the Church's social agenda, so that a stronger bridge might be formed between liturgy and social justice. Michel was deeply influenced by his three year apostolic work with native Americans. This influence revealed itself in the new emphasis of the magazine.

body of Christ. Day insisted that every number of *The Catholic Worker* include an article or column on some aspect of the liturgy on the progress of the liturgical movement.[83]

Besides the New York house of hospitality, other CW houses of hospitality were opened in some of the larger cities around the United States where economic hardship was most acutely present. In a detailed letter from a staff member at the CW house in St. Louis, Missouri, we have a good description of the role which liturgy played in daily life, at one of those houses of hospitality.

> The Catholic Worker unit here has been aware for long of the place and importance of the liturgy in its program. The reading of Compline at the meetings has been part of the regular procedure here for the past two years, just as in the center at New York. Now, however, with the opening of the coffee line over two hundred destitute men appear each morning, who offer a rich field for liturgical practice. Not only has a chapter of the League of the Divine Office been established among the older members of the unit, but several surprising things have happened among the unfortunate men themselves who come to the shop.[84]

The author writes of how the daily practice of liturgical prayer has formed and evangelized the unemployed and destitute who came seeking help: "We were made bold by the excellent spirit in so many of the men to carry the liturgical spirit even more intimately into our

---

[83] The editors of the *CW* wrote to the *OF* editor: "We are overwhelmed with gratitude at your generosity in sending us the entire list of publications of The Liturgical Press. They arrived this morning, and the office staff has been sitting around ever since devouring them eagerly and profitably. Nearly all our friends who are interested in social justice from a Catholic point of view, from the very beginning of the paper, have been people equally interested in the Liturgical Movement—a fact which rather surprised us at first, as we hadn't realized that the relation between the two was so widely appreciated. But by now we are well accustomed to having most of the all-day discussions in our office come around eventually to the doctrine of the Mystical Body of Christ. So you can imagine the eagerness with which your donations will be seized upon by the many people who make use of the all-too-meagre facilities of our office and library. We hope we may have some small share in spreading a knowledge and love of the liturgy in this country, and humbly trust, too, that our work may have some share occasionally in your prayers. Very respectfully yours, The Editors, *The Catholic Worker*." *OF* 8 (1934) 284. This was a practical example of Michel's work for a "social regeneration" which would flow out of the liturgy and aim at transforming the whole society, based on the practice of the early Church, where the relationship between the eucharistic table and the needy was a lived reality.

[84] Joseph McDonald, "A Liturgical Apostolate," *OF* 12 (1938) 272–3.

lives." The writer then describes fifteen minutes of scriptural reading each day during lunch and dinner. Speaking of such reading, he states: "It penetrates our day in a peculiar way, and has carried a new kind of life into the shop and among the men on the coffee line. Seldom is one seen to leave before the end of the reading."[85]

The author then described how several people had expressed interest in joining the CW staff at the Eucharist: "The idea has been adopted and each morning many of these men walk in a body to Mass before allowing themselves the coffee and rolls . . . It is hoped that the morning Mass will in time become a *Missa recitata* for the unemployed." The older members had already begun a monthly celebration of the dialog Mass and were hoping to celebrate that liturgy with greater frequency. The letter concludes by mentioning that each of the weekly meetings at the CW house in St. Louis were given over, at least in part, to a discussion on the liturgy and its function in their lives.

A national gathering of Catholic Workers, held in Detroit from 3–5 September 1938, began with the dialog Mass with general Communion, and focused entirely on the spiritual foundations of Catholic social activism. Topics included the Mystical Body of Christ as it acts liturgically; interracial justice, which included a "sacrifice-banquet" with the black community of St. Peter Claver Church, Detroit; the issue of labor and the spiritual solution to the problem. A report on that gathering concluded:

> We were especially struck by the number of those (laity) who made use of intermission periods to recite parts of the divine office; several of the younger members, we discovered, recite all of the hours whenever they can possibly do so. There are of course others who still can see little relation between, let us say, praying Compline and feeding the poor, but the general religious outlook is strongly liturgical among quite a number of the Catholic Worker groups.[86]

An interesting article entitled "Helping the Hobo to God" sought to evaluate reasons for the liturgy's appeal to so many homeless who crossed the threshold of the CW house in Cleveland, Ohio. At the outset, the author wrote: "If the average layman is largely indifferent to the meaning of the liturgy, what chance is there with these homeless men . . . most of whom have forgotten how to bless themselves?" Against all odds, the liturgy had a tremendous appeal and served as the path back to the Church for the homeless individual.[87]

---

[85] Ibid., 273.
[86] "The Apostolate," *OF* 12 (1938) 523.
[87] William Gauchat, "Helping the Hobo to God," *OF* 15 (1940) 386.

Several reasons for liturgy's popularity among the group were suggested. First, the strong character of the liturgy was more compatible with the individual's own rugged spirit and character than the sentimentality of private devotions of the day. The second reason given was with regard to the search for community among the homeless.[88] Further, the author suggested that since the homeless were unaccustomed to the practice of private devotions, they did not have to unlearn these habits and so were free to embrace liturgical prayer more readily. Like all the other CW houses, the Cleveland community concluded each day with Compline.

The author concluded by noting the lack of class distinction at the Lord's table:

> The poor who have nothing, and are despised by everyone for having nothing, can offer to God a gift of infinite value in the Mass. At Mass the poor are rich, and the rich are no more than the poorest of the poor. The Mass takes us from the humanity of Christ to his divinity, from earth to heaven. These are the "rejected stones" of which we hope to build with God's help a new spiritual edifice.[89]

The Campion Propaganda Movement

The Campion Propaganda Movement began as an offshoot of the New York and Boston CW houses, under the leadership of Dorothy Weston and Thomas Coddington. The Campionites were convinced that the social and liturgical ideals of the CW required a strong attack on the American status quo. They took the lead in militant demonstrations in 1934 and 1935, which gave the CW some unwanted publicity. They engaged in street confrontations with pro-Nazis who broke picket-lines and were anti-Catholic, inciting anger and even some minor physical assaults on CW members. Initially, Dorothy Day was impressed with the zeal of the group, particularly with their refusal to strike back when they were attacked. By the middle of 1935, however, those incidents were increasing, and Day believed that the Campionites,

---

[88] "The feeling of 'togetherness' characteristic of liturgical prayer touches souls that have long been separated from their fellows, their brothers, and that have suffered the loneliness of being without God." Ibid., 386–7. This point confirms Steven Recken's thesis cited earlier in this chapter *(supra p. 112, n. 20)*, that a fundamental goal of those who lived and suffered through the depression was that of "fitting in," of being accepted by the community, of knowing the security of human support since the depression had robbed them of all other hope of economic security and success.

[89] Ibid., 389.

despite their official non-violent stance, were in fact, provoking violence. In addition, Coddington encouraged Day to curtail the soup-line operation, expand fund-raising operations in parishes, and remove some of the "bums, deadbeats and freeloaders" who were involved with the CW, in order to help improve the CW's image. Day refused to comply, reaffirming the centrality of the poor within the movement. Further, she stopped reporting on Campionite demonstrations in the *CW*. After a futile attempt to have Day removed and take over the paper, the Campionites left in the winter of 1936 to establish their own movement and journal. Since Virgil Michel supported the founding of other American Catholic social movements, it is not surprising that he was involved with the beginnings of the Campion Propaganda Committee, as well.[90]

Unlike the CW which existed as an independent movement within the American church, the Campionites focused their efforts on parish renewal, primarily in the New York and Boston metropolitan areas. They encouraged greater lay participation in the liturgy by promoting the Divine Office and the dialogue Mass, as a firm grounding for the social renewal of the Church.[91] Moreover, they established maternity guilds, classes in Gregorian chant and liturgical Latin, religious education and recreational programs for children, and parish assistance for the needy. They initiated the weekly "Parish Liturgical Bulletin" in 1936, as a way of spreading news of the liturgical renewal on the parochial level.[92]

The Campion Propaganda Movement never enjoyed the life-span of the CW, primarily because its leaders lacked the pragmatism required of organizers and executives. For instance, one summer in the Berkshire mountains, the Coddingtons hosted a ten-day institute on liturgy and sociology. Unfortunately, the couple forgot to arrange for beds,

---

[90] Piehl, 124. Extensive correspondence in the archives at St. John's Abbey, Collegeville, reveals that Michel attempted to mediate the dispute between Day and Coddington, as he was a friend of both. Although those attempts at mediation were unsuccessful he continued to support both movements.

[91] They identified themselves exclusively as a lay movement: "We are a lay group . . . This means that we do not accept priests or clerics in major orders, or religious as active members, but only as advisors, spiritual directors or teachers. We feel that the initiative should come from the layman and the laywoman and that much of the Campion action can only be done by laypeople." "Campion Pamphlet No. 1: The Organization, Development, and Aims of the Campion" (1936). The Catholic Worker Collection (W-9), Marquette University Archives, Milwaukee, Wis.

[92] Letter of Albert H. Coddington, Obl. O.S.B., to New York pastors (ca. 1936). Catholic Worker Collection (W-6), Marquette University Archives.

food, and bathing facilities for those participating in the institute. Such inexperience explains why their journal, *Liturgy and Sociology*, was also unsuccessful, despite its creative plan and the employment of well-respected authors.[93]

There was a potential off-shoot of the Campionites. Cornelius Bates, a parish priest at St. Mary's in Durand, Michigan, had some early contact with Coddington and the Campion Propaganda Movement. Bates' dream was to take the ideas inherent within the Campion Movement and use them to begin a lay community founded on the basis of the liturgy that included the profession of vows.[94] In encouraging Bates to pursue his plans, Virgil Michel noted the potential complimentarity of both groups.[95] Unlike the Campionites or the CW, however, Bates' plan for a liturgically-based religious community never materialized.

Friendship House

Friendship House (FH) was founded in Toronto in the early 1930s by the Russian baroness Catherine De Hueck, another pioneer in the work of social justice. Like the CW, FH was a safe haven for the poor and destitute. She wrote:

> To the original premises, the St. Francis House, came tired, hopeless men in search of shelter and food. Panhandlers, transients, tramps, bums, hobos, people called them. To us they were all Brothers Christopher. The upper rooms, where the children used to be, were transformed into dormitories. Only ten beds could be placed there. No one was ever asked

---

[93] Hughes, *The Monk's Tale*, 135–6.

[94] "I have a strong notion of attempting to build up a kind of lay religious organization on the basis of the liturgical life. Briefly—a central nucleus of priests who would become specialists in liturgy, sociology, etc., and who would become a school to teach the lay part of the organization. This lay group would devote all its time, energy and resources to the work of building up a liturgical center which would naturally overflow into social action." Letter to Virgil Michel, 30 September 1936, SJAA: Z-22.

[95] "Your group as I understand it would really be a religious order with vows even while the members are working at secular occupations out in the world. Your idea strikes me as being a very worthwhile one, though it is quite novel in its way. However, it is a move that is in line with various other things happening today . . . the first thing that is necessary is to be able to get a few lay people who are willing to try your scheme. If you start with a movement of priests and instruct them . . . there is too much danger of a larger venture failing in its very start. All these movements grow very slowly and with small beginnings." Letter to Cornelius Bates, 3 October 1936, SJAA: Z-22.

any questions. All were received as God's ambassadors, for that is really what the poor are. Food was shared and food was begged.[96]

The beginnings were not easy. Although De Hueck had the support of Archbishop Neil McNeil of Toronto, there was resentment on the part of local residents including the clergy, at the presence of a house for the homeless. While the dedication was there, De Hueck and her volunteers were disillusioned as their ministry in Toronto took shape. They were ready to give up completely when Virgil Michel arrived sometime between 1934 and 1935, and visited them in a run-down storefront on Portland Street. Sitting down on a broken chair, he addressed the group:

> How fortunate you are . . . This is what I have been dreaming about. You are discouraged. You need the Mass. You must persevere by all means. You have a vocation. Study the Mass, live the Mass. Between two Masses you can bear everything.[97]

Their situation improved. They gained increasing respectability in Toronto, and in 1938 opened another house in Harlem, New York City, which De Hueck recognized as a place of tremendous need where many knew constant suffering, especially those in the black community.[98] Other houses were opened in Chicago; Marathon City, Wisconsin; Ottawa and Hamilton, Ontario.

Like Dorothy Day and Peter Maurin, the baroness was convinced that liturgy could transform society, attributing her liturgical knowledge and awareness to the guidance and inspiration of Virgil Michel. She learned well, for she was always seeking connections between the Christ encountered in the liturgy and the Christ encountered in the streets. She wrote:

> In the liturgy we learn to know Christ. And if we truly know Him, we shall recognize Him everywhere, but especially in His poor, and we shall set our faces toward liberation of Him from the yoke of injustice and

---

[96] Ibid., 15.

[97] Interview with Catherine De Hueck, Washington, D.C., 5 February 1953. Quoted in Marx, 379.

[98] "Harlem of Churches . . . Harlem of brothels . . . where vice lives side by side with heroic virtue. There is no ghetto wall around Harlem, like the one Hitler built in Warsaw. There is worse—an invisible, impregnable, unbreakable wall that forever divides its inhabitants from the rest of the world. It was not built with hands. It was erected by human minds and hearts . . . each brick a prejudice . . . each bit of mortar an act of intolerance." De Hueck, *Friendship House*, 1.

pain, helping to bring about the reign of Christ the King in this world.
And with it order, peace and love, so that we shall be able to say: "I saw
Christ today, and He was smiling."[99]

De Hueck believed that the purpose of liturgical participation was to
improve our collective sight in order to better recognize the Christ who
lived in the poor and dwelled on the streets:

> And so it goes on! Eternally born anew in the stable, facing poverty, cold
> and hunger, spending His youth in narrow dirty streets between noisy
> trucks, overcrowded tenements, persecuted, forgotten, derided, abused,
> exploited, sold for thirty pieces of silver, neglected, beaten, spat upon
> and crucified over and over again, *Christ walks the earth in His poor.*
>   But there is worse. Those who have eyes can see His bloody face in the
> hearts of men, His body, bowed by the heavy cross, fall in exhaustion on
> the hard pavement of our streets. Oh, for thousands of Veronicas to wipe
> that holy Face in the hearts of men![100]

For the baroness, the service of justice demanded courage, given
through love and faith, both of which are found in the Eucharist.
Grounded in the liturgy, De Hueck had a unique way of seeing into the
human condition with a singular compassion for the downtrodden:

> Why did they call him a Communist? He only asked for justice. So he
> was picketing to get justice. But was there such a thing as justice in this
> world? Did people know what it was to do hard work and always be
> hungry, and see those that one loved be hungry and cold too?[101]

De Hueck's friendship with Virgil Michel contributed mutually to
their respective apostolates as was the case in Michel's friendship with
Dorothy Day. De Hueck wrote to Michel on 30 June 1938:

> I value your letters very much as I value your friendship and interest in
> my work . . . So when I write about all these things to you, it is because
> in my human weakness I hope for just such a letter as you have written,
> for it helps me and gives me courage to go on . . . As to the liturgy, you
> are right again . . . I often wonder how it is that Catholics, good pious
> Catholics, prefer novenas to Mass. How is it that the children of light do
> not seem to need the source of all light daily? How is it that we speak of
> Catholic Action, and any other Christian action, going forth into the heat
> of the battle without Him who is the very reason for our battle?[102]

[99] De Hueck, "I Saw Christ Today," 310.
[100] Ibid.
[101] Ibid., 308.
[102] Marx, 379.

In an interview, some years after Michel's death, De Hueck stated: "Father Virgil foresaw the laity as the spearhead of the Church in coming times . . . Without him there may not have been a Friendship House movement at all."[103]

The Grail Movement

The Grail, founded as a women's movement on 1 March 1929 by the Dutch Jesuit, Jacques van Ginneken, was brought to the United States in 1940 by Lydwine van Kersbergen and Joan Overboss. There was an earlier contact with American Catholicism, however. In 1936, van Kersbergen had written to Dorothy Day, having heard of the efforts of the CW. The two began to correspond, and this was to be the beginning of a long-lasting relationship between the Grail and the CW.

The arrival of the Grail on American soil coincided with the first national liturgical week held at Holy Name Cathedral, Chicago. At the very outset, the two women made fast contact with liturgical pioneers and promoters. Like other lay movements at that time, the Grail began a training program for what we would call today "lay ministry," which they centered at Doddridge Farm in Libertyville, Illinois (near Chicago). This training program, which drew upon the expertise of liturgical leaders like Ellard, Diekmann, and Hillenbrand, had two primary goals. First, it aimed to make the liturgy live for those who were participating. Second, it aimed at carrying the spirit of the Eucharist throughout the day. Members read and discussed Guéranger and Parsch and devoured periodicals like *OF*.

In Holy Week of 1941, the Grail sponsored a retreat for young women at Doddridge Farm. They recited the liturgical hour of Prime each morning, followed by a sung Mass. They celebrated Tenebrae on Tuesday, Wednesday and Friday with an English recitation of the psalms by the women while participating clergy sang the lamentations. The retreat included a seder supper of roast lamb, bitter herbs, and unleavened bread on Holy Thursday night, Stations of the Cross outdoors in the fields on Friday, and the renewal of baptismal promises on Holy Saturday night with each member holding a lighted candle. This retreat marked the beginning of the Grail movement in the United States; from then on, the movement held great force, combining a deep formation in Christian spirituality and culture with outreach to the needy. Projects for ministry included working with black Americans, re-Christianizing the American culture, ecumenical work, a ministry to married persons, and a department of "Catholic Culture"

---

[103] Ibid.

(e.g., press and film) which, they said, might expand into a center at the movie industry headquarters in Hollywood. Their ministry was rooted in the liturgical life of the Church. Each year a two-week summer course was sponsored at the farm, which always included solemn Vespers chanted antiphonally in English (while the priests recited them in Latin) and a "mystery play" on the final evening, which served to illustrate the theological points made by Ellard in his talks.[104]

The unity which existed between the liturgical and CW movements existed between the liturgical and Grail movements, as well. Conferences at that 1941 retreat were given by Gerald Ellard. In turn, at the 1941 Liturgical Week in St. Paul, Minnesota, Joan Overboss gave an overview of the Grail and stressed that the lay apostolate must always be grounded in the liturgy, using daily life at the Grail as an example.

The Grail eventually came into conflict with the archbishop of Chicago, Samuel Stritch. The movement functioned quite democratically, operating on principles of equality and shared responsibility. Grail members participated in Catholic Action, but raised some questions about the CA premise which stated that the laity worked in cooperation with the hierarchy. Archbishop Stritch was not pleased with the description of the lay apostolate given in the Grail's publicity for its 1942 summer course. "It would be more Catholic," he responded, "to add a line to their statement saying something like 'lay apostles working in subordination to the Hierarchy . . .' The program of Catholic Lay Action is not planned by them but, as the Popes say, is given by the Hierarchy."

An additional conflict arose over liturgical language. That same advertisement read: "together we will celebrate the Holy Mysteries." Stritch responded:

> In the language of the Church, the faithful assist at Mass, and uniting themselves to the Priest, offer Holy Mass to God, but they do not celebrate Mass, which essentially consists in Acts of exclusively priestly power.[105]

Stritch found the Grail's concept of participation to be problematic, whether that was their desire of "transforming the world" socially, or their understanding of active liturgical participation. The archbishop concluded:

---

[104] Jean Kalven, "Living the Liturgy: Keystone of the Grail Vision," *U.S. Catholic Historian* 11 (1993) 22, 29–33.

[105] Letter to van Kersbergen, 24 May 1942. Quoted in Alden Brown, *The Grail Movement and American Catholicism 1940–1975* (Notre Dame: University of Notre Dame, 1989) 34.

> The Church is not a social program; the Church Catholic means: a super-
> natural life, union with Christ, and from that all other activities should
> flow.[106]

Despite occasional hierarchical obstacles, the work of the Grail continued. Like the CW or FH, the Grail imaged in miniature the potential
of the whole Church in the United States to live as the body of Christ.
Speaking of the Church or, even more directly, of the Grail as the Mystical Body of Christ met with some resistance by those who advocated
an individualistic piety, and "who regarded time after communion as
a moment of private conversation with God." Nonetheless, leaders did
not fail to stress that the theological principle of the Mystical Body was
absolutely integral and liturgy was the key to such integration. In
learning about the liturgy, Grail members also experimented extensively to create a celebration which was fully participatory:

> Those to whom the Dialogue Mass was something new, found it a joy-
> ous event to chant the Offertory verse as we slowly filed up to place our
> own host in the Ciborium, and the idea of our offering ourselves with
> the priest and with Christ to God became very real.[107]

Like the NCRLC, the Grail movement emphasized a return to nature, and their academic programs expanded to include a "Rural Life
School." Speakers included lecturers like Luigi Ligutti, a pastor from
Granger, Iowa, who assisted unemployed miners and their families,
both Protestant and Catholic, in securing government funding for the
building of homes under the New Deal legislation. Throughout the
1930s he was a strong advocate of rural workers and became president
of the National Rural Life Conference in 1941. He called for the integration of farming with a lively religious practice, advocating a return
to rural life as a healthy environment for the living out of the gospel.

Consistent with the desire to integrate liturgy and life, worship at
the Grail moved outdoors, with a ritual created to bless a new vineyard on the property. This included a procession from the chapel
across the fields, led by a processional cross and a white banner. Following the blessing, participants prayed for the great vineyard of the
Church, for its dead branches and also for its new branches (catechu-
mens). They prayed for the hierarchy, its strong branches, and for "the
hurt and wounded branches in the winepresses of the world." The
presider dismissed the assembly with words from the Song of Songs:
"Catch me the little foxes that spoil the vines." "It is your task," he

---

[106] Brown, 35.
[107] Kalven, 29, 36.

said, "to catch the little foxes of materialism and Godlessness that eat their way among the grapes, the members of the Church."[108]

During Christmas week of 1942, Martin Hellriegel offered a course at Doddridge Farm on the lay apostolate, suggesting that the way of evangelizing the world was not through an overly pious approach which would divide the evangelizers from their hearers. Something else was needed:

> To convert the world, we need an entirely different type . . . women with intelligence and holy impertinence . . . women with vision and radical conviction, women who are determined to live on principle twenty-four hours a day.[109]

Predictably, Hellriegel drew on the liturgy as the wellspring for an active lay apostolate, speaking of the three tables of Christian life: the banquet table of the Eucharist, the dining room table of everyday, and the feasting table of heaven. His words led one member to remark: "Our eating should become a sacred ceremony, both in the family and in the Christian community." Reynold Hillenbrand and H. A. Reinhold also became involved, lecturing on the priesthood of the baptized and liturgy as the base for social justice. Dom Ermin Vitry instructed them in liturgical chant. Dorothy Day spent a sabbatical with the Grail. While Doddridge Farm and later Loveland (Grailville), Ohio, were not intended to function as liturgical centers, they soon became nationally known for their liturgical innovations and for their attempts at the integration of liturgy and life. The Grail attracted a large following of clergy and laity who came to witness the liturgical experimentation, not unlike the interest witnessed in Hellriegel's experimentation at O'Fallon, Missouri, some years earlier.

Despite the beautiful liturgies, the Grail's primary focus was the social transformation of a materialistic culture which needed to hear the call to conversion again, perhaps in a new way. This was their task as lay apostles, as women of the Grail. Additional courses were offered on liturgy and culture, along with the role of woman in a Christian social reconstruction, all giving credibility to the establishment of the Grail as a center of formation for the lay apostolate. In 1944, the national headquarters were permanently relocated in Loveland, Ohio, and their apostolate of education for lay ministry and social activism continued with force for many years to come. Interest in the liturgical apostolate continued, as well, and the Grail community served as a

[108] Ibid., 36–7.
[109] Ibid., 39.

testing ground for new liturgical texts and actions. Many members participated in the national liturgical weeks and some went on to study at the Notre Dame Summer School of Liturgical Studies, continuing the organic relationship between liturgy and justice, an inspiration which they attributed to the vision of the liturgical pioneers and promoters.

Christian Family Movement

In 1943, the Christian Family Movement (CFM) was born in Chicago. As a couples' movement, focused on strengthening the witness of the Christian family as an apostolic force within society, the group adopted the cell technique of the Belgian canon Joseph Cardijn's Jocist movement which was already in use in branches of Catholic Action.[110] In many respects, CFM was the couples' or adult branch of CA in the way that other groups (e.g., high school or college) had their own unique branches of the movement. Reynold Hillenbrand was influenced by Cardijn's inquiry method ("observe, judge, and act") and was instrumental in the founding of CFM in Chicago. The Jocist movement was brought to the United States by the Holy Cross priest, Louis Putz, and established the University of Notre Dame as a center for Catholic Action. With Putz's collaboration, Hillenbrand promoted the establishment of CFM in Chicago. Jocist cells traditionally separated women from men, so that even married couples who belonged to the same movement were unable to share membership in the same local cell. Pat and Patty Crowley, the first executive directors of the movement, found such separation rather odd.[111] In 1947, couples cells were established, usually composed of four couples per cell.

They were not alone in their innovation. At the same time another couples' movement was formed in South Bend, Indiana. In 1949, when CFM held its first convention at Childerly Farm outside Chicago, there were thirty-seven couples who took part. *For Happier Families,* the CFM journal, was initiated in that same year, and immediately sold twenty-

---

[110] See Joseph Cardijn, *Challenge to Action,* E. Langdale, ed. (Chicago: Fides, 1955).

[111] Patty Crowley recalls those early years with amusement. In 1943, at a family renewal day at Lake Forest, Illinois, near Chicago, the married couples who attended that gathering were not permitted to sleep in the same room. Those family renewal days were, in fact, the beginning of the Cana movement which, unlike CFM, focused its efforts on better participation in parish life as married couples, but lacked the broader social concern which was inherent within CFM. Out of Cana grew the pre-Cana movement, which prepared young Catholic couples for marriage. Interview by author, 10 December 1994, Chicago, Illinois.

five hundred copies. The movement expanded rapidly. Records show that in 1952, there were five thousand couples participating, not only in the United States, but in seven other countries, as well.

Scripture and the liturgy were the basis for the social outreach of CFM couples. Weekly CFM meetings began with fifteen minutes on the Scriptures and another fifteen minutes on the liturgy, followed by the forty-five minute inquiry in which the group carried out the "observe, judge, and act" principles. In that third segment, they often discussed some aspect of Catholic social teaching,[112] then strategized some localized response.

CFM was strictly a lay movement. Meetings took place in the homes of CFM couples, rather than in parish halls. Although each cell had a priest-chaplain, the meeting was organized and led entirely by the lay leaders. At the end of each meeting, several minutes were allotted for "chaplain's remarks" before all participants concluded with the singing of Compline. The sung *Missa recitata* was celebrated at all CFM conventions. CFM members participated in the annual liturgical weeks and in the Vernacular Society, and followed closely the progress of the liturgical movement.

Social outreach of CFM varied, depending on the local needs of each geographical area where cells were found. Among issues that occupied the Chicago CFM group, interracial justice was of paramount importance, and soon became a national CFM concern, as well.[113] South Bend cells focused their activism on the need for a school to serve retarded children in the area, recreation facilities in a neighborhood where such facilities were lacking, and baby-sitting services for couples who were in need of an evening out together. The organization became increasingly ecumenical long before Vatican II.

---

[112] As a student at Trinity College in Washington, D.C., Patty Crowley was very much influenced by Monsignor John A. Ryan of The Catholic University. Ryan's lectures were not overly stimulating. Lectures consisted of little more than his reading aloud out of his own book, *Questions of the Day*. Students quickly learned that when they were able to get Ryan to close the book and talk from his own experience, the classes were much more interesting. So, Crowley and the other students were faithful to the task of getting Ryan to close his book. It was such conversations which had a great effect upon Crowley. Interview of 10 December 1994.

[113] This was the case from the beginning. In 1944, Pat Crowley invited Ann Harrigan, an associate of Catherine De Hueck at Friendship House, to come to the meeting of the men's group and discuss the work of Friendship House and the issue of interracial justice. Harrigan was invited precisely to recommend some concrete action in which the group could engage. As a result, many CFM members became involved in Friendship House as volunteers. Crowley, Interview.

Responses in a 1952 CFM questionnaire indicated greater devotion to the liturgy, greater application of the Scriptures, more apostolic service, and a deepened spirituality with a greater realization of the responsibility toward others as effects of CFM on individual members.[114]

PART TWO:
THE LITURGICAL PIONEERS AND SOCIAL JUSTICE

Part Two focuses on the social thought, the pastoral experience, and the writing of Virgil Michel, Hans A. Reinhold, and Reynold Hillenbrand. These three pioneers stand out among all the others as champions of the liturgy's social dimension, for tirelessly addressing the intrinsic link between liturgy and social justice. While other liturgical leaders caught a glimpse of such a vision, it was Michel, Reinhold, and Hillenbrand who lived and taught this essential relationship inherent within the liturgy. And because of what they were advocating, all three individuals were caught in the midst of assorted controversies and suffered because of their convictions.

The Legacy of Virgil Michel

Virgil Michel was a man of extraordinary talent. When he died suddenly in 1938 at the age of forty-eight, those who knew him in one particular area of expertise were surprised to learn of his many other accomplishments. Not only was he founder of *OF* and The Liturgical Press, he had also been an English and philosophy professor, dean at St. John's University, Collegeville, a violinist in the St. John's orchestra, and a baseball and tennis star. He also coached St. John's Preparatory School athletics, worked as a translator, and wrote on such varied topics as race relations and women's issues, economics, art, and education. He even wrote a novel. Of all those interests, it was his unifying vision of the revival of liturgical worship in America, along with a rediscovery of the Church's social mission and the renewal of Catholic education, that was his greatest contribution to the American church and society.[115]

In 1916, as a graduate student in education and philosophy at The Catholic University of America, Washington, D.C., Michel was interested in the development of American philosophical thought. He chose as the topic of his doctoral dissertation: "The Critical Principles

---

[114] Jay P. Dolan, *Transforming Parish Ministry: The Changing Roles of Catholic Clergy, Laity, and Women Religious* (New York: Crossroad Publishing Co., 1989) 248–9.

[115] R. William Franklin, and Robert Spaeth, *Virgil Michel: American Catholic* (Collegeville: The Liturgical Press, 1988) 20–1.

of Orestes A. Brownson." Brownson (d. 1876), in his earlier years, had written a great deal on the philosophical and religious foundations for a healthy American society, and spoke positively of an appropriation of theology in terms of American culture. He wrote on the relationship between Catholicism and culture. He studied atheism and secularism in American society. Interestingly, Brownson was a convert to Catholicism and both a contemporary and friend of American Catholic reformer Isaac Hecker. Brownson's own commitment to justice had a deep and lasting effect on Michel.[116]

Brownson also reflected on the role of the layperson in Church and society, advocating a spirituality that was peculiarly American. According to Michel, Brownson was "one of the most prominent figures that the Catholic laity in the U.S. can point to."[117] Brownson believed that through baptism, the laity were brought into "a community of apostolic faith and authority."[118] Brownson defended lay activism and freedom within the Church since freedom was the only true path to genuine religious piety, as far as Brownson was concerned. He was convinced that the old style spirituality, which emphasized nothing more than holy obedience, had to be changed to meet the challenges of the modern age in a democratic society. In calling for a new spirituality that integrated obedience with liberty, Brownson was aware that his positions were not easily received by everyone in the Church.[119]

[116] In the conclusion to his doctoral dissertation, Michel wrote: "His concern for the betterment of society and for the uplift of the lower classes shows him to have been fully alive to the justice of the agitations going on in the United States . . . He was not satisfied with reveling in abstract theories, however, and earnestly pleaded for practical application, an example of which we see in his sociological conception of literature." Marx, 11–13.

[117] Michel, "Brownson, A Man of Men," *Catholic World* 125 (1927) 756.

[118] Patrick Carey, "Lay Catholic Leadership in the United States," *U.S. Catholic Historian* 9 (1990) 229.

[119] "He who ventures to assert that the clergy are only functionaries in the church and for the church, that the laity are an integral part of the church, and not mere 'hewers of wood and drawers of water' to the hierarchy, with neither voice nor souls of their own, is at once suspected of wishing to democratize the church, of having Congregational predilections or reminiscences, if not of being animated by an unavowed hostility to the hierarchical constitution of the church herself. It is hard to protest against an extreme in one direction, without being suspected of wishing to run to an extreme in another. Hence it is that they who propose changes or ask for changes demanded by the progress or changes in civilization, are sure to be misunderstood, misrepresented, and suspected of disloyalty to Catholicity." Carey, 230. Such was often the case with the liturgical pioneers and others who were advocating the doctrine of the Mystical Body of Christ in the 1930s.

What, specifically, were the ideas which Brownson and Michel held in common? Four major themes emerge: (1) the nature and mission of the Church; (2) the role of the laity; (3) the role of Catholic thought in the modern world with the commitment to social change; and (4) the commitment to social reform.[120] Brownson argued that the Church was a dynamic and lived reality, calling for communion among its members with Christ at the center. As such, the Church's mission was vital and dynamic.[121] He stressed the fundamental equality among all Church members. This was the very theology of ministry that would undergird Michel's contribution to the liturgical and social apostolates and to the task of integrating those two apostolates into one.

As a young monk, Michel exhibited a keen sensitivity to the conditions and needs of the times, recognizing the need for changes in societal structures, and considering how Benedictine monasticism might contribute to societal reform. It is probable that his graduate studies in Washington during World War I where he served as a military chaplain, and the secular educational environment of Columbia University, New York City, also had some effect upon the shaping and evolution of his social thought. Michel likewise volunteered to be sent to the Bahamas missions—an offer which the abbot refused.[122] All this was prior to his European sojourn. He did not abandon his social consciousness when he boarded the ship for Europe; rather, that passion for justice continued to burn within him as he pursued philosophical and liturgical studies at Rome and Louvain, and as he made pilgrimage to the great European liturgical centers at places like Maria Laach and Mont César.

Upon his return to the United States in 1926, he was determined to pursue that harmonious relationship of liturgy and life in the Mystical Body of Christ, clearly inspired by the insights of Orestes Brownson.

---

[120] Seamus Finn, "Virgil Michel's Contribution to Linking the Liturgical and Social Apostolates in the American Church: A 50 Year Perspective" (Ph.D. diss., Boston University, 1991) 40.

[121] "The Church, as St. Augustine says, is the body of Christ, and the body of believers in union with him are the whole Christ, totus christus, as the soul and the body united in their living union are the total man. The charter of the Church is in her internal constitution and life, as the living body of our Lord, and her rights and powers are in and from him living in her, and speaking and operating in and through her as his own body, or the visible continuation or representation on earth of the Incarnation. We say his own body; for the Church is not a foreign body, having relation with him only through the medium of external commission. She is his spouse, flesh of his flesh and one with him, having her personality in his divine person." Brownson, "Derby's Letters to his Son" (1865). Finn, 41.

[122] Marx, 14–16.

This was especially the case after 1935 when Michel resumed his editorship of *OF*, redirecting the magazine to deal more explicitly with issues of social justice and culture. There was, however, a more experiential component in Michel's life which moved him further along the path to promoting the integration of liturgy and justice.

Michel had been overwhelmed by the challenges offered in those early years of the liturgical movement. He told a colleague in 1929: "The possibilities of doing good are almost overwhelming us."[123] By early 1930, he was suffering from complete exhaustion, and in April of that year he suffered a nervous breakdown. What followed was two months of hospitalization, an experience of "the dark night of the soul," where he suffered from severe headaches, was unable to sleep, unable to read, and unable to celebrate Mass. For most of the two following years, Michel was unable to pray the Liturgy of the Hours, and so was assigned three rosaries as his daily prayer. Upon leaving the hospital in June 1930, he was sent to the Chippewa Indian Reservation in northern Minnesota to rest and engage in a minimal amount of pastoral ministry. This experience became formative in shaping his understanding about social justice and its relationship to the liturgy.

The first three months were spent in recuperation, but by September Michel was able to begin some pastoral work centered around Cass Lake where he remained until September 1931. Thinking that he had recovered, the abbot called him back to St. John's to resume teaching philosophy. It soon became clear, however, that he had not recovered, so he was sent back to the Chippewa, this time to minister at White Earth. He remained there until the beginning of August and then returned to Cass Lake for a lighter pastoral assignment. At Cass Lake, Michel invited a native American family to live with him for the year. They remained together until he was called back to the monastery in September 1933 to become dean of the college.

Michel approached his ministry among the Chippewa with the same level of intensity and dedication that he had given to the liturgical apostolate. He learned their language, hunted deer and bear with them, ate their food, and worked and recreated with them. To increase membership in the parish, he went into bars and spoke informally with patrons, inviting them to come to church and take a look. His psychological problems continued during those three years. He continued to suffer from insomnia and headaches as well as depression. He frequently signed his letters: "In Passione Domini." Such experience proved redemptive, however. Life among the Chippewa filled him

---

[123] Marx, 161.

with a greater awareness of the many injustices which were a daily reality for the poor. His later writings on the evils of poverty and the call to a simple life-style grew out of this experience.[124]

Michel studied the Chippewa culture and learned of what we now call "Native American Spirituality." He had recognized the presence of Christ in their culture, in their poverty, in their simplicity, and he encouraged them to recognize the same. He became convinced that the credibility of the Church and of his own ministry would best be served through lay leadership. As native Americans, lay leaders had an advantage over Michel in the promotion of evangelical and liturgical programs among the Chippewa. For instance, in emphasizing the tradition of First Friday devotions, it was the lay leaders who would go through the community on Thursday, visiting homes and reminding people that liturgical events and other devotions would be taking place in the church on Friday, and that they were invited and encouraged to participate.

Michel reorganized the missions with a concrete program of social and spiritual reconstruction. From 21 to 25 June 1933, for example, Michel organized the twenty-third annual convention of the Catholic Chippewa Societies of northern Minnesota, calling it "a great religious spectacle and a real spiritual success." It was the largest convention of that type ever to be held. He would have been happy to spend the rest of his life ministering among the Chippewa, so when he returned to Collegeville in 1933, he did so reluctantly.

In considering the formation of Michel's social consciousness, then, we can point to two primary influences. Academically, it was the philosophical and religious thought of Orestes Brownson, along with Beauduin's influence upon him during studies in Europe. Pastorally and experientially, it was his encounter with poverty and personal struggle brought on by his illness and fulfilled during those three years on the reservation. Returning to Collegeville and to the work of the liturgical apostolate, those combined factors made a difference in the agenda of the liturgical movement.

Michel believed that American Catholics had become too materialistic and individualistic:

> As long as the Christian is in the habit of viewing his religious life from the subjectivist and individualist standpoint, he will be able to live his daily life in terms of the prudent individualism and subjectivism without any qualms of conscience.[125]

---

[124] Ibid., 162–4.
[125] Michel, "Liturgy and Catholic Life," 136. Quoted in Marx, 218.

Liturgy was the solution to individualism, capable of opening the eyes of American worshipers to the possibilities of a truly Christian culture. For this reason, he saw the liturgical movement as the primary apostolate. Inspired by Brownson's ideals and by the liturgy itself, Michel believed that the solution to the social problems of his day was the formation of an American culture that was truly Catholic—a culture which would embody the principles of the doctrine of the Mystical Body of Christ. Speaking of the supernatural communion which existed in the Mystical Body, he suggested that such a relationship was "the best model and guide for all social organizations of men."[126] The lack of a clear understanding of the Mystical Body would perpetuate the dichotomy between the sacred and secular in American culture.[127]

That dichotomy was evident on all sides. Michel saw the Catholic presence lacking in most of the modern day mediums of communication: cinema, press, advertising, contemporary literature. A culture infused with the true Christian spirit could transform human behavior into Christ-like behavior, embracing gospel values and casting aside conflicting values of materialism, selfishness, and individualism, all of which fractured the unity of the body of Christ. He wrote in 1935:

> We have as a whole, little or no understanding of what Christian culture really is, and have also lost much of the instinct of what it should be, since we have been living through centuries of a declining Christian sense and a growing pagan atmosphere of life.[128]

The individualism which was so much a part of American culture stood in sharp contrast to the kind of community and shared responsibility which typified life among the Chippewa and which expressed

---

[126] Michel, "Natural and Supernatural Society," *OF* 10 (1936) 243–7; 293–6; 338–42; 394–8; 434–8.

[127] "And so while many Catholic Christians mind their own business, the injustices suffered by share-croppers, the gross discriminations against negroes (even at times within the walls of Catholic churches), economic oppressions of all sorts, crying court injustices, violent vigilante antics based on the principle that might is right, etc., go on, with hardly a prominent Catholic voice raised in protest. How the Church Fathers of old would have made the welkin ring with the righteous indignation of the Lord and with their incessant denunciations on the one hand and guiding exhortations on the other. They knew of no compromise between Christ and this world. Why hesitate today, when we all know that the support of Church and school come not from the coffers of the wealthy but from the mites of the poor?" Michel, "Social Injustices," *OF* 11 (1937) 79.

[128] Michel, "The Liturgical Movement and the Future," *America* 54 (1935) 6.

what it meant to live in the body of Christ.[129] Thus, Michel became a strong critic of individualism, writing frequently about its destructive influence in American society.[130]

While many in government and business continued to praise the values of capitalism, Michel had little tolerance for its promotion as a cure for the social ills of the 1930s.[131] In responding to one article which appeared in *Catholic World,* calling Christ "the first preacher of capitalism as the most workable thesis for society," Michel wrote: "What blasphemy! As if there were anything really Christian about our modern Capitalism."[132] And given the extent to which such individualism was present in American society, it held obvious implications for American Catholics when they would gather for worship. Like the rest of society, many Catholics in the United States suffered from the same tendency to dichotomize. Religion remained largely a private affair and there was little indication that Catholics had any unified vision of common life in the body of Christ.[133]

In order to respond apostolicly, then, Christians needed to be culturally educated as well as religiously informed, and it was the liturgy that would be "the basis of social regeneration."[134] The living of the liturgical life would provide the needed energy for such cultural contact and communication. There was no middle of the road in such a commitment to Church and culture:

> . . . too long have sincere Christians looked upon their spiritual life as something shut up entirely within themselves and have tried to harden themselves against the evil influence of the world even while leaving that same world to itself. We must be with Christ or against Him; we

---

[129] He explained: "There is only one answer I know of to the problem of the balanced harmony between the individual and the social: *The Mystical Body of Christ.* There the individual retains his full responsibility, the fullest possibility of greater realization of his dignity as a member of Christ; yet he is ever a member of the fellowship of Christ, knit closely with his fellow members into a compact body by the indwelling Spirit of Christ: *There* is the pattern of all social life lived by individuals." "Natural and Supernatural Society," 244–5.

[130] For a summary of Michel's critique of American individualism, see Finn, 63–75.

[131] Michel defined capitalism as follows: "An economic system that rests on the priority of production over consumption for the purpose of rationalized profit in a free market and free money system." *The Nature of Capitalism* (St. Paul: Wanderer Publishing Co., 1936) 16.

[132] Michel, "What is Capitalism?" *The Commonweal* 28 (1938) 6.

[133] Michel, "Are We One in Christ?" *ER* 81 (1934) 395–401.

[134] Michel, "The Liturgy the Basis of Social Regeneration," *OF* 9 (1935) 536–45.

must either affect the world in which we live or else the world will affect us.[135]

Consistent with this integrated view of Christian life, Michel argued for the equality of women and men, including shared apostolic partnership: "Women are born to be in their own way apostles, not only examples, of Christian ideals and life."[136] He contended that it was the pioneers of early Christianity and not the pioneers of the womens' movement in this country, who first advocated the feminist agenda. Early Christianity offered a radical witness in freeing women from slavery and from subjection to men, which had been normative in pagan Greece and Rome. Further, women assisted Jesus in his earthly ministry, helped the other apostles in spreading the gospel, and had an influence in public life. Deaconesses assisted in administering baptisms, instructing Christians in times of persecution and preparing them for the sacraments, and in works of mercy. Some of these women were themselves martyred. Michel's biographer summarized his reflections on the role of women in early Christianity in these words:

> Women, like men, actively participated in the Church's worship and the lay apostolate since they shared as members of the Savior's Body in the same priesthood.[137]

Michel always substantiated his own theories and plans with the teachings and practice of the early church. In calling for the full and active participation of women in the liturgical movement and even more fundamentally, in the apostolic mission of the contemporary Church, he remained consistent in his reliance on early-Church sources.

In 1934, as an educational contribution to the restoration of a Christian social order, Alphonse Matt began what came to be known as The Social Institute at St. John's. This was a program of adult education aimed at training lay leaders in Catholic social teaching, in cooperation with the Central Catholic Verein. It consisted of a series of weekend conferences, featuring professors from St. John's as lecturers. Virgil Michel was among those lecturers but soon came into conflict with the local bishop, Joseph Busch of St. Cloud, who accused Michel of promoting CA without an official mandate. The situation grew increasingly

---

[135] Quoted in Marx, 262.

[136] Michel, "The Liturgical Movement and the Catholic Woman," in Central Catholic Verein of America, *Annual Report,* 58. On the underestimated contribution of women to the liturgical movement, see Nathan Mitchell, "The Amen Corner: A Mansion for the Rat," *Worship* 68 (1994) 64–72.

[137] Marx, 262.

tense as the bishop eventually requested copies of Michel's lectures before he gave them, and proceeded to critique numerous points within
each lecture. Eventually the situation improved as the bishop established his own CA program in St. Cloud, allowing the Social Institute
to constitute a part of it.

Michel viewed the theme of the Mystical Body more as a spirituality, as a way of living in society, than as theological doctrine. In this
way, he differed from his colleagues in Germany from whom he had
borrowed the concept in the first place. Of course, while the German
theologians discussed in the previous chapter helped to retrieve the
doctrine of the Mystical Body, that doctrine did not originate at the
Tübingen school of the nineteenth century. Rather, this was a classi-
cally Pauline theme. As Kenneth Himes notes, Michel's own employment of this doctrine was consistent with Pauline usage.[138]

Michel believed that the contemporary Church was called to take on
the form and shape of the Mystical Body, paradigmatically expressed
in the Eucharist. Since the Mystical Body was not merely a supernatural reality but a model for a renewed human society, the retrieval of
this theme as a fundamental eucharistic spirituality challenged Christians to view themselves not merely as organically linked to Christ, but
to all who shared life in that same body. And the liturgy was to be the
wellspring of such organic union. Obviously, this organic union had
strong social implications for Christian responsibility in daily life.
Quite simply, liturgy demanded justice. In fact, liturgy was justice in
action because it embodied that ideal and just society: the reign of
God. Thus, the reunification of liturgy and justice was essential to a
healthy ecclesiology. Michel believed that once the laity had recovered
a sense of the richness of the liturgy which had been taken from them
in previous centuries, they would likewise come to see the importance
of the work of justice in the Church's mission. It was more than a co-
incidence, Michel often said, that the liturgical renewal promoted by
Pius X should be followed by a five-hundred page text by Pius XI, promoting CA. Unless one understood the Church as Mystical Body continuing Christ's mission through the apostolic life of every member,
grasping the full significance of the liturgical life, laity would be incapable of grasping the full import of their role in the body of Christ.[139]

---

[138] Himes, 203.

[139] Marx, 194. Promoting full and active participation among the laity was not
warmly welcomed by all sectors of the clergy. One priest wrote: "The Liturgical
Movement aims to take the very heart of the priesthood away from us clergy and
give it to the lay ones." Letter, *Sentinel of the Blessed Sacrament*. Quoted in "Communications," *OF* 5 (1931) 197.

The renewal of the social order would come when the Church lived as the Mystical Body of Christ with full and active liturgical participation.[140] The Christian, then, was called to live the life of Christ daily as an unceasing act of worship. While such a life was lived more intensely in the liturgy, the call was the same whether one was standing in the liturgical assembly on Sunday morning or at work during the week. For the Christian, every action was already a social action, because the believer shared membership in the body of Christ. Positive actions helped the body to grow in stature. Negative actions diminished. Herein lies the connection between liturgy and justice for Virgil Michel: that worship should continue in the streets and the marketplace, at work and at home. Christian life was to be an unceasing act of worship. When believers failed to live worshipful lives in other situations, they had knowingly or unknowingly accepted the secularist dichotomy of the culture which tended to keep religion separate from the rest of life.[141] This was often the reality in parishes where cultural tensions continued among believers who worshiped in the same eucharistic assembly. One striking example of such incongruity comes from a historian who framed the experience of being a black Catholic in the south earlier in this century:

> One summer, when I was eight years old and lived in the Midwest, my family took a trip South to a small town on the Gulf Coast. I was born there and most of my relatives had been settled there for generations. I had three encounters with racism on that trip, the first when I wanted to drink from a water fountain meant for whites only and the second when I tried to play on a beach off limits to blacks. The third incident of the summer of my education took place on a Sunday, in a Catholic church. For some reason we had missed Mass at the black church and went

---

[140] "He who lives the liturgy will in due time feel the mystical body idea developing in his mind and growing upon him, will come to realize that he is drinking at the very fountain of the true Christian spirit which is destined to reconstruct the Social Order." Michel, "With our Readers," *OF* 5 (1931) 431.

[141] Michel wrote: "One cannot steep oneself in the true meaning of the Mass as corporate worship to be participated in by all and enact the dedication of oneself to God with Christ in sacrificial prayer of the Mass, and yet remain a cold-blooded individualist in one's life outside the precincts of the altar. Similarly, one cannot become social-minded in regard to the large economic problems of our day—unless one's interest is purely academic or 'scientific'—without adverting to the fact that such social-mindedness has its proper place in the religious life of the Christian. The two go hand in hand. It is impossible to remain individualistic in prayer and sincerely social in daily life, or to remain individualistic in daily life and become sincerely social in prayer." "Our Social Environment," *OF* 12 (1938) 318.

instead to a white church, which my grandfather, a carpenter, had helped build years before. We crowded into a half pew in the back with the only other black worshipers. The pew was too small to seat us all, so during Mass we had to take turns kneeling and sitting. In front of us two white men had a whole pew to themselves. The message was obvious: they belonged there; we didn't. Hot, tired, and angry I couldn't understand how something so unfair could happen in a church. Then we went to Communion. Since we were seated in the back, we brought up the rear of the line to the altar rail. But as we knelt, there were still some white communicants waiting to receive the Host. To my amazement, the priest passed me by, not once, but twice, until he had distributed Communion to all the whites. Then he returned to me. That Mass, my mother commented afterward, hadn't done her a bit of good since all she felt during the service was hate. I didn't say anything. I just felt humiliated and betrayed.[142]

Michel employed the example of the offertory procession in the early Church as a concrete example of the union between the marketplace and the liturgical assembly. Everyone brought something of his or her own to the altar—bread or wine, olive oil, some other product. No one brought his or her gift in isolation, but rather all joined together in that same procession, offering their gifts as a single offering to God. While some of the bread and wine was laid on the altar to be used for the liturgy itself, the rest of that one offering was laid aside on tables for the poor and needy. Thus, in the direct service of God through their common sacrifice, they were indirectly serving the needs of their brothers and sisters. This was active liturgical participation in the Mystical Body of Christ.

In Michel's opinion, one of the limits of the earlier European liturgical movement was that it lacked the justice dimension. While Beauduin was an obvious exception to this, Michel's thesis was accurate.[143] He was convinced that the future of the liturgical movement

---

[142] A. Raboteau, "Black Catholics: A Capsule History," *Catholic Digest* (June, 1983) 32–3. See also John T. McGreevy, *Parish Boundaries: The Catholic Encounter with Race in the Twentieth-Century Urban North* (Chicago: The University of Chicago Press, 1996).

[143] In the words of H. A. Reinhold: "We had no Virgil Michel in Germany. The close inter-connection of the liturgical revival with social reform . . . was never expressed in that forceful way in which you see it in the writings of the late Dom Virgil and *Orate Fratres* . . . Maria Laach, Guardini, Parsch and Klosterneuburg only occasionally pointed out the necessary social consequences of a true liturgical revival among our Catholic people . . . America is in an enviable position . . . While in Germany the leaders of the liturgical and social revival, both strong and powerful movements, never really met and sometimes antagonized and criticized each

held little promise if it did not unite with the social apostolate, stressing the relationship of liturgy to the rest of life.[144] And the liturgy's social dimension was found in its ability to "evoke, shape and enact new attitudes and ideas in the life of the worship."[145] Put differently, society was not changed until the individuals themselves were challenged, changed, transformed. It was in the liturgical assembly that believers heard that call to conversion together. Michel wrote:

> Today, the natural social bonds have been disrupted . . . It is not too much to say that the revival of true social human life will be achieved only under the inspiration of the liturgical life, since the specific divine purpose of the latter is to transform human nature after the mind of Christ and inspire it unto a life replete like His with love of God and man.[146]

The liturgy revealed such challenges in its high ideals, emphasizing the subordination of one's will to the demands of the gospel and the community, and in the fundamental truth of the paschal mystery: that the life of the Christian is ever a life of dying and rising with Christ. Such demands were not intended to deny individuality or diversity, but they were intended to challenge narcissism and selfishness.[147] The practice of the early Church exemplified the radical living out of the gospel which the membership in Christ's body calls for, and Michel often referred to such examples in his writings and lectures. Christians of those early centuries brought to the Eucharist the fruits of their work—their gifts employed in the liturgy and alms for the poor. In those gifts they offered themselves to God and in dedicating themselves to God they were likewise dedicated to the service of the human community.[148]

---

other—here you have a close cooperation of the two, a unity of both, right from the start." "Liturgy, True Remedy," *Social Forum* (December, 1938). Quoted in Marx, 180.

[144] See Michel, "The Liturgical Movement of the Future," *America* 54 (1935) 6–7.

[145] Himes, 208.

[146] "Social Aspects of the Liturgy," *Catholic Action* 16 (1934) 9, 11.

[147] "Far from depreciating or suppressing the values of individuality and personality, the Mystical Body of Christ gives these their best possible realization. The responsibility that each member has, not only for his own self, but also for the good of the whole Body, is the highest personal responsibility that the individual man can be privileged to share; it is implicitly the highest possible acknowledgment of the true dignity and value of the human person." Michel, "Natural and Supernatural Society," 434–5.

[148] See Michel, "The Layman in the Church," *The Commonweal* 12 (1930) 123–5.

In addressing baptism, Michel often lamented the fact that Christian initiation was almost always treated negatively, as freedom *from* original sin. According to Michel, the far more significant aspect of baptism was its positive emphasis—freedom *for* service in the Christian community—the commissioning for ministry within the Church with its inherent social responsibility. Confirmation, he argued, carried with it the responsibility for the social environment in which the Church functions. Through their initiation into Christ, strengthened through full and active liturgical participation, women and men served as an effective leaven in the marketplace. In referring to the words of the baptismal rite, Michel said:

> As Christ is ever the Way, the Truth, and the Life—King and Teacher and Priest—so must every member of his body as an "other Christ" be in some degree king and teacher and priest unto himself and unto others. Can he otherwise really be said "to have part with Christ?"[149]

This power was exercised through liturgical participation, to be sure, but such participation must lead the believer into Christian service. True enough, the liturgy did not offer a concrete plan for social justice, but it did provide a model of communion which left no room for economic injustice or racial prejudice, no room for distinctions between rich and poor, because all are of equal value in the body of Christ.[150] In the words of social activist, Monsignor John J. Egan:

> . . . Michel and his followers spoke of the liturgy as a school of social justice. This did not mean simply that preachers spoke on social problems. Here the liturgy is once again crucial. In the liturgy, properly celebrated, divisions along lines of sex, age, race or wealth are overcome. In the liturgy, properly celebrated, we discover the sacramentality of the material universe. In the liturgy, properly celebrated, we learn the ceremonies of respect both for one another and for the creation, that allow us to see in people and in material goods, "fruit of the earth and work of human hands," sacraments of that new order which we call the justice of the Kingdom of God.[151]

[149] "Liturgy and Catholic Life," 78.

[150] Michel wrote: "The liturgy does not offer a detailed scheme of economic reconstruction, or anything of that kind. But it does give us a proper concept and understanding of what society is like, through its model, the Mystical Body. And it puts this concept into action in its worship and wants us to live it out in everyday life. The liturgy furnishes an admirable basis along social lines." Letter to Martin Schirber, O.S.B., 27 November 1935. Quoted in Marx, 205.

[151] Egan, "Liturgy and Justice: An Unfinished Agenda," a paper delivered at the Liturgical Symposium, Boston College, 21 June 1983, later published in *Origins* 13 (1983) 399–411.

Those high ideals of the liturgical pioneers and their colleagues in Catholic social movements were not easily realized in the average parish. While liturgical pioneers were preaching social justice and social activists were advocating a liturgically-based social outreach, most parishes, especially in east coast cities like Boston, New York, and Washington, would have found such talk completely foreign to their experience. And when there was talk of liturgical renewal in parishes, it often consisted of concern about a new style of vestment, such as the conical chasuble or longer surplices, and had less to do with more fundamental issues like the relationship of liturgical participation to daily life. Virgil Michel quoted an article which had appeared in the *Catholic World:*

> Never has the writer or any of his intimate friends heard a sermon on the practical application of the living wage doctrine, on the duty of distributing surplus wealth, on the protection of women and children in industry, on the obligation of employers and employees to cooperate, on the duty of the state to promote industrial harmony.[152]

He continued:

> I know of a recent instance where a priest did preach on social justice in one of our largest cities, and he shielded himself behind abundant quotations from the papal encyclical. He received a letter from a prominent parishioner, a most faithful church-goer, who told the priest he should stay with the preaching of religion and not meddle in economics, otherwise she would attend church elsewhere after this, and she was even ready to tell the pope the same if he did not mind his business better![153]

The ideal was very far, indeed, from the reality of normal parish life, but this did not discourage the leaders of the liturgical movement from promoting it. Virgil Michel died in 1938, but the social vision of the liturgical movement continued through the leadership of H. A. Reinhold, Reynold Hillenbrand, and others.

Hans A. Reinhold

Known by friends and associates as H.A.R., Hans Ansgar Reinhold was born in Hamburg, Germany in 1897, ordained a priest in 1925, and came to the United States in 1936 when he was forced to flee because of his strong criticism of Nazism. His protest against anti-Semitism remained strong, even after his arrival in the United States, and he

[152] Michel, "Social Injustices," 78.
[153] Ibid.

became a strong advocate of justice. His liturgical interest came from time spent at Maria Laach as a novice, and from association with liturgical leaders like Odo Casel, Abbot Ildefons Herwegen, and Romano Guardini. From Europe, he began correspondence with Dorothy Day, whom he had met on a visit to New York in 1933. He was deeply impressed by the witness of the CW, and by its desire to integrate liturgy with justice, since this was his own desire as well. Day invited him to come to New York and to work on a Catholic refugee committee.[154]

Upon arrival in New York, ecclesiastical authorities, especially Chancellor Francis McIntyre (later Cardinal Archbishop of Los Angeles), considered him a suspicious character and watched him closely.[155] He was forbidden to speak within the archdiocese. His anti-Franco sentiments were well-known, labeling him a troublemaker. After several months in Manhattan he was exiled to Brooklyn, where he received a better welcome. Work with refugees led him into ecumenical relations and to acquaintances with Paul Tillich and Reinhold Niebuhr. His troubles followed him, so he continued to move—to Middle Village, Queens; to the Benedictine Portsmouth Priory in Rhode Island; to Seattle, Washington, to work as a seamen's chaplain; then on to Sunnyside, in the Diocese of Yakima, Washington, where he remained until his retirement.[156]

The year before Virgil Michel's death, Reinhold was in Boston where he met another Benedictine from Collegeville, Emeric Lawrence, at the home of a friend. Lawrence was deeply impressed with Reinhold, so, after Michel's death, when the *OF* editorial board met to choose a successor for the writing of Michel's regular column, "Timely Tracts,"[157] Lawrence recommended Reinhold.[158] Three

---

[154] Joel P. Garner, "The Vision of a Liturgical Reformer: Hans Anscar Reinhold" (Ph.D. diss., Columbia University, 1972) 26–7.

[155] For an interesting account of his problems with the Archdiocese of New York, see *H.A.R., The Autobiography of Father Reinhold* (New York: Herder and Herder, 1968) 105–7.

[156] Garner, 27–33. Reinhold's autobiography is helpful in providing background about his travels around the United States, his association with others in the social and liturgical movements, and his often problematic dealings with the American hierarchy. See "Part Two: America" in *H.A.R.*, 105–49.

[157] "Timely Tracts" was a column in *OF* which addressed issues of social justice in a pragmatic and often forceful way, speaking directly, for example, to the issue of racial injustice and calling for societal change.

[158] Lawrence wrote: "The afternoon of his funeral a crushed group of young monks gathered in Fr. Godfrey Diekmann's room in the monastery. It seemed like the end of the world for all of us. It was taken for granted that Fr. Godfrey would be the editor of *Orate Fratres*, since he had been managing editor under Fr. Virgil for

months later, he took up the task, which he continued for fifteen years until 1954.[159]

H.A.R. began by reflecting on Michel's leadership and activism:

> I have again glanced over most of his tracts. I am struck by an observation. They are all imbued with the spirit of an almost prophetical criticism and earnestness. And there is nothing of the bitterness or sharpness one might expect from an impatient reformer. Father Virgil had that holy impatience which is the true mark of a man "who sees," who has a vision of a more perfect world. But yet, he was prudent and charitable, merciful and ready to understand. Whatever he had to say in his timely tracts, his fingers close on the beating pulse of the Church's life, he was pervaded by a spirit of true reform, a striving for the better. Sometimes he had to rebuke self-complacement "show Catholicism," based on a wrongly conceived *esprit de corps,* or the superficiality of his co-religionists who substituted efficiency, worldly means, statistical achievement, commercialism and competition with non-catholic agencies for spiritual, humble, supernatural, and simple policies.[160]

Reinhold's contact with the Catholic Worker community and with the writers of *The Commonweal,* encouraged him in his passion for a justice rooted in the liturgy. Rather than losing momentum with Michel's death, the social agenda of the liturgical movement, along with its relationship to the other Catholic social movements of the 1930s and 1940s was strengthened, thanks to the leadership of Reinhold and others. Like Michel, Reinhold had also been steeped in the solid tradition of German ecclesiology, and was convinced in the primacy of the incarnation, leading to an organic view of Church and societal life.

For the first seven years of his assignment, Reinhold focused the *OF* column on the theme of liturgy and society. He wrote in 1945: "While we all know that the liturgical movement is a task and a hard one, we do not all seem to know that the new social order is part and parcel of our task."[161] Reinhold's sacramental world view had no problem

---

years. But who was to continue Virgil Michel's Timely Tracts, the most dynamic and 'practical' feature of the magazine? 'Why not Hans Reinhold?' I asked, and, if I never had another good idea the rest of my life, that was enough." Garner, 33.

[159] For an annotated bibliography of Reinhold's articles in *OF,* see Sandra L. Lindsey, "Accents of Candor and Courage: H. A. Reinhold in the American Liturgical Movement," M.A. Thesis: Theology, University of Portland, 1992, 113–50.

[160] "Dom Virgil's Columns," *OF* 13 (1939) 223. See also Reinhold, "Denver and Maria Laach," *The Commonweal* 45 (1946) 86–8.

[161] Reinhold, "A Radical Social Transformation is Inevitable," *OF* 19 (1944) 367.

incorporating a liturgical perspective with regard to society. In fact, Reinhold believed that such a liturgical perspective was essential:

> There is little "atmospheric" relation between a period which has a *"liturgical" mind,* and its *vision (and realization) of a society* equally sound in the set-up. How can a generation which has a clear grasp of the mystical body be entirely estranged from an equally organic conception of secular society, unless this generation forgets about the supreme anti-manichean principle of the liturgy: *consecrare mundum,* its task to integrate the incarnation.[162]

With his sacramental world view, H.A.R. spoke of "civilizing" and "consecrating" the world, suggesting that such terms when used analogously, were correlative. In other words, like Virgil Michel, Reinhold argued that the liturgical practice of the Christian must flow into daily life. In the face of oppression and injustice, be it racial, economic, or other, the Christian could not afford to sit back and remain indifferent. If a new social order would be established, it would necessitate critical voices within the body of Christ whose liturgical participation would give them the courage to speak out against injustice and abuses within the American economic system.[163] If liturgy was celebrated in a vacuum, devoid of passion for suffering humanity or unconnected to American life, then it was simply "a beating heart without blood vessels to carry the blood to our fingertips and toes."[164]

In the spirit of Michel, Reinhold made connections between the grassroots participation of the cooperative and liturgical movements, challenging his readers to think "liturgically" in their daily participation in secular society:

> The family, the parish, professional organizations, credit unions and cooperatives, labor and insurance unions, closer knit townships, city districts and communities with greater democracy in them, more participation of the "political laity" in the pseudo-liturgy of the "political clergy" or professional politicians, are things which form a surprising parallel to our own liturgical renaissance. It all looks very much like our own movement reflected in a secular mirror.[165]

He called for a depersonalized view of property and ownership which would put the values of the common good over and above personal

---

[162] Reinhold, "Liturgical Fascism," *OF* 16 (1941) 217.
[163] Garner, 160–1.
[164] Reinhold, "Freedom of Worship," *OF* 17 (1943) 131.
[165] Reinhold, "Liturgy and the New Order," *OF* 15 (1940) 78.

advantage and gain.[166] Like Michel, Reinhold made the distinction between individuality and a narcissistic individualism, suggesting that within the liturgy, there was a balance between collective and individualistic tendencies: "Our liturgy reflects a healthy and moderate balance of both tendencies, the individualistic and the collectivistic trend in person and society."[167]

Reinhold argued for a radical Christian witness which emerged within the community "from below"—from the people themselves—from their participation in worship. Such witness, he insisted, could not be imposed "from above." When liturgy in the local church was lived and celebrated authentically, when it was truly an expression of the assembly which gathered to celebrate, then would its power be morally transformative.[168]

From the first theme of liturgy and society, came the second theme which occupied his energies, namely liturgy and social action:

> Therefore it will always be a test for true liturgical spirit if those who stand up for it at the same time serve the poor in houses of hospitality, help organize parish cooperatives, lead in labor movements, or come from such practical professions as doctors, nurses, housewives, teachers, and priests. As long as we see fruits with the flavor of the gospels in the very parishes which stress liturgy, we need not worry.[169]

Reinhold was a strong believer in parish life and made wide use of pastoral experience in his writings and lectures. He relied heavily on his own ministry in maritime chaplaincy, in work with refugees, in education, in ecumenism, and in parish life, as he developed his theory on the integration of liturgy and justice. Those ministries gave added credibility to his words, because he spoke with experience and not from lofty ideals far removed from average Catholics.

Inspired by the witness of Dorothy Day whom he considered a mentor, and by Peter Maurin, H.A.R. urged American Catholics to allow their parish worship to flow very directly into service of the poor with the establishment of shelters for the homeless:

---

[166] See Reinhold, "Depersonalized Property," *OF* 15 (1940) 273–5; and "Collective Ownership is Collectivism," Ibid., 225–7.

[167] "Collective Ownership is Collectivism," 227.

[168] "The liturgical experience of a living parish necessarily leads to a New Order, rising from the minds of free Christians not forced on them by decrees, chekas, or gestapos . . . How can people who have seen and experienced the 'organism feeling' of a new living parish or its new family in Christ fail to grasp the idea of a new, organic order of society?" Reinhold, "Liturgy and the 'New Order,'" 79.

[169] Reinhold, "Popular Christianity," *OF* 14 (1940) 169–70.

If the floods of living water, descending from the altar into the parish, spilling over into a house for pilgrims (whom we call hoboes) and guests, for wanderers and the poor, would that not be a sermon from the roofs and house tops? A rectory basement, an old school, a barn will do for a beginning.[170]

Not only did H.A.R. preach about social justice through his writings and lectures, he also put those words into practice. Several months after writing that article on houses of hospitality, he spoke with Dorothy Day about opening a house of hospitality in Seattle. After talking with the bishop, permission was granted. At the same time, he became involved with the trade unions in the northwest and saw a relationship between issues of labor and liturgical renewal:

. . . nowhere more than here will it be disastrous if we continue to keep the laity in liturgical apathy and inactivity. How can we expect a worker to feel responsible for the Church, to stand up and assume responsibility, to feel that his brethren *are* the Church in their factories, slums, homes, unions, local papers and organizations, if they are allowed to take as much part in the performance of the liturgy as they take part in a movie, as more or less, mere interested spectators, who pay for a "show" and enjoy or dislike it?[171]

H.A.R. was likewise an outspoken advocate of interracial justice. African-Americans, he contended, called the American church to rejoice in its own diversity and challenged desires for rigid uniformity. In this way, the liturgical movement that also called for diversity shared a kindred spirit with African-Americans.[172] Reinhold and his colleagues in the liturgical movement responded directly to what had become a uniquely American issue, and argued strongly that there was no room for racial prejudice within the Mystical Body of Christ.

---

[170] Reinhold, "House of God and House of Hospitality," *OF* 14 (1939) 77–8. As his biographer notes, Reinhold knew that the ones who would most benefit from such social outreach would not be the poor, but would be those who served them. Garner, 168.

[171] "ACTU and Liturgy," *OF* 14 (1939) 33–4. See also John Cort, "The Labor Movement: Labor and the Liturgy," *The Commonweal* 51 (1949) 316–8.

[172] "The liturgical movement, so full of color, life, music, and a definite religious 'formedness' feels a kindred spirit. When all women look, talk, dress, make-up, and think as the *Woman's Home Companion* suggests, when their radio announcers have scared them into the universal likeness of Hollywood and that non-existent spectre of imitation-cafe-society of New York, we heed the example of courageous Negroes to be ourselves." H. A. Reinhold, "Let Us Give Thanks for our Colored Brethren," *OF* 17 (1942) 172–3.

Reinhold made the connection between the action of the Eucharist and the action of the marketplace, demonstrating an intrinsic relationship between the two. He had little sense that a "hunger and thirst for justice" was of great significance for most American Catholics, arguing that if Catholics truly understood the significance of their liturgical participation, then they would be compelled to follow through on their pursuit of social justice. He wrote:

> The poor at my side must be an alarm to me. If the colored parishioners are discriminated against, the sacrament must inflame me. The beauty of the liturgy and its sacred order must be a thorn in my side if at the same time the socio-economic order of my country is a mockery of the Gospel and if Christ's friends, the poor, are ignored while the well-washed, well-dressed, well-housed and respected are given practical preference as the "good Catholics."[173]

Not one to mince words, Reinhold's words were credible and concrete, and people listened. As a result, his influence in the American liturgical movement was great, particularly in calling American Catholics to think "liturgically" in their schools and offices, in their banks and factories, when they encountered the poor and unemployed, and to do the work of justice as a result. His words were prophetic, and like most prophets, he paid a price for what he preached, suffering greatly as a result.[174]

Reynold Hillenbrand

Reynold Hillenbrand was also of German stock. His grandparents emigrated to the United States from southern Germany in the mid-nineteenth century settling in Bristol, Wisconsin. Hillenbrand's parents moved from Bristol to Chicago, where he was born in 1904. The

---

[173] "A Social Leaven?" *OF* 25 (1951) 517. In that same article, he states: "Since we are members of that Mystical Body, which prolongs the incarnation, the state of the body social is a liturgical concern. We who claim to live by the sacraments must be found in the forefront of those who work for a new society built according to the justice and charity of Christ. Between shallow activism and naive optimism, this worldly and natural, on the one hand, and, on the other, an awareness of our duty to lay down our lives for justice's and charity's sake in order to implement what we do in sacred signs, there is a world of difference" (518–9).

[174] He wrote in the epilogue of his autobiography: "Sorrows now are mainly behind me, and my consolations are many. There are both fond and painful recollections . . . With fond recollections go fond hopes, and with painful reminiscence is the knowledge that the way of pilgrim progress is measured with sorrow. The road is wider now, and the goal is closer to sight." *H.A.R.,* 150.

Hillenbrands were parishioners of St. Michael's German Catholic Parish where Reynold also attended school. Not surprisingly, as a German Catholic institution, St. Michael's was known for its strong social consciousness, publishing a weekly paper, *Weltbuerger,* a journal dedicated to social issues, and supporting the magazine of the German Catholic Verein, *Central-Blatt and Social Justice.* In addition to the commitment to justice, St. Michael's was known for an active liturgical life, with a solid commitment to liturgical music. This included regular Sunday Vespers, daily benediction, and street processions on important feasts.[175]

During the Depression in the academic year 1930–1931, Hillenbrand was a doctoral student at St. Mary of the Lake Seminary. He then studied in Rome from 1931–1932 and indicates in his lectures that he heard Pius XI explain *Quadragesimo Anno* during that time.[176] Like other liturgical reformers, Hillenbrand was steeped in the ecclesiology of the Tübingen school and in the doctrine of the Mystical Body of Christ. His writings indicate as well, that he was clearly influenced by *Quadragesimo Anno* along with *Rerum Novarum.* He was also influenced by Virgil Michel and by the publications of The Liturgical Press, so that in 1937, as rector of the seminary, he invited Michel to come and speak to the students—an invitation which Michel accepted.[177] Like Reinhold and Michel, Hillenbrand criticized the secularism and individualism of American society, all of which had led to economic injustice. And like his colleagues, he believed that the solution to such disunity was the restoration of an organic society founded on "the true Christian spirit of self-sacrificial love."[178] He, too, encountered opposition in pro-

[175] Robert Tuzik, "The Contribution of Msgr. Reynold Hillenbrand (1905–1979) to the Liturgical Movement in the United States: Influences and Development" (Ph.D. diss., University of Notre Dame, 1989) 1–2, 5.

[176] Hillenbrand, "Notes for Talks on Labor and Social Justice" (unpublished manuscript), Hillenbrand Papers (6/26), University of Notre Dame Archives.

[177] Hillenbrand wrote: "I know very well that our students were not becoming familiar with the liturgical literature that your Press issues. I acquired a good deal of it, which I made available for examination to the men who were ordained this spring. Next year we shall do things more systematically. I shall obtain the Christ-Life Series so that the men will know what it is before they leave. I should like to see much deeper interest in the *Orate Fratres* and I think it will come in time. We are glad that you came to the Seminary; it did the students a lot of good." Letter to Virgil Michel, 28 June 1937. Quoted in Marx, 157–8.

[178] Tuzik, 47, 162. In his tenure as rector of the seminary (1936–1944), he invited colleagues like Donald Attwater, Paul Bussard, William Busch, Dorothy Day, Godfrey Diekmann, Catherine De Hueck, Gerald Ellard, Martin Hellriegel, Maurice Lavanoux, John La Farge, and H. A. Reinhold to the seminary to offer lectures or

moting the doctrine of the Mystical Body. His loyalty to the popes and their teachings saved him from being labeled a radical.

In 1938, Hillenbrand established the first Summer School of Social Action for priests—a move which grew to such an extent that Chicago became the center of American Catholic Action in the United States. He was insistent that this school, soon to receive national attention, offer courses on the liturgy. Ellard was one of the lecturers in the 1939 summer school, offering what he called a "Public Worship Clinic." In that program, he defined liturgy as corporate worship of the whole Mystical Body of Christ, and called for an official translation of the Mass in the vernacular, greater use of the dialog Mass, and fewer (black) Requiem Masses. Those summer schools were an important instrument in promoting the liturgical renewal with an emphasis on the relationship between liturgy and justice.

In 1940, Hillenbrand served as co-chairperson of the first national liturgical week, held at Holy Name Cathedral in Chicago. That experience led him, the following year, to establish the first Summer School of the Liturgy at St. Mary of the Lake Seminary, which included courses on Catholic Action, and liturgy and peace. Unlike the summer schools of Catholic Action, the primary emphasis here was on the liturgy. At the same time, the program logically attended to liturgy's dialogical counterpart, social justice. Hillenbrand was taught that the liturgy was "the social exercise of the virtue of religion or the public worship of the Church." Through his ministry, that is exactly what his students came to believe and live.[179]

Chicago was undoubtedly the center of social Catholicism for the American church, not only in terms of social action, but including liturgical renewal, as well. This was due, in large part to the prophetic leadership of Reynold Hillenbrand and to subsequent leaders like John Egan and others whom he influenced. Like Reinhold and other prophetic types, Hillenbrand was not always welcomed by his own. Some found his ideas difficult to accept, among whom were the more traditionally-minded largely Jesuit faculty whose own piety was more focused on personal sanctification. He had additional problems, some of which brought him into conflict with the archbishop. The close proximity of the Grail's Doddridge Farm led him into contact with that social movement, and he became one of their lecturers. This did not please Archbishop Stritch whose tensions with members of the Grail

---

courses. Once again, such a list reveals the close collaboration which existed between the liturgical and social apostolates of that period.

[179] Ibid., 46–72.

have already been discussed. On 15 July 1944, Hillenbrand was removed as seminary rector and "promoted" to a pastorate at Sacred Heart Parish in Hubbard Woods, Illinois, only to be replaced by an older more traditional rector. Despite the conflicts, under Hillenbrand's leadership a new generation of socially conscious clergy was trained who then instilled that same vision in their parishes. This led some pastors to complain about the perspectives and critical opinions of their new associates.

What could have been an experience of failure and disappointment for Hillenbrand became a new challenge to implement on the parish level the ideals and principles of liturgy and social activism he had been teaching at the seminary. Everything he introduced in the parish regarding liturgical and social reform he did with a thorough catechesis beforehand. Within one year he introduced the dialog Mass, along with liturgical preaching at all the Masses on such topics as active participation in the liturgy and Catholic social teaching. Some parishioners gathered in the church at 6:00 a.m. during the week to pray Lauds together before going to work, and then again at 6:00 p.m., on their way home, for the celebration of Vespers. Hillenbrand began a parish music program and established a parish library to educate parishioners on ideas about the liturgy and the demands of social justice, the Mystical Body, lay apostles, CA, and the like. As a result, Sacred Heart was transformed into a model parish.

Through his life and ministry as a liturgical pioneer and social reformer, Hillenbrand challenged his hearers to work toward the elimination of injustice in the workplace, toward the elimination of racial prejudice, toward the restoration of married and family life, and toward responsible political stewardship. The 1943 national liturgical week focused directly upon the relationship of liturgy and society. Hillenbrand gave one of the talks, entitled "The Spirit of Sacrifice in Christianity." He said:

> We cannot be content merely to share in the renewal of Christ's death and resurrection but must bring the effects of it to society—into all of life, into all social relationships: to the Negro, therefore, who cannot find employment, whose housing is cruelly overcrowded, who cannot enter a Catholic school; to the sharecropper who, in the phrase of Pius XI, has no hope of ever obtaining a share in the land; to the workers who earn too little to rise from their proletarian condition to the security of owning property; to the dispossessed laboring masses of the empire-colonies and of the Far East, whose groans mount to heaven. As a case in point, the average industrial wage in India is only $60 a year; we need to remember this after the war. We must bring the effects of the altar to them. Christ died for all; all are beneficiaries of his justice and charity. We

sacrifice with Christ; all must be the beneficiaries of justice and charity at our hands.[180]

Hillenbrand concluded his remarks with a strong reference to the Mystical Body of Christ:

> The mystical body provides the compelling reason, the driving force to set things right. The Body is one, a living Whole. What one group suffers, all suffer—whether that be the politically enslaved in the South Seas, the economically exploited in Bolivia, the starving in China, the racially disenfranchised at home. We must see Christ in all His members, and at the same time remember all men are destined to be His members. We must have a deep, intimate, living conviction of it. And we will acquire that conviction at Mass, where we are one at Sacrifice![181]

Hillenbrand often spoke of racial prejudice as a concrete example of where American Catholics were called to unite their liturgical participation with social activism: to work against racial injustice, to recognize black Americans as brothers and sisters and respond directly to their needs. He put into practice the social justice he advocated.

CONCLUSION

Several interesting points emerge in this chapter. First, German Catholics in the United States were central to the promotion of a socially conscious liturgical renewal. The liturgical movement would have looked very different indeed, had German Catholics not arrived on American shores. It was German or German-American pioneers like Hellriegel and Michel who promoted the doctrine of the Mystical Body as integrative to liturgy and life. It was German or German-American pioneers like Reinhold and Hillenbrand who spoke out forcefully for social activism that was grounded in the Church's liturgical life. It was German organizations like the Catholic Verein which were the first to initiate Catholic social outreach in the United States. The German contribution cannot be underestimated.

Second, Chicago was a center for much of this activity. The Liturgical Conference was founded in Chicago and the first liturgical week took place there in 1940. Catholic Action (CA), the Young Christian Workers (YCW), the Christian Family Movement (CFM), the Grail, the

---

[180] Hillenbrand, "The Spirit of Sacrifice in Christian Society: Statement of Principle," in *National Liturgical Week 1943* (Ferdinand, Ind.: The Liturgical Conference, 1944) 106.

[181] Ibid., 108.

St. Benet's Bookshop (to be discussed in the next chapter), the Vernacular Society were all centered within the Archdiocese of Chicago. The Catholic Worker (CW) and Friendship House (FH) soon found a home, as well. Reynold Hillenbrand rightly deserves credit for Chicago's leading role in American Catholic liturgical and social activism, but Chicago's centrality was not only because of Hillenbrand. Although liturgists and social activists like Dan Cantwell, Jack Egan, Pat and Patty Crowley, Bernard Laukemper, Ed Marciniak, Joseph Morrison, Sara Benedicta O'Neill, Nina Polcyn, and John K. Ross-Duggan were influenced directly or indirectly by Hillenbrand, they made very significant contributions on their own. Together, these Chicago Catholics formed a network that extended far beyond the shores of Lake Michigan.

Third, the liturgically-based social activism discussed in this chapter was largely private initiative, with little or no help offered from the supposed leadership. These activists had to solicit funding for their own projects, and publicize their own events. This was grassroots social activism.

The liturgical pioneers and promoters saw the relationship between liturgy and social concern as absolutely fundamental to the future success of the movement: liturgical renewal which did not connect to real life was a dead issue. They consistently promoted a strong social consciousness, even to the point of personal suffering on their part. More to the point, liturgical participation that failed to address the needs of the weaker members of the Mystical Body of Christ was no participation at all. In reflecting on the beginnings of the American liturgical movement, H. A. Reinhold wrote:

> The same men and women who beg for more vernacular, who strive for sanctity through a more intense living in the sacramental world of the liturgy and through their ascetic efforts, must be the ones who do not only give alms—person to person or in drives—but who help unions, sit on employers' councils and housing committees, in interracial groups and Catholic Action centers, who campaign for medical services for the strata that cannot afford them, who oppose demagoguery and injustice to the freedoms needed by man, and make the cause of enslaved nations a matter of their own heart.[182]

The liturgical movement needed the multi-faceted social action movement for the credibility of its own message. The social movement, in turn, needed the liturgical movement for spiritual grounding and direction. John Egan remarks:

[182] Reinhold, *The Dynamics of Liturgy*, 19.

. . . what the best of the social activists taught us was what the best of the pastoral liturgists practiced: that the primary object of our concern must be the *whole* person, the person considered not merely as a statistical victim of systemic injustice or even as merely a subject of the Church's sacraments; but the person in their whole existence, with a personal history and a world of relationships all their own.[183]

These movements, then, shared a profound interdependence.[184] While there are many interesting facets to the liturgical movement in the United States, it was precisely its social consciousness that became its hallmark when viewed from other parts of the world. The issues that surfaced were peculiarly American, thus a peculiarly American liturgical agenda emerged and developed—one which incorporated those principles. And the fundamental principle that grounded the American movement, and likewise linked it to other movements within the Church, both domestic and international, was the doctrine of the Mystical Body of Christ.

---

[183] Egan, 13.

[184] Egan believes that this was more the ideal than the norm, claiming that those who bridged the gap between the liturgical and social movements were relatively few. Many liturgical leaders missed the social justice aspect in their promotion of a liturgical revival, in Egan's estimation. Virgil Michel, H. A. Reinhold, and Reynold Hillenbrand were, of course, exceptions to this, in that they labored tirelessly for the integration of these two important dimensions of ecclesial life. Interview by author, 15 December 1994, De Paul University, Chicago.

CHAPTER FOUR

⁂

The Liturgical Movement and Education

INTRODUCTION

In the words of one writer: "The end of the liturgical movement is education toward the worship of God."[1] This was true enough, since that fundamental goal of full and active participation could only come about when American Catholics understood the nature and importance of their participation in the liturgical assembly. Resistance to change often stems from ignorance and a lack of information, rather than anything else. Thus, the way to encourage full and active liturgical participation was to educate, to catechize the people liturgically about their role as baptized members of the Church, and their responsibility within the Mystical Body. When one thinks of the American liturgical movement and education, one thinks of publications like *Orate Fratres;* of the celebrated liturgical weeks which gathered thousands of participants; of summer programs like those offered at Collegeville or Notre Dame. Liturgical catechesis in the 1930s and 40s, however, was far more expansive, emerging in elementary schools and bookstores, in home study groups and elsewhere. While this chapter will explore the more prominent means used by the liturgical pioneers and promoters for communicating their message, it will also examine other lesser known avenues of liturgical catechesis. In addition, we shall look at the relationship between the liturgical movement and catechetics, a relationship which had its own inherent tensions.

The chapter is divided into four primary sections: (1) tools used for liturgical education; (2) liturgical education in schools; (3) liturgical

---

[1] F. Arnold, "Liturgy in the School," *The Catholic Educator* 24 (1953–54) 169.

adult education; (4) the beginnings of academic programs in liturgy in the United States.

Virgil Michel and his colleagues believed that the liturgy itself was the fundamental formative instrument in bringing about change in Church and society—liturgy as the "basis of social regeneration." In other words, the best way to learn about the liturgy and liturgical participation, was to participate actively in its celebration. But the reformers were also aware that this participation was enhanced when it was informed; and if the movement was to have a lasting impact it needed to employ other media for communicating the message, for catechizing the people as to their participative role in the Mystical Body. While liturgy was the primary locus for such spiritual formation, a secondary formative and educative level was needed. As Christians were deprived of exercising their own baptismal priesthood in the liturgical assembly for centuries, so, too, were they deprived of a solid liturgical understanding. As Paul Marx has remarked:

> A study of the origins and development of the liturgical renaissance in any country will show that everywhere the obstacles are the same: ignorance of the people, lack of liturgical literature and properly trained teachers, and, not infrequently, clerical indifference and opposition.[2]

Liturgical education was recognized as an important forerunner to liturgical change. Some pioneers learned sooner than others that reform without preparing the people beforehand was absolutely futile. In the 1930s and 40s as in our own time, there were parish leaders who attempted to introduce liturgical changes without preparing parish members beforehand. At the second liturgical week, in 1941, a priest from Wisconsin made an intervention on that very point:

> Father Winzen in his paper stated that we shouldn't throw ourselves wildly into the liturgical movement; not to put the cart before the horse. Well, I am afraid that's the way I started in the liturgical movement. It was the result of a visit I made to England, where I became attracted to the liturgical movement in that country. Principally, I had seen some beautiful "liturgical" altars. When I came home I looked at our altar. It was a cheap one with a lot of niches on it that looked like "cracker boxes." I went around and raised some money, removed this altar and put in a beautiful "liturgical" altar. The people thought I was going Protestant, and the next thing I knew they had gone to the Bishop and told him so. The result of that was, the Bishop moved *me*.[3]

---

[2] Marx, 219.

[3] Intervention by Father Hodik, in *Proceedings: 1940 National Liturgical Week* (Newark: Benedictine Liturgical Conference, 1942) 80.

The speaker learned his lesson. In the next parish, he began by instructing the people about the liturgy, about the call to "full and active participation." Gradually the liturgy grew, and parish members began living that which they were professing. Liturgical renewal in that second parish involved the whole community in the process. The difference between the approaches used in the first and second parishes was remarkable. Education needed to be a crucial part of American liturgical renewal if the renewal was to have a lasting effect.

The American church was educated about the liturgy through periodicals and other texts, through study groups of lawyers or nurses and through formal courses, through radio broadcasting, and public speeches in such unlikely places as the Boston Common. The message was also communicated through bookstores and pamphlet racks in churches, through the social movements discussed in the previous chapter, through liturgical days and weeks. The medium of the message was rich and varied, drawing in people from many different facets of American church and society.

The Cultural Context:
American Catholic Education in the 1920s and 30s

As has already been mentioned, Catholics in the early part of the twentieth century came largely from immigrant groups, making higher education an impossibility for many. This began to change in the 1920s when the average rate of increase in enrollments at Catholic colleges each year was nineteen percent.[4] Forty-three percent of students attending Catholic colleges for women in 1930 were enrolled in institutions which had only opened their doors for the first time in that same decade. The growth in the American Catholic population was reflected in a tremendous increase in enrollment across the country, but also demanded some major changes in the running of those institutions, including the adoption of the credit-hour system, course offerings and electives, and institutional accreditation. These were new concepts in the 1920s.[5]

Catholic education was viewed as possessing many fine qualities that were lacking in other secular institutions—a sense of tradition, a way of appropriating and analyzing the events of life. What Catholic education needed, however, was a way of integrating these different

---

[4] In 1916, there were 8,304 full-time students enrolled in Catholic colleges; by 1950, that number jumped to 112,765. Dolan, *The American Catholic Experience*, 399.

[5] Philip Gleason, *Keeping the Faith: American Catholicism Past and Present* (Notre Dame: University of Notre Dame Press, 1987) 142.

elements. With the arrival of neoscholasticism in the 1920s, Scholastic philosophy became the bridge which was able to integrate and connect the various educative factors within Catholic academic circles.[6] This was so because Scholastic philosophy had always been closely identi-fied with Catholic faith and ideals, based, however, on reason rather than dogma. It was not surprising that in 1929, the Jesuit dean of the graduate school at Marquette University suggested that the teaching of Scholastic philosophy should take precedence over and above all other course offerings, with a view toward creating a truly Christian society in the United States.[7]

Religion as an academic subject, however, was only beginning in the 1920s. When one spoke of teaching religion in that period, it almost al-ways meant the catechism, unless, of course, one was a seminary stu-dent. John Montgomery Cooper, a professor at The Catholic University in Washington, D.C., in 1909, was probably the first to begin teaching the subject of religion as an academic discipline within American col-leges or universities. Even in the 1920s, professors were debating whether or not courses in religion were worthy of receiving academic credit. Many of these educators had been impressed and influenced by the example of John O'Hara, C.S.C., who as Prefect of Religion (and later president) at The University of Notre Dame, made the teaching of religion an evangelical campaign to promote frequent reception of Communion and growth in popular piety and religious devotions. In 1937, only three out of eighty-four Catholic colleges surveyed offered the possibility of an academic major in religion.

Cooper continued to develop a more pastorally-oriented, pragmatic approach to religion, writing catechetical materials for use in the class-room. He argued that college religion needed to differ from that which was taught in seminaries, become less dogmatic and abstract and more pastoral, inviting students to reflect on their lives and to appropriate what they were learning in light of their own experience. In such a way, Cooper was establishing the foundations for what would become the School of Religion and Religious Education at The Catholic Uni-versity.

Fulton J. Sheen, himself schooled in philosophy at Louvain, Bel-gium, integrated Cooper's technique with neoscholastic philosophy. Catholics, Sheen argued, needed to be educated in two worlds—the sacred and the secular—the world of the Church and the world of

---

[6] Although the Catholic Theological Society of America was not founded until 1945, the American Catholic Philosophical Association was established in 1926 and its journal, *The New Scholasticism,* soon followed in 1927.

[7] Gleason, 143.

secular society. This was necessary in order to bridge the gap between the two, and for Catholic laity to evangelize secular society where they lived and worked. In a 1929 address to the National Catholic Educational Association, entitled "Educating for a Catholic Renaissance," Sheen dynamically and enthusiastically presented his case, calling for an organic unity within society which could only be brought about through an integrated search for truth in the Catholic context. Already, one can begin to see some connection to the message of Virgil Michel and the other liturgical pioneers at roughly the same time. It is no surprise that Sheen chose the image of the Mystical Body of Christ as the integrative principle on which to base his plan. Sheen helped to popularize the Mystical Body doctrine for thousands of Catholics in the 1930s and 40s.

In 1939, the task of organic integration in Catholic institutions of higher learning reached a new level. In that year, the National Catholic Educational Association announced that theology rather than neoscholastic philosophy was to be the integrative discipline in Catholic higher education. This was the first time that teaching theology to undergraduates had ever been suggested in the United States.

An immediate problem arose as to how theology might best be taught. The key figures in the debate were Gerald B. Phelan, director of the Pontifical Institute of Medieval Studies in Toronto, and Francis J. Connell, C.SS.R., of the Redemptorist seminary in Esopus, New York (later at The Catholic University of America). Phelan made the distinction between religion and theology as "the science of divine faith," while Connell argued more in terms of apologetics—preparing students to witness to their faith through an emphasis on the Mystical Body and Catholic Action. Despite his emphases, Connell did include dogmatic and moral theology as areas to be included in college theology courses. John Courtney Murray, S.J., then responded to the two by presenting his "Necessary Adjustments to Overcome Practical Difficulties." Murray called for a total reform of theology, since seminary theology focused on "the demonstrability of truth from the revealed Word of God," while what college students needed was something far more pragmatic: "the liveability of the Word of God." Murray suggested that what was needed was a more fundamental theology that was "wholly oriented toward life."[8]

John Courtney Murray was right. Catholics were, in general, deprived of such "liveability of the Word of God." While it is true that the catechism was known by many, the experience of many Catholics remained a matter of catechism questions and answers, laws to be

[8] Gleason, 146–7.

observed, commands to be followed. This was true whether the issue was liturgical participation or decisions that needed to be made in daily life. Weekly confession, with its focus on the individual and his or her behavior, became a way to clear one's record and start over again, but a deeper understanding of the corporate demands of Christian faith was neither encouraged nor understood. While preaching often assisted many Protestant congregations in this endeavor, this was not the case in Catholic circles. One non-Catholic observer offered the following comment:

> The sermon is of minor importance in the Catholic Sunday morning service or Mass. It is usually no more than eight to ten minutes in length. It is prefaced by the priest's reading of a selection from the Scriptures. Usually the reading is rapid and sometimes intoned almost as if it were liturgy. The Scripture reading is seldom used as a basis for development of the sermon. The sermons are usually straight, rational expositions of doctrine with much less general use than the Protestant pastors employ of devices to interest and persuade (such as illustrations, narrative, dramatic figures of speech, personal witness). The role of the priest in the service is primarily that of performance of the ritual, not of instruction.[9]

There was much work to be done in the area of Catholic theological, liturgical, catechetical, and biblical formation. When we consider the educative and catechetical work of the liturgical pioneers and promoters, they were not alone in calling for something new. Indeed, the American church itself was undergoing something of a transformation in other areas of ecclesial renewal. Theology was just beginning to come into its own as a unique and integrative discipline, as a way of viewing life and the world. Just as liturgy for many Catholics signified rubrics, obligation, and something divorced from daily life, so, too, were religion and theology identified strictly and solely with the catechism. The call for an informed liturgical awareness, then, did not happen in a vacuum, but in union with other calls for a new understanding of what it meant to be American and Catholic.

American Catholic historian Jay Dolan has described the relationship of the liturgical movement to the theological, biblical, and catechetical renewal which took place within the United States, in this way:

> The basis for liturgical renewal was a new theology of the Church . . . It was a more biblical, less institutional, type of theology, which emphasized the spiritual nature of Catholicism. Its focus was Jesus Christ, not the saints; its chief prayer was the Mass, not the novena; it encouraged

---

[9] Dolan, *The American Catholic Experience,* 392.

a social spirit, rather than individualism; it sought to foster community, rather than isolation; it stressed the public quality of religion, not the private.[10]

It follows naturally that these pioneers in the different areas of Church renewal—biblical, liturgical, and catechetical—recognized that they shared a common, fundamental task of renewal within the American church. Of course, such an integrated vision was not shared by everyone. Some theologians called for an integrative theology while failing to see liturgy as part of the same piece, while some liturgists focused strictly on the renewal of Christian worship and ignored other important facets of American ecclesial life. "Tunnel-vision" is not a problem endemic to our own time.

Reformers like Virgil Michel, William Busch, Gerald Ellard, Hans Reinhold, and numerous others, however, caught the vision and lived that integration in their own lives and work. An interdisciplinary consciousness on their part gave added credibility to their instruction. Michel had a doctorate in philosophy as well as a background in education. He served as Dean of Studies at St. John's, in addition to his liturgical pursuits. The scope of Michel's correspondence demonstrates his varied competencies. One finds extensive correspondence between Michel and Mortimer Adler at the University of Chicago regarding plans for the Great Books Program. There was correspondence with the University of Chicago philosopher, Richard McKeon. In 1937, there was also extensive correspondence with Theodore Vermilye and The Church Unity Octave Council in New York regarding the possible organization of an Anglican-Roman Catholic Dialogue in the United States. Such diverse interests clearly enhanced Michel's role as liturgical educator and helped him to bridge many gaps. Busch was a seminary professor, and with his proficiency in languages was able to translate the best materials coming out of Europe for an American public. Ellard was a trained theologian and seminary professor, and was, by far, the scholar among the group. Reinhold was an educator, and bridged many gaps between theory and praxis, popularizing many of the more scholarly materials through his writings in *Orate Fratres*. As a team of liturgical educators committed to full ecclesial renewal within the United States, these colleagues exemplified the very Mystical Body which they were promoting. The weakness of one was the strength of another. Together, in pooling their creative resources, the message was communicated and the movement grew.

---

[10] Ibid., 389.

Tools for Liturgical Education

Michel, Busch, Ellard, and other colleagues knew well that their biggest obstacle to initiating a liturgical revival within the American church was a serious lack of quality printed material on the liturgy. There were books and pamphlets available on the Mass and other sacraments, but they tended to be devotional in style and over-emphasize an individualistic piety. Already in Europe, there were some fine publications being released, primarily in German and French, which would do a great deal to help the cause if only they were translated and made available to American Catholics. Moreover, the pioneers recognized the importance of communicating their own message. It would not be enough simply to translate books written in Germany, Belgium, France, or Austria. There was a need for their own publishing to communicate the richness of the Church's liturgical heritage in a peculiarly American way, addressing the pastoral issues germane to the United States. The pioneers immediately began writing and publishing their work to make texts available for the liturgical education of American Catholics. The primary project of the liturgical apostolate was the founding of an American liturgical periodical, *Orate Fratres*.

Orate Fratres

Jay Dolan has rightly called *OF* "the bible of the liturgical movement."[11] Virgil Michel often said that the greatest obstacle to liturgical renewal in the United States was misinformation. There was an obvious need for liturgical instruction in order to correct misunderstandings and assist the movement's growth. *OF* grew out of such a need. Founded in 1926, the magazine became a major vehicle for the promotion of the ideals and goals inherent within the liturgical apostolate.

In a letter sent to *America* which appeared in the edition of 25 April 1925, Gerald Ellard asked: "Why not an American Journal of Liturgical Studies?"[12] Ellard's letter received much attention and stirred a great deal of enthusiasm. It was not until Christmas of that year, however, that Ellard met Virgil Michel for the first time with Martin Hellriegel at O'Fallon, Missouri.[13] It was at that Christmas meeting where plans for

---

[11] Dolan, *The American Catholic Experience,* 389.

[12] Gerald Ellard, "Open Up the Liturgy," *America* 33 (25 April 1925) 37.

[13] Ellard learned of Michel through Hellriegel, and of his plan to begin a national liturgical periodical. He wrote Michel to express delight at the news and to offer publicity in the pages of *America,* since that journal was "eager to get liturgical matter of all sorts." Ellard wrote: "What has definitely been decided upon for the pub-

the journal were seriously discussed and *OF* was launched. Even prior to Ellard's piece in *America*, William Busch had written a number of articles on the liturgy in *America* and *The Commonweal*, and especially in *The Catholic Bulletin*, the weekly paper of the Archdiocese of St. Paul, calling for a liturgical movement. And Michel, of course, was already dreaming of similar possibilities upon his return from Europe.

It is important to remember that Michel's desire was to spend his life primarily in the field of philosophy. Thus, he envisioned his own role in the liturgical apostolate as one who would perhaps initiate the project, but then assist from the sidelines. Regarding the journal, he was afraid that if *OF* were published at Collegeville, the bulk of the burden would fall upon him. So he asked Abbot Alcuin to assign a number of monks to the apostolate. He wrote over a third of the first volume of the magazine, and composed the first three publications of the Popular Liturgical Library. The abbot appointed him the first director of The Liturgical Press as well as its chief financial officer. Michel had virtually no experience in any of these areas so he had to learn quickly.

In presenting the plans for *OF,* he wrote:

> The review we are planning is not to be merely Benedictine in tone or scope. It will devote itself entirely to the liturgical movement, both theoretically and practically envisaged. Our editorial staff includes eleven persons outside of the monastery (one of these also a Benedictine) all but one or two of whom have for some time been well acquainted with the liturgical movements in Europe. We expect to launch the review with the beginning of the next ecclesiastical year . . .[14]

The foreword to *OF* laid out, even more clearly, the goals and objectives of this pioneer liturgical periodical:

> Our general aim is to develop a better understanding of the spiritual import of the liturgy . . . We are not aiming at a cold scholastic interest in the liturgy of the Church, but at an interest that is more thoroughly intimate, that seizes upon the entire person . . . affect[s] both the individual spiritual life of the Catholic and the corporate life of the natural social units of the Church, the parishes, so properly called the cells of the corporate organism which is the entire living Church, the mystic body of Christ.[15]

---

lication? A monthly, bimonthly, quarterly, or what sort of publication? To what class of people will it make its most direct appeal? Has a name been chosen for the organ? Is the ground being prepared in any positive way for its reception?" Letter of 5 November 1925. SJAA: Z-24.

[14] Marx, 110.

[15] "Foreword," *OF* 1 (1927) 1–2.

As for the title of the journal, that was addressed in the first volume:

> "How did you come to choose that title?" The question has been asked
> repeatedly of the organizers of *Orate Fratres*. Taken literally, it has no sat-
> isfactory answer. The title simply suggested itself without forewarning
> the moment the idea of a liturgical review was accepted. But reflection
> confirmed the appropriateness of the title, for the words of the "Orate
> Fratres" prayer of the Mass, exhortation and response together, are a re-
> markable summary of the liturgy and of the ideas behind the liturgical
> apostolate.[16]

Michel was convinced that if the American church leaders could be
reached, taught, and influenced, then the message would be effectively
communicated to the rest of the Church. So, the magazine was initially
aimed at clergy and religious, seminarians and the more educated
laity—all those who were in a position to influence others. It was designed to combine sound scholarship within a pragmatic, pastoral
framework which would become a hallmark of the American movement. It endeavored to keep readers informed not only of liturgical activities and developments in the United States, but throughout the whole
world. In that first volume, Michel wrote: "its invitation is extended to
all Catholics of whatever rank, to cooperate in the liturgical apostolate
by whatever means lie within the possibility of the individuals."[17]

Despite Michel's desire to use the journal as a means of influencing
the right people, it was not initially easy to make the right contacts.
The only commercial advertising which took place was the sending of
15,000 letters to clergy. Progress was slow and it took great effort simply to convince those in positions of leadership that such a liturgical
journal was worth supporting.[18] Nonetheless, the magazine continued

---

[16] "Editor's Corner," *OF* 1 (1927) 90.

[17] "Editor's Corner," Ibid., 29.

[18] Donald Attwater, Michel's counterpart on the other side of the Atlantic, shared
similar frustrations in England, where his own efforts at liturgical writing were not
always well-received: "At the end of twelve months the 'Catholic Times' stopped
my monthly liturgical article, alleging that the two columns were wanted for
'news.' I thought this might be a tactful way of telling me that they did not like my
contributions; but no: no other liturgical matter has taken its place." In responding
directly to the problem of expanding the *OF* readership, Attwater continued: "Certainly 1650 subscriptions to 'O.F.' cannot be anywhere near enough, but I quite appreciate that a chief difficulty is getting at the right people. Doubtless this can be
done only by judicious advertising, as I suppose the United States is (are?) too huge
for circularizing to be practicable short of a million dollar capital!" Letter to Virgil
Michel, All Saints Day, 1927. SJAA: Z-22.

to take shape and its existence soon came to be applauded throughout North America and beyond.[19] While beginning with only 800 subscribers in 1926, mostly from the middle and far west, that number doubled in one year to 1,680 subscribers, of which 1,531 were paid at a rate of $2.00 per year. The magazine grew to 4,000 in 1938, and to 10,000 subscribers by the mid-1950s.[20] On the occasion of its twenty-fifth anniversary in 1951, Godfrey Diekmann orchestrated a subscription campaign to raise the number to 5,000. By the end of that calendar year, in November 1951, subscriptions totalled 5,400. By October 1953, subscriptions had risen to 7,300, and in June 1954, the total reached 8,884.

It was not uncommon for the *OF* editors to receive letters commenting on the value of the magazine as a tool in promoting the liturgical movement on the local level.[21] At the Catholic Junior College in Grand Rapids, Michigan, the Catholic Action study group even used the journal as a text for studying the liturgy, with a series of corresponding discussion questions drawn up by the leader.[22] Despite the extensive publicity directing the magazine to a clerical audience, there were a surprising number of lay people among those early subscribers. In fact, it was often an embarrassment to some leaders within the movement that lay members of the Church responded with far greater interest and enthusiasm than their clergy. Thus, in numerous places throughout the United States, it became the task of parishioners and

[19] Records reveal that between March 1928 and September 1930, over 10,000 sample copies of the magazine were sent to priests and bishops throughout the country. Religious communities and diocesan staffs were consulted as to how the journal might be expanded and improved. By 1929, the journal, along with other publications of The Liturgical Press, were being received in twenty-nine different countries. Monks of St. John's Abbey, "The Liturgical Press" (unpublished manuscript, n.d.), SJAA: F-20, 3–4.

[20] In 1941, Godfrey Diekmann noted that forty-five per cent of subscribers were clergy; thirty-five per cent were religious; and twenty per cent were laity. Hughes, *The Monk's Tale*, 116.

[21] One priest wrote: "When I first saw a copy of *Orate Fratres,* something like eight years ago, the liturgy meant little more than rubrics, and the mystical body had no practical meaning for me, although (I am now ashamed to say it) I had previously studied and taught the *Summa* of St. Thomas Aquinas. There are without doubt many others whose experience has been similar to mine. I have profited greatly from your review. I hope my people have profited likewise from the inspiration and guidance that *Orate Fratres* has given me." (Rev.) S., "Comments on the Tenth Anniversary of *Orate Fratres,*" *OF* 11 (1937) 138.

[22] See Burton Confrey, "Using *Orate Fratres* to Introduce the Liturgical Movement," *OF* 6 (1932) 175–81.

other lay activists to educate the clergy as to the importance of the liturgical movement and to instruct their pastors in the principles which the liturgical pioneers were promoting.

As the editors learned of the interests and needs of their readership, the magazine's format evolved and was adapted accordingly. The early years of *Orate Fratres* focused largely upon the restoration of the assembly's active participation in the liturgy through sound catechesis. This was attended to in greater detail with editorials and articles which addressed lay spirituality and Church doctrine as revealed through liturgical texts, the role and meaning of symbols, the liturgical calendar, a return to scriptural and patristic texts as legitimate sources of intelligent participation, and the promotion of liturgical hymns and chants.

The first change in format came in 1930. This included an overall expansion of the magazine, along with the inclusion of additional departments. A more significant change came in 1935, when the entire focus of *OF* took on a more socially-oriented direction and consciousness.[23] This reflected Virgil Michel's own growth in social awareness, aided in no small part by his several years spent on the Chippewa reservation in northern Minnesota. The inclusion of the social dimension within worship developed in union with other issues of liturgical reform, like advocating use of the vernacular; evening Masses; celebration of the Eucharist facing the assembly; the size and placement of the altar; and the participation of the laity in the Liturgy of the Hours.

Part of the magazine's expansion included the introduction of a new section entitled "The Apostolate," which was initiated to deal pragmatically with those concrete issues of pastoral practice and liturgical reform. Michel explained that while the movement in Europe had made great progress on the theoretical level, it was less effective on the pastoral level. Through "The Apostolate," and indeed, through the entire journal, the editors hoped to have a serious impact in effecting pastoral change lest the American movement be left solely in the realm of theory.

While we now accept and recognize the importance of approaching liturgics and liturgical renewal in an interdisciplinary manner, this

---

[23] Michel wrote: "As firmly as we were convinced nine years ago of the claims we made for the spiritual importance of the liturgical movement, so firmly are we now convinced also of the following wider views: 1) unless there is a Christian cultural revival, Christian dominion of the world will yield more and more to the neo-pagan . . .; 2) a genuine liturgical revival must result also in a Christian cultural revival; 3) no cultural revival is Christian unless it is animated by and flows from the liturgical spirit." "Nine Years After," *OF* 10 (1936) 5–6.

would have been considered a radical concept in the early years of this century. Nonetheless, Virgil Michel was convinced that the future of the liturgical movement depended largely upon its openness to those other disciplines within ecclesial and the wider social life which were in relationship to Christian ritual. *OF* broke new ground in insisting that the magazine was to be interdisciplinary, in that it was to address those other important areas which were relative to the liturgy:

> Our hopes, indeed, do not exclude other aspects of the liturgy, all of which may combine and should combine to emphasize its essential function in the spiritual life. Many and varied interests meet in the liturgy. The latter is a great mine of the widest cultural life. There are the literary, musical, artistic, historical, even ethnological and archeological aspects, all of which are worth fostering, and all of which are replete with interest and value in life.[24]

Unlike other church periodicals which maintained the "status quo," *OF* remained on the "cutting edge" of American church life in the 1930s and 1940s. In this way it differed substantially from other journals such as *The Ecclesiastical Review* or the *Homiletic and Pastoral Review*. Its articles were often controversial, particularly the "Timely Tracts" of H. A. Reinhold, as letters representing many different sides of the spectrum indicate.[25]

Under Godfrey Diekmann's editorship, the name of the magazine was changed to *Worship*, on the occasion of its twenty-fifth anniversary. Basically, those involved in staffing and editing the magazine found it rather ironic that a periodical that was seriously pushing vernacular in the liturgy was doing so under a Latin title, so they made the move, but not without a few fireworks in the process. Several went so far as to cancel their subscriptions. Others simply wrote the editor in protest. The problem was two-fold. First, the shift to an English title clearly suggested a very determined position on the vernacular issue

---

[24] Marx, 124.

[25] One letter which Godfrey Diekmann and H. A. Reinhold especially enjoyed, stated the following: "I hope your publication will stop publication. It has become a medium for unwise purveyors of thought, especially dark-age monks, and mouthing nuns, who would do more good to stay in their cloisters and say their prayers, instead of trying to introduce novelties to confound the lay people." "Disgusted," Letter to Editor (1943) (SJAA: #1166). Diekmann wrote to Reinhold: "Enclosed copy of a letter received today. I would love to publish it just as it is, including mistakes—provided you and Gerald Ellard, both honored by the attack, give your approval . . . that 'dark-age monks, and mouthing nuns' one is delicious." Letter to H. A. Reinhold, 4 October 1943. Ibid.

on the part of the editorial staff. Since the *OF* readership was not in complete agreement on the issue, such a clear endorsement of the vernacular was viewed by some as problematic. Secondly, the word "worship" was considered a Protestant term. Catholics did not talk about worship. They spoke about Mass, or the sacraments, or making a novena, but never about "worship." The title was too ecumenical as far as some were concerned. One reader wrote:

> To the Editor: Don't change the name. That's not the trouble—make your articles factual and realistic instead of dreamy and wishy-washy. Emphasize the Latin—leave the women and the vernacular alone—they are not and should not be in the picture.[26]

With twenty five-years of experience and ever-increasing notoriety throughout the United States, *Worship* remained an important educative tool in American liturgical renewal.[27]

The Liturgical Press

Michel's plan, which was conceived during his European sojourn, was to develop a "Popular Liturgical Library" requiring the translation into English and the publication of some of the best European liturgical classics in a popularized, pamphlet form. He wrote to Abbot Alcuin:

> Just think how it would help to transform the mentality towards the liturgy at home, not to think of the possible providential work that lies before us in the whole English-speaking world.[28]

Although some Catholic publishers at the time had published occasional liturgically-related texts, there were not yet any serious liturgical publishers in existence. And although *OF* could fill some of that void with the publishing of liturgical articles (even lengthy articles which appeared in a series of divided parts), there was still a need for a center that would facilitate the publication of longer and more classical liturgical texts from the great European liturgical masters.

---

[26] "Communications," *OF* 25 (1951) 474.

[27] Edited by Diekmann and designed by Frank Kacmarcik, the journal won the Catholic Press Association award for the best-edited publication in both 1951 and 1952. In 1953, Kacmarcik completely re-designed the layout and format of the magazine, and in 1954, *Worship* was named one of the "Catholic Magazines of Distinction," ranked fifth among all periodicals. Editor, "The Apostolate," *Worship* 28 (1954) 377–8.

[28] Letter of 18 January 1925. Quoted in Marx, 37.

St. John's already had a printing press which the monastery had inherited from the *St. Cloud Tribune* when it was terminated in January 1889. This included a complete set of type, three presses and other accessories. Nonetheless, the press was small and it was unrealistic to anticipate any large production of liturgical publications with such a limited operation. Given the situation, Michel asked Joseph Matt of St. Paul, Minnesota, for help. Matt was the publisher of the large German weekly *Der Wanderer* and was helped by the monks of St. John's in establishing his own paper. Matt's facilities were under-utilized. Although quite an extensive press with the most modern equipment, Matt's operation printed nothing more than *Der Wanderer* and its weekly English equivalent. Michel asked Matt to include *OF* and the pamphlets of the Popular Liturgical Library as part of the printing responsibility of the Wanderer Press and Matt agreed. Thus, in April 1926, The Liturgical Press began its work.

In April 1926, even before the release of the first issue of *OF*, the Wanderer Printing Company had delivered 5,000 copies of the first publication, *Offeramus*, a manual for the dialog Mass. In July of that same year, 3,000 copies of Romano Guardini's *The Spirit of the Liturgy* arrived with the help of another printing company in St. Paul, McGill and Warner. By the 1st of August, 2,000 copies of Lambert Beauduin's *Liturgy: The Life of the Church* were ready for distribution. Michel's fear about the uncertainty of the publishing enterprise caused him to be initially cautious in the number of copies that were printed. *The Gift of Life* (Rite of Baptism) was published in June 1927, followed by *Seal of the Spirit* (Confirmation) in October. The *Funeral Mass and Burial Service* was published in June 1928. These ritual texts, printed by the Wanderer, appeared in pamphlet form and were sold for 10 to 15 cents each.

The beginnings of The Liturgical Press were not easy. The only means of advertising available was the back cover of *OF*. Total sales for the 1926–27 fiscal year were $5,076, representing a loss of $440. The first time that The Liturgical Press made any profit whatsoever was in the fiscal year 1930–1931, when their volume of business increased to $12,200. The financial losses can be explained, at least in part, by the fact that inventory was not taken, and, as would be expected, sales were not able to match printing costs in that early period of operation. Further, in an effort to make the published materials available to as wide an audience as possible, Michel and his colleagues desired to sell the pamphlets as cheaply as possible. They were more interested in promoting the liturgical movement than in making a profit.[29]

---

[29] "The Liturgical Press," 1–3.

Those early years of The Press, then, were limited to the publication of *OF*, the Popular Liturgical Library, and *Sponsa Regis* (later *Sisters Today*), and did not expand into the publication of books. In fact, in 1937, when Michel finished his text, *The Liturgy of the Church*,[30] it was published by the Macmillan Company in New York. The first book-publishing venture of The Press came in that same year, ironically, with the publication of Abbot Alcuin Deutsch's *Manual For Oblates of St. Benedict*. Due to the peculiar nature of such a monastic text, it was agreed that it would best be handled by a monastic publishing house. A second book was published two years later, Ulrich Beste's *Introducio In Codicem*, a thousand-page text on Canon Law. In both cases, the printing was done by the Abbey Press of St. Meinrad, Indiana. When those two texts appeared, the name "St. John's Abbey Press" was used to distinguish the material from liturgical works. Such a distinction was continued for a number of years until all was subsumed under The Liturgical Press in the 1950s. With the successful publishing of a thousand-page work like the *Introducio*, a number of monks at St. John's agreed that they were capable of expanding their efforts at book publishing. The abbot was less convinced, however. He acknowledged the presence of a number of other American Catholic publishers, such as Bruce publishers, P. J. Kenedy and Sons, and Sheed and Ward, just to name a few, and he did not want to compete with what was already in existence since some of those publishers were themselves struggling. Furthermore, he felt that The Press should remain small since many of the monks at St. John's were already over-extended.

While Virgil Michel served as director of The Press in those early years, the business management of the operation was delegated to a number of monks, especially Dunstan Tucker, Roger Schoenbechler, and Rembert Bulzarik. Bulzarik had been in the printing business before he entered the monastery and brought well-established business management skills to his work. With such a background, Bulzarik was a key figure in the expansion and future success of The Press. He had the kind of shrewd business sense that Virgil Michel lacked. While supporting the efforts of the liturgical movement, he argued that The Press should not go bankrupt in the name of promoting liturgical renewal. With such convictions, Bulzarik kept The Press afloat and tempered Michel's idealism with the facts and figures of the publishing

---

[30] The book was a collection of a series of lectures which Michel had given at the Pius X School of Liturgical Music, New York City, in the summer of 1936. Michel wrote in the foreword: "They (the lectures) are therefore popular in presentation and content, and are in no way the product of expert liturgical knowledge, of which I am quite innocent." *The Liturgy of the Church* (New York: Macmillan Co., 1938).

business. With Michel's death in 1938, Godfrey Diekmann took over as director. Since Diekmann had already worked very closely with Michel in the work of The Press, along with the continuing business skills of Rembert Bulzarik, the transition was natural and The Press continued to flourish.

Despite Abbot Deutsch's reluctance to expand The Press into book publishing, he agreed to allow the publishing of the *Short Breviary* in 1941. This became a milestone for the future liturgical publishing of the monastery. Despite its cost and limited appeal, the book sold over 25,000 copies. The publishing of that text became the definitive turning point that The Press would no longer deal strictly in pamphlets, but would now include books as well. Evidently, the success of the *Short Breviary* convinced the abbot that such efforts by The Liturgical Press were fulfilling a need which was not being met by other Catholic publishers—the publishing of materials and the making available of texts that were firmly devoted to the renewal of liturgy within the American church.

With the development and growth of the liturgical movement in the United States came the expansion of The Liturgical Press. With a growth in gross income from $35,000 in 1942–43, to $67,000 in 1946–47, profits continued to increase. Under the leadership of Ronald Roloff, another monk at St. John's, The Liturgical Press building was erected in the summer of 1951. A second development under Roloff's direction was a drastic improvement in the artistic and textual quality of what was being produced. With the arrival of Frank Kacmarcik in 1950 to become a member of the faculty at St. John's University, came a distinctively more professional and artistic design to the publications of The Press. This was not only the case with the covers of *OF* or *Worship*, which Kacmarcik continues to design, but with all the other books published at Collegeville, as well. It was also at Roloff's suggestion that Latin titles previously employed by texts of The Liturgical Press began to be changed to English. A newer edition of *Offeramus* was changed to *Our Mass*, which included a Kacmarcik cover and a text printed in red and black. This was the first time that a Latin title had been changed in favor of English—a change which yielded very favorable results.

As the liturgical movement continued to make an impact on American ecclesial life, and as The Press grew in fame, the Wanderer Printing Company could no longer compete with the large orders being requested for such texts as *Offeramus* and *Gift of Life*. In 1946, the printing of *Offeramus* ran to 40,000 copies while there was demand for 120,000 copies of the baptismal text, *Gift of Life*. Thus, The Liturgical Press entered into a new business partnership with the Webb Publishing Company of St. Paul, Minnesota. And with the increased *OF* readership and *Sponsa Regis,* new printers were sought for those journals. North Central Publishers took over the printing of the new *Worship* in September 1952, while Sentinel Publishers of St. Cloud, Minnesota, assumed responsibility for the printing of *Sponsa Regis.* All was eventually subsumed by the Sentinel Publishing House. To this day, *Worship* continues to be published by Sentinel Publishers. In the fiscal year 1952–53, The Press more than doubled its income from the preceding year.[31]

Other Liturgical Publications

Even though *OF* was the primary journal of the liturgical movement, there were other journals which educated American Catholics about the liturgical renewal taking place throughout the whole Church and particularly in the United States. *Liturgical Arts,* founded in 1931, addressed issues of liturgical art, architecture, and music. This will be discussed in the next chapter. *Altar and Home* was founded in 1933 at Conception Abbey, Missouri. Already in the 1920s, the monastery at Conception was becoming known as a center of monastic liturgical revival under the leadership of Patrick Cummins, O.S.B. Cummins was greatly influenced by Michel, as the extensive correspondence in the Virgil Michel papers at St. John's Abbey indicate. Cummins received encouragement from Michel as well, especially when he encountered a less than positive reception from his confrères at Conception in introducing the dialog Mass in 1926. Michel had intended to initiate a more popularized version of *OF* in the 1920s. That dream, while not fulfilled by Michel himself, was fulfilled through the efforts of the monks at Conception Abbey. Under the leadership of Raymond Meyerpeter, O.S.B., *Altar and Home* was initiated as a popular liturgical weekly for the family. The magazine was first edited by Henry Huber, O.S.B., and given its strong liturgical emphasis through the contributions of Bede Scholz, O.S.B. The title of the journal was recommended by Bonaventure Hirner, O.S.B.[32] *Altar and Home* was directed to the kind of average Catholic audience that a more scholarly periodical like

---

[31] "The Liturgical Press," 5–11.

[32] Cummins encouraged the abbot at Conception to send Bonaventure Hirner and Bede Scholz to Collegeville for their theological studies. Both were influenced by Michel, especially Scholz. When Michel recognized Scholz's keen interest in the liturgy, he took Scholz on as a type of protégé, instructing him in liturgics and keeping him informed regarding the efforts of the liturgical movement. Scholz brought this expertise back to his monastery in 1930 and became a strong force in liturgical developments at Conception Abbey. Marx, 149.

OF was unable to reach. The goals were the same: to encourage full and active liturgical participation on the part of the whole Church. The ways of communicating those goals, however, were simplified, providing a more pastoral and pragmatic approach. Concretely, this journal attempted to bridge the gap between the Sunday liturgical assembly and domestic life.

The *Catholic Art Quarterly* was founded in 1937, assisting teachers of art in the Catholic school system. Although this journal had less of a liturgical focus than *Liturgical Arts,* liturgical concerns are evident in many of the numbers of that journal. The lesser known *Living Parish* was founded in 1940, and sought to address peculiarly parochial concerns regarding liturgical renewal.

Liturgical Catechesis Through The Catholic and Secular Media

Early in the history of the liturgical movement, mass media was employed to assist the educative efforts of the liturgical pioneers. Many Catholic periodicals around the country began including a regular section on liturgical renewal. This was often the case with diocesan newspapers, depending on the local ordinary. If the bishop was favorably disposed toward the liturgical movement, then the newspaper of that diocese was more likely to carry articles on issues of liturgical reform, either to educate the people liturgically, or simply to keep them informed of developments within the movement. *The Davenport Messenger,* for example, stands out as a Catholic paper which gave extensive coverage to liturgical interests over the years.

Coverage was not limited to Catholic periodicals. In those years, as is often the case with newspapers today such as *The Los Angeles Times, The New York Times,* or *The Washington Post,* there was one day of the week set aside for coverage of "religion." Depending on the newspaper and the geographical location, certain papers covered liturgical developments, as well. Radio broadcasting offered another avenue of liturgical education. Whether in newspapers or on the radio, coverage was due, at least in part, to the influence of prominent members of the Catholic laity who had themselves become involved in the workings of the liturgical movement. Arthur T. O'Leary was one such layman. He was president of the Catholic Laymen's League of Orange and Rockland Counties, New York, when he wrote to Virgil Michel in 1938. In that letter, he noted that for three years he had been responsible for providing material for the Catholic feature of the church page that appeared each Saturday in the five daily secular papers of those two counties. There was no charge for printing the weekly piece in any of the five papers. Having already addressed issues of Catholic education and rural life, he wrote of his plans for a complete series of fifty-two weeks on liturgical renewal:

> If this can be put over in the manner in which I plan, I don't have to tell you of the prospect that it opens up for the Liturgical Movement. I don't know whether it would be evolutionary or revolutionary, but in any event it would certainly be in keeping with the present cockeyed world if we were permitted to establish a precedent for the propagation of the Liturgical Movement at the expense of and through the business acumen of the secular press.[33]

O'Leary wrote Michel seeking advice on how best to present the material. He saw great value in the use of the secular media to promote the liturgical movement:

> I am convinced that these secular channels, which reach about one hundred thirty thousand readers in communities where Catholics are one in six, are available, and can be successfully used to educate our own Catholic people on the Mass, provided, of course, the subject is presented in quite a different fashion from that to which we are accustomed in books or publications outside of those of your own Order or group. In these counties, I suppose that no more than one Catholic in a hundred reads any Catholic publication. From my own experience of at least eight years with various groups in the city and in the country, I know that the subject can be made a popular one. I believe that it can be done through these newspapers.[34]

O'Leary was a good strategist. He recognized the influence of the secular press upon American Catholics and the potential for using such a medium in the task of liturgical renewal. In many respects, O'Leary typified the kind of "lay apostle" Virgil Michel was looking for. Michel and the other liturgical pioneers knew well that the future of the liturgical movement would only be successful to the extent that "lay apostles" were set on fire with the spirit of that same mission to become, themselves, promoters of full and active participation in the liturgy. Only in that way would the message of liturgical renewal gain credibility, not only in convents and seminaries, but at the very grassroots level of the American church.

---

[33] Letter to Virgil Michel, 11 July 1938, SJAA: Z-26. The plan for the series included sections on "a) Sacrifice; b) Priesthood; c) Mystical Body of Christ, i.e. corporate aspects of Christianity-Holy Communion and unity; d) The True Significance of the Mass; e) The Laity and Loss of Active Sharing in the Mass; f) The Mass Structure; g) The Prayers of the Mass; h) The Church's Prayers Outside the Mass and the Church's Year; i) Externals of the Mass."

[34] Ibid.

Radio broadcasting was also utilized as a means of communicating the message. Vincent C. Donovan, O.P., gave a series of fifteen minute talks on the Mystical Body and the liturgy in 1929, on WLWL, Brooklyn, New York. A brief musical interlude followed Donovan's presentations, after which the speaker returned to the microphone to respond to questions called in from listeners. In 1930, the Boston Catholic Truth Society Radio Hour ran a series of commentaries on liturgical renewal. In that same year, a Benedictine of St. Mary's Abbey, Newark, delivered a series of short talks on the liturgical movement aired during the Paulist Radio Hour and heard throughout the New York metropolitan area. Another liturgical series was aired over WIP in Philadelphia.[35]

As Michel encouraged those with whom he ministered in the northern Minnesota Chippewa community to appropriate the mission and catechize their peers, so too in the liturgical movement. Use of the media encouraged such shared responsibility. Like the goal of full and active liturgical participation, the catechetical task of liturgical renewal was to be a cooperative effort, embodying that same principle. And if this cooperative venture of liturgical education was to reach the whole spectrum of the American church, then catechetical efforts could not be limited only to adult circles, but needed to be included in the formative education of the young as well, since they too were called to share in the same apostleship. As a result, a series of catechetical texts were developed as a way of promoting the ideals of the liturgical movement from the earliest years of a child's formation. It is to these texts that we now turn.

The Christ Life Series

The impact of *OF* along with publications of the Popular Liturgical Library was significant, not only among clergy and interested laity, but also among communities of religious women whose primary mission was that of education. Inspired by such publications, two of those women, Estelle Hackett, O.P., and Jane Marie Murray, O.P., began to imagine the possibilities of a liturgically-based religious education. In March 1929, they travelled from Marywood, the Dominican motherhouse in Grand Rapids, Michigan, to Collegeville, to consult Virgil Michel about how best to initiate such a liturgical formation among children in grade school. The meeting proved to be important, and a welcome response to Michel's own desires to develop a more integrated approach to religious education. Michel knew that such integration

---

[35] Letters of F. Benedict to Virgil Michel, 26 October and 5 December, 1929. SJAA: Z-22.

did not come about through the memorization of answers to questions in the catechism, as was the standard religious pedagogy of the time. If the religious, psychological, emotional life of the child was to mature in a healthy and balanced way, something new needed to emerge—attention to aesthetics and to symbol, and to the concrete application of religious truths in light of human experience. He wrote:

> Think now, to what pains the catechist must go to illustrate the myster-ies of our holy faith in such a matter that the child-mind can sufficiently grasp them, and then reflect on the treasury of picturesque symbolism in the liturgy, which is the plastic presentation of all dogma, our faith in word and deed! Would not our catechism lessons become a living and vital everyday experience, if they were built up on the daily or familiar liturgical acts, if the supernatural truths were taught as caught from the prayers and rites of the Church?[36]

Michel, Hackett, and Murray agreed that a new type of integrative text was needed for the teaching of religious education, based on the liturgical year. Michel, with his predictable determination, told the sis-ters to return to their rooms after that first meeting, and to compose the first lesson of that new text which they would then critique together when they met the next morning. The result was a five-part series, en-titled *With Mother Church*. These five small liturgically-based texts were "laboratory manuals," intended to be used in conjunction with catechisms on the elementary and high school levels.

Through the dedicated efforts of Hackett and Murray, religious edu-cation on the primary and secondary levels began to include a grow-ing sensitivity to issues within the liturgical movement as well. But just as Michel's efforts would have been difficult if not impossible without the support of an abbot like Alcuin Deutsch, those Dominican women were encouraged in their pursuits because they were fortunate to have a superior like Eveline Mackey, O.P. Under Mackey's leader-ship, the Dominicans at Marywood caught the liturgical spirit early in the movement's history. In a 1929 letter read in all convents, Mackey wrote:

> In the name of the Divine Victim of the Holy Sacrifice of the Mass, I beg you to take up the teaching of the Liturgy at once. Use as a text our new Laboratory Manuals in Religion called WITH MOTHER CHURCH. En-courage each of your pupils to have his own book . . . In order to help the teachers to do this work to the best advantage, I wish that the Prin-cipals of schools would subscribe for ORATE FRATRES, and all the

---

[36] "Editor's Corner," *OF* 3 (1928) 157–8.

Sisters become familiar with the Daily Missal. The Motherhouse will assist you in every way possible.[37]

To assist the promotion of such a liturgical spirit in Marywood schools, Mackey sent sixteen Dominicans to the first liturgical summer school at Collegeville that same year.

The response to *With Mother Church* was enthusiastic. It soon became clear, however, that such manuals were hardly sufficient. While they helped in raising some liturgical issues or in calling attention to various liturgical elements, feasts, and seasons, they failed to deal substantively with the fundamental issues of liturgical renewal. Further, these two catechetical pioneers soon realized that many of the Dominicans who were assigned the task of teaching religious education were largely unaware of the liturgical movement and its precepts. More work was needed, perhaps a whole new series of texts—not a laboratory manual, but a textbook for each grade which would integrate liturgy with religious education. While Hackett and Murray agreed that *With Mother Church* was insufficient, they considered themselves theologically incapable of writing a much larger textbook series for each grade. When they told Michel that such a series would better be written by a priest, Michel insisted that the work be done by them.[38]

In October 1929, encouraged by their Benedictine colleague who served as editor of the series, Hackett and Murray began a two-fold project of writing their texts. The fundamental task would be *The Christ Life Series* for the primary grades, and *The Christian Religion Series* for high school students. The latter was to be a secondary project and, in fact, did not emerge until after Michel's death. The content was to be a combination of catechetical doctrine, biblical history, and liturgy, including art and music. The primary supposition was that the liturgy itself was the fundamental locus for religious education and that Christ was the primary teacher. This relationship between the liturgy as formative and religious instruction in the classroom was addressed in a statement of purpose, composed to promote use of the series:

> . . . the religion course should have a solid liturgical basis. More than that, the liturgy must be the very fibre of its being. The liturgy is not merely a phase of religious instruction; it is the life of Christ in His Church; it is the glorious triumphant Christ teaching and sanctifying His

---

[37] Letter of 3 September 1929, SJAA: Z-22.
[38] Marx, 153.

members who are of good will. It is through the sacred liturgy that Christ instructs and transforms souls into Himself. The work of the teacher in religion, then, is to bring children to a conscious participation in the sacred liturgy, wherein Christ Himself teaches and sanctifies them.[39]

Pedagogically, the method utilized questions, assignments, and projects, and was designed to encourage the living out of one's baptism through personal involvement on the part of the child, attempting to demonstrate the relationship between religious faith and the rest of life.[40] Before actually publishing the series, the texts were used experimentally as a pilot project in a number of Catholic grade schools throughout the United States.[41]

While initially applauding *The Christ Life Series* as something new and creative, many who used the texts considered them far too advanced for their students. Indeed, there were some who considered the texts too advanced for the faculty as well. Part of the problem was that an entirely new pedagogical method was being introduced for which the teachers were largely unprepared. A more basic problem was that, quite simply, many found the material in the texts too abstract, with long sentences and concepts too difficult to grasp. As a result, the series had to be reworked and rewritten numerous times. By April 1937, only 45,515 of the 159,490 copies printed had been sold, and the total sales were not much greater than 100,000 books.[42]

---

[39] "Fundamental Character and Purpose of the Christ-Life Series" (unpublished manuscript) SJAA: Z-29. This relationship between a formative liturgy and religious instruction in the classroom surfaced some tensions as the liturgical movement matured, primarily between liturgists and catechists. There were some liturgical pioneers who believed that if Christians of all ages were included in the liturgy, then the liturgy offered sufficient religious instruction in itself, and there was little need for catechetics. Gerard Sloyan, Telephone interview by author, 2 January 1995.

[40] Michel, "Advantages of the Christ-Life Series," Memo to the Macmillan Company, 26 Jan 1934, SJAA: Z-22, 6.

[41] One school which experimented with the texts was The Convent of the Sacred Heart in Grosse Point Farms, Michigan. Because the series was so well-received, a summer institute was organized at Grosse Point Farms (17 June–3 July 1935), featuring Michel, Hackett, and Murray as faculty. Three courses were offered: 1) Life in Christ; 2) The Christ Life Series; and 3) The Teaching of Religion. Participants received two college credits for each thirty-hour course. There was a charge of $12.00 for each course and an additional fee of $7.00 per week for those who chose to reside at the Convent. SJAA: Z-22.

[42] Marx, 237.

William Busch once made the comment that the series arrived twenty years too early. This may have been true on a number of levels. When the books were being written, Hackett and Murray were just becoming involved with the liturgical movement themselves. Although they were dedicated to liturgical renewal and were convinced of the potentially integrative role that liturgy could play in religious education, they were just beginning to understand that link between liturgy and religious education in those early years. A similar series would have looked much different twenty or thirty years later, with all the benefits of trial and error that were part of the liturgical movement's history. Today, *The Christ Life Series* is often held up as a very successful liturgically-based catechetical series. Those who speak so glowingly of the Series, however, have not studied its contents very carefully. Closer examination reveals that despite its references to liturgical feasts and seasons, despite its liturgical illustrations, the liturgy fails to be a unifying force in the work. Gradually, Jane Marie Murray grew in her own liturgical understanding, became increasingly involved in the liturgical movement in the 1940s and eventually a board member of the Liturgical Conference.

Despite its flaws, *The Christ Life Series* was a first step towards the integration of liturgy and religious education. Its primary contribution was in opening the door for future work on the relationship between liturgy and catechetics. Our discussion now moves from educational texts in primary schools to texts on the collegiate level, with Ellard's more successful *Christian Life and Worship*.

Christian Life and Worship

The first liturgical textbook to appear on the collegiate level was Gerald Ellard's *Christian Life and Worship*, published in 1933 by the Bruce Publishing Company of Milwaukee and reprinted in 1934, 1940, and 1950. The book, designed by the Catholic Worker artist, Adé Bethune, contained twenty-seven chapters, along with an extensive bibliography. In addition, a short reading list was included at the end of each chapter. Besides treating historical and theological aspects of the Eucharist and the other sacraments, along with the Liturgy of the Hours, the text also treated the Bible, the basic tenets of Christianity, and issues within the American liturgical movement. The book was hailed by the general editor as "marking a new era of liturgical studies in our colleges."[43] It was not intended to be the definitive word in

---

[43] Joseph Husslein, "Preface By The General Editor," in Gerald Ellard, *Christian Life and Worship*, (Milwaukee: Bruce Publishing Co., 1950) vii.

liturgical collegiate studies, but seen, rather, as a first step in the publishing of other liturgical textbooks. As the greatest scholar of the American liturgical movement, Ellard put the best of his skills to work in the writing of *Christian Life and Worship*. The book was grounded and developed on the principle of the Mystical Body of Christ. Ellard relied heavily on patristic sources, citing numerous liturgical texts and other documents of the early Church.

The fact that *Christian Life and Worship* was printed in four editions suggests something of its popularity as a college text, although it was also recommended and occasionally used with adults in liturgical study groups. That book, however, was not without its flaws. With the early editions of the book, both students and professors complained that the text was unmanageable, especially the early chapters. Ellard accepted the criticisms and worked at making his text more intelligible. The early editions of *Christian Life and Worship* also contained a number of historical inaccuracies. These too, Ellard corrected. In fact, for the 1950 edition, he completely revised and enlarged the entire text, responding to written criticisms he had received over the previous seventeen years, and to his own critique of the book. In his preface to the 1950 revised edition, Ellard noted that a national survey of college religion texts ranked *Christian Life and Worship* third out of one hundred texts on the college and university level. A Minnesota college department of religious studies even organized itself under the title of the book.[44] Ellard's widely used text knew no rival on the collegiate level and college religion departments supporting the liturgical movement favored the Ellard text over all others.

Liturgical Education in Schools

With a growing liturgical consciousness emerging in the 1930s throughout the United States, liturgical pioneers and promoters labored to instill that same liturgical awareness in Catholic students of all ages and academic disciplines. As we shall see, the introduction of liturgics into academic institutions took various shapes. It was occasionally included in religion courses and even then, its format differed tremendously from place to place. There was a notable difference among those school administrators and faculty members who were regular subscribers to *Orate Fratres*. In most cases, those who were aware of the work being done at Collegeville and elsewhere focused on the more significant liturgical issues: baptismal priesthood in the Mystical Body of Christ, full and active liturgical participation, and the

---

[44] Ibid., xv–xvi.

relationship between liturgy and Catholic Action. In other cases, the focus was on rubrics and externals. This section begins with a consideration of liturgical catechesis on the primary level.

The issue of liturgical catechesis in primary schools received a good deal of attention early on in the liturgical movement's history. After all, children were potentially future promoters of the liturgical movement. In writing of the liturgical sense inherent within the early Church, one teacher remarked that children had been robbed of such an awareness as the liturgy gradually became more and more the property of the clergy. She wrote: "To religious instructors, therefore, belongs the task of attempting to reestablish this *liturgical consciousness.*"[45] In 1931, religious educator Peter Resch wrote:

> No amount of detail is spared to lead our youth to an early acquaintance with the history, liturgy, art, rubrics, theology, etc. of the Holy Sacrifice. Grade pupils now learn some of the intricacies of the ordo and the Church calendar, practice psalmody and Gregorian chant, are made to appreciate the art of altar and sanctuary building and vestment structure, are introduced into the deeper mystic signification of the ceremonies and so forth.[46]

Resch's enthusiastic description of one school was hardly expressive of the norm throughout the rest of the United States. Some liturgical pioneers argued that too many religious educators were using the liturgy as a subsidiary of the catechism, rather than as the basis upon which all theological doctrine was founded. In 1926, one religious educator addressed the unfortunate subordination of liturgy to catechetical instruction:

> The liturgy . . . has very little connection with the rest of the curriculum . . . Very much of the trouble is due to our inclination to regard the liturgy as a means of explaining the catechism rather than as the basis upon which the teaching of the catechism should be founded. The liturgy is supernatural experience which, together with the natural experience of everyday living, should be the starting point of religious education.[47]

[45] M. Bernarda, "The Liturgy Taught Through Formal Discussion," *The Catholic Educator* 18 (1947–48) 244. The writer argued for a more socially-oriented pedagogy when teaching liturgy in elementary schools, since the liturgy itself was fundamentally social in character.

[46] Peter Resch, "On Teaching How to 'Pray the Mass,'" *Journal of Religious Instruction* 2 (1931–32) 12. Resch suggested that despite the quantity of such liturgical information, a more qualitative unity was lacking.

[47] George Johnson, "The Liturgy as a Form of Educational Experience," *Catholic Educational Review* 24 (1926) 529.

The simple memorization of liturgical data in catechism format was found to be a very inadequate means of promoting a liturgical awareness in the classroom.[48] Liturgy itself was its own best liturgical educator. While the catechism over-emphasized the rational, intellectual powers of understanding and memory, liturgy had a far greater formative power with its appeal to the emotions, the senses, and the will. In a 1930 presentation to a conference of elementary school teachers, religious educator Joseph Kempf made his own plea based on Augustine and the practice of the early Church:

> St. Augustine wrote of the use of liturgical actions which accompany instruction, and we still have a remnant of the old practice in the ceremonies of Holy Week and of Baptism . . . It is a long time between St. Augustine and Pope Pius XI but all the time the Church has urged the liturgy for religious training. As a matter of fact, before catechisms were put in the hands of the faithful, the liturgy was the principal means of training in religion.[49]

In Kempf's estimation, liturgy's appeal to the senses and the emotions was precisely its richness, in that it was able to reach the depths of human experience far more profoundly than the catechism-based approach with its limited appeal only to the intellect. Kempf admitted that feelings and emotions were often looked upon with suspicion, but that such suspicion was due, in large part, to a confusion between sentimentalism and genuine affective religious experience. True worship of God was only complete when the Church prayed with the full use of all the senses:

> Service with our whole heart, our whole soul, our whole mind, and our whole strength. Merely intellectual considerations leave us cold, whereas an added appeal to the emotions stirs us to action.[50]

Thus, teaching liturgy strictly as a matter of questions to be memorized and soon forgotten was not the answer. If, indeed, the liturgy did make an appeal to the senses, to the emotions, and to the will of the assembly, then it needed to find a permanent place in the teaching of religion, where those senses, emotions, and will would be stirred into service. In calling for liturgy as a means of religious education—for religious instruction in and through the liturgy—Kempf was not arguing

---

[48] See Editorial, "What Is Wrong With Our Teaching of the Mass," *Journal of Religious Instruction* 13 (1942–43) 323–5.

[49] Joseph Kempf, "The Place of the Liturgy in the Teaching of Religion," *Journal of Religious Instruction* 1 (1931) 138–9.

[50] Ibid., 140.

for the abolition of the catechism, but rather that the catechism find its foundation in the liturgy.[51]

Like the evident fragmentation between faith and daily life, the same fragmentation could be observed in religious education of the 1930s. The separation between the teaching of religion and the living out of one's faith in daily life could best be remedied by a return to the liturgy as the unifying force between human and religious experience:

> Much of what we do as religious teachers has been written on the water
> . . . If we seek an explanation, we might discover that the divorce which
> exists between the teaching of the faith and the living of the faith, be-
> tween the religion lesson and daily experience, suggests one of the main
> reasons. I am now advocating the liturgy as the best channel of making
> religious doctrine bear down upon life . . . The divorce between the the-
> ory and practice of religion is healed by the liturgy . . . Before the era of
> the catechism, the people learned their theology by praying and living
> with the Church. The liturgy was then the catechism, the theology of the
> people, and it remains today the most striking, most widespread, most
> popular, and most easily understood witness of our faith.[52]

Thus, an important goal of liturgical catechesis was the promotion of liturgical living, where in understanding the social nature of the liturgy the student came to appreciate the social nature of Christianity.[53] Liturgical catechesis was crucial to make the distinction between personal and corporate prayer, lest students view the liturgy as another type of personal devotion where an individual prayed for her or his own needs and forgot the whole body of Christ. The key to an integrated religious instruction was the Mystical Body of Christ.[54]

---

[51] In the words of Damasus Winzen: "Christian doctrine and the sacraments belong together. Doctrine without the sacraments is empty. Sacraments without doctrine become mechanical." "The Liturgical Movement and the Confraternity of Christian Doctrine," *Journal of Religious Instruction* 12 (1941–42) 567.

[52] John T. McMahon, "Suggested Liturgical Program for Schools I: Stemming the Leakage," *Catholic Educational Review* 29 (1931) 451–4. See also McMahon, "Suggested Liturgical Program for Schools II: The Mass is the Center," *Catholic Educational Review*, 513–26.

[53] See Theresa A. Doyle, "The Teaching Sister and the Liturgical Front," *Journal of Religious Instruction* 14 (1943–44) 211–19.

[54] See U. Alfred, "The Liturgy and Catholic Education," *Journal of Religious Instruction* 16 (1945–46) 625–6; see also Louis Putz, "The Need for Developing in the Pupil An Awareness of His Role in the Mystical Body," *National Catholic Educational Proceedings* 51 (1954) 426–31.

In a 1936 address to participants in the Missouri Catholic Educational Conference, Martin Hellriegel offered his audience some concrete suggestions for the promotion of liturgical living among their students, beginning with the Mystical Body. This doctrine needed to be presented in a concrete, simplified way to help students understand that membership in Christ's Mystical Body was foundational for liturgical participation. Other suggestions included the need to provide a thorough explanation of the Mass; teaching students how to use the Missal; encouraging corporate participation in the Eucharist through the *Missa recitata;* the restoration of a principal Sunday parish Eucharist, along with the restoration of Sunday Vespers or Compline; a thorough study of the liturgical year; teaching about the key relationship between liturgy and daily life, particularly life in the home—a type of liturgical spirituality.[55] Under Hellriegel's direction, Holy Cross Parish Elementary School in St. Louis was nationally known for its impressive liturgical curriculum. Parents and some of the faculty began expressing their concern, however, that while the children were well-versed in Gregorian chant and in the feasts and seasons of the liturgical year, they were less trained in the fundamentals of mathematics and grammar.

Tensions were not limited to Hellriegel's parish in St. Louis. Throughout the country, liturgists and catechists argued about how best to catechize American Catholics of all ages. Some believed that the goal was to impart knowledge, providing history and facts. The problem with such an approach, however, was that too often the externals of the liturgy became the focus while ignoring the internal action of participating in the Mystical Body of Christ. In such situations, the divorce between liturgy and life continued.

For Virgil Michel, teaching liturgy was not about imparting such knowledge but far more significantly, about leading students to a deeper understanding and appreciation of their own role as baptized members of Christ's Mystical Body, and therefore as worthy participants in the eucharistic assembly. The externals were merely expressions of the internal. Attention to the externals risked becoming knowledge for knowledge's sake, whereas true knowledge of the liturgy and liturgical participation could never be measured by facts and figures.[56] Michel appealed for a return to an integrated liturgical catechesis which emphasized quality rather than quantity:

---

[55] Martin Hellriegel, "The Spread of the Liturgical Movement," *Journal of Religious Instruction* 7 (1936–37) 213–4.

[56] This is well-demonstrated by an exchange of letters between Virgil Michel and Franklyn Kennedy, a newly-ordained priest at St. Rose Parish, Milwaukee, Wis-

What happens in concentrated form in the Mass when it is intelligently and wholeheartedly participated in must unfold itself in detail through all the moments of our life between Mass and Mass, regardless of whether we can attend the Sacrifice daily or only on Sundays. The Mass is at once cult, creed, and code—worship, dogma, and life—and no teaching of it that does not embrace it in its totality is in any sense adequate.[57]

It was the personal conviction and example of those doing the catechesis, their living the liturgy in daily life, which was as important as the material itself.[58] Even if the material were very well-presented, it would mean little to the students unless they were able to witness in the catechist that same desire to participate fully in the liturgy as a baptized member of the Mystical Body. Active participation was part of a teacher's preparation to effectively instruct the students in the liturgy.

In educating young students about the richness of the Church's liturgy and their own responsibility as active participants, they would themselves become "lay apostles" in promoting the liturgical movement among their families and friends. This would secure a more liturgically literate American church in the future. This was Virgil Michel's desire.

A 1929 survey on the teaching of liturgy in high school offers some interesting data on what was taking place within only a few years of the inception of the American liturgical movement. It polled a select number of high schools around the country, and the writer admitted that there were still many secondary schools which offered nothing on the liturgy in their curriculum. Despite that reality, the survey showed

---

consin. Kennedy was concerned about how best to teach the Mass to children of the fifth and sixth grades of the parish school, since the curriculum called for such a study. Kennedy wrote about how well the students had been trained in the liturgy: ". . . a fifth grader startled me by showing me precisely how the priest holds the chalice at Offertory—the proper height, position of the hands, and the like." Michel responded: "To teach the children by making them memorize the externals of the Mass seems to us (editors of *OF*) superfluous and starting at the wrong end. Because it does not enter into the heart of the matter." Letters of 16 September and 19 September 1929, SJAA: Z-22.

[57] Michel, "Adequate Preparation for Teaching the Mass," *Journal of Religious Instruction* 8 (1937–38) 596.

[58] ". . . The teacher's own personal living of the Mass in his or her life both in and out of church, is the most important factor, truly the *conditio sine qua non*, for proper teaching of the Mass. It is, therefore, also the most important element in a teacher's preparation." Ibid., 597. See also Michel, "Knowledge Requirement for Teaching the Mass," *Journal of Religious Instruction* 8 (1938) 765–70.

that two out of every three high schools polled were teaching liturgy. Eighteen of those schools had introduced liturgy as a separate course in the curriculum while others that responded affirmatively had incorporated liturgy into the teaching of religion. In all cases, teaching the Mass held the primacy of place in the course structure. Half of the schools polled were using the Latin-English Missal, usually the *St. Andrew Daily Missal,* as the textbook for that part of the course.

The survey did not limit its scope to the Mass. Other topics included the Liturgy of the Hours, sacraments, sacramentals, music, devotions, Christian symbolism, architecture, and the Church's ritual books. Those who organized the survey were surprised at the large number of institutions already attempting some treatment of the liturgy on the high school level. Those same results led the organizers to recommend a one-semester course on the liturgy in senior year of high school which could then be continued at the university level.[59]

High school teachers, like their colleagues on the primary level, often lamented the fact that they were unsure about how best to present liturgical material to their students. Their focus was almost exclusively on the Mass. Although the Catholic Action study clubs did address issues like the Liturgy of the Hours, this was less the case in the classroom. Teachers complained of a general lack of interest on the part of the students whom they taught. While, no doubt, such disinterest could be explained by sheer adolescence, it was also true that the language often employed to present liturgical material was stilted. It was abstract and overly pious, and failed to attract the average American teenager.

One of the biggest supports for the high school teaching of religion was Gerald Ellard. Even though Ellard's own work focused primarily on the college or university level, he also spent time teaching in Catholic Action summer schools where he encountered groups of adolescents who were exposed to the liturgical revival taking place in the United States. Moreover, Ellard addressed numerous teachers' conferences, offering strategies for more effective liturgical teaching. Ellard encouraged teachers to find ways of making the material concrete, and to simplify liturgical concepts.[60]

At one such conference, Ellard argued that the term "sacrifice" was problematic, in that it signified one thing in everyday usage and something quite different in the codified language of worship. In everyday

[59] Maurus Ohligslager, "An Investigation of the Teaching of Liturgy in Catholic High Schools," *Catholic School Interests* 8 (1929) 187–9.

[60] See Ellard, "What To Emphasize in Teaching The Mass," *Journal of Religious Instruction* 5 (1934–35) 11–6.

usage, sacrifice signified "giving up," as a negative self-privation, whereas in the language of worship, the same term was better and more positively described in terms of "giving." "The natural language of love," he wrote,

> is the sign-language of gift-giving. Love never feels that words can do it justice. So at all age-levels, at all cultural levels, the world over, human love calls to human love in the language of giving.[61]

Ellard spoke of love as mutuality, where the assembly gathered in worship offered the "sacrifice" to God together in love, and received the gifts of God in that same spirit. In the code of love, according to Ellard, the offering of food and drink signified the offering of oneself without limit or condition, "since food and drink are life's very sustenance."[62] With such examples, Ellard encouraged his hearers to think creatively so as to make the message of the liturgical renewal more acceptable.

In the late 1940s, Joseph Munier reported that the dialog Mass had been adopted in one form or other in high schools around the country, that students had often been well-trained in their vocal participation, that the Missal was frequently introduced in freshman year of high school with intensive training in its use, and that seniors were involved in preparing the altar and vestments for the Mass itself. Munier was concerned that too often these same high school students failed to grasp the deeper significance of their actions, of their corporate action as the Mystical Body of Christ. They were well-trained in the externals, but the central act of the worship itself managed to escape them. And they were not being challenged to live liturgically. Munier wrote of his experience on high school days of recollection:

> The students give a wonderful demonstration of vocal participation in the morning Mass, then react to the retreat talk on the central action of the Holy Sacrifice with complete surprise as though they were hearing a new idea.[63]

Munier expressed his concern about a recent survey of Catholic college students. The poll noted that the majority of college students who went to Mass did so only out of a sense of duty, and spoke of their own physical, albeit passive presence at Mass, but nothing more:

---

[61] Ellard, "Teaching the Mass in High School," *National Catholic Educational Association Proceedings* 38 (1941) 340.

[62] Ibid., 341.

[63] Joseph Munier, "The Catholic High-School Student and the Mass," *The Catholic Educator* 19 (1948–49) 107.

Not one student expressed or even suggested the conviction that he was there to offer with the priest the Body and Blood of Christ to His Heavenly Father. Some of these students were from secular high schools. All of us who are convinced that the Mass is the highest expression of religion, the necessity of our lives, the heart of the mystical body, must be deeply concerned and anxious to meet the problem.[64]

Aside from the formal classroom situation, there were other opportunities for liturgical catechesis on the high school level.[65] In the last chapter, we discussed the various branches of CA on all levels including high school. Those weekly study clubs and summer schools of CA contributed greatly to catechizing teenagers on the liturgical renewal, inviting their participation in the various projects of the liturgical movement. In general, greater liturgical interest was found among those who participated in extra-curricular activities. Those involved in movements like CA as high school students became animators of liturgical renewal when they moved on to college or university to continue their studies. It is to the efforts at liturgical education on the college level that we now turn.

When college and university students of the 1930s and 1940s became actively involved in the extra-curricular study and discussion of liturgy, working together and even teaching one another, the promotion of the liturgical movement and its principles enjoyed greater success. There was also the treatment of liturgy in the classroom, promoted by Ellard, Busch, Reinhold, Diekmann, and others, but the enthusiasm for those courses came from students' involvement in extra-curricular activities where together they grew to recognize their own role in the Mystical Body of Christ. This had obvious implications for a more dialogical, participative experience of worship when these students gathered for liturgical prayer.

In 1927, just after the founding of *OF* and The Liturgical Press, William Busch wrote Michel, telling of his course on the liturgy in St. Paul, Minnesota. The course was offered to sisters in the Teacher's College, and included a history of Christian worship with special attention to the catechumenate and the sacraments, as well as the Liturgy of the Hours and the liturgical year.[66] In that same year, at Marygrove

---

[64] Ibid.

[65] Occasionally, liturgists were invited to give a series of lectures on the liturgy, either to students, to teachers, or to both. Martin Hellriegel, for example, gave a number of lectures at St. Elizabeth Academy in St. Louis in 1928, where the *missa recitata* had just been introduced the previous fall. As noted in *Orate Fratres:* "All of the girls are using the *St. Andrew's Missal,* including a few Protestant girls who attend the Academy, and that on their own initiative." *OF* 3 (1928) 64.

[66] Letter to Virgil Michel, 21 October 1927, SJAA: Z-22.

College in Detroit, Michigan, courses in religion began to include some study of the history of liturgy, as well, although that study was limited to the Mass, aided by the use of missals. Students were encouraged to become promoters of the liturgical movement in their own parishes and on campus.[67]

In 1928, the National Catholic Alumni Federation took up the issue of the teaching of liturgy in colleges and universities. Edward Dore, president of the federation, consulted Virgil Michel about how this group of prominent Catholics might best assist the efforts of the liturgical movement on college campuses. At Michel's recommendation, they invited a certain Father Power to their convention on 21 April 1928 at the Waldorf Astoria Hotel in New York City to speak on the topic: "Liturgy in Catholic Colleges."[68]

A Holy Cross sister at St. Mary's College, Notre Dame, Indiana, wrote to Virgil Michel in 1930, noting that the liturgical movement had taken hold on that campus, both in the classroom and in extra-curricular study clubs devoted to the liturgy. Student enthusiasm with the liturgical projects on campus soon gained attention in St. Mary's monthly student publication, *The Chimes. Orate Fratres* was mentioned as a staple both in the classroom and in the study clubs.[69]

In 1934–1935, the University of Notre Dame held a series of informal evening lectures and discussions in one of the student dormitories, Walsh Hall, to help students to better understand the Mass. Eighty-one percent of the students at that university expressed the desire "to know the Mass as well as the priest." A number attributed their boredom and their disinterest in becoming more participative to the fact

---

[67] The school weekly, *The Watch Tower,* sponsored a series of essays on the liturgy. Essays focused primarily on the Mass and the liturgical year. Letter of Virgil Michel to Mary Judith, 3 April 1930, SJAA: Z-25.

[68] In that address, Power argued for the introduction of a course on "The Liturgy of the Church." Letters of Edward Dore to Virgil Michel, 7 February, 17 March, and 24 March, 1928, SJAA: Z-24.

[69] Letter of M. Benedictus to Virgil Michel, 3 March 1930, SJAA: Z-22. In 1932, Gerald Ellard reported that forty colleges and universities had introduced courses in the liturgy within the previous decade. He noted, however, that not all of the courses were reflective of the kind of issues which American liturgical pioneers were promoting. Some were still caught up in the externals and few reflected the "new style." By "new style," Ellard meant reference to the Mystical Body of Christ; the liturgical movement as a whole; the symbolic nature of liturgy; and the sacramental nature of Catholicism. Ellard, "The Liturgy Course in College: Its Present Content," *Journal of Religious Instruction* 3 (1932–33) 690–1, 695. See also Ellard, "The Liturgy Course: A Proposed Outline," *Journal of Religious Instruction* 3 (1932–33) 783–91.

that they failed to understand the true significance of the Mass. These gatherings held on campus gradually drew more interest from among the students. In addition, lectures on the liturgy were also given in theology courses; pamphlets on the liturgy were distributed on campus; the *Religious Bulletin* ran a nine-part series on the history of the Mass and its significance; and the Notre Dame Council of the Knights of Columbus undertook the task of popularizing the Missal on campus.[70] A number of students in two dormitories in particular, Walsh and Badin Halls, stated that the *Missa recitata* helped them in understanding the fuller significance of the Mass as the celebration of the whole Church.[71]

At roughly the same time, the Calvert Club of the University of Chicago, the Catholic organization on campus, was sparking interest in the liturgical movement on Chicago's south side, which led to their sponsoring a three-day symposium at the Lillie estate, near Wheeling, Illinois. While liturgy was not the only item on the agenda, it did figure prominently in the proceedings of that gathering. Aside from the symposium's academic component, there were a fair number of liturgical celebrations. In addition to celebrating Mass together, the group gathered together twice, for the celebration of midday prayer and then before retiring, night prayer. The educative component consisted of talks on the nature of liturgy and the work of the liturgical movement, along with talks on labor, science, and Christian marriage. Pamphlets were distributed to participants, informing them about the liturgical apostolate at Chicago's St. Benet's Bookshop, run by one of Chicago's leading pioneers at the time, Sara Benedicta O'Neill. Such interest was not uncommon on college campuses, and these smaller special-interest groups often had significant effect on the wider university community.[72]

Francis Cahill, a senior at Boston College in 1938, organized a small team of peers to travel around and talk about the liturgy to various groups on campus and throughout the Boston metropolitan area.[73]

---

[70] They donated $100 for the wholesale purchasing of missals which could, in turn, be sold to students for $1 each. Within six months, more than 800 missals were sold. These texts then became another tool in the project of liturgical education on campus. *Bulletin of the University of Notre Dame: Religious Survey of Undergraduates 1935–36* (Notre Dame: University of Notre Dame, 1936) 15–6.

[71] *Bulletin of the University of Notre Dame: Religious Survey of the Undergraduates 1937–38* (Notre Dame: University of Notre Dame, 1940) 13.

[72] "The Apostolate," *OF* 11 (1937) 518–9.

[73] Cahill wrote about their goals: ". . . to make engagements at almost every single Catholic College and high school around here. Then we will proceed to lec-

Cahill and his associates had read some of Virgil Michel's material and were so impressed that they decided to become liturgical promoters themselves. It was not an easy task, however. He wrote Michel of his frustration in promoting the liturgical movement in Boston: "It is very difficult to give you an idea of what a liturgical group is up against in this city." Cahill then proceeded to outline their plan for the lectures, which they had first to submit to Cardinal O'Connell for approval.[74] Michel advised the group and sent them a number of books and pamphlets to assist their efforts.

At St. Mary's College, Notre Dame, Indiana, and St. John's University, Collegeville, just to name two institutions, there were liturgical study clubs through the 1940s. At some schools, like Nazareth College, Nazareth, Michigan, the clubs called themselves "the Liturgy Commission," and chose texts to read together in the course of a year's study program. In 1944, the Nazareth group chose Von Hildebrand's *Liturgy and Personality*. One member presented a synopsis of the chapter to the group, highlighting key elements and raising some questions for consideration, followed by an open discussion.

Mercyhurst College, Erie, Pennsylvania, began its own study group at about the same time, centered on the history of the Mass and the promotion of liturgical participation on campus. Group participants held annual "missal drives." By 1944, ninety percent of students on campus owned their own Missal. The Mercyhurst group also initiated daily Compline on campus, and numbers of those attending increased greatly.[75]

Godfrey Diekmann developed a fairly elaborate program of liturgical formation on the college campus at St. John's in 1944. The schema was divided into sections on Eucharist, the college chaplain, the Catholic college curriculum and the liturgy, means for promoting the

---

ture at all the parishes. I intend to have an open forum after the lectures so the people can ask questions and I can then figure out just how much they know and how interested they are in the liturgy." Letter to Virgil Michel, 17 September 1938, SJAA: Z-23.

[74] The outline was divided by speaker. Following an introduction on the nature of liturgy and the purpose of the "liturgical team," as they called themselves, the first speaker addressed the essentials of Christian worship: prayer and sacrifice. The second speaker lectured on the mystical body of Christ. The third member of the team defined the liturgy, the liturgical year, and liturgy of the hours, and spoke about the efforts of the liturgical movement. The final speaker addressed issues of liturgy and ritual, and the social aspects of the liturgy. Ibid.

[75] "Liturgical Bulletin," 1:1 (October, 1944) St. John's University, Collegeville, Minn. SJAA: F-20, 1-2.

liturgical spirit on campus, and a general program to prepare students for future parish life. While the program was geared primarily to the students at Collegeville, it was endorsed by the Commission on the Liturgy of the National Federation of Catholic College Students, which gave its ideas a wider hearing in Catholic colleges around the country.[76] Several colleges worked at bridging the gap between college and adult education by offering a series of adult courses on the liturgy taught by college faculties. Such was the case with the Education for Leisure Program held at Rosary College, River Forest, Illinois. Courses met once a week for a series of ten weeks and there was no charge for the instruction. Topics in 1936–1937 included "Use of the Breviary," and "The Missal and the Liturgy."[77]

On occasion, liturgical study groups on college campuses invited prominent liturgical leaders to lecture on the revival taking place around the country. Algin Kuchera, chaplain at St. Paul's University Chapel, Madison, Wisconsin, invited H. A. Reinhold to lead a "liturgical week" on campus from 26–31 October 1940. There had already been a growing interest in learning more about the liturgy among students at the university, thanks to the efforts of a study group initiated by the chaplain. Kuchera believed that a leader like Reinhold would instill enthusiasm for the liturgical renewal by offering a series of lectures and discussions in the course of a week.[78]

The teaching of liturgy in seminaries meant the teaching of rubrics. Great emphasis was placed on the proper training of those who were preparing for diaconal and presbyteral ordination—proper, that is, in the sense of a rubrical correctness when presiding at a liturgical event. As early as 1920, Edwin Ryan presented a paper on "The Teaching of Liturgy in the Seminary," suggesting that the issue was far more significant than simply rubrics, and proposing serious liturgical study within seminary academic programs.[79] There were a good number of seminarians throughout the United States who did catch the liturgical spirit and became promoters of the movement. This was the case both in diocesan seminaries as well as in theologates of different religious

[76] Godfrey Diekmann and D. Hackert, "Liturgy On The College Campus," SJAA: F-20.

[77] "The Apostolate," *OF* 11 (1937) 229–30.

[78] Letter of H. A. Reinhold to Godfrey Diekmann, 16 August 1940, SJAA: #1166.

[79] Roger Schoenbechler, "Liturgy in our Seminaries: Some Practical Suggestions," in *National Catholic Educational Association Proceedings* 35 (1938) 578. See also Martin Hellriegel, "Liturgy and the Minor Seminaries," *National Catholic Educational Association Proceedings* 33 (1937) 550–6; John Ford, "Teaching Liturgy in the Seminary," *National Catholic Educational Association Proceedings* 44 (1947) 119–30.

orders. Those seminarians shared Ryan's call for liturgy's place within the seminary curriculum.[80] It took some time, however, to convince bishops and seminary rectors of such a value.[81]

Pioneer William Busch was himself a Church history professor at The St. Paul Seminary. He admitted that at his seminary, liturgical life and enthusiasm for the American liturgical revival among his students paled in comparison to the Benedictines at Collegeville. Despite the absence of liturgical courses there, the success of a liturgical study club was noted.[82]

In 1927, the Jesuit theology students at St. Louis University organized a liturgical seminar, including weekly meetings where Jesuit scholastics took turns at presenting papers on the liturgy, followed by discussion. In 1928, William Puetter, S.J., reported that topics for the seminar included the liturgical movement, the history of the Mass, the social nature of the liturgy in light of the Mystical Body of Christ, a comparison between the Oriental and Latin rites, the history and development of the liturgical year, and sacraments in the Mystical Body. The seminar then established a "liturgical bulletin board" in the community, where participants kept their Jesuit confrères updated on news of the liturgical movement and on particular aspects of the liturgical year (e.g., the stational churches in Lent). Hellriegel was cited as a key advisor to the group.[83]

Students at the Redemptorist seminary in Esopus, New York, inaugurated a "liturgical academy" in 1931, meeting each Saturday to hear lectures on the liturgy, followed by shorter talks applying the liturgy to particular aspects of daily life. Moreover, once a month, usually on Thursday evenings, members of the faculty made presentations on the relationship of liturgy to dogma, missions, preaching, and other areas. The work of the academy led to the publishing of a small in-house publication, *Dominus Vobiscum,* twenty pages in length and issued according to the liturgical seasons, where short articles appeared on different

---

[80] See Basil Stegmann, "Importance to Seminarians of the Present Liturgical Movement," *National Catholic Educational Association Proceedings* 29 (1932) 609–19.

[81] As early as 1928, the editors of The Liturgical Press sought to make contact with seminary faculties: "We would like to bring seminary students into closer contact with the Church's liturgy and can think of no better method than an appeal to the professors of liturgy." Letter to The Professor of Liturgy, Theological Seminary of St. Charles Borromeo, Overbrook, Philadelphia, PA, 1 September 1928, SJAA: Z-23.

[82] Letter to Virgil Michel, 17 October 1929, SJAA: Z-23.

[83] Letter to Virgil Michel, 3 March 1928, SJAA: Z-24.

aspects of the liturgical movement, along with editorials, and a "question box."[84]

The arrival of the liturgical movement at seminaries in the United States usually came through student initiative, explaining the early presence of liturgical study clubs in many of those institutions, while a formal recognition of liturgy as a serious academic discipline did not emerge until much later. A great deal depended upon the openness of the local bishop and the seminary rector. Hillenbrand's tenure as rector of the seminary at Mundelein offers the example of an outstanding exception. Students who studied theology during the Hillenbrand years at Mundelein were profoundly influenced as to the importance of the liturgical movement and overall liturgical renewal in American ecclesial life. There is a significant lack of information available on liturgical education in American seminaries during this period, probably because most seminaries continued to limit liturgics to the study of rubrics. The American Catholic presbyterate in the 1930s and 1940s would have looked very different, indeed, if there were more seminary rectors like Hillenbrand. Unfortunately, this was not the case.

Liturgical Adult Education

American Catholics responded to the liturgical movement in many different ways. Some responded with sheer disinterest or with suspicion. Others, however, were dissatisfied by the poor quality of liturgical celebrations in their own parishes, and were stirred by the possibility of something better. Liturgical education of adults offers, perhaps, the best example of the varied and creative form that liturgical catechesis took on the local level. Before exploring those examples, however, we look briefly at a fundamental principle which the liturgical leaders consistently held—the fundamentally formative character of the liturgy itself.

From the very beginning, leaders of the liturgical movement argued that liturgy, well-celebrated, was the best and most fundamental form of adult education which the Church could offer American Catholics:

> To many uninstructed Catholics the religious year is just a succession of Masses. We attended Mass last Sunday, and we shall go on attending Masses on Sundays and holidays. Year after year, we hear the "same old Mass." To too many Catholics this seems to be the fact. What a splendid opportunity there is to live anew with the whole Church the life of Christ . . . The educational instrumentalities of the Church are not con-

---

[84] Thomas Kelly, "Liturgical Academy at Esopus," *OF* 9 (1935) 426.

fined to the catechism and catechetical instruction . . . It has been re-marked that the one great cause of religious ignorance, if not the great-est cause, is the ignorance of the liturgy.[85]

Virgil Michel cautioned those who wanted to use the homily as a di-dactic tool for teaching about the liturgy, arguing that the liturgy itself held its own power to form and even instruct the Christian community in the Mystical Body. He suggested that the real challenge was to re-trieve the formative, instructional power of the liturgy, rather than to explain didactically liturgical symbols that were considered too weak to speak for themselves. He wrote to his confrère, Patrick Cummins, on this matter:

> The whole Mass of the Catechumens (second part of it) is instructional, yes, but that instruction is in the very Epistles and Gospels themselves . . . Practically, for our people, there may be no instruction except the homily—but that is due to the fact that the priests' praying of the Mass of the Catechumens means nothing to the people.[86]

While the liturgy itself was, in its essence, a school of Christian for-mation, many in the liturgical movement came to agree that preaching within the Mass offered a great opportunity for adult education. Such preaching was not limited to discussion of full and active liturgical participation, but also included the demands which this participation placed upon the community, thus making the connection between liturgy and daily life. One finds many reports of preaching on the liturgy itself. This was the case not only within the United States, but also in mission territories where Americans, influenced by such sources as *OF,* sought to promote the same renewal.[87] Parish missions in the liturgical seasons of Advent and Lent offered another opportu-nity to liturgically catechize American parishes.[88] Preaching on the

---

[85] Editorial, "The Liturgical Year and Adult Education," *The Catholic School Jour-nal* 30 (1930) 290–1.

[86] Letter to Patrick Cummins, O.S.B., 17 January 1928, SJAA: Z-24.

[87] One example comes from Eugene Bork, S.J., who worked at the Catholic Mis-sion in Punta Gorda, British Honduras. Bork wrote to Michel about his liturgical preaching at the mission. On Sundays, he preached three times on the Mass. Bork noted: "I see that it (the liturgical instruction) is also bringing new faces to the church among older people." Letter to Virgil Michel, 9 August 1929, SJAA: Z-22.

[88] For example, a series of five Lenten sermons, preached at St. Francis Xavier Church in St. Louis, by Joseph F. Kiefer, S.J., focused on membership in the Mysti-cal Body of Christ and its implications for the life of the community and the indi-vidual. "The Apostolate," *OF* 8 (1934) 329.

liturgy also was included in the format of preached retreats for religious.[89] Occasionally, bishops who were supporters of the liturgical
movement required liturgical instruction to be given in all parishes of
a given diocese during Sunday Mass.[90]

Like other aspects of the liturgical movement, study clubs did not
have an easy beginning. In 1927, Bernard Benson, a frequent correspondent with Virgil Michel and with the *OF* editors, expressed his
frustration with attempts at sustaining a liturgical study club in San
Francisco:

> I am strong for the study club idea, but it is a hard matter to interest
> people in it and even when one succeeds in that, it is something else
> again to get them to go to the library and dig up the material for pre-
> sentation. In my own little club which has dwindled to two others be-
> sides my wife and me, the whole burden falls on me. The Third Order of
> St. Francis is taking up the study of the Mass in the men's counsellors'
> meeting, starting this month. The Reverend Director doesn't expect to be
> able to get any number of men to prepare the material, but that remains
> to be seen.[91]

Despite those difficult beginnings, study clubs gradually yielded success as news of the liturgical movement spread within American
Catholic circles.

---

[89] In a letter to Virgil Michel, a Benedictine confrère from St. Mary's Abbey,
Newark, New Jersey, wrote about his own work in preaching retreats: "I try to give
one daily instruction on the liturgy . . . While endeavoring to give them a better
understanding of the liturgy . . . I have also tried to bring them to participate in it
more actively." Letter of F. Benedict, O.S.B., 1 November 1926, SJAA: Z-22.

[90] William A. Griffin, Bishop of Trenton, New Jersey, wrote a pastoral letter to this
effect: "The course of instructions . . . will begin on the first Sunday of October and
continue every Sunday thereafter for twelve or fourteen months. Even in large city
parishes with a close schedule of Sunday Masses, the regular announcements will
be sufficiently curtailed to allow for at least a ten- to twelve minute instruction at
each Mass . . . Assistance at Mass can be realized only in one way, namely, by
ACTIVE PARTICIPATION with the human priest and with Christ in the Holy
Sacrifice. Help to 'reestablish all things in Christ.' Be in very truth 'members of one
another.' Take a personally active part in offering the Mass . . . Save your private
devotions for other times . . . in assisting at Mass, prove to yourself and your
neighbor . . . that you are consciously exercising your great privilege of membership in the mystical body—our Holy Church." "Letter to the Beloved of the Clergy,
the Religious and the Laity, 24 September 1946." SJAA: #1163.

[91] Letter to Virgil Michel, 7 April 1927, SJAA: Z-22. Two years later, Benson reported that he was still having problems increasing interest and membership in his
study club, which dwindled to only five members. He wrote, however: "We are not

In 1934, The Liturgical Press published a study club outline for those groups wishing to learn more about the liturgy and the goals of the liturgical movement.[92] Volumes of *OF* between 1926 and through the 1940s, reveal a plethora of study clubs throughout the United States that chose to take up the issue of liturgical renewal. In most cases, these groups focused on other issues as well, but they decided that a given year or a series of months would be given over to liturgical study.[93] In other cases, clubs sponsored a lecture or series of lectures on behalf of the liturgy.[94]

Moreover, there were a number of professional societies which organized their own programs of liturgical education. In 1934, the Minneapolis-St. Paul chapter of the National Catholic Federation of Nurses formed a liturgical study club focused primarily on the Mass.[95] The Middle West Chapter of The National Catholic Alumni Federation held a series of forums on the liturgical movement.[96] In October, 1934, the Catholic Teacher's Institute held at Peoria, Illinois, a small liturgical institute. Led by Hellriegel, the entire program was devoted

---

discouraged for it is an idea that must grow, just like the idea you are at work on." Letter of 30 November 1929, SJAA: Z-22.

[92] *Liturgy and the Liturgical Movement* (Collegeville: The Liturgical Press, 1934). The outline was designed to be used in a "unit course," and included chapters with the following headings: "1) Introductory: The Liturgical Movement; 2) The Catholic Liturgy; 3) Liturgy The Life of the Church; 4) Active Participation of the Laity in the Liturgy; 5) Liturgy and the True Christian Life." Appendix 1 offered help in learning how to use the Missal, while appendix 2 offered suggestions for essay-papers. The outline was complete with its own methodology of how best to proceed in studying the material, and included an extended bibliography of recent liturgical works. The methodology included the recommendation that study club participants write essays on the various topics they were discussing, and that each discussion always be summarized with several practical conclusions, and an explanation of how these practical conclusions are to be put into practice. Ibid., 4.

[93] The Barat Association of Cincinnati, Ohio, an organization of working women, chose the topic of liturgical renewal for their monthly study sessions during the year 1929. Normally, about seventy to seventy-five women were in attendance at each meeting and they used *OF* as the primary text for the course. Elizabeth Grace, "The Lay Folk and the Liturgy," *OF* 4 (1930) 573.

[94] In 1934, for example, the Liturgical Arts Society sponsored a series of lectures on six Tuesday evenings between October and March, focusing on liturgical participation. The lectures were held at the Centre Club, 120 Central Park West, New York City. "A Program of Liturgical Study," *America* 51 (1934) 557.

[95] "The Apostolate," *OF* 8 (1934) 281.

[96] Ibid., 329. In the same year, the New York chapter of that same organization organized a Lenten series of lectures on the liturgy, given by two Jesuits, Wilfrid Parsons and Gerard Donnelly. Ibid., 280.

to the liturgy as related to parish, school, and convent life.[97] The convention of the Minnesota Council of Catholic Women devoted the entire afternoon session of 24 October 1934 to the issue of liturgical study clubs.[98] At Manhattan College in Riverdale, New York City, the Alumni Society took up the study of the liturgy as their project for the 1936-37 academic year. The project consisted in the alumni offering a monthly lecture on the liturgy to the entire student body with a follow-up discussion one week later, including students, faculty, and alumni.[99]

The movements and organizations discussed in the previous chapter —Catholic Action, The Catholic Worker, The Grail—had a component of liturgical education as part of their own regular order. Often, these groups would sponsor large lectures on the liturgy which they opened to non-members. For instance, in 1941, The Chicago Catholic Worker organized a twelve-week series of classes on the liturgy which were so well-received that a number of participants had to remain standing for the entire session. Those who planned the course expected a much smaller group, since classes were held on Friday evenings. Many drove from great distances to attend and there was great diversity in the kinds of people who participated.[100]

Study clubs also came into existence on the parochial level. These parish study clubs often chose a particular aspect of the liturgy to be explored each year. In 1934, members of the liturgical study group at St. Boniface Parish, Minneapolis, met twice a month to pursue the theme: "The Mass: Our Sacrifice." At St. Brendan's Parish, New Haven, Con-

---

[97] "The Apostolate," *OF* 9 (1935) 34.

[98] Members of the different study clubs in Minneapolis-St. Paul came to the convention, and following a presentation on the clubs' function by F. Gilligan of St. Paul Seminary, club members demonstrated to the several hundred convention participants a model liturgical study club session. Their model session demonstrated a study of the ordinary of the Mass. Ibid., 35–6.

[99] Lecture/study topics included: "the laity and the loss of the liturgy: cause and cure; the significance of the Mass: what it is (gift of God) and what it is not (popular misconceptions); Mass structure and prayers; Catholic Action and the Mass (including the intimate connection between the liturgical movement and Catholic Action); the Mystical Body and the Mass." Letter of Arthur T. O'Leary to Virgil Michel, 14 December 1936, SJAA: Z-26.

[100] Participants were described as follows: "We noticed many ordinary workers in the group, a few newspaper people, several social workers, a sprinkling of unemployed, and a goodly number of professional men and women. The course was led by Gregory O'Brien, and covered such topics as the mass, the liturgy of the hours, and lay priesthood. The classes always ended with the singing of compline by the entire group, followed by a social." "Notes Along the Way," *The Chicago Catholic Worker* (February, 1941) 8.

necticut, the group met weekly to hear lectures on the liturgy in general, and on the liturgical movement.[101] In some cases, parish groups began to sponsor parish-wide and even diocesan-wide lectures.[102] At St. Vincent Ferrer Parish, New York City, Vincent C. Donovan, O.P., gave a very popular series of weekly lectures in the church on different aspects of the liturgical movement and its call to renewal, which drew increasingly large numbers of men and women from around the city.[103]

An interesting model of adult education and the study of the liturgy is offered in the Christian Family Movement (CFM), already discussed in the previous chapter. While the other social movements within the American church promoted greater liturgical promotion through praying together the Liturgy of the Hours, experimenting with the dialog Mass, or holding occasional lectures or study sessions on the liturgy, CFM was consistent in keeping the component of liturgical education one of the three major parts of every CFM meeting. Several thousand couples were involved in the early 1950s.[104]

Unlike other lay organizations that invited a priest to lecture on the history of the liturgy, CFM couples who led the meetings were responsible for preparing beforehand, so as to present the academic material on the liturgy as accurately and thoroughly as possible. In fact, all participants were encouraged to prepare for each meeting:

> Not only couples who are going to lead the meeting but every couple should beforehand go over the questions of the Gospel, the Liturgy, and the Social Inquiry. This preparation should be made well in advance of the meeting.[105]

[101] Those lectures were given by B. M. Donnelly and discussion followed. "The Apostolate," *OF* 8 (1934) 280–1.

[102] Many of these study groups also began to include Compline as a regular component of the meetings. Godfrey Diekmann, Letter to Clifford, 21 November 1940, SJAA: #1163.

[103] "The Apostolate," *OF* 11 (1937) 229.

[104] Following the opening prayer, CFM meetings always began with the biblical component where a Scripture passage was read, then applied to daily life through discussion. Liturgical study constituted the second component, including a brief presentation and discussion. The third component was that of social inquiry, where participants followed the "see, judge, and act" principle, and where topics chosen sought to raise social consciousness (e.g., regarding family spending), and then lead to some type of social action. The meetings concluded with a preview of the following meeting, then the chaplain's remarks, then prayer (usually sung Compline), and the chaplain's blessing. Patty Crowley, Interview by author, 10 December 1994, Chicago, Illinois.

[105] *Christian Family Movement Annual Inquiry Program* (1953–54) University of Notre Dame Archives: CFM Papers, 16.

Liturgical topics covered a wide range of material. In 1948, the married women's federation took Pius XII's encyclical on the Mystical Body as the foundation for their liturgical study:

> At the meeting, it is discussed sentence by sentence, and sometimes word by word. The leader tries to bring out the meaning of the text . . . The study of the Encyclical is not concluded when all the members of the group know the meaning of the text. Just as in the New Testament discussion, the leader asks for application of the passages. For example, in an early paragraph, Pius XII remarks that one of the factors leading to the renewed interest in the doctrine of the Mystical Body is the frequent reception of Holy Communion. In applying this, one member commented that we ought to think of the reception of Holy Communion as something we do as members of the Mystical Body, as something that unites us not only to Christ, but also to His members. Others spoke of family Communion in the same way. We feel it is important to conclude each liturgy discussion with an explicit suggestion that we begin to think differently or act differently (or both) in view of what we have read.[106]

In 1953–54, CFM chose the Mass as its focus of liturgical education. The study/inquiry text for that year began:

> "The Mass," Pius XII tells us, "is the source and center of our spiritual lives." No one person could explain what this means for each of us in our daily living. Our lives vary. We are husbands, wives, fathers, mothers, office workers, farmers, clerks, factory workers, teachers, skilled workers, executives, laborers, white collar workers. Yet each must worship God by his daily work.[107]

Throughout that year, CFM cells around the United States dealt with different aspects of the Eucharist, for example, "The Mass is something done together; participation in the Mass; why sing at Mass?; the Mass is the great teacher; offering ourselves with Christ; how can we make our daily lives a continuation of the Mass?"

A closer reading of CFM materials reveals that while liturgical study was central to CFM meetings, the treatment of liturgical topics was rather uneven. In some cases, the liturgical issues discussed were quite substantive, even revolutionary. In other cases, however, the focus was on externals. Such inconsistency does not discredit their attempts at liturgical study, nor their desire to model their lives on the liturgy.

---

[106] "Gals Spur Action In Varied Fields: Reports On Best Use of the Liturgy," *ACT* (May 1948) 3.
[107] *CFM Annual Inquiry Program* (1953–54) University of Notre Dame Archives: CFM Papers, 2.

The list of examples of adult liturgical education could go on. In the examples already given, however, one can recognize that such adult education experienced largely through small discussion groups, was manifold in existence, and varied in size of the group, methodology, and interest. Despite such variety or perhaps because of it, news of a liturgical renewal spreading throughout the United States came to be heard in many different corners of the American church. Such a fact can be easily demonstrated by the thousands of people who attended the liturgical weeks of the 1940s and 1950s, but also in more obscure ways. The liturgical weeks are a well-known hallmark of the American liturgical revival. But liturgical education also happened in lesser known, more localized ways—in study clubs, for example. These groups and locally sponsored events, then, bear their own testimony to the growth of the American liturgical movement on the grassroots level.

The great success of liturgical weeks in Belgium was well known to the American pioneers, generating an enthusiasm for fuller participation in the liturgical movement. Although the first national liturgical week was held in 1940, an earlier event took place on 25 July 1929 when St. John's Abbey, Collegeville, hosted the first national liturgical day. Over four hundred participants took part, of whom one hundred and fifty were religious women and one hundred were priests. Besides participants from different parts of the United States, there were several international participants from the Bahama Islands; Saskatchewan, Canada; and the Philippines. The speakers were already well-known to *OF* readers and addressed familiar topics: Alcuin Deutsch, "Renewal in Christ"; Martin Hellriegel, "Survey of the Liturgical Movement"; William Busch, "The Missal and the Breviary: Sources of Spiritual Life"; Basil Stegmann,"Practical Ways of Living the Liturgy"; Victor Siegler, "Introducing the Mass to Children"; Roger Schoenbechler, "The Chant in Parish Churches." A discussion followed each of the presentations. The 1929 liturgical day was intended to be a prelude to a full-scale national liturgical week. Michel and his colleagues believed that a national liturgical week was still too premature in 1929, so they opted for a one-day event which held the possibility of greater success.[108]

A second national liturgical day was held at Collegeville on 22 October 1930, which featured, among other presentations, one talk by John Harbrecht on "The Social Value of the Liturgy," a talk by Alcuin Deutsch on "The Liturgy as a Factor in Higher Education," and a third

---

[108] "The First National Liturgical Day in the United States," *OF* 3 (1929) 322–40.

talk by Sister M. Estelle, O.P., co-editress of *The Christ Life Series,* who addressed the topic "The Liturgy and Religious Instruction in the Grades." This event was likewise well-attended, with a number of different geographical areas represented.[109]

A number of liturgical study days surfaced in the 1930s, in predictable cities like St. Louis and Chicago, organized by leaders like Hellriegel and Laukemper. There were other liturgical days on college and university campuses, usually organized by chaplains who had become promoters of the liturgical movement. When the first national liturgical week was held in 1940 in Chicago, Hellriegel assisted the Catholic Alliance of St. Louis in organizing a liturgical day for those unable to attend the larger national event:

> During the week of October 21, Catholics from every part of the country will gather in Chicago to observe Liturgical Week. In keeping with this widespread manifestation of interest in the ritual and prayers of the Church, St. Louis will have its own meeting on October 20 to be known as Liturgical Sunday. A picked group of interested people, especially young men and women from the schools, sodalities, and Catholic organizations, is being invited to attend a Dialogue Mass and discussions throughout the day led by national and local leaders in the Liturgical Movement.[110]

The Catholic Alliance described the aims of the liturgical day: "To promote among Catholic lay-groups and organizations a knowledge of the Liturgy as an essential part of any program of Catholic social action." Although those study days were smaller and not as significant as the larger national gatherings of the 1940s and 1950s, their existence was important, paving the way for the larger and more elaborate national weeks of the Liturgical Conference.

The liturgical weeks represent the liturgical movement's coming of age in the American church.[111] Registration statistics indicate that the weeks drew large numbers of participants as they moved around the country. At the first national week held in Chicago, 1,260 people attended: 391 lay men and women, 320 clergy, 533 religious women, and 16 brothers. The largest number of participants were from the geographical area where the week was held, with a different location each

---

[109] "Our Second Liturgical Day: 22 October 1930," *OF* 5 (1931) 36–40.

[110] Letter of the Catholic Alliance of St. Louis, 9 October 1940, Marquette University Archives, Milwaukee.

[111] A full presentation of the history of the national liturgical weeks can be found in Lawrence Madden, "The Liturgical Conference in the USA: Its Origin and Development," Doctoral diss., Theological Faculty, University of Trier, 1969.

year. Statistics show that only several hundred participants travelled great distances to attend the liturgical weeks each year. At the 1940 Chicago meeting, for instance, 893 of the 1,260 registrants were from the state of Illinois.[112]

While a number of the pioneers collaborated on the beginnings of the liturgical weeks, the leadership of the project came from another Benedictine, Michael Ducey, who in July 1939, at a meeting of key Benedictine liturgical leaders at Lake St. Clair, Michigan, founded what would become the Benedictine Liturgical Conference. Their goal was to promote the importance and value of liturgy in American Benedictine communities. One of their first projects was to promote the idea of sponsoring national liturgical weeks similar to the *semaines liturgiques* held in Belgium. Liturgical interest was confirmed in autumn of that same year during a catechetical congress in Cincinnati, when the time allotted for the section on liturgy was too brief. This resulted in the recommendation of a national congress where the subject of liturgy could be treated more systematically.

In January 1940, the Lake St. Clair group met at St. Procopius Priory, Chicago, to organize plans for a national liturgical congress, followed by a second meeting on 18 April, where the group of five (including Godfrey Diekmann) met with Cardinal Stritch, requesting permission to hold the first national liturgical week at Holy Name Cathedral in Chicago. Permission was granted, and immediate preparations for the week were given over to Joseph P. Morrison, rector of the cathedral.[113] The "week" was actually a four-day congress, keynoted by Reynold Hillenbrand. In recounting the liturgical movement's history, beginning with its European roots, he began his address:

> A generation from now, with peace unbroken let us hope, we who are here tonight, and a great many others, shall look back on this week as fraught with some historical importance. For the first time, the week focuses widespread national interest into one national meeting. It unifies this interest. And, in a sense, for the moment it makes it corporate, because it draws isolated efforts of many into common deliberation, common sympathy, common effort.[114]

[112] *Proceedings: 1940 National Liturgical Week* (Newark: Benedictine Liturgical Conference, 1941) 241. The 1941 Liturgical Week in St. Paul, Minnesota drew 1,345 participants; 1942 at St. Meinrad, Indiana, 1,357 participants. The 1947 week in Portland, Oregon had 2,023 participants, while the 1948 meeting in Boston drew 3,537 registrants. The largest, however, was the St. Louis liturgical week in 1964, which gathered over 20,000 participants.

[113] Madden, 18, 22–3.

[114] *Proceedings: 1940 Liturgical Week*, 5.

Indeed, Hillenbrand was right. A major goal of such national gatherings was liturgical education. Another equally important aspect, however, was to offer mutual support to liturgical pioneers and promoters, many of whom felt isolated in their own efforts. Talks centered around the basic theme of the week: "The Living Parish: Active and Intelligent Participation of the Laity in the Liturgy of the Catholic Church." The 1941 week had as its theme, "The Living Parish: One in Worship, Charity, and Action"; "The Praise of God" was the topic of the 1942 St. Meinrad gathering. The 1943 meeting returned to Holy Name Cathedral in Chicago and marked the move from the Benedictine Liturgical Conference to the Liturgical Conference, lest the project be viewed solely as a monastic concern. That year's theme was "Christian Sacrifice." In 1944, at the first liturgical week outside the midwest, participants at the New York liturgical week focused on the issue of "Liturgy and Catholic Life." The following year, in the aftermath of the war, the St. Louis Liturgical Week addressed this issue: "Catholic Liturgy in Peace and Reconstruction." The 1946 Denver Liturgical Week had as its theme, "The Family In Christ." Other aspects of liturgical renewal as related to daily life were treated in subsequent liturgical weeks through the 1970s.

A more extensive historical study of the liturgical weeks would take us beyond our purpose here. Suffice it to say that those national weeks were a moving force in the popularization of the American liturgical movement and in educating American Catholics toward liturgical renewal. The well-orchestrated eucharistic and non-eucharistic liturgies central to those gatherings were educative in themselves, since organizers recognized the fundamentally catechetical role of the liturgy. Many of those participants, galvanized as they returned to their homes, took up the task of educating others about the liturgical revival happening within the United States.

When American Catholics gathered to learn about the liturgy and to teach one another through adult study clubs, they normally met in homes, or occasionally at the parish house. They sponsored lectures in large city hotels and at prestigious social clubs in cities like New York, Boston, San Francisco, and Chicago. There was, however, another locus for liturgical activity, for study, discussion, and learning; it was the Catholic bookshop.

When the liturgical movement began to grow in the late 1920s, and pamphlets (and later books) began to be published, the pamphlet rack in the back of parish churches was encouraged as the best means of selling those educative texts. A good deal of reference to church pamphlet racks is found in the early editions of *OF*. In fact, editors of The Liturgical Press began promoting their own Popular Liturgical Library through the use of church-rack pamphlets. Moreover, clergy began writing Virgil Michel and the editors of The Liturgical Press about using the pamphlet rack as a tool in liturgical education.[115]

In the late 1930s, a lay woman, Sara Benedicta O'Neill began a more creative venture in Chicago: the St. Benet's Library.[116] The library began in the living room of her parents' home and in February 1943, moved to the newly-opened Sheil School of Social Studies.[117] Catherine De Hueck had educated and greatly influenced the school's founder, Bishop Bernard J. Sheil, and the school was opened at her suggestion. It was located in the headquarters of the Catholic Youth Organization at 31 East Congress Street, Chicago. Within a few months, over two thousand adults were attending evening classes on topics such as "God, Liturgy, Survey of Science, Practical Writing, the Negro in America, Mathematics for Everyday Use, and Panel Discussions on Women in Wartime." In accord with Sheil's desires, no fees were charged for the courses and all were welcome, regardless of color or creed. In the basement of the building, Sheil provided space for a library, and later bookstore, under the name of St. Benet and under the direction of Sara O'Neill. She soon invited the collaboration of other women in the enterprise, and its fame and popularity grew, long outlasting the Sheil School. Much more than a bookstore, St. Benet's became a nationally-known catechetical and liturgical center which drew visitors from across the United States.

A Benedictine oblate of Monte Cassino, O'Neill maintained Benedictine connections throughout her entire life. She was a personal friend of the abbot of Bruges, in Belgium, and made a number of visits to the great monasteries of Europe. Her knowledge of foreign languages both facilitated her travels and enhanced her appreciation of the monastic liturgical revival taking place on the European continent. A close friend of Catholic publishers, Frank and Massie Ward, she was

[115] "The thought has struck me that the publications from your press relative to Liturgy would be profitable to put in the Church rack . . . A copy of the following is requested: 'Orate Fratres,' 'Liturgy, the Life of the Church,' 'My Sacrifice and Yours,' 'The Liturgical Year.' I am hoping to put the book rack to profitable use this year, and wish to obtain the most useful books for that purpose. It is my intention to give talks on the subjects, and then refer the people to the article or book in the book rack that they might profit more thereby." The Liturgical Press records show that twelve copies of *OF* 1 were sent, along with the other books requested, and the writer was billed accordingly. Priest of St. Bernard's Parish, Detroit, Michigan, Letter to the Editors of the Liturgical Press, 4 August 1927, SJAA: Z-22.

[116] For a summary of O'Neill's achievements, see "Benet Library Founder Observes 80th Birthday," *New World* (25 March 1949).

[117] See "Sheil School Opens Doors," *New World* (22 January 1943).

also well-read in Catholic theology, and was convinced that a serious program of adult education was greatly lacking in the American Catholic church. New life was emerging, however. The liturgical movement and the Catholic Worker were growing, and *The Common-weal* magazine was coming into its own as a progressive voice within American Catholicism. O'Neill knew all the key figures in these important developments.[118]

O'Neill's interests were many and varied. She was an early ecumenist, and often asked why the Christian churches did not do more to collaborate on projects of mutual interest. She was also a member and benefactress of the St. Anscar League for the Conversion of Scandinavia. She was, in the words of her colleague and successor in running the bookstore, Nina Polcyn, "the precursor of the eco-feminist movement," one who was deeply involved with the Council of Catholic Women and called for the rightful place of women in American church and civil society. An aggressive personality, she was not one to back down from her convictions. Like so many other liturgical pioneers and promoters, O'Neill attributed her passion for liturgical reform to her experience of the liturgical renewal taking place in monastic Europe. She was more educated and informed than most American clergy at the time, and she challenged priests in a number of ways, for example, in discontinuing the celebration of memorial Masses for the dead throughout the week, and restoring the celebration of the Mass of the day.

Much impressed by the celebration of the Liturgy of the Hours in Benedictine monasteries, O'Neill educated American Catholics as to its richness, suggesting that this was the prayer of the whole Church. She encouraged others to learn more about the Office of the Dead, and then to take this up as a ministry on the occasion of the death of parish members:

> There is another Office in the Church besides the little Office and the big Office. There is the Office of the Dead. That I have been very much interested in for a long time, and I found that most Catholics haven't any idea what the Office of the Dead is. So for several years my library group and myself have been doing just what Father Bussard suggested. We have been saying the Office of the Dead in English when we attend the wake of a deceased friend, because we want the Catholic people there to learn it, to know something about it. You will hardly believe me, but this is true: Recently, a Catholic who heard us for the first time, asked a member of the household if that was a Catholic service![119]

[118] Nina Polcyn Moore. Interview by author, 15 December 1994, Evanston, Illinois.

[119] "Discussion: October 23," in *Proceedings: 1940 National Liturgical Week* (Newark: The Benedictine Liturgical Conference, 1941) 159–60.

As we saw in the previous chapter, many of these pioneers knew one another. So, not surprisingly, O'Neill and Catherine De Hueck were also friends. As the library's size and popularity began to grow, De Hueck recognized that the library could be far more influential if it were more centrally located. With her own strategic plan for adult education in Chicago, De Hueck convinced Bishop Sheil that such a library was just what the Sheil Center for Social Studies needed. De Hueck's plan included a strategy for the evangelization of the entire United States, beginning with Chicago. She gave Sheil an outline of her plan, encouraging his support, and he agreed. In witnessing the St. Benet Library's continued growth in popularity and importance, Sheil moved the library out of the basement to the ground floor, providing a significantly larger space and paying the salaries of two employees. With that move, the library took on more the nature of a bookstore, selling periodicals like *Orate Fratres, The Catholic Worker,* and *The Commonweal.* The St. Benet's Bookshop was the only place in Chicago where *The Commonweal* was available in those years.

Nina Polcyn Moore came to know Sara Benedicta O'Neill through Catholic Worker circles and gatherings of *The Commonweal* Catholics, as they were often labeled. Polcyn Moore first met Dorothy Day in 1934, while picketing at the German Consulate in New York City. She recalls being impressed by the fact that Day insisted upon one hour of prayer each day as a necessary and integral part of their picketing together. From 1937 until 1941, Polcyn Moore lived and worked at the Catholic Worker House in Milwaukee, after which time she stayed on in Milwaukee, teaching in a local school. One day, a call arrived from Sara Benedicta O'Neill, asking Polcyn Moore, with her usual forceful tone, to assist in the St. Benet's project. Another friend and colleague of Polcyn Moore's, Margaret Blaser, was also invited. The two agreed and moved to Chicago. Initially, Blaser worked as the bookstore's accountant, which was not one of O'Neill's strong points. Polcyn Moore began her tenure in Chicago on 1 January 1943, teaching in the Sheil School and also working in the bookstore. Besides her liturgical interests she promoted a labor union at the Sheil School, an idea which Sheil himself opposed, afraid that he would be the only bishop with a labor union. He was a difficult employer, always on the scene and constantly checking up on his employees.[120]

Like Virgil Michel, Dorothy Day, Catherine De Hueck, and other reformers, O'Neill sought to bridge the gap between liturgy and life, between liturgical reform and social activism, and she came to recognize the potential for the St. Benet's Bookshop as a center for liturgically

---

[120] Nina Polycn Moore, Interview by author.

and socially minded Catholics alike. With a larger staff and with its notoriety spreading well beyond the confines of Chicago, the St. Benet's Bookshop became known throughout many parts of the United States as a center for liberal Catholicism, and, in particular, as a meeting place for liturgical pioneers and promoters. O'Neill, Blaser, and Polcyn Moore hosted Compline in the back of the bookshop each Saturday evening at the end of the workday. Since the shop was centrally located in "the Loop," it was convenient to office workers and Saturday shoppers. About twenty people arrived each Saturday with their briefcases and shopping bags, and sang Compline. At the first liturgical week in Chicago, O'Neill made an intervention describing that weekly event:

> . . . I am the one who has the tea parties in the library. We have all classes of piety and liturgicalness at the library and I generally, at 5:30, invite the godless ones to get out if they don't want to sing Compline. A number of them, particularly two very fine individuals, simply will not say it because we have been saying it in the Latin and their particular hobby is that it should be said in the vernacular. So, we compromise and satisfy the laity. We have been saying the Psalms in English, but we most liturgical ones insist upon singing the Latin hymns and the *Nunc dimittis*. By the way, Mary Perkins was the one who first showed us how beautiful the canticle is when it is sung.[121]

Following Compline, many in the group then walked across the street for dinner together at the Congress Hotel before returning home. Polcyn Moore remarked: "Customers must have thought they had entered something crazy. Reinhold felt it (Compline in the bookshop) was inappropriate."[122]

Study groups held weekly meetings at the bookshop to discuss such topics as participation in the Mystical Body; the promotion of vernacular in the liturgy; the Liturgy of the Hours. Before the advent of air travel, Chicago was the train-hub for the United States. Because O'Neill was so well-connected and the bookshop so well-known, when O'Neill heard that Dorothy Day, Godfrey Diekmann, H. A. Reinhold, or Frank and Massie Ward would be passing through, she quickly organized a lecture and discussion in the bookshop itself. As numbers attending such events grew, those lectures moved to a conference room at the Congress Hotel, across the street, in order to accommodate the crowds. Interesting people were always passing through their doors from the east and west coasts and the south of the

---

[121] "Discussion: October 23," in *Proceedings: 1940 Liturgical Week*, 155.
[122] Interview by author.

United States. Martin Marty, Jaroslav Pelikan, and Reynold Hillenbrand were all regular customers. At one point Marty even did a window display for the shop on an ecumenical theme. Hillenbrand advised Chicago priests and bishops to stop into St. Benet's on their day off and browse. "Maybe you'll even learn something," he would tell them. "If nothing else, buy a book. If you don't read it, you can always use it to prop a window open." Many priests and bishops did visit, and, as Polcyn Moore remarks: "We educated them all. This was a women's movement."[123]

The St. Benet's Bookshop became a center for the League of the Divine Office, and was the regular meeting place of the Vernacular Society. O'Neill was a pioneer of both. She and her colleagues also knew and supported the Christian Family Movement and other Jocists. The bookshop became a major supporter of the annual liturgical weeks, providing a display of books at each year's gathering. This, too, helped to publicize bookstore projects. They were among the biggest distributors of books published by The Liturgical Press and Hellriegel's Pio X Press in the United States.

Much to the disapproval of Sara O'Neill, the bookshop came to list liturgical art among its sales. O'Neill voiced her discontent from the very beginning: "There'll be too much 'kitsch' and you'll burn with Benzinger." She hated tasteless liturgical art.[124] O'Neill's opinion changed, however, when she began to see the high quality of liturgical art sold in the shop. Polcyn Moore travelled to the great European monasteries and brought back the best and most distinctive liturgical art available at the time. The shop carried Beuronese art and the highly respected work of Ilse Von Drage. O'Neill remained ever-present in the bookshop and insisted on being in charge until her death on 11 January 1954, at the age of eighty-five. Her obituary noted that, from the beginning, St. Benet was "a library and a bookshop in the marketplace." Sheil called O'Neill "one of the most important women in Chicago," because of the bookshop's influence in Chicago and beyond.[125]

In 1954, due to financial problems with a number of social projects within the Archdiocese, the Sheil School closed and was reorganized as a center of adult education under the direction of Msgr. Daniel Cantwell, himself a social activist and supporter of the liturgical

---

[123] Polcyn Moore, Interview by author.

[124] Polcyn Moore, Interview by author. For a description of 'kitsch', see Joanna Weber, "The Sacred in Art: Introducing Father Marie-Alain Couturier's Aesthetic," *Worship* 69 (1995) 243–62. Weber notes: "'Kitsch' is equated with watered-down sentimentality, devoid of any truth, a conglomeration" (249).

[125] "Sara Benedicta O'Neill," *Amen*, (1 July 1954), 20.

movement. The St. Benet's Bookshop was then purchased by Nina Polcyn Moore who sold the shop in 1973 to two women, blood-sisters, who then turned the shop into a short-lived vestment business. The shop closed its doors permanently in 1977. As expansion continued, Polcyn Moore and her colleagues moved to an even more central location at 300 South Wabash. In her eighty-first year, reflecting back on the bookshop, Nina Polcyn Moore commented: "It was a ministry of education. We prayed for those who entered our doors."[126]

There were similar centers in other parts of the United States that animated enthusiasm for the liturgical movement, and assisted in the task of adult education in liturgy and other areas of Church renewal. The Paraclete Bookshop, on the upper east side of New York City, was founded by Elizabeth Sullivan on 2 October 1942. Like Sara Benedicta O'Neill, Sullivan was heavily involved in the projects of the liturgical movement and a regular participant in the annual liturgical weeks. She eventually became president of the Liturgical Conference and was said to be a colorful character, sitting and puffing on her cigarette, strong in communicating her views to others on the board.[127] She was also a great supporter of *The Commonweal* and of the kind of pastoral issues which *The Commonweal* promoted. Although it was a much smaller operation than St. Benet's, the Paraclete was established with the same desire to promote adult education among American Catholics, and to be an educational center for New Yorkers interested or involved in the liturgical movement, the Catholic Worker, and the like. Sullivan remained involved until her death in 1978.

A similar concept was operative in the Thomas More Bookshop in Cambridge, Massachusetts. Along with carrying periodicals like *Orate Fratres* and serving as a distributor for The Liturgical Press, it mobilized and educated *The Commonweal* Catholics in the Boston area, giving them a greater understanding of liturgical and social developments within the American church.

In that same period, women of the Grail movement owned and operated the Junipero Serra Bookshop on Maiden Lane in the center of San Francisco. Besides selling the latest in liturgical texts, the Junipero Serra was the meeting place for roundtable discussions, which so much characterized the Grail's educational apostolate in the late 1940s and 1950s. Topics included the different facets of renewal within the American church, and did not exclude the progress of the liturgical movement. This apostolate of the Grail at the Junipero Serra created

---

[126] Nina Polcyn Moore, Interview by author.
[127] Robert Rambusch, Interview by author, 3 January 1995, New York City.

something of an educational center for progressive Catholics in the San Francisco Bay area.[128]

Academic Programs in Liturgy

As study clubs and the national liturgical weeks (along with centers like the St. Benet's Bookshop) served as means of liturgical education, a more extensive commitment was seen in the growth of liturgical summer schools and eventually academic degree programs in liturgical science. Although the first American degree program in liturgy was initiated at the University of Notre Dame only in 1947, there was already a course in liturgy being offered as part of the regular summer school curriculum at that same university as early as 1930. Participants were normally women in religious communities who taught on the primary and secondary school levels.[129]

St. John's Abbey offered a liturgical summer school from 24 June to 3 August 1929.[130] The 1929 session included courses on "The Spirit of the Liturgy" and "The Sacramental Life of the Church" (Virgil Michel, O.S.B.); "The Liturgy and Catechetical Instruction" (Basil Stegmann, O.S.B.); "Liturgical Music and the Parish: Principles and Organization" (Ermin Vitry, O.S.B.); "Gregorian Chant" (Innocent Gertken, O.S.B.). Other courses were included on music technique.[131] Similar courses were offered in the 1931 liturgical summer school, along with two new courses, one, a "Daily Liturgy Lesson," the other, "Church Latin for Beginners."[132] Like Notre Dame, the Collegeville program drew largely upon religious women as their primary student body.

[128] The author is indebted to John Coleman, S.J., for this information.

[129] In a letter to Virgil Michel, Benzinger Brothers Publishers reported that a certain L.V. Broughall, C.S.C., was to lecture on the liturgy in the 1930 summer session. A total of twelve hundred students was expected. The letter noted that Broughall had consulted Benzinger about their missals, and other pertinent liturgical books, for instance, Bulzarik's *Living With the Church* and Grimaud's *My Mass*. Alfred Benzinger spent an hour with Broughall going through various liturgical texts. Benzinger invited Michel's assistance as well: "If there is anything you can take up with him by correspondence in the way of orienting him along these lines, we feel that he would be sincerely grateful." Letter of 16 June 1930. SJAA: Z-23.

[130] Benzinger Brothers wrote the directors of the Liturgical Summer School inquiring about the possibility of displaying their books which had been advertised in *OF* in some form of an exhibit. The staff responded favorably. Letter to Liturgical Summer School, 24 April 1929, and response of 30 April 1929, SJAA: Z-23.

[131] "Liturgical Summer School Held at St. John's University 24 June to 3 August 1929," Course Listing. SJAA: F-20.

[132] "Liturgical Summer School Held at St. John's Abbey, 26 June to 5 August, 1931." SJAA: F-20.

In the late 1930s and early 1940s, groups like the Grail and the Campionites organized summer schools that treated liturgical subjects. In 1937, the Campionites organized a "farm-summer school" which consisted of five two-week sessions between 20 June and 29 August. Subjects treated included liturgy and sociology, liturgy and life, and the Mystical Body of Christ. There was one hour of lecture and discussion on each subject daily, along with the full participation of all students in the singing of the liturgical hours and the celebration of the Eucharist.[133] And those groups were not alone. Encouraged by the great success of the first national liturgical week in 1940, Hillenbrand organized a three-week liturgical summer school at St. Mary of the Lake Seminary, Mundelein, Illinois, from 14 July until 1 August 1941. The program, limited to priests, included four classes per day excluding weekends, and daily discussions each evening. The purpose of the summer school was to "refresh the liturgical doctrine in the minds of the priests and to discuss with them a more intelligent and active participation on the part of the laity." Faculty consisted of such liturgical leaders as William Busch, Gerald Ellard, Godfrey Diekmann, Martin Hellriegel, and H. A. Reinhold. Subject matter included a study of the Mass and the other sacraments, the liturgical movement, the liturgical year, parish participation, liturgy and social action, the dialog Mass and the "high Mass," Gregorian chant. In addition, each priest was offered the opportunity of demonstrating his liturgical presiding style for the sake of critique by the faculty and his peers.[134]

Six years later, the liturgical summer school at the University of Notre Dame was founded by Michael Mathis, C.S.C. Mathis was not a liturgist in the strict sense. His background was that of a missionary and hospital chaplain. But in 1936 Mathis was presented with the first volume of Pius Parsch's *The Church's Year of Grace*, which had a deep influence upon him. He continued reading more about the liturgy and in 1937, was asked to organize something on campus for the missions. He gathered students together for a study of the Missal and soon introduced them to the *Missa recitata* as well. Within a few years he became convinced that the liturgy itself was the best tool for instructing students. Mathis introduced what he called the "Vigil Service," where students gathered together to sing morning prayer and to be catechized through the reading of the Scriptures and patristic texts.

As early as 1940 Mathis proposed to the provincial administration of the Indiana Province of the Congregation of Holy Cross the establishment of a school of missions and liturgy at Notre Dame. Finally, in

---

[133] "The Apostolate," *OF* 11 (1937) 374.
[134] Letter to Godfrey Diekmann, 1 May 1941, SJAA: #1164.

1946, Mathis' provincial superior, John C. Cavanaugh, C.S.C., gave permission for the establishment of a liturgy program at the University of Notre Dame. The permission granted was not for the opening of a school of liturgy, but for the establishment of a modest program within the undergraduate curriculum in the summer of 1947. Given his convictions about the educative, formative power of liturgy itself, the daily order of his liturgical institute included a full liturgical schedule:

5:40 a.m.	Lauds
6:00 a.m.	*Missa cantata* with a homily
9:00 a.m.	Terce (optional)
4:00 p.m.	None (optional)
7:10 p.m.	Compline and Benediction.

All these liturgies were held in Sacred Heart Church on campus. The three courses offered were entitled: "The History of the Liturgy"; "Some Aspects of the Liturgy"; and "Gregorian Chant." The "Aspects" course was pastoral in focus and taught by a number of professors. Godfrey Diekmann lectured on "The Christian Way of Life: The Sacramental Way"; Willis Nutting, "A Layman Looks at the Liturgy"; H. A. Reinhold, "Ecclesiastical Places: Churches and Cemeteries"; Reynold Hillenbrand, "The Place of the Liturgy in Catholic Action"; Bernard Laukemper, "Station Church and Latin Masses"; Bede Scholz, "The Ecclesiastical Year"; Damasus Winzen, "The Scriptural Background of the Ecclesiastical Year"; and Gerald Ellard, "Aims and Objects of the Liturgical Movement." Each evening at 5:00, "the liturgical forum" took place, comprising a presentation by the "Aspects" lecturer of the week, followed by discussion.[135]

Mathis was quite successful in his ventures during that first summer. There were eleven students who took the history course for credit and twenty-two auditors; twenty-six credit students for the Aspects course and thirty-six auditors; and eight credit students for the Chant course and fifteen auditors. Mathis soon pushed for a Master of Arts Degree program in liturgical studies, but his proposal was rejected because the university believed that such a program was not sufficiently academic. Mathis' second attempt at a proposal was successful in 1948. The program continued to grow. In 1951, with the help of his former student, Michael P. Grace, Mathis secured an annual subsidy of $10,000 per year from the Michael P. Grace II Trust Fund. This allowed Mathis to bring some of the best liturgical scholars of Europe to the summer liturgical faculty of Notre Dame: Donald Attwater, Louis

---

[135] Robert J. Kennedy, *Michael Mathis: American Liturgical Pioneer* (Washington: The Pastoral Press, 1987) 4–7, 12.

Bouyer, Jean Daniélou, S.J., Balthasar Fischer, Pierre-Marie Gy, O.P., Johannes Hofinger, S.J., Josef Jungmann, S.J., Christine Mohrmann, Hermann Schmidt, S.J., and others. These were in addition to the American liturgical pioneers already mentioned. One student during those early years has observed that because of the largely European faculty, Mathis' program failed to emphasize the strong connection between liturgy and social action which was so much a hallmark of the American movement and much less characteristic of the European call to liturgical reform.[136] In 1965, the Mathis program was expanded into the Graduate Program in Liturgical Studies and has awarded over fifty doctorates in liturgy to date, an even number of Catholic students and students of the other churches.[137] There is no question as to the central role which the Notre Dame liturgy program has played in the advancement of serious academic study of the liturgy in the United States.

While Mathis was developing his program in the late 1940s, William Leonard, S.J., was preparing to announce his own liturgical summer school on the east coast. Launching his "Social Worship Program" in 1948 at Boston College where he was professor of theology, Leonard integrated the joint concerns of liturgy and social activism. The brochure for the summer school stated:

> *You have noticed*—the profound interest in social worship manifested everywhere in America during recent years.
>
> *You have heard*—about the Encyclical published last Fall by Pope Pius XII giving direction and a powerful spur to this movement.
>
> *You know*—of the modern resurgence of the doctrine of the Church as the mystical body of Christ which has become for twentieth century Catholics the heart of Christian sociology, the mainspring of Catholic Action, the basic premise of our hope for a just world order.
>
> *You understand*—that social worship is nothing more than the mystical body at prayer.
>
> *You will therefore be interested*—in the announcement that Boston College will offer, during the coming summer, the Social Worship Program.

The summer school was advertised in conjunction with the ninth liturgical week which was held in Boston. Co-educational classes met from 28 June through 7 August and covered the following courses: "The

---

[136] Kevin Seasoltz, O.S.B., Interview by author, 28 November 1994, St. John's Abbey, Collegeville, Minnesota.

[137] James F. White, *Roman Catholic Worship: Trent to Today* (New York: Paulist Press, 1995) 100.

Church as the Mystical Body," "The Encyclical 'Mediator Dei,'" and "Social Worship in Practice."[138] Despite a prestigious faculty including such noted liturgical pioneers as Jesuits Gerald Ellard and Clement J. McNaspy, Boston College refused to give academic credit to those attending the summer program. This resulted in low student enrollment.[139]

CONCLUSION

There are several points raised in this chapter which should be highlighted. First, in the thinking of the liturgical pioneers, Jesus Christ was the primary teacher and the liturgy was the school of prayer and Christian living. This was not only the case with the proclamation of the Word or the preaching, but in the entire liturgical act with all its symbolic richness. Sunday after Sunday, in encountering Christ and the members of Christ's body in the liturgical assembly, the Church grew in recognition and understanding, at least ideally, of its own vocation as the body of Christ in the world. Thus, the liturgical pioneers promoted well-prepared, well-celebrated liturgy as the best educational tool.

Second, the reformers were realistic enough to recognize that a didactic component was also needed. Liturgical education on the local and national level was necessary to bring about true liturgical reform. For centuries, Catholics were deprived of a thorough understanding of their role as active participants within the Mystical Body of Christ. They had learned that the liturgy properly belonged to the clergy, and that their own role consisted in being passive observers. Understandably, members of the Church acted accordingly and personal devotions took on greater significance. Michel and his colleagues soon realized that liturgical renewal would be impossible without serious catechesis.

Third, the United States did not represent one culture, but many. And like the pluralism of many different cultures within American society, so too was there a diversity of pedagogical models in American liturgical education. As an immigrant population, many Catholics in the 1920s and 1930s were not as well-educated as other Americans. Catholic colleges and universities were only beginning their expansion in those years. Even within the various immigrant groups, there were significant differences as to liturgical background and education. Some immigrants were better prepared than others to hear the message of

---

[138] University of Notre Dame Archives: Vernacular Society Papers, 38:2.

[139] Leonard, *The Letter Carrier,* 127.

the liturgical reformers. Thus, the promotion of liturgical education required a multi-faceted approach, responding in different ways to elementary, secondary, university, and seminary education, and to the various groupings within the realm of adult education. That plurality gave the liturgical educators a wider hearing, allowing the message to be carried to many different corners of the American church.

Fourth, like the Mystical Body itself, the pioneers promoted a type of education where all members of the Church learned from one another. The movement had large numbers of clergy and religious among its members, but they were not the only liturgical leaders and educators. In some cases, parishioners educated their clergy. The women of the St. Benet's Bookshop enlightened bishops, along with Hillenbrand alumni. CFM couples presented talks on liturgical renewal to their peers in their movement. University students and alumni mobilized to promote liturgical education. What one sees in the educational efforts of the movement, then, was an attempt to involve the whole American church, to engage the talents and expertise of all Church members. It was Michel's call for all Church members to become "lay apostles."

Fifth, we have seen that the task of liturgical education was not easy. There were many challenges in attempting to convince American Catholics that the liturgical movement was more than a fad—more than a "midwestern, German invention." Among clergy and seminarians, it was difficult to convince them that liturgical education meant far more than simply being instructed in matters of rubrics. In summer programs of liturgical study, it was not easy convincing university administrators that liturgics was a serious academic discipline. As a result, most administrators denied academic credit to liturgical courses offered in those early years.

The key to all of the educative efforts of the liturgical reformers was integration. In promoting the kind of liturgy which was intrinsically bound to the rest of life, where those who shared in the Eucharist were called to serve the weaker members of that same body of Christ, reformers recognized that education had its own part to play in that same integration. They called for the employment of the social sciences and the arts. They consistently pointed to the relationship between liturgical education and other forms of American ecclesial renewal. It was that unified vision of liturgical and ecclesial renewal which educated American Catholics to their rightful place within the liturgical assembly and strengthened the movement in its efforts.

CHAPTER FIVE

✿

The Liturgical Movement
and the Arts

INTRODUCTION

This final chapter will explore the relationship between the liturgical movement and the arts: art, architecture, and music. Some explanation of terms is in order. In its most fundamental sense, art is the creative, human expression of beauty. Although the mediums of art, architecture, and music are distinct, all three constitute art in the broader sense as creative human expressions of beauty. In this sense, then, architects and musicians are also artists.

Nevertheless, the term "art" is usually employed in a restricted sense to describe the mediums of drawing and painting, sculpting and the like. Art museums, for example, normally do not contain objects related to music. The liturgical pioneers and promoters made those same distinctions between art, architecture, and music, and so those distinctions will be made in this chapter. When Virgil Michel and his associates wrote about art or more specifically, liturgical art, they were normally referring to the interior decoration of churches: to paintings and sculpture, liturgical vesture and flowers; those elements that created or constituted the liturgical environment in which the Church gathered for worship. Liturgical appointments such as altar, ambo, and font, were normally considered part of the architectural plan, although they obviously needed to be treated equally from the perspective of art as focal objects within the liturgical space. The plural term "liturgical arts" was used more inclusively for all the artistic mediums that contributed to full and active liturgical expression. This included the building where the Church gathered, as well as the artistic elements of the liturgical environment and music.

One final distinction needs to be made. On occasion, the pioneers made reference to liturgy itself as art. This concept, promoted initially

in the German liturgical movement by Abbot Herwegen, was continued in the United States by Virgil Michel and others. The sense is
metaphorical. Liturgy was art in that it was a creative, human expression of beauty offered to God as a "living sacrifice of praise." Consequently, liturgical participants were described as artists not in a literal
sense, but as those who through their varying liturgical roles contributed to that unified work of art which was the liturgy. As artists,
liturgical participants were called to mirror the beauty of the body of
Christ in daily life.

While it is true that the liturgical arts did not flourish with any notoriety until the 1950s, pioneers and promoters of the liturgical movement did not leave this area unattended. Thanks to Virgil Michel, H. A.
Reinhold, and others who were capable of bridging gaps between the
ecclesial and artistic worlds, at least some Catholic artists found their
way into the liturgical movement and caught its spirit. Examples include Maurice Lavanoux, the Liturgical Arts Society, Catholic Worker
artist Adé Bethune, Justine Ward, Mother Georgia Stevens, and the
work done on Solesmes chant at The Catholic University in Washington and the work of the Pius X School of Liturgical Music in New York.

This chapter opens with a consideration of the arts within American
culture in the 1920s and 1930s, then looks more specifically at religious
art of that same period. Following the introductory section, the chapter is divided into three major parts: (1) the liturgical movement and
art; (2) the liturgical movement and architecture; (3) the liturgical
movement and music.

The Arts in the United States in the 1920s and 1930s

The early years of this century were a period of expatriation of
American artists, not only for painters and sculptors, but also for musicians and writers. Examples include Hemingway, Fitzgerald, Cop-
land, and Thompson, all of whom had left the United States for
Europe.[1] Those were challenging times for artists in the United States
since many Americans failed to appreciate the contribution of the arts
in society. Artists were often depicted as eccentrics. Further, the arts
were viewed as a women's activity. In a 1929 artistic survey which
focused on the town of Muncie, Indiana, Helen and Robert Lynd reported that "music, like poetry and the other arts, is almost nonexis-
tent among men."[2]

---

[1] See Editor, "Shall Artists Run to Europe?," *Literary Digest* 100 (1929) 23–4.

[2] Helen and Robert Lynd, *Middletown: A Study in American Culture* (New York:
Harcourt, Brace, and World, 1929); quoted in Andrew Yox, "An American Renaissance: Art and Community in the 1930s," *Mid-America* 72 (1990) 108.

Slowly, the arts became more acceptable within the culture. Statistics substantiate this claim. From 1910 to 1920, the number of artists and art teachers within the United States rose from 34,000 to 35,000, and the number of musicians and teachers of music rose from 130,000 to 139,000. In the next decade that number increased from 35,000 artists and art teachers to 57,000, while the number of musicians and music teachers increased from 139,000 to 165,000, representing a total increase of almost thirty percent in the 1920s.[3] Artistic stereotypes began to change, as well. Several articles challenged the image of the artist as eccentric, while other writers suggested that an artist was capable of being happily married.[4]

For some, the artist—the composer, the poet, the painter or sculptor—stood as a prophetic model who challenged the status quo, calling the United States to free itself from the shackles of materialism and selfishness. This message received an even wider hearing with the onset of the Great Depression. Church and family assumed a greater significance as Americans searched for the security of belonging to a given community. While larger businesses and corporations were strongly criticized during the depression for their competition and greed, artists, like the cherished institutions of Church and family, escaped such a critique. This was because artists were viewed as being non-materialistic themselves. Some in the intellectual community saw a unique vocation for artists to raise the social awareness of other citizens, calling Americans to greater social responsibility.[5]

In 1934, under the leadership of President Franklin D. Roosevelt, New Deal programs strengthened the artistic movement. Sixteen thousand paintings were sponsored in the 1930s. Symphony orchestras increased in that decade to over two hundred and sixty as Americans grew in appreciation of classical music. By the end of the 1930s, classical music radio programs had over ten million listeners. There was also a significant growth in literature, which compared favorably with what was accomplished in the successive four decades.[6]

---

[3] U.S. Department of Commerce, Bureau of the Census, *Abstract of the Fourteenth Census of the United States* (Washington: Government Printing Office, 1923) 494; U.S. Department of Commerce, Bureau of the Census, *Abstract of the Fifteenth Census of the United States* (Washington: Government Printing Office, 1933) 317–8.

[4] See Avery Strakosch, "I Married An Artist," *Saturday Evening Post* (3 October 1936) 27–8.

[5] See Suzanne LaFollette, "The Artist and the Depression," *The Nation* 137 (September, 1933) 264.

[6] Yox, 113.

The 1930s saw the growth in Gothic architecture around the country, conveying the grand splendor of western civilization, along with its Christian idealism. This was especially the case of new buildings erected on American college campuses. The classical style of architecture also became popular in the 1930s for libraries and public buildings.

Thus, while the 1930s were a time of tremendous economic hardship for most Americans, they were also a decade when the American arts came into their own. In 1941, the novelist John P. Bishop expressed the matter even more strongly: "the future of the arts is in America."[7]

Our study now moves from a general survey of the arts in American culture to a consideration of art in its more limited understanding—paintings, sculpture, drawings—as distinct from architecture, music, or other artistic mediums. Specifically, this next section will consider the state of art in Catholic churches of the United States in the early years of the liturgical movement.

American Religious Art in the 1920s, 1930s, and 1940s

Despite the great emergence of American art in the 1930s, art grew up outside the Church and continued to be held with a certain amount of suspicion from within it. This was not so in Europe. In France, Georges Rouault created his famous "Miserere" series between 1922 and 1927. Catholic artists in Switzerland and Germany who had produced quality secular art also produced quality liturgical and religious art in that period. But in the United States, there was little serious activity. One *OF* editorial noted: "Why—already commercial (religious) art is trying to make the rugged Don Bosco look as elegant as Mr. Eden."[8] An *Art Digest* editorial referred to the "blasphemy of ugliness" in Catholic churches, stating that "bad art continues to characterize the Catholic Church in America."[9]

One writer for the *Christian Social Art Quarterly,* Franz Mueller, commented on the poor quality of "religious art" available in the United States in the 1930s. He wrote:

> No, Jesus Christ cannot be confused with a film star. The "Prince of Peace" is by no means a sentimental ranter in stage costumes and the "Child of love" is something more than a second Shirley Temple or rejuvenated Jackie Coogan.[10]

[7] John P. Bishop, "The Arts," in *The 1940s: Profile of a Nation in Crisis* (ed.) Charles Eisinger (Garden City, N.Y.: Doubleday and Co., 1969) 236.

[8] "The Apostolate," *OF* 12 (1938) 329.

[9] Peyton Boswell, "The Valiant Few," *Art Digest* 11 (1937) 3.

[10] Franz Mueller, "Heretical Conceptions of Religious Art," *The Christian Social Art Quarterly* 1 (1938) 4.

When liturgically-minded shopkeepers like Nina Polcyn Moore went looking for quality religious art, they travelled to European monasteries to find it. As late as 1948, John La Farge noted that the quality of Catholic art in the United States was not much improved:

> The fact that Catholic religious art in this country is as yet very unsatisfactory, to say the least, that it certainly does not correspond either in its content of thought and emotion or even in its technical skill with the dignity and competence that our Faith would demand is so much of a truism that it would only be wearisome to labor the point.[11]

The Liturgical Movement and Art: Liturgical Environment

Critics of the liturgical movement claimed that it was concerned solely with the artistic externals of the liturgy—vestments, candles, flowers—elements considered by many to be unimportant. Michel and his colleagues labored to demonstrate that the movement was, indeed, substantive, and that the goal of full and active liturgical participation was far more exhaustive than the type of vestments worn or the color of the flowers. Thus, the very beginning of the liturgical movement in the United States did not reveal an immediate concern with the liturgical environment—statuary, paintings, stained glass, vesture—in the way that it dealt with the more fundamental issue of liturgical participation. The hesitance about saying too much too soon on matters artistic might well be explained simply by good strategizing by the movement's pioneers. Nonetheless, Michel and his colleagues remained passionate about the issue of art in the liturgical environment.

Liturgical pioneers recognized the contrast between artistic growth within American culture and the sad state of affairs within the Church. They also recognized the success of the European liturgical renewal in its relationship to modern art and architecture and hoped for a similar breakthrough in the United States. Virgil Michel was influenced by the European liturgical art and was the first American Catholic to lecture on the topic of liturgical art, following his return to the United States. Writing on the topic in 1927, Michel stated: "Among the many [Catholics], almost all understanding has been lost."[12] A solid understanding of liturgical art needed to be restored within the American church, but it had to be an understanding that saw art as a servant of the liturgy.[13]

---

[11] John La Farge, "Catholic Religious Art" (August, 1948), in *A John La Farge Reader* (ed.) Thurston Davis (New York: The America Press, 1956) 38.

[12] "Editor's Note," *OF* 1 (1927) 182.

[13] Michel wrote to Maurice Lavanoux: "I judge from your statement that you must have an excellent library on liturgical art. Have you any ideas seeking for

Many American Catholics found it difficult to distinguish between genuinely liturgical art and the more broadly-interpreted religious art. Jacques Maritain helped to articulate a spirituality of Christian art, suggesting that art was visual theology. Christian art was doubly difficult, because being both an artist and a Christian offered tremendous challenges in the contemporary world.[14] Maritain described the tension in terms of "art of the Church, or sacred art," and "religious art." Many fine pieces of religious art had no function within the walls of the church itself. In other words, just because art happened to be religious, that did not necessarily imply that it automatically deserved to find a place within the worship space. Genuine sacred art had the power to evangelize while poorly executed art could potentially destroy or at least distort the message.

Maritain offered three criteria for determining genuine liturgical art. The first was "orthodoxy." If art was to function as a servant of the liturgy and a tool for evangelization, it needed to conform to the doctrinal truths which the Church preached. The second element was that of "liturgy." Liturgical art needed to conform to norms and regulations of liturgical usage, according to the proper authority on such matters. The third element offered was "inspiration." Liturgical art needed to proceed from an inspiration "neither academic, nor formalist, nor archaic, nor sentimental, but truly and authentically religious."[15]

John La Farge wrote that American Catholics needed to ask themselves about the function of religious art:

> There is a question as to how much real influence on Catholic life paintings and statues do really exert. Holy souls spend a lifetime in intimate companionship with atrocious works of art and yet find in them simply a mild stimulation to virtue or a means of fixing their attention on certain revealed truths, and are not affected for good or evil by the defects of the production. On the other hand, people can live amidst the most magnificent art and derive from there little benefit or even remain pure materialists.[16]

---

expression that might be appropriate for an article in *Orate Fratres?* We can offer no large honorarium and have been so stocked with materials that we have not yet started with articles on Liturgical Art. But if something suitable presents itself we make room for it, since we do not want to wait too long before saying something on the subject." Letter of 1 February 1929, SJAA: Z-25.

[14] See Jacques Maritain, *Art and Scholasticism* (New York: Charles Scribner's Sons, 1930).

[15] Jacques Maritain, "Reflections on Sacred Art," *LA* 4 (1935) 131–2.

[16] La Farge, "Catholic Religious Art," *LA* 16 (1947–48) 120.

What was the function of art within the liturgical environment? Was it to serve simply as a background for worship—as an adjunct or simply as an afterthought to the architecture of the church building? Was it to be simply the work of the artist, art on a religious theme with absolutely no connection to the liturgical prayer of the Church? Was it to function more as the *ikon*, where the image of a painting received a certain veneration by the assembly, and was therefore planned directly to assist in the concentration of worship, reverence, and liturgical ceremony? These were questions which needed to be asked by the liturgical pioneers as they called for a higher quality of American liturgical art, and as they called for greater union between art and worship. These were likewise questions to be asked by pastors and artisans together as they considered the communities for which the art would be created. Speculative thinking of this sort—corporate reflection between pastors and artisans—was more the exception than the norm in American parishes.

La Farge distinguished between the objective function of art and its subjective aim. Too often, the subjective aim included the notion of being "pleasant, consoling, comforting, or uplifting." He equated that subjectivity with America's cultural desire to be entertained—the desire for "immediate and palpable enjoyment."[17] Indeed, the same critique of subjectivity could be used when speaking about problems of liturgical participation in general, particularly in the post-Vatican II American church.

Along with objectivity and subjectivity, there needed to be a healthy balance between practicality and creative abstraction. If art were merely practical, then it would be "cheap and ugly," and would cease to be art. On the other hand, if art lacked a certain practicality, then it would "degenerate into dilettantism or aestheticism." A practical dimension within art maintained its connection to both secular and ecclesial life. With the rise of individualism and subjectivism in American culture, art risked being privatized, divorced from the social aspects of life. A degree of practicality protected art from such a demise. The ultimate goal was a harmonious blend between the objective and the subjective, the liturgical and the artistic within the worshipping community. This meant the removal of all extrinsic elements.[18]

Those who promoted quality liturgical art agreed that the goal was not to impose extrinsic artistic elements on the liturgy, rather to allow artistic beauty to emerge from within the liturgy itself. The best way

---

[17] Ibid., 121.
[18] Michel, "Liturgy and Art" (written in 1936), *Catholic Art Quarterly* 19 (1955–56) 24.

for liturgical artists to do this was to study the liturgical documents, along with liturgical history and symbolic traditions, in order to recognize the proper role of art within Christian worship. When liturgical art functioned properly, it was not superfluous but intrinsic to the very act of liturgy itself, because it united with the other liturgical elements.[19] The emergence of modern liturgical art attempted such a synthesis.

Art is intrinsically related to liturgy for one very good reason: liturgy itself is art in a broader, metaphorical sense. This was the thesis of Ildefons Herwegen, abbot of Maria Laach, years before the founding of the liturgical movement in the United States. Herwegen argued that liturgy "developed" into a work of art in that it bore within itself the seed of beauty which was bound to flourish. Life was implied in the bearing of a seed, which in turn implied a living tradition. And a living tradition implied a living art. Such a relationship between liturgy and the arts was natural in the early Church, but was lost in the late renaissance with all its philosophical and religious upheavals.[20]

Virgil Michel continued Herwegen's thesis:

> For the spirit of the liturgy is the supreme expression of the spirit of art. In the liturgy we find embodied in the highest degree some of the characteristics that are common to all art. The liturgy is essentially the external embodiment of an interior soul and spirit. In fact, in its sacramental mysteries it is above all else the incarnation of the truly Divine, the making present of the supernatural in its own mystical but real actuality . . . There is likewise something mysterious and mystical about all art. By means of the external all true art brings us into contact with the unseen, with the spiritual. It, too, is the embodiment of something that is essentially more than the merely external or corporal. From this standpoint the liturgy is the most precious, the richest art, since its inner reality at its best is the Divine itself.[21]

As liturgy and art shared this intrinsic connection, and as the Christian was called to live the liturgy and to be the body of Christ in daily life, so too was art a further extension of that same sacramental principle. Michel spoke of the Christian as an artist called through baptism and through ongoing liturgical participation to express the qualities of truth, goodness, and beauty—qualities which we attribute to God—in

---

[19] Gerald Phelan, "Aestheticism and the Liturgy," *LA* 4 (1935) 87–90.

[20] See Herwegen, *The Art Principle of the Liturgy,* (trans.) William Busch (Collegeville: The Liturgical Press, 1931).

[21] Michel, *The Liturgy of the Church* (New York: The MacMillan Co., 1938) 317.

daily life. Christ embodied those attributes to the full. The Christian was thus bound to be "another Christ," embodying those same qualities of truth, goodness, and beauty. Michel wrote:

> Every Christian is then an artist in showing forth in his life, through the grace of Christ, the truth, and the goodness, and the beauty of the Christ-life, the splendor of the truth of God.[22]

Some social activists of the 1930s and 1940s questioned the liturgy-art relationship, claiming that art was something belonging only to the rich. Virgil Michel dismissed such a critique:

> Art is thus not something that belongs to the idle and rich; it is something that follows naturally from the genuine life of a member of Christ. No great riches are required for art; only the qualities of soul that make the Christian a genuine image of God.[23]

Social activist and Catholic worker artist Adé Bethune concurred with Michel. In doing the ordinary tasks of life—washing dishes, doing laundry—Christians performed an art and consequently shared in the creative art of God. Those commonplace actions were an image of the eternal life which all Christians shared through baptism. In common elements the art of God was recognized. "We are like a cup," wrote Bethune, "And Christ is inside filling it." The result is that cups and jars "are raised to great dignity." So, the art of a meal shared together among Christians, in the home of one or another, is linked with the Eucharist and therefore rich in significance. The habitations of Christians, whether shacks or castles, are likewise rich in significance, "because we can see in them an image of the temple of God." In calling for participation in "the creative art of God," Bethune concluded:

> If we can discern in the reverent and holy usage of common things and in the sacred performance of common works, an image of our worship of God, it is not difficult to discern in our devotion, our respect, our hospitality towards our common fellow-man an image of the respect, the devotion, and the hospitality we owe God. Our art, the very excellence of our workmanship, stands as a living testimony of the holy love and reverence which we have for one another and which integrates us one to the other whether inferior or superior, deserving or undeserving, proud or humble, clean or dirty, young or old, known or unknown, into one body, living one life.[24]

[22] Michel, "Art and the Christ-Life," *Catholic Art Quarterly* 5 (1941) 2–5.
[23] Ibid., 3.
[24] Adé Bethune, "This 'Here' Life," *The Christian Social Art Quarterly* 3 (1940) 7–8, 10.

Like the liturgy, art was not intended to be a museum piece, but a vibrant, living tradition, responsive to the signs of the times. In a paper delivered at the 1944 liturgical week in New York City, Maurice Lavanoux noted that discussions on both liturgy and art were often explosive, perhaps because both were living traditions: "liturgy is life . . . art is life." Lavanoux was responding to those within the American church who wanted to keep both liturgy and art in the realm of archaeology where they were safe, not tampered with, and had little effect on contemporary life. Both liturgy and art challenged the "status quo," and were organically-linked living traditions.[25]

The organic relationship between art and liturgical participation was described as sharing the same foundation, love, similar to the relationship between nature and supernature. Just as art was international, capable of bridging gaps that divided nations and peoples, so too liturgy was "supra-national," in that it was one great collective action uniting all people to one another through their union with Christ. Art was elevated to its highest dignity in the performance of liturgical worship just as nature reached its true destiny in its union with the supernatural.[26]

Connections between liturgical participation and liturgical art were not always easily recognized. Editors of the journal *Liturgical Arts* were challenged to keep the doctrine of the Mystical Body and the issue of liturgical participation in the forefront of their readers' minds. Many members of the Liturgical Arts Society were concerned primarily about the "externals" of worship, and needed to be reminded of the foundations of liturgical art in the Mystical Body. Bringing such matters to the Society's consciousness created a certain amount of tension in those early years.[27]

The Liturgical Arts Society shared the same fundamental goal as the liturgical pioneers. Its leadership was convinced that the primary

---

[25] Lavanoux, "The Liturgy, Art, and Common Sense," *LA* 13 (1944–45) 54–5.

[26] Michel, *The Liturgy of The Church*, 318–9.

[27] Susan White, *Art, Architecture, and Liturgical Reform: The Liturgical Arts Society (1927–1972)* (New York: Pueblo Publishing Co., 1990) 87. The Society attempted to settle the matter with the following statement: "Properly understood, the liturgy is *both* the internal homage of the soul *and* its outward bodily expression by means of words, chant, ceremonies, etc., in the forms ordained by the Church for her . . . public worship! The aims of the Liturgical Arts Society have always stressed these two aspects of the liturgy without which what has become known as the Liturgical Movement might well be more aesthetic speculation of an unbalanced insistence on externals without corresponding spiritual foundation." "Editorial," *LA* 14 (1946) 128.

means of achieving full and active liturgical participation was to convince the assembly that they were a fit *subject* for participation in the Mass. Had this been readily accepted and had "intelligence and willingness of the layman . . . not been generally underestimated,"[28] full and active participation might already have been a reality.

The union of art and liturgy needed to be organic rather than accidental, and that could only happen when the smaller merged with the greater, when liturgical art took its inspiration from the liturgy, and when art lost itself in the liturgical action in order to find its highest meaning. According to Michel, art as a servant of the liturgy was merely an instrument, "a means, but a means in which the liturgical action reaches its highest perfection of expression that created mind can give it."[29] Accordingly, Michel cautioned against too strong an emphasis on the art itself:

> In general, however, we shall continue fighting shy of too great emphasis on the externals . . . but shall continue to stress the inner nature of the liturgy above all. This is the source of greatest misunderstanding of the liturgy by bishops and priests, even Benedictines. Once the true inner spirit is caught, the externals will almost take care of themselves. On the other hand we might stress the externals without ever getting at the true internal spirit, and thus end by being mere aesthetes and not true children of God.[30]

Virgil Michel described liturgy as a living art where the human and divine act together. The liturgy in action was living art of the highest quality. As such, the relationship between liturgy and art was not extrinsic or artificial but organic. In this manner, art was participative, contributing to and symbolically expressive of the call to liturgical participation which was at the heart of the movement.

Not all Christian art, even good quality Christian art, was necessarily liturgical art.[31] Liturgical art needed to be inspired by the liturgy in its ideas and ideals. Michel pointed to a very pastoral problem regard-

---

[28] Editorial, *LA* 13 (1944) 2.

[29] Editorial, Ibid., 319.

[30] Letter of Virgil Michel to Matthew Britt, 9 September 1929, SJAA: Z-22.

[31] John Sellner wrote: "Art . . . is not necessarily fit for the Church simply because it is artistic. In fact it fails to be artistic when it is out of place . . . A man travelling through a certain city was looking for a Church. Finally he espied an exquisite little Gothic building, and asked a passerby what that Church was. 'That's no church,' he was told; 'that's a gas station.' Art loses its intrinsic value if its out of place." "Worship of God in Church Music," *The Christian Social Art Quarterly* 3 (1940) 9.

ing the construction or renovation of worship spaces and the type of art designed for those spaces:

> . . . in many instances, the artistic features of our churches are deter-
> mined not by the traditional wisdom of the liturgy, but by the individu-
> alistic quirks of pious donors, who litter the church walls, or even the
> altar itself, with ornaments and statues of all sorts, entirely unrelated to
> the aims and spirit of liturgical relationship.[32]

In its service of the liturgy, liturgical art shared the same purpose as the liturgy itself: to give glory and praise to God, and to sanctify the liturgical assembly, rather than call attention to itself. Thus, like all ser-vants of the liturgy, liturgical artists engaged in an apostolic function, since the artist served as a mediator of Christ's presence in the assem-bly. Michel reinforced the ministry of the artist in this way:

> The Christian artist, perhaps more than any other Christian, is always a
> lay apostle. He is *ex professo* an apostle of the liturgical spirit in his very
> vocation.[33]

Predictably, the recognition of an artist's role as a servant of the liturgy would come through a deeper understanding of his or her member-ship in the Mystical Body of Christ:

> If he (the artist) is going to fabricate decorations that are fitting for the
> dwelling place of the Head of the Mystical Body he must first be deeply
> imbued with his own dignity as a member of that Body of which Christ
> is the Head.[34]

Michel also described the liturgical artist as a "Christian educator," since liturgical art led Christians to the truths of the faith. The artist possessed an apostolic function since liturgical art helped to fulfill the purpose of the liturgy.[35]

Like the artists who crafted it, a work of liturgical art was also a ser-vant of the liturgy, leading participants into the very experience of the holy. But even when art was well executed, it was not always easy to convince artists that their art was not an end in itself. Eric Gill, the well-known English engraver and type designer, argued that liturgical

---

[32] Michel, "Liturgy and Catholic Life" (manuscript, 214), quoted in Marx, 277. Parts of "Liturgy and Catholic Life" appeared in *OF* as a series between 1939 and 1941.

[33] "The Apostolate," *OF* 11 (1937) 183.

[34] G. Ryan, "Art in the Liturgy," *The Christian Social Art Quarterly* 2 (1939) 7.

[35] Michel, "Liturgy and Art," 27.

art was public art and should not over-emphasize the personal or subjective whims of the artist.[36]

If art was to be a servant of worship and reflect the dignity of the Mystical Body of Christ, then the purchasing of cheap imitations such as manufactured liturgical art made available through catalogs, was unsatisfactory.[37] The use of original and natural materials was encouraged at all cost. Liturgical art was not limited to icons or statuary but included all elements which contributed to the creation of the liturgical environment.[38] Put simply, liturgy was an experience of beauty, and therefore liturgical art needed to express that beauty most profoundly.

To promote quality liturgical art, the pioneers advocated an integrated vision which harmonized the worship space with the liturgical act itself, and with those who participated in that action. Consequently, to bring about such integration, it was considered essential to deal with those who were primarily responsible for the creation of the liturgical environment—the artists themselves. The contribution of artists was an important ministry within the Church and the pioneers assisted American Catholics, especially the artists themselves, in recognizing that reality.

[36] See Susan White, *Art, Architecture, and Liturgical Reform,* 112–4.

[37] Maurice Lavanoux called for a de-centralization of good sources of liturgical art: "sources which could call upon first rate sculptors, painters, ceramists, enamelers, silversmiths, wood carvers, stained glass craftsmen, and so forth. Is not something wrong with the existing set-up when a pastor in the State of Washington, for example, feels he must write to New York, or even to Chicago, for information? Could we not have regional centres? . . . And I do not mean sources supplied by the 'church goods' manufacturers." "A Panel Discussion at the National Catholic Building Convention, Chicago, 1 July 1948," *LA* 17 (1948–49) 30.

[38] In a letter to Virgil Michel, Adé Bethune wrote of her commencement of a liturgical vesture business in New York City and Newport, Rhode Island, which would be dedicated to the creation of artful, dignified liturgical vesture. The letter points to the marked difference between catalog liturgical art and that which was crafted and fashioned by an individual artist: ". . . Did I tell you about my attempts at 'baptizing' my mother's business? She has a very busy workshop, as you may know, of linens, lace, lingerie, etc. . . . Well, at New Year's I concocted 2 chasubles with her and studied the problems of silk, cost, colors, style, etc. Since then we've already had 4 orders! . . . Let Barclay St. watch out—for 'Thames Street' will be a great rival. Boy can we beat Barclay St.—at its own prices even! I figured out ways of making such simple vestments that all the money can go into the quality of the silk and the simple workmanship, as *none* is wasted on fake ornament. Even using the best silk, the vestments come to only $32 to $41 and using the less expensive silk I should think they could be made for $20. I don't think Barclay St. sells ample vestments for less!—and even those are so carelessly thrown together that it makes

The Liturgical Arts Society

As liturgical leaders were developing a theory of the apostolic function of liturgical art in the midwest, the practitioners of those arts were responding to the call on the east coast with the founding of the Liturgical Arts Society. In 1925, Everitt Radcliffe Harman, a thirty-two year old Benedictine from Portsmouth Priory, Rhode Island, arrived at Portsmouth's founding abbey, Fort Augustus, Scotland, to begin theological studies. Prior to entering the monastery, Harman had completed a degree at the Massachusetts Institute of Technology School of Architecture. In his two years abroad, he observed with great interest the artistic renewal taking place at Fort Augustus, Beuron, Maredsous, and elsewhere in Europe, and recognized the potential for a similar renewal in the United States. Determined to promote that same artistic renewal within American Catholicism, on returning to Portsmouth in 1927 Harman organized a retreat for a small group of New York and Boston artists, architects, and draftsmen, many of whom had studied at such prestigious schools as Harvard, Yale, Princeton, and Columbia and all of whom were wealthy. Together, they shared a common frustration at the generally poor quality of religious art within the American church.[39]

At that first retreat held at Portsmouth Priory in 1927, Everitt Harman put forth his plan. He proposed "A Benedictine Oblates Guild of Architects, Artists, and Craftsmen," primarily to encourage the creation of quality liturgical art and architecture and to challenge the "status quo." One "Letter to the Editor" in the periodical *Liturgical Arts* described what the guild was against:

> prison stone churches looking like jails on the outside and either wedding cakes or vaudeville theatres in the inside . . . cardboard chasubles and lace curtain albs and surplices, against gold fringe frontlets and female angels in pink and blue dance frocks, against fret-saw shrines and confessionals, against factory statues in "natural" colors tattooed with gold-leaf "decorations" on religious habits, against wood painted to imitate grained marble, against any and every sort of imitation.[40]

One of the members, Maurice Lavanoux, was concerned that the wealth and prestige of the group, along with the agenda which had been set, would present serious obstacles to the relationship between liturgical art and social justice. Unable to present a cohesive plan, the

---

my heart bleed to see such sloppiness and vulgarity." Letter of 15 March 1938, SJAA: Z-22.

[39] S. White, 1–2.

[40] Benjamin Musser, "Letter to the Editor," *LA* 1 (1932) 78.

guild disbanded within one year because of a debate over whether or not members should become Benedictine oblates or remain independent. A more realistic plan was then presented, and the Liturgical Arts Society was established in the New York apartment of Idesbald van der Gracht, in 1928, as an effort to "devise ways and means for improving the standards of taste, craftsmanship, and liturgical correctness in the practice of Catholic art in the United States."[41] Van der Gracht had been one of the members of the Portsmouth guild, and nine of the original guild members were among the founders of the Liturgical Arts Society. This was a lay organization which included women and men from all walks of ecclesial life. Virgil Michel served as one of the early advisors to the group.[42] Members of that society were committed to the creation of art and architecture which would serve the liturgical assembly and would give artistic expression to what their participation professed. The Liturgical Arts Society insisted that objects of art employed in the Church's liturgical prayer be in harmony with that worship, thus contributing to the renewal of the true Christian spirit in ecclesial and civil life.

One artist who successfully grasped that harmony between worship and art was Eric Gill. A promoter of the social art movement in England, Gill was one of the major influences on the development of American liturgical art and an early member of the Liturgical Arts Society. Like the Impressionists, the social art movement originated in the nineteenth century as a protest movement against neo-classicism. Social artists separated themselves into communes as a way of living more organically the relationship between art and human community. Gill devoted his life to creating religious art which was imaginative and of the highest quality, and became an example for members of the Liturgical Arts Society and other artists, as well.[43] Through his association

[41] Masthead, *LA* volumes 1:1 to 40:3, quoted in White, viii. Founded in 1931, *LA* was the primary publication of the Liturgical Arts Society and was published quarterly.

[42] In a letter to Michel inviting his membership, L. Bancel La Farge wrote: "Just now we are working to organize the following groups: architects, painters, sculptors, craftsmen (iron workers, glass makers, etc.) and literary men having liturgical knowledge and interests. We wish to learn if you are impressed with the idea and willing to join the movement. Knowing as all of us do the dimensions of the Catholic building program in the United States, there can be no doubt that the opportunity is great and that the need for better work is imperative." Letter of L. Bancel La Farge to Virgil Michel, 22 March 1930, SJAA: Z-25.

[43] See Eric Gill, *Art Nonsense and Other Essays* (London: Cassel and Co., 1929); *Beauty Looks After Herself* (New York: Sheed and Ward, 1933); and *Art and a Changing Civilization* (London: John Lane, 1934).

with the British liturgist, Donald Attwater, Gill came to know Virgil Michel, and became an early artistic advisor to *Orate Fratres*, assisting especially with cover designs and regularly offering a critique of the magazine's layout and design. On occasion, he wrote on the liturgy itself and submitted those articles to Virgil Michel for his critique.[44] A socially-minded artist who was imbued by the liturgical spirit, Gill's influence was substantial within the early years of the American liturgical movement. The American liturgical artist, Frank Kacmarcik, who did not become involved in the liturgical movement until 1950, was deeply influenced by the work of Eric Gill.[45]

Artists like Gill and, later, Kacmarcik, bridged many gaps between art, worship, and social justice. Others took up the work also. As an artist and liturgical pioneer strongly committed to the Catholic Worker, Adé Bethune assisted that same integration.[46] Bethune, a Belgian, was influenced by Beauduin's efforts in her own country. Coming from a liturgically-active Belgian school, she was disappointed with the impoverished liturgical life in New York. After becoming involved in the Catholic Worker, Bethune was encouraged by Dorothy Day to pursue her liturgical interest. Day orchestrated Bethune's participation in the Catholic Action Summer School where she studied liturgy with Gerald Ellard.[47]

Another contributor to such integration was John La Farge, S.J. La Farge was chaplain to the Liturgical Arts Society and also editor of *America*, the Jesuit weekly, in addition to being a social activist. Together, these concerns led him to involvement in the liturgical movement. His many articles in *America, Liturgical Arts,* and *The Commonweal,* reflect an integrative vision uniting liturgical participation, liturgical art, and social reform. *LA* modelled that same integration. Although it served as the journal of the Liturgical Arts Society, it did not limit its scope strictly to art and architecture in the liturgical context. Like *OF* and *The Catholic Worker,* we find in this artistic journal the same integrated concerns for liturgical participation and social responsibility, and for the role that art played in such concerns.

As chaplain to the Society, La Farge was concerned about the alienation from the Church experienced by many artists. This concern is

[44] Letters of Eric Gill to Virgil Michel, 25 April, 25 May, 26 July 1938, SJAA: Z-24.

[45] Frank Kacmarcik, Interview by author, 22 November 1994. St. John's Abbey, Collegeville, Minnesota.

[46] See Judith Stoughton, *Proud Donkey of Schaerbeek: Adé Bethune, Catholic Worker Artist* (St. Cloud: North Star Press, 1988).

[47] Adé Bethune, Interview by Nancy Roberts, 26 April 1983. Marquette University Archives, Catholic Worker Collection (W-9), Milwaukee, Wisconsin.

evident in many of his writings. In one article in *America*, La Farge argued that the root of an artist's spiritual problems was the inability to appreciate the sanctity of the art itself, a sanctity revealed only when the artist attended to the mystical or contemplative side within his or her life. That mysticism, nourished and celebrated in the liturgical assembly with other members of the Mystical Body of Christ, helped artists to see their work in its proper perspective. La Farge admitted that due to a variety of reasons, many artists did not easily find their place within the liturgical life of the Church.[48]

Maurice Lavanoux argued that part of the problem with religious art in the United States was precisely the equation of the spirituality of the artist with his or her professional artistic ability. Too many clergy, in Lavanoux's estimation, equated artistic excellence with "the personal piety and goodness of the artist." Among well-known artists whose secular work was already exhibited in various museums, it was seldom the case that their religious art reached the same high level of quality. This was perhaps the case, in Lavanoux's estimation, because those artists felt the need to conform to the poor standards already established for American religious art.[49]

Liturgical Artists and Alienation from American Society and Church

Numerous letters to the editors to *OF* and *LA* in the 1930s and 40s expressed the conviction that liturgical artists were, in general, unrealistic in their approach and incapable of responding adequately to the pragmatic demands of average parishes. Some argued that the new and creative liturgical art displayed and promoted by *LA* failed to touch the human experience of average American Catholics:

> You are fighting a good fight, but it seems to me that you are still a little in the clouds . . . Who will have the courage to put in his church a painting like "The Disciples of Emmaus," . . . by Daniel O'Neill? Or a mosaic by Elsa Schmidt? They may be great artists but their work cannot enter our churches.[50]

Another writer in *LA* noted that too often the incorporation of art into a new worship space was the last thing to be considered. The writer suggested that it was crucial for the pastor to deal directly with the

---

[48] La Farge, "Religious Problems of the Catholic Artist," *America* 58 (1938) 547–8. See also "Further Thoughts on Christian Art and Artists," *America* 59 (1938) 42–3.

[49] Lavanoux, "Catholics and Religious Art," in *Catholicism in America: A Series of Articles from* The Commonweal (New York: Harcourt, Brace, and Co., 1953) 202.

[50] Luigi Scioccheti, "Letter To the Editor," *LA* 19 (1950–51) 79–80.

artist, engaging him or her in the process from the beginning, rather than considering the art as an afterthought in the construction of a new church. The pastor and liturgical artist, along with the architect and others involved, could learn and work toward consensus on the art most appropriate for the worship space being discussed.[51] In arguing for quality liturgical art that was expressive of the particular worshiping community, one writer contended that "art must be brought back to the people." He continued:

> The artist has become separated from the society in which he exists— retiring to an "ivory tower" where he produces esoteric displays of technique for an audience of equally esoteric critics and fellow artists. The result of this decadence has been the isolation of the individual major arts—painting, sculpture, and architecture. Each artist in his field is content to compete with the other. In other words, integration of the arts as the byzantine, gothic, and renaissance worlds knew it, is no longer in existence.[52]

Artists recognized their separation from the community, but attributed its cause to art's prophetic role within society, not easily received by the community precisely because art confronted uncomfortable issues and themes which most people would rather avoid:

> To a great extent, indeed, the artist now occupies the place of the persecuted saint of another day . . . Ultimately art is concerned with one value and one value only: truth. But truth is an ethical value—perhaps the supreme ethical value. Modern art is unpopular because it has pursued this value to the exclusion of all sentiment and compromise.[53]

Opinions differed on reasons for the estrangement of artists from the Church and on possible solutions. One letter in *America* called for the establishment of an art commission in every diocese to assist both liturgical artists and pastors in healing the rift by establishing artistic norms for each local church.[54]

The Liturgical Arts Society retreats for artists and architects were another way of inculcating a better liturgical understanding within that professional group and of attempting to heal the division between the art world and liturgical assemblies. The advertisement for one retreat noted:

---

[51] R. Hurley, "Letter to the Editor," *LA* 21 (1952–53) 65–6.
[52] James Wines, "Letter to the Editor," *LA* 22 (1953–54) 130.
[53] "Editorial," *LA* 19 (1951) 54.
[54] G. B. Werner, "Church Goods," *America* 63 (1940) 718.

Such retreats, if based on the liturgy, will, besides promoting the personal holiness of the artists, at the same time tend to impart that inspiration which is required in him who would produce real liturgical art. They would become schools for the formation of artists who will learn to know the true principles of ecclesiastical art and to apply them in their work.[55]

The retreats were organized twice a year in different monasteries around the United States.[56] Portsmouth Priory, Rhode Island, became a national center for liturgically-minded artists and architects much in the way that Collegeville served as a national center for the entire American liturgical movement.

In addition to the liturgical retreats, summer gatherings of artists, poets, liturgists, and dramatists were initiated in the late 1930s for the exchange of ideas and common study. In a letter to Virgil Michel, Sarah Taylor explained the 1937 summer program, which was to be held at Clark's Island in Plymouth Harbor, Massachusetts. Taylor wrote:

A group within the Boston Chapter of the Catholic Poetry Society of America is promoting a summer colony to foster creative activities, spiritual, liturgical, poetic, musical, dramatic and philosophical . . . Recently Pulpit Rock where the Pilgrims are reputed to have held their first Sabbath and one of the most historical spots in the Mayflower territory, was blessed by a Jesuit at the invitation of the proprietor. Now "The Old House," a colonial farmhouse with capacity for a dozen or more persons, has been made available for the colonists to occupy from July 1 through Labor Day 1937.[57]

Whether a retreat for liturgical artists or a summer art colony, such gatherings helped to bridge the gap between art and American Catholicism. Many artists and pastors lived in a world which dichotomized art and worship. They failed to recognize the intrinsic relationship between the two and saw art as ornamentation, as something added to the liturgy rather than organically emerging from the worship of a given community. Thus, in addition to focusing on the artists themselves, liturgical reformers directed their efforts toward highlighting the unique intrinsic connection between liturgy and art.

The Synthesis of Modern Liturgical Art

Playful new art forms were emerging at the beginning of this century, emphasizing the abstract over the real. With its roots in Picasso,

[55] Editor, "A Liturgical Retreat for Architects and Artists," *OF* 7 (1932) 86.
[56] Ibid., 87.
[57] Letter of 14 November 1936, SJAA: Z-22.

modern art emerged in New York in the early years of the twentieth century as a protest movement against representational art. By principle, modern artists negated any intelligible subject matter, but not any intelligible meaning. In negating subject matter, modern religious art returned to the basics, to the core of Christian faith. Certain materials—concrete, for example—made new structural forms possible, along with new combinations of color and texture. Thanks to new methods of illumination, there were lighting effects which had never been seen before. Why not bring these discoveries and concepts of beauty to the service of God in the liturgical assembly? When asked to define modern art at the National Catholic Building Convention in 1948, liturgical artist Emil Frei responded with one word: "simplicity."[58] Modern art proved to be a threat to many—a stripping away of what many held sacred—and was quite controversial within American Catholic circles in the 1930s and 1940s.

On the one side of the issue, artists were arguing that something new was emerging: an uncluttering of excessive ornamentation which distracted liturgical participants. Those in the art community challenged the American church to be open to a simplification of the liturgical space.[59] Modern liturgical art was capable of forging the synthesis between the liturgical and the artistic. Like the liturgical movement, modern liturgical art was responding to the signs of the times and expressed the social and religious themes of the liturgical movement. On the other side, however, some American Catholics argued that modern art was diametrically opposed to tradition, much in the same way that critics of the liturgical movement contended that it, too, was not sufficiently tradition-bound.[60] Joseph E. Ritter, archbishop of St. Louis, offered his support to artists and called the American church to greater artistic tolerance:

[58] Editor, "A Panel Discussion," 33.

[59] "I am pleading that decoration for decoration's sake, and stunty combinations of crucifix and candlesticks, be confined to shrines. I am stating that, at the high altar, the liturgical revival needs designers with a stern sense of relative values, a sophisticated restraint and a lighter touch. Could we not have less crowing and flapping of wings over altar designs merely because they are rubrically correct? Should not the criterion be liturgical motivation, not 'grand effects' which smother the rite?" Wellington Schaefer, "Letter to the Editor," *LA* 16 (1947–48) 136.

[60] Maurice Lavanoux responded: "We must not be swayed by the pronouncements of those who see the devil in any creative work of art that is a bit out of the ordinary. Some of you may remember Father Gillis' syndicated warning of pending doom in his effusion entitled—no less—'Atheism and Modern Art.' Such utterances can do great harm, particularly if they are taken seriously by those in authority." Editor, "A Panel Discussion," 30.

> Surely it is not the tradition of the Church for art to be something static, or for the artist of our day serving religion to be confined to imitating the designs of past centuries . . . The connotations of the word "modern" has led timid souls to equate it with a denial of the past . . . Let us take the word "tradition." It is often understood as a static frame of mind, as opposed to modern, whereas it is really a dynamic force, a continuing force.[61]

Writing in *LA*, artist Leopold Arnaud pointed to the nineteenth century as the time when the paradigmatic shift in artistic creativity within Christian art could be pinpointed:

> Until the nineteenth century, art was naturally and unconsciously contemporary. While continuously expressing the permanent dogmas of the Church, Christian art was constantly changing in form, vocabulary, and iconography in compliance with the changes in social requirements, philosophic ideals, and aesthetic concepts, so that it was always a spontaneous, creative art, animated by the vitality and living flexibility of the Church.[62]

With the nineteenth century came new archaeological discoveries and a new fascination with the reconstruction of classical antiquity. Secular art was inspired more by archaeological discoveries than by the earlier creativity which had been its hallmark. At the same time, the Church was reexamining its own origins and history, and it held creativity in greater suspicion. Those who were suspicious of creativity appealed to tradition, but so did modern liturgical artists:

> With the understanding that the word "tradition" has nothing in it of "convention" or "routine," that it excludes neither conflict nor problems, evolution nor struggle, I like to call myself a traditional artist. The true tradition as much in the ways of living as in the arts and the professions, implies a continuous renewal. And these renewals do not appear without ebb and flow, without sudden fits of intense disgust or exaggerated preferences.[63]

Another artist suggested that American Catholics' inability to sufficiently appreciate modern liturgical art was consistent with the American culture's artistic illiteracy. As noted earlier in this chapter, by the 1930s, art—even modern art—had become a more acceptable medium in the United States. This was less the case within the American church,

---

[61] Joseph Ritter, "Toward a Living Climate of Religious Art," *LA* 23 (1954–55) 4.
[62] Leopold Arnaud, "The Living Tradition in Christian Art," *LA* 9 (1941) 47.
[63] Joep Nicolas, "The Credo of An Artist," *LA* 9 (1941) 50.

perhaps because American Catholics were still largely an immigrant group. Ides van der Gracht, one of the founders of the Liturgical Arts Society, attributed the poor quality of American liturgical art to "the low socio-cultural status of immigrant priests."[64] There was a stark difference on the European continent, where Catholics in France, Germany, and Switzerland responded much more readily to modern artistic developments. In Griffin's view, the prejudice toward modern liturgical art was due to ignorance. He called for tolerance:

> What about tolerance? . . . tolerance to investigate the new work with the equipment which qualifies you to make an investigation. This must be instilled from the teaching. Art is a science, and the elements of the physics of this science must be understood, but this must be counter-balanced by the individual perception.[65]

Supporters of modern liturgical art argued that resistance was understandable. Fundamentally, people resist change, and so whatever arguments were used, negative reactions toward modern liturgical art were to be expected. Through education, however, people were capable of change. Beginning with the early years of a child's schooling, the education of American Catholics about the history and symbolic significance of modern religious art would provide a better understanding of the role of art within worship, as well.[66] Maurice Lavanoux argued that, aside from education, too many clergy spoke for their parishioners without seriously surveying their congregations as to their needs or wishes.[67]

---

[64] S. White, 135.

[65] Griffin, "Letter to the Editor," *LA* 17 (1948–49) 71.

[66] "Behind all the tawdry religious art is the working proverb of most business— 'Give the public what it wants!' . . . Most Americans want white bread just because they are used to it. They need the food values of whole grain bread, but very few prefer to eat it. This can be corrected by education, especially in the young . . . Aesthetically, Catholic children are weaned on trash." Melville Steinfels, "Modern Religious Art," *Catholic Art Quarterly* 7 (1944) 4.

[67] "It is a fallacy to offer as an excuse for bad work the *hint* that it is *what the people want*. Can we not say, rather, that members of an average congregation seldom have an opportunity to express their opinion on these matters? They seldom have the opportunity to make comparisons, they grow up among the relics of past mistakes, and they are led to believe that such relics are the normal apparel of any Catholic church. On the basis of my experience in quite a few instances, I feel that many a parishioner would welcome a change, provided, of course, the whole business is decently explained to him." Editor, "A Panel Discussion," 30.

If modern liturgical art was to be the synthesis of the liturgical and the artistic, its promoters had their difficulties in gaining an acceptance of their cause by the majority of American Catholics. Well into the 1950s, liturgists and artists continued to lament the sad state of liturgical art within the United States. Unlike countries such as Germany, where the National Episcopal Conference issued formal support for the liturgical arts in the late 1930s, American Catholic artists continued to be held in suspicion by many within the American church. The topic of church architecture sheds more light on this tension.

The Liturgical Movement and Architecture

The goals of the liturgical movement were not easily realized in American church architecture of the 1920s and 1930s. A modern liturgical movement needed a modern liturgical architecture that would better reflect the goal of full and active liturgical participation. The birth of modern Church architecture comprised one part of the larger movement in modern architecture, so, it is essential to begin by briefly discussing the modern architectural movement.

The modern architectural movement was firmly established by the time the liturgical movement in the United States came into existence in 1926. Like the modern art movement, the modern architectural movement was a revolt against false architecture that blended assorted architectural styles into one or attempted to imitate historical styles of the past—the neo-classical and neo-Gothic revivals, for example— which had separated architecture from the life of the community. That movement within architectural design emerged as one artistic response to the social problems of the world. Through socially-minded modern architects, architectural projects of urban planning and urban renewal, along with an overall desire to create public spaces that reverenced the life of the community, were the architectural community's contribution to the social restoration of secular and religious society.

The origins of the movement can be traced back to the nineteenth century, to engineers such as Thomas Telford and Marc Seguin, and to the influence of the French *Ecole Polytechnique,* founded in 1794. In the nineteenth century, a new architectural style emerged, not in prestigious academies and lofty embassies, but in very commonplace environments like the waterfront of St. Louis and the department stores of Chicago. By the beginning of the First World War, American architect Frank Lloyd Wright was already exercising considerable influence on the American architectural scene.

The liturgical movement and modern architectural movement in Europe first came together in the Paris suburbs in 1918, to create a modern church building at Le Raincy, thanks to the leadership and the foresight of the pastor, Abbé Nègre. After consulting several ecclesiastical architectural firms and receiving cost estimates that far exceeded the parish budget, Nègre invited the consultation of Auguste Perret, a secular architect, well-known as a master of reinforced-concrete construction. The design produced was large enough to accommodate two thousand congregants, and the cost was far less than the other estimates. The design was approved, construction began in 1922, and the church was completed and dedicated the following year. If the decisive date for the beginning of the pastoral liturgical movement in Europe was the Malines Conference of 1909, then the 1923 consecration of the church of Notre-Dame du Raincy marks the beginning of the movement in modern liturgical architecture.[68] Despite its significance, however, Perret's work was virtually ignored for thirty years, until the 1950s when he received his next commission to design another church. Switzerland and Germany soon followed the lead in modern church architecture. Influenced by Perret, Karl Moser designed St. Anthony, Basel, in 1927. Fritz Metzger's St. Charles Church, Luzerne, using the one-room type plan—a common feature of Swiss church architecture—offered another example.[69] In Germany, dialogue between theologians and architects developed, and the basic theology and principles of modern church architecture were formulated through the influence of Maria Laach and the contribution of liturgical leaders like Romano Guardini. Those individuals were not simply concerned about the possibility of new materials and structural systems in

---

[68] Peter Hammond, *Liturgy and Architecture* (New York: Columbia University Press, 1961) 52–4. The plan reflected the basilica model of the early church, except without a separate choir. The church was designed as one single integrated space and the elevated altar was centrally placed, bringing it closer to the assembly. With the use of concrete, pillars were thin and did not obstruct the assembly's view of the table, ambo, and presider. The ambo was placed on the north side of the church. The baptistry was located to the left of the entrance of the church. A small chapel stood on the right of the entrance. The design was applauded for its honest integrity of style. It was simple, uncluttered, and devoid of unnecessary ornamentation.

[69] According to Peter Hammond: "Switzerland was the only country in western Christendom which, by the late thirties, had created a living tradition of church architecture. There is still no other country where modern churches of real quality take their place so naturally among the best secular buildings of the day. The 'ecclesiastical' architect does not exist. The finest Swiss churches are the work of the same architects who have created some of the most outstanding schools, hospitals, and houses of the last thirty years. The Church has learned how to speak the language of the living." Hammond, 62.

church construction; more importantly, they were concerned about the essential function of the *domus ecclesiae* with its contemporary expression in modern architecture.

One of the leading theorists in this regard was Rudolf Schwarz, an associate of Guardini's in the "Quickborn" Catholic Youth Movement in Germany. Schwarz designed his churches on two fundamental principles. First, one begins designing a church from a reality based on faith rather than art. Secondly, one who designs a church must be "absolutely truthful in . . . artistic language by saying nothing more than we can say in our times and nothing which cannot be understood by our contemporaries."[70] H. A. Reinhold wrote:

> I think Rudolf Schwarz has made the church anew *a house for* divine worship, not an autonomous, architectural expression of religious feeling, *religiöses Weltgefühl.* That is a step forward.[71]

Dominikus Böhm's cruciform church at Ringenberg, completed in 1935, was famous for its extreme simplicity, its free-standing stone altar in the center of the transept, and the possibility for the one presiding to stand behind the table and face the assembly. While it is beyond the scope of this study to concentrate on modern church architecture in Europe, the brief summary given of European developments is helpful when considering the growth of modern church architecture within the United States.

Modern American church architecture developed much more slowly than in Europe. In fact, in the words of liturgical and architectural designer, Robert Rambusch, "In the United States, art and architecture grew up outside of the church."[72] While something new was emerging on the European continent, tasteful Gothic continued to be the architectural style employed in American churches in that same period—the 1920s and 1930s. Further, the kind of theological and architectural collaboration taking place in Germany was still in its nascent stages in the United States.

American liturgical pioneers who had travelled through Europe were very much impressed with the congruence between liturgy and church architecture. Michel, Busch, Reinhold, and others, longed for that same congruence on American shores. In April 1927, while addressing a group of architects in St. Paul, Minnesota, Michel called for

---

[70] Ibid., 55–6. Schwarz designed the Church of Corpus Christi, Aachen, in 1930, and the village chapel at Leversbach, near Cologne, in 1934.

[71] Reinhold, "The Architecture of Rudolf Schwarz," *Architectural Forum* (January, 1939) 24.

[72] Interview by author, 3 January 1995, New York City.

a church architecture in harmony with the participative goals of the liturgical movement. In that address, Michel acknowledged that American churches were, in fact, constructed in pioneer conditions, often in immigrant communities with insufficient funds. Too often the concern with the building of churches focused on the practicalities— the cost of the construction, methods of ventilation, and the response of the people to the design. Too seldom was there any reference to art. Michel deemed this a natural consequence of a pioneer church within which nothing else was possible. Acknowledging the obviously limited resources of those who constructed American church buildings, Michel said:

> . . . this youthful country was strewn with churches that (sic) are products of the art of construction, but not of the higher art of architecture.[73]

As the country continued to develop, however, American Catholics could no longer be content with a merely pragmatic view of church architecture. Theoretically, American Catholics needed to ask themselves: "What is the social mission of architecture?" More specifically, what was the role of churches in the social mission of architecture? Indeed, such a question was consistent with the message of liturgical leaders who advocated the social dimension of worship. According to Michel:

> Catholic churches, as works of architectural art, must pursue religious perfection as expressed in the Catholic ideals of worship . . . Architecture is more truly a sermon in stones that preaches the ideals and truths of the Catholic religious life even as these are preached from the pulpit in the official Catholic worship.[74]

Church architecture was deeply symbolic with its own inherent language. This was evident in the early Roman basilicas and in the great Christian churches of later centuries:

> Then the churches preached sermons in living stone; then the church building spoke, to those who knew and understood its language, of the truths of life, of time and eternity, of the mysteries of Christianity.[75]

---

[73] "The Catholic Spirit in Architecture: An Address to the Gargoyle Club of the Twin Cities," 5 April 1927 (unpublished manuscript) SJAA: Z-32, 2. Sections of this paper were later published in an article entitled "Architecture and the Liturgy," *LA* 5 (1936) 13–8.

[74] Ibid., 6.

[75] Ibid., 8.

Michel attempted to articulate the symbolic meaning of churches of the 1920s and 1930s, using the example of church facades that were often left unadorned, yet were richly colorful and bright inside. This contrast symbolized the Christian community because the interior beauty of the Christian heart mattered more than the external beauty.

That symbolism continued in considering the church building as the gathering place for the Mystical Body of Christ. Christ had said of himself: "I am the door," and through him people enter the reign of God. The church portal was itself representative of Christ. In entering through that portal on Sunday morning, members of the Mystical Body of Christ were entering more deeply into the life and mystery of that same Christ. It was for this reason that the baptismal font was placed at the entrance of the church, so that the believer, once baptized, could look beyond the vestibule of the church to the altar. Michel pointed to the church building itself as a central architectural symbol, because it symbolized the whole Mystical Body, "the total community of faithful living the life of Christ." The individual bricks and stones represented the individual members of the body of Christ, incorporated into "the unitary structural church." Members of the Mystical Body were those "living stones" who were gathered day after day, from one generation to the next, within its walls. The church building reminded believers about their call to live as Christ's unified body in the world, as "one body, one spirit in Christ." In this way, church architecture contributed to the goal of full and active liturgical participation.[76]

Often, in the 1930s and 1940s, the concern of church architecture primarily regarded the exterior. Once the exterior of the church had been completed, the interior could be finished quickly by ordering the necessary furnishings from a church-goods supplier. Moreover, artists and architects were often held in suspicion by clergy, so it was the pastor who would complete the architectural project by choosing the furnishings and, occasionally, even the art for the interior. The result was an obvious imbalance between exterior and interior, much to the consternation of the artists and architects involved.[77]

---

[76] Ibid., 10–12.

[77] Henry Clifford wrote: ". . . Could not the pastor follow more definitely the advice of his architect, employing him not only for the shell but also for the interior of his church as well? Here the question of expense is most intimately involved, but surely a better balance could be maintained between the items of construction and decoration. Is it not poor policy to spend vast sums on a superior tile roof to protect the body from rain while leaving only enough to furnish the sanctuary with undignified statues calculated to scandalize the soul?" "Letter to the Editor," *LA* 11 (1942–43) 93.

Within the church building, the altar was symbolic of Christ and the central symbol of Christian worship:

> The altar should be to the church what the Mass is to worship. The altar should be the central unifying factor in the entire church. Pillars should not hide it from view; and so the side aisles should be narrowed down to mere corridors and the central space widened. Nor should there be three altars on almost an even line; the central altar should dominate completely.[78]

Maurice Lavanoux noted that, ironically, often the altar seemed to be an afterthought once the construction of the church had been completed:

> After all, the altar is the reason for the building of the church, and not vice-versa. We should, therefore, see to it that sanctuaries are properly planned to allow for adequate circulation and also that the altar stands free from the wall . . .[79]

Operating under the premise that "where there is an altar, there is a church," Eric Gill argued, as well, for the central placement of the altar, surrounded by the assembly:

> . . . The altar is the chief thing and if we are going to make the Holy Sacrifice the centre of our worship, it is natural that it should be the centre, physically as well as in our minds. From the point of view of the building, a cruciform church of brick and stone is the simplest to build, . . .

---

[78] Michel, "The Catholic Spirit in Architecture," 30.

[79] Editor, "Church Leaders Guide Movement, States Lavanoux: Architect Says That Liturgy Rules Have Approval of Authorities," *The Michigan Catholic* (2 December 1937). In another place, Lavanoux recounts the story of designing a church some years before as a junior draftsman: "I asked about the definite location of the altar and the size. I was informed that such details were left for the pastor and sometimes the boss to decide and that I should not ask embarrassing questions. Being of a curious mind I followed the matter through and found that the church had been planned without much thought of the altar or of other necessary appurtenances in the sanctuary. Finally, I discovered that a church goods salesman with his catalogues had called on the pastor, and the result was the purchase of an altar that was too large for the space provided and the design of which—if it could be called design—violated all the canons of decent work. The altar was a combination of wood, plaster composition, and imitation marble. Furthermore the construction of this altar violated all the rules I could find, and when I asked questions on that score, I was told again not to worry about such matters, since they were distinctly within the province of the clergy, and if anyone should remonstrate with the pastor, it must be his bishop and certainly not a mere draftsman." "Because It Is the House of God," *LA* 8 (1940) 62.

but for God's sake, let us put the altar in the middle and get the people all round and taking as much part as they can.[80]

Another architectural issue for American liturgical pioneers concerned placement of the organ and choir, consistently located upstairs in the gallery or "choir loft." There were two reasons for the choir's location. First, music was not considered a ministry. It was performance. Second, women were not permitted to enter the sanctuary in those years. Michel addressed the issue on a number of occasions and called for the placement of the choir in front of the assembly, behind the chancel.[81] The argument for the placement of the choir and organist was to promote their visibility, since they too shared a ministry within the liturgical assembly and should fulfill that ministry in the midst of the assembly, rather than upstairs in a separate gallery.[82] Normally, galleries were places for passive spectators rather than active participants. Amidst a liturgical agenda that promoted full and active participation, such galleries seemed clearly out of place. Too many choirs, in the thinking of the liturgical pioneers, saw their role strictly as musical performance, and then as passive spectators during the rest of the liturgy. In placing the choir near the altar, singers would be "tempted to *respond* to the celebrant rather than *compete* with him."[83]

Whereas new architectural forms were beginning to emerge in Europe in connection with the liturgical revival taking place there, American architects continued to rely on the neo-Gothic style quite popular in the United States during the 1920s. Michel criticized this architecture as possessing a "tendency towards an individualizing art." In contrasting Gothic and Romanesque architecture, he wrote:

> Gothic art is indeed religious and inspirational; but it is not collective and unifying . . . If the Gothic church symbolizes the liberated, almost over-bold flight of the individual mystic soul to God, the Romanesque church symbolizes the slow, steady, composed and ordered upward trend of the Church militant in its totality.[84]

---

[80] "Letter to the Editor," *LA* 8 (1939–40) 58.

[81] See "The Catholic Spirit in Church Architecture," 30.

[82] Lavanoux spoke to seminarians and faculty at the Archdiocese of Detroit's Sacred Heart Seminary: "Would it not be well to plan our churches so as to allow the placing of the choir near the altar and not in a gallery at the rear of a church? This plan might have the added advantage of doing away with organ recitals and the warbling of enthusiastic sopranos or the bellowing of tenors which result in nothing more than an unholy competition with the priest at the altar." Editor, "Church Leaders Guide Movement."

[83] Editorial, *LA* 17 (1949) 78.

[84] Michel, "The Catholic Spirit of Architecture," 28.

H. A. Reinhold described the difference between Gothic and modern churches in this way:

> Like the basilica, our modern churches are centered on the two myster-
> ies of rebirth and growth, Baptism and Eucharist. In Gothic cathedrals
> liturgy is sunk at the bottom of a sacred sea of soaring forms, a small
> planet surrounded by large trees. We are swept upward by the striking
> features of this style: it is the architecture of the lone mystic communing
> with God without community or sacrament.[85]

Despite the critique of Gothic and neo-Gothic in liturgical circles, many architect-members of the Liturgical Arts Society were employed by firms which relied heavily upon that architectural style. It is not surprising, then, that they advocated the use of the neo-Gothic in the construction of new church buildings as the best way to celebrate and symbolize—in stone—the true Christian spirit. Thus, the early volumes of *LA* featured articles on the design and construction of some recently completed neo-Gothic churches such as the Episcopal Cathedral of St. John the Divine in New York City. Given the geographical location of the Society and the architectural firms that its members represented, the churches tended to be located in the New York metropolitan area. Neo-Romanesque designs like the Church of the Holy Child in New York City, and neo-Byzantine designs like the Church of the Precious Blood in Astoria, Queens, New York City, were also encouraged in the early volumes of *LA*.[86]

European artists and architects were occasionally commissioned to come to the United States and design liturgical art and architecture in a particular style known in Europe at the time. Beuronese artist, Clement Frischauf, O.S.B., for example, received one such commission. Frischauf worked on the Church of St. Anselm in New York City.[87] Under the direction of Desiderius Lenz, O.S.B., the art produced by the monks of Beuron, Germany, had significant influence in the United States. Through the American liturgical pioneers and promoters, Beuronese art, especially its mosaics, became well-known. Participants in the American liturgical movement often sought after Beuronese art for their churches. The *OF* editors explained their promotion of the Beuronese school in this way:

> This special type of religious art, so highly developed in our day as to
> constitute a recognized school of its own, has found its chief inspiration

---

[85] Reinhold, *The Dynamics of Liturgy*, 87.
[86] S. White, 149–50.
[87] Colman Barry, *Worship and Work* (Collegeville: The Liturgical Press, 1993) 332.

in the liturgy of the Church and the daily liturgical life so faithfully followed out by its monks. Their art is really an expression of their life.[88]

Michel and his colleagues called for a new liturgical architecture that would embody the fundamental principles of the Mystical Body—the unity which linked Christians with God and with the whole human community. Church architecture would then express a living tradition as a powerful and prophetic symbol of the reign of God within American society:

> By ever preaching and sowing into men's hearts the seed of the unifying bond that ties them all to God and to each other in an intimate social fellowship, this art of arts will transmit the solid values of traditional civilization, and dispense for the present and future the healing balm that was never more needed, the solid foundation of social peace and weal. Thus church architecture will on the one hand perform the apostolic mission it assumes by its union with religion, and on the other hand fulfil most perfectly the cultural mission it has in common with all art, that of being at once the conserver of the best values of the past, the inspirer of the present, and the prophet of a bright future.[89]

Michel's dream was not easily realized. As with modern art, there were also tensions between modern and classical architecture within the American church.[90] Indeed, the modern art and architectural movements shared common ground: a protest against the imitation of art and architecture of earlier periods, along with a desire for simplification. Serving as chair of the 1948 National Catholic Building Convention in Chicago, Maurice Lavanoux addressed the tension between modern and classical architecture:

> The first thought I would like to submit concerns the fruitless controversy between pseudo-modern architecture and pseudo-archeological

---

[88] "The Apostolate," *OF* 5 (1931) 571–2. In his autobiography, one Beuronese artist who produced liturgical art for American churches gives additional information on the origins of Beuronese art: Willibrord Verkade, *Yesterdays of an Artist-Monk* (New York: Kenedy and Sons, 1929).

[89] Michel, "The Catholic Spirit in Church Architecture," 34.

[90] One scathing critique of modern church architecture is found in Henry Hope Reed's "Toward a New Architecture?" He described the modern architect as "the eternal rebel," as "forever trying to shock." He continued: "Originality at all costs is the surest way to shock . . . The hunger to be original is the strongest force behind the modern plague." Condemning modern church architecture for "the complete absence of visual pleasure," he called it "the new Puritanism." *LA* 24 (1956) 53–6.

architecture. I feel it is a fruitless controversy and, as a matter of fact, it really does not exist; discussion on this level merely clouds the issues . . . Times change and so does man's outlook change regarding the external aspects of life as a whole. We need only be ourselves, be honest in our convictions, and plan according to the requirements of our day . . . That is surely not a revolutionary idea. Is it not true that the Church lives by that dynamic tradition? If we look at art and architecture in this manner, we soon realize that an archaeological and sentimental approach is left behind—precisely where it should be.[91]

Those who failed to understand the need for a new liturgical architecture argued that those new buildings were incapable of competing with the artistic quality and grandeur of the great Gothic and Romanesque churches of Europe and North America. They complained that, while the new structures were functional and often economical, they failed to communicate with gracious language. Virgil Michel responded that it was not enough that a church simply be "artistic." He wrote in *LA:*

We may of course admire the art of a church during off moments, but we should not be doing so during worship. The art of a church should call the attention of worshippers to itself as little as a priest's sermon should be directed to eliciting the admiration of the people for the eloquence of the preacher. Both church and sermon must go deeper than that, else they are not Christian in the sense of exercising the mediatorship of Christ.[92]

Like liturgical ministers, the liturgical arts were also called to be transparent, rather than call attention to themselves. In promoting a new liturgical architecture, H. A. Reinhold defended modern European designs:

Their conception of "holy emptiness" is nothing negative. They conceive architecture as something which serves a purpose and is a humble handmaid of Christ and His mysteries. These white walls, the local stone and the brick floors, these plain altar blocks, these plain *things* serving the holy mysteries, are liturgical in a unique sense. The "emptiness"—an element which our times hardly appreciate—conveys to us a feeling of true grandeur, although the material of the church building and its sacred furniture is very plain and strictly local.[93]

---

[91] Editor, "A Panel Discussion," 30.

[92] "Unless the Lord Build the House," *LA* 6 (1937–38) 65.

[93] Reinhold, "A Revolution in Church Architecture," *LA* 6 (1937–38) 125. With direct reference to American churches, Reinhold asked: "Does the church show a

The issue of materials used figured prominently in the modern architectural debate. Maurice Lavanoux argued that style was far more important than the type of materials used,[94] though not all American Catholics were sympathetic to such a position.[95] The most controversial of all materials being promoted was the use of reinforced concrete. Concrete had been used with great success in the modern European church structures already discussed, but the use of concrete in church-building proved far more troublesome in the United States. Some believed that concrete was too cheap and pedestrian to be worthy of church architecture. For others, it was simply cold and unattractive, unlike stone which bore its own potential for beauty and grandeur. In other words, it over-emphasized the functional and potentially eclipsed the artistic.[96] H. A. Reinhold reminded critics that the great masterpiece of Hagia Sophia in Constantinople (modern Istanbul), was in cast concrete, reinforced with thin layers of brick.[97] The issue

---

truly Christian spirit of poverty? (A dignified poverty, not shoddiness or destitution.) Or is ostentation to be paid for by grinding the faces of the poor through mortgage-paying generations of both priests and parishioners? . . . Or is this church (as it well might be) a temporary shelter, a tent of the migratory Christ and his flock, and one which shows that we have no abiding city here below?" *The Dynamics of Liturgy*, 88.

[94] "Response to H. A. Reinhold," *LA* 8 (1939–40) 39.

[95] Henry Ellis of Portland, Oregon, who described himself as "an average parishioner," wrote the following: "If there is not enough money available for an expensive material, such as granite or marble, then let the construction be of wood or brick or other acceptable contemporary building material. It is most honorable to fit the material to the purse, and the basic law in choice of construction materials would seem to lie in allowing them to say just what they are. If our parishes can afford only wood, or brick, or concrete, then the message of wood, brick, concrete, telling the Christian truths in terms of what God has made and man fashioned, will have a more worthy influence on succeeding generations of faithful than mere size purchased at the expense of durability and merit. The sincerity of our religion ought to be one with the sincerity of our intentions and our good works, and no less so in the case of art and architecture which become, as it were, the artist's tangible expression of his faith." "Letter to the Editor," *LA* 17 (1948–49) 48.

[96] "To the modernist, ferro-concrete is the providential instrument of liberation whose logic makes for an architecture without memories. We know something of its uncompromising characteristics. Its satisfactions are frankly limited to an unrhetorical rendering of function on a theory that beauty inevitably follows. It is another point of difference, for traditionally beauty in architecture is the *felicitous* expression of function and as such implies the enlistment of the imagination." Charles Maginnis, "The Artistic Debate," *LA* 12 (1944) 82.

[97] "Letter to the Editor," *LA* 8 (1939–40) 39.

was not easily resolved, and one finds many references to the debate in periodicals such as *LA* and *OF*.

Michel, Lavanoux, and others reminded their hearers that the Church was fully the Church, whether it gathered together in a barn or in the most elegant cathedral, whether the building was made of concrete or marble. It was the unity of the Mystical Body of Christ that church architecture was meant to foster. As with modern liturgical art, and so, too, with a new liturgical architecture, pioneers promoted a unified vision of liturgy and life that included art and architecture, music, and especially the community who claimed membership in Christ. Liturgical leaders encouraged architects to collaborate with the assemblies for whom they were designing the churches, and with their parish leaders.

Such unity typified the liturgical movement and kept it from becoming an "arty affair for the delectation of aesthetes."[98] While the liturgical movement, in general, was viewed by some American Catholics as being strictly concerned with the externals of Church life, artists and architects bore the brunt of that critique. Lavanoux labored to demonstrate that, on the contrary, liturgical artists and architects were likewise concerned about pastoral matters (for example, about financial problems) when a parish community was building a new church.[99] He also expressed concern that in some situations, the parishioners themselves initially paid for architectural mistakes when the church was built, and were then being asked to pay a second time in order to make a particular worship space more "liturgical." He saw this as a moral issue, particularly since Americans were just beginning to find their way out of the Great Depression in the late 1930s.[100]

---

[98] Editor, "Church Leaders Guide Movement."

[99] "a sensible and logical consideration of the liturgy qualifies building problems and this, in turn, reacts on the congregation in terms of funds which, in turn, react on the pastor in terms of annoying references to money, etc. . . . In other words, building for the Church should take into consideration the liturgical requirements, the budget, and competent professional advice. All these combined have a definite apologetic value. Harry B. (Binsse) is always after me because I stress common sense and logic in all these matters and he tells me that many—priests and laymen—do not work according to common sense." Letter of Lavanoux to Virgil Michel, 31 July 1937, SJAA: Z-25.

[100] "A week ago I went to Schenectady with Harold Rambusch in answer to a call from a pastor who wanted to clean up his church. His funds are limited and both Rambusch and I took that into consideration in our discussions. I had previously met this pastor and had given him an outline of my thoughts on the general subject of church building and remodeling. Well, we went over the matter very carefully and I don't know yet what will be done—but the point is this: about 60

The pioneers advocated a serious program of education in liturgical architecture on local and national levels, recognizing that the ongoing debate between architects and clergy was more the result of misunderstanding or ignorance than malice. A recommendation was made for seminary courses in art and architecture, since those future leaders of the American church would need to be intimately involved with architectural projects after their ordination.[101] Programs such as the National Catholic Building Convention were held to gather together "pastors, mothers general, and others interested in building and remodeling, as well as representatives of the business industry, and to prepare the former for a better understanding of the problems involved in these projects."[102]

H. A. Reinhold was clearly the most architecturally literate of all the liturgical pioneers, as his writings reflect. He stressed the importance of the function and a careful consideration of the use of the space, noting by way of example, the substantial difference between a parish church and a monastic or convent chapel. An abbey church, for example, should clearly show the prominence of the choir stalls, since the choral office was a significant element in the life of the monastic community. Reinhold emphasized the importance of two foci in the floor plan of every church: the font and the altar. His reason was simple:

---

percent of what he has to spend now to put things in order represents what was done badly in the first place. Therefore the whole thing in my mind takes on a bit of a moral aspect because the money misspent in the first place and the money required now to repair the damage comes from the people—and this in a parish which has to pay out about $300.00 a week to pay off the debt. You can see what all that can mean when multiplied by the number of parishes in this country where the work is done much in the same manner." Letter to Virgil Michel, 20 July 1937, SJAA: Z-25.

[101] The Curator of Paintings of the Philadelphia Museum of Art wrote: "Is it not possible for seminaries to have at least one course in aesthetics with accent on church architecture and church decoration? The pastor of a church is so much king of his own castle that he ought to be better prepared to meet the difficulties of creating a dignified and uplifting background for the liturgy. If this is not feasible or acceptable, my second suggestion would be for the pastor to consult recognized art authorities in his district. The United States is well supplied with museums whose staffs are always ready and eager to be consulted on matters of taste and decoration. In questions of doctrine one normally turns to the Church for advice. In return, why are not the museums and their staffs consulted in the field of aesthetics?" Henry Clifford, "Letter to the Editor," *LA* 11 (1942–43) 92–3.

[102] "Editorial," *LA* 16 (1948) 66.

Christians are pilgrims, on the road, in via, to Heaven. Hence, the natural place for the congregation is between these two foci.[103]

He argued against fixed seating for the assembly, because it immobilizes the congregation and creates a psychological barrier to full and active liturgical participation. He called for the presence of the choir in front of the assembly, and spoke of architectural arrangements for mixed choirs of men and women.[104] Reinhold recommended a private chapel for the reservation of the Sacrament, which was more conducive to prayer and private meditation. Regarding the baptismal font, he called for a return to the use of "constantly flowing fresh water."[105]

In 1948, during the second session of the Notre Dame summer program in liturgical studies, Reinhold taught the first five weeks of an eight-week course on the principles of liturgical architecture. The last three weeks of the course were taught by Walter Knight Sturges, a professional architect, focusing on the problems of contemporary church architecture and the architectural practice of that period.[106] The Liturgical Arts Society played its own very prominent role, both in the artistic and architectural education of the clergy, and in the liturgical education of artists and architects. The Society's periodical, *LA*, contributed significantly to that education, along with the Society's meetings and the network of relationships established between artists,

---

[103] Reinhold, *Speaking of Liturgical Architecture* (Notre Dame: Liturgical Programs of Notre Dame, 1952) 5.

[104] While accepting the Church's requirement of a screen on occasions when women sang in choirs, Reinhold still argued for the choir's placement in front of the assembly. He wrote: "We found the choir in ancient basilicas in front of the altar—an ideal location for a vested choir of men. In these days of mixed choirs the location near the altar has to be concealed from the view of the congregation, e.g., behind a grill, yet so close that immediate contact between priest and choir is always available; the members must be able to receive Holy Communion before the congregation." Reinhold, *Speaking of Liturgical Architecture*, 18.

[105] He wrote: "The average holy-water stoop is hardly representative of cleansing water . . . The Church can certainly bless running water as well as stagnant water." Reinhold, *The Dynamics of Liturgy*, 81–2.

[106] Walter K. Sturges, "Brick and Mortar Grace," *LA* 17 (1948) 12–3. The course included a review of modern European and American churches, "especially such radical new approaches as the buildings designed by Barry Byrne, Moser, Rudolf Schwarz, and the Swiss school, together with their new sculpture, mosaics, paintings, and minor arts in their groping toward contemporary expressions on the one hand and approaches toward the service of mysteries in their essence on the other." Reinhold, "Liturgical Arts at Notre Dame," *LA* 17 (1948) 13.

liturgists, and pastors. In most cases, those who understood the goals of the liturgical movement were equally at home with the modern artistic and architectural revival within the United States.

The Praxis of Modern Liturgical Architecture

Despite the cautious climate in the United States regarding modern church architecture and its late arrival in the American liturgical revival, there are several examples of creatively designed and well-executed churches that should be mentioned.

One of the earliest examples of distinctly American church architecture comes from the Chippewa reservation in northern Wisconsin. The church was not of the modern architectural style we have been discussing, but reflected the sound liturgical principles that would soon be promoted by the liturgical pioneers: a church building symbolizing the Mystical Body of Christ gathered together in worship. The pastor, Fr. Philip P. Gordon, himself a Chippewa and one of the first native American Catholic priests in the United States,[107] built the church in the form of a tepee, and incorporated artistic design common to the Chippewa in the interior. The church was built in 1922 after the previous church was destroyed by fire. Gordon dreamed of a church building that would symbolize the Chippewa community who would worship within its walls, connecting the important symbols of the Chippewa with Christian ideals. Such a church building was to be "a connecting link which would sagely bring Indians from paganism to Catholicism . . . the only way to reach the Indian's heart."[108] In order to raise money for the new church, Gordon collected $30,000 from friends of those who lived on the reservation.

The Chippewa were enthusiastic about the project, and they did much of the work on the building. While Alexander C. Eschweiler, a Milwaukee architect, designed the church in collaboration with Gordon, the carpenters and masons were all Chippewa.[109] Together, they

---

[107] While Gordon was not directly involved with the liturgical movement, he had a close relationship with the Benedictines of St. John's Abbey, Collegeville, and with the University of Notre Dame. He was a social activist, and travelled to Washington, D.C., on a number of occasions to lobby for the rights of the Chippewa and, indeed, of all native Americans.

[108] Paula Delfeld, *The Indian Priest: Father Philip B. Gordon, 1885–1948* (Chicago: Franciscan Herald Press, 1977) 70–1.

[109] The non-Indian architects and window designers sought Gordon's counsel in interpreting Native American symbolism and suggesting in what way art and architecture might best be unified to incorporate both native American and Christian symbols. Ibid., 72.

carried granite rock from the fields and woods of the reservation. The roof was made of rough cedar shingles that were hewn from trees near the lake. The stained glass windows included traditional native American symbols such as the rising sun, arrows, crossed pipes and tobacco with the cross above.[110] The wooden rafters inside the church were stained in bright red, blue, and orange—colors that were typically used among the Chippewa. Deerskins hung in front of the confessionals and in front of the altar. Altar cloths with traditional Native American designs and symbols were woven by women in the parish.

In 1933, Sacred Heart Church in Pittsburgh, Pennsylvania was built. The architect, Carlton Strong, was given full authority to build "a liturgical church." Working in collaboration with the pastor, the two engaged the expertise of a number of European and American theologians and designers. Although the church was designed in the neo-Gothic style, it was known for its use of genuine materials and for the fact that "everything in the Church of the Sacred Heart has a signification":

> There is no artificial window, no synthetic marble, no ornamental columns standing about without doing any work, no counterfeit decoration for the mere sake of decoration.[111]

The church was constructed from the "inside out," giving primacy of concern to the liturgical space—the altar, ambo, font, placement of ministers and assembly—and only later, the exterior. The choir was located in front of the assembly, "just outside the sanctuary." The baptismal font was located in a separately designed area, "in its proper liturgical place," near the entrance to the church. The floor of the sanctuary contained a map of the world with the inscription from Malachi: "In every place there is sacrifice and there is offered to my name a clean oblation." The parish liturgical schedule included Sunday afternoon "Compline," and sound liturgical principles were followed in use of the worship space.[112]

---

[110] One newspaper reported: "Indian psychology has been taken into consideration in working out the symbolic designs of the stained glass windows by George W. Mueller of the Milwaukee Mirror and Glass Works. Realizing that few of the Indian parishioners were able to read, Mr. Mueller planned the windows so that each shall speak to Indians in familiar terms." Ibid., 71.

[111] Philibert Harrer, "A Liturgical Parish," *OF* 7 (1933) 447.

[112] For example, "Announcements are never made from the pulpit. The word of God, and only the word of God, has a place in this pulpit. To avoid any temptation to digress into the financial standing of the parish and the like, the Fathers have the announcements printed in attractive style and distributed to parishioners after the

A more celebrated architectural accomplishment came one decade later, in 1942, with the construction of St. Mark's Church, Burlington, Vermont. Under the leadership of the new pastor, William A. Tennien, and with the help of a firm of young Burlington architects, Freeman, French, and Freeman, they designed and constructed a church that began with the liturgy and moved outward. The architects began by considering the altar—its design, size, and placement—and from there considered the rest of the building. Since the altar was considered central to Christian worship, it was placed directly in the center of the church, allowing, in 1942, for the celebration of the Eucharist with the presider facing the assembly. The assembly was gathered around the altar in three sections, each section seating one hundred and sixty persons. The fourth section, behind the altar, contained the ambo, as well as the choir, the organ, and the entrance to the sacristy. Lavanoux remarked:

> The keynote of the design is simplicity. Whenever any element was discussed, the question was always asked "Can we do without it?" If so, it was eliminated. The result is that everything has a definite purpose. Mere decorative doodads were banished, but all elements used were as beautiful as possible, within budgetary limitations and type of materials used.[113]

The tabernacle continued to be placed on the altar, yet it was designed deliberately to be low, so as not to obstruct the view of the assembly during the eucharistic prayer.[114]

LA carried an interesting exchange of letters between Reinhold and Tennien, the pastor of St. Mark's. In praising the work accomplished at that Burlington parish, Reinhold disapproved of the division of the congregation into three parts, as only one third of the assembly would be in the direct sight of the one presiding. Tennien responded to one phrase in Reinhold's letter that suggested it was the pastor's goal to "have his 'parish family' in front of him." Tennien wrote:

> Now if Father Reinhold means that my first principles are to have my parish family in front of me for the celebration of the mass, then he has assumed something which is contrary to fact. From the "pastoral-theological" point of view, I have never thought of those offering mass

---

Masses . . . The attendance at the Sunday Masses is close to forty-five hundred, many of whom are 'outsiders.'" Ibid., 452–3.

[113] Lavanoux, "Saint Mark's Church, Burlington, Vermont," *LA* 11 (1942) 82.

[114] "After all, why should a tabernacle be so high when the sacred vessels it contains are so low? Why should not the tabernacle be considered for what it is—a receptacle for the sacred vessels?" Ibid.

with me as being in front of me, but rather gathered round me . . . That is, in designing Saint Mark's all our thinking was concentric with the altar at the centre . . . In our long narrow churches, about two thirds of the congregation never *see* the mass; and so it matters very little whether the celebrant faces them or not. Now a solution such as Saint Mark's brings about a much greater visual-presence of the congregation. The church seats 480 people, yet no person is more than ten pews distant from the altar of sacrifice.[115]

The pastor continued by explaining the rationale for the central location of the altar:

What we wanted to do was to pick up the mass and hurl it into the very midst of our congregation; we wanted it to have the force of a bomb exploding—which is what the mass has. That is best achieved by pulling it out of its seclusion at the far end of a deep sanctuary, at the far end of a long church, and dropping it down among the people who are offering it. Saint Mark's is our inadequate gesture in that direction, and our weak protest against the *status quo*.[116]

In 1949, Barry Byrne, an apprentice of Frank Lloyd Wright and one of the better known American liturgical architects, designed and saw to completion the Jesuit Church of St. Francis Xavier on the campus of Rockhurst College, Kansas City, Missouri. Taking his inspiration from the early Christian Antiochene symbol of the fish, Byrne designed the church in the form of a fish. While it gained a great deal of attention and won several awards from an architectural and artistic standpoint, it was criticized from a liturgical point of view for giving greater attention to the unique design of the building than to the needs of the liturgical assembly who would be worshiping there.[117]

In 1950, H. A. Reinhold put his own creative energies to use in the design of St. Joseph's Church in Sunnyside, Washington. Reinhold placed the baptismal font with the altar in the center of church. The main entrance was through a side narthex. In addition, a small chapel was provided for daily eucharistic celebration, since the number of weekday congregants never warranted full use of the larger liturgical space. The choir was placed in the front of the assembly, on the side of the sanctuary. The materials used for the liturgical appointments—

---

[115] William Tennien, "Letter to the Editor," *LA* 12 (1943) 49–50.

[116] Ibid.

[117] Peter Hammond wrote: "Barry Byrne's well-known church in Kansas City . . . is another example of a fundamentally mistaken approach to church planning. Often it is found in combination with the other false approach—the concern with structure rather than function." Hammond, 82.

altar, font, ambo, tabernacle, candlesticks, lighting—were modest but well-designed and well-executed.[118] Another example came in 1953, with the radical design and construction of Blessed Sacrament Church, Holyoke, Massachusetts. The church was designed to be octagonal and the altar was placed in the center of the octagon. Eight rows of pews surrounded the altar.[119] The design was radical because, unlike most other American churches built at that same time, this architectural plan symbolized and articulated the theology of the Mystical Body of Christ, and facilitated the goal of full and active liturgical participation. The greatest architectural triumph for the American church in that period, however, came with the building of the monastic church at St. John's Abbey, Collegeville. Since its construction was only begun at the end of the historical period of our study—1954—our discussion will be limited to the architectural plans for the abbey church.

In the spring of 1953, Marcel Breuer was chosen from a large pool of his colleagues to be the chief architect for the new church at St. John's Abbey. Following a series of open meetings where the merits of each architect were discussed, the building committee and senior council submitted a prioritized list of five names to the abbot. Breuer was at the top of the list. He was selected, in the words of Abbot Baldwin Dworschak, because "he struck us as being not only an outstanding architect, but a simple, straightforward, sincere and rather humble person."[120]

Following eight months of preparation, Breuer presented his plan to the monastery on 28 January 1954. The design presented a modern structure, expressive of the monastic life at St. John's, but also of the contemporary church in the United States. It was the first American church to use reinforced concrete. Plans were announced to the public in 1954, and quick reactions surfaced from all sides. Although some responses were negative, the overwhelming response, both in the United States and beyond, was positive. Breuer's plans were featured in fifteen magazines in the United States, France, Italy, Spain, Cuba, and Japan. Lavanoux called Breuer's plan "truly a milestone in the evolution of the architecture of the Catholic Church in this country." He continued:

> Even an inkling of these plans is sufficient to induce joy and hope for the future of the arts in the United States . . . And the fact that all this

---

[118] Lavanoux, "Catholics and Religious Art," 206–7.

[119] James F. White, Interview by author, 22 November 1994, University of Notre Dame, Notre Dame, Indiana.

[120] Barry, 337.

should happen at Collegeville is significant, since the background of sound liturgical scholarship and practice at the Abbey is known throughout the world . . . Here we have the logical sequence: the liturgy first, in all the daily splendor of the ceremonies and of loving observance; then the arts closely integrated to the liturgy and practiced by those who take part in that liturgy, from which it draws its inspiration and substance.[121]

Architectural Forum described Breuer's plans in this way:

. . . A thin cowl of concrete into walls and roof over this monastic church, creased into folds for structural stiffness. And in front of the church will stand a symbolically modern bell tower for this 1,400 year old client—a pierced banner of reinforced concrete. The structural system sought by Architect Breuer was one with which he could return to the clarity and honesty of the Romanesque which he admires above all other historical styles ("Gothic already hides and fakes.") He found his opportunity in a continuous concrete slab, molded and dented into a kind of modern graining, a simpler version of the UNESCO structure with the same acoustical advantages (especially important to the chanting of the monk's offices). There will be no hung ceiling, no plastered finish. The concrete will be faced with granite on the outside, but inside will be left with the scars of the framework still on it to contrast ruggedly with a gilded ceiling and red brick floor.[122]

The monks at St. John's were sufficiently confident in their own liturgical understanding, not allowing themselves to be intimidated by what American Catholics might expect church architecture to resemble or express, so they encouraged Breuer in his creativity. Consistent with the agenda of the liturgical movement, they returned to the sources— the liturgical understanding of the early Christians—and the abbey church was designed accordingly, in a contemporary American context. One example of this was the placing of the baptistry at the entrance, with a skylight above and surrounded by glass walls and gardens. There was even the possibility of opening the baptistry to the outdoors, depending always on the cooperation of the Minnesota weather. This was intended to resemble the concept and use of the atrium in early Christian basilicas. Most important, however, was its signification of initiation into the Church: first baptism, followed by full admission to the Church, culminating in the Eucharist.[123]

---

[121] Lavanoux, "Collegeville Revisited," *LA* 22 (1954) 46.

[122] Editor, "A Benedictine Monastery by Marcel Breuer," *Architectural Forum* 101 (1954) 148–56, quoted in Barry, 339–40.

[123] Barry, 340.

St. John's Abbey Church, along with the other examples given were exceptional. In general, American church architecture of superior quality did not emerge until much later. Aside from the artistic and architectural caution which existed within the American church, another reason for the slow development of church architecture was purely sociological. The period following the Second World War saw the suburbanization of Catholicism. With the G.I. bill, the United States government built freeways and offered financial support for the creation of new residential areas and the building of homes in the suburbs. New parishes were founded and new churches needed to be built. These communities, however, often lacked the finances for such construction. In many cases, they also lacked liturgical taste. A number of parishes began by building a school and using the school gymnasium as a temporary place of worship until sufficient funds could be obtained for the building of the parish church. Often, the parish church was never built and the school gymnasium was converted into a worship space.[124]

Architects like Pietro Belluschi of the Massachusetts Institute of Technology, Marcel Breuer of New York City, Barry Byrne of Evanston, Illinois, and Joseph D. Murphy of St. Louis, all made their contributions, but it would not be until Frank Kacmarcik came onto the scene in the mid to late 1950s that modern church architecture truly took its rightful place within the liturgical movement, with the creation of high-quality, uniquely American structures for the gathering of the Mystical Body of Christ.

The Liturgical Movement and Music

At the beginning of the twentieth century, there was little congregational singing in most American parishes. Over the centuries, as members of the assembly gradually lost their active role in the liturgy, chant ceased to be the musical prayer of the assembly. Certain ethnic parishes were exceptional in continuing their strong tradition of congregational singing, often with an equally strong corporate consciousness. Most other American parishes were less developed musically, at least from a liturgical perspective.[125] Many continued to employ the operatic, overly emotional type of religious music that prevailed at the

---

[124] Steven M. Avella, author of *This Confident Church: Catholic Leadership and Life in Chicago, 1940–1965* (Notre Dame: University of Notre Dame Press, 1992). Interview by author, 10 December 1994, Archbishop Cousins Catholic Center, Milwaukee, Wisconsin.

[125] See Paul Westermeyer, "Twentieth-Century American Hymnody and Church Music," in *New Dimensions in American Religious History,* Jay P. Dolan and James P. Wind, eds. (Grand Rapids, Mich.: Eerdmans Publishing Co., 1993) 175–207.

time.[126] The music was usually performed by a choir and had little to do with the liturgy itself.[127] Hymnody was generally viewed as a Protestant custom. Organists, choirs, and soloists performed as the parish members "heard Mass." Already in the nineteenth century, however, the monks at Solesmes undertook the challenging task of studying chant through a comparison of hundreds of medieval manuscripts. Their work proved to be foundational for the restoration of chant in the twentieth century.

A turning point came on 22 November 1903 when Pope Pius X issued his *motu proprio: tra le sollecitudini,* calling for a reform of Church music.[128] Issuing the decree in the first year of his pontificate, he called for a return to Gregorian chant as recovered by the monks of Solesmes, in order that all Catholics could participate more fully in the liturgy. That document served as a kind of *magna carta* for the liturgical movement in its call for the restoration of congregational singing. While many popes wrote decrees on sacred music, Pius X wrote more on that topic than all the popes combined.[129] The document reflects its historical period in continuing to insist, for example, that women were forbidden to sing in choirs. Nonetheless, the document challenged the

---

[126] "In the nineteenth century . . . composers . . . began to compose works for no particular purpose except people's amusement. That removed music from its earlier relation to the whole of life, to festivals, celebrations, praise of God, events of state, and play. Further, as composers felt they had to express their religious feelings, the congregation became an audience. Simultaneously, church music was isolated: concert music was considered too worldly, so contemporary pieces were seldom performed in church, and a new thing called a 'sacred style' developed." Ibid., 177.

[127] One 1951 editorial noted: "It was not so long ago that the average High Mass for instance on Sunday morning lasted for more than two hours during which the officiating priest spent most of his time at the sedilia waiting for the singers to complete page after page of text repetitions to the accompaniment of free organ parts and orchestra (the orchestra on the 'big' feast days!)." "Historical and Liturgical Cycles," *The Caecilia* 79 (1951–52) 42.

[128] The document is virtually identical to Pius X's *votum*—which the then Cardinal Giuseppe Sarto sent to the Congregation of Sacred Rites in Rome in August of 1893, prior to entering Venice as its Patriarch on 22 November 1894. The *votum* was the precursor of his pastoral letter on church music which he then issued on 1 May 1895. Angelo De Santi, S.J., collaborated on all three documents. The original manuscripts of both texts are found in the archives of *La Civiltà Cattolica* in Rome, and show the texts written in De Santi's hand. Corrections are found in the hand of Pius X. See Robert Hayburn, *Papal Legislation on Sacred Music: 95 A.D. to 1977 A.D.* (Collegeville: The Liturgical Press, 1979) 212–22.

[129] Hayburn, 195.

use of overly theatrical music, and called for a return to music that was truly liturgical.

Moreover, the *motu proprio* gave grounding to diocesan regulations on Church music throughout the United States. Dioceses issued "white" lists of approved liturgical music and "black" lists of music not permitted in churches.[130] Those who understood the situation best, however, recognized that the imposition of regulations would not solve the problem:

> What we need is not more "White Lists of Approved Music," but more, and many more, competent choirmasters who are able to select suitable music without specific directions from the diocesan authority, and more choirs capable of singing in inspiring fashion.[131]

When the liturgical movement was launched twenty-three years after the promulgation of the *motu proprio,* that document had borne little fruit in the United States. Congregational singing, when introduced, was often viewed as something superfluous to the liturgy itself. Some complained that congregational singing interfered with their private devotions, while others argued that the inclusion of added congregational participation unnecessarily lengthened the celebration of the Mass.[132] Most American parishes showed little recognition of the recommendations of the *motu proprio.* American Catholics continued to resist chant as cold and uninteresting, compared with the more emotionally-charged operatic music in vogue during those years.

In 1940, Gerald Ellard wrote that "the vast majority of American Catholics have still to experience the joy of participating in a High Mass sung with whole-souled enthusiasm by the entire congregation."[133] He noted: "The choir is not a caste into which one per cent or so of the parish membership is predestined; singing one's prayers to God is not a monopoly of a closed-shop, church gallery group." Rather, members of the assembly needed to be convinced that "theirs is the right to do most of the singing at all liturgical functions."[134] As

---

[130] See Editor, "'Black List' of Forbidden Music—Music That Is Contrary to the 'Motu Proprio' of Pope Pius X Because Unliturgical in Every Respect and Inartistic From a Musical Standpoint—Masses," *The Monitor* (San Francisco, 19 December 1925) 1–2.

[131] Alastair Guinan, "Modern Mass Music," *The Commonweal* 19 (1934) 353.

[132] See Mary L. Allen, "Chant and the Lay Apostolate," *The Caecilia* 74 (1946–47) 192–4.

[133] Gerald Ellard, *Men at Work and Worship* (New York: Longmans, Green and Co., 1940) 146.

[134] Ibid., 153.

one writer put it, "the Church as a temple of worship is no more a concert hall than it is an art gallery."[135]

While liturgical pioneers called for congregational singing which they claimed was the most active way of participating in the liturgy, the emphasis was primarily on Gregorian chant rather than on hymnody. Some Catholics argued that they were singing liturgically when they joined in the corporate singing of sentimental Marian hymns such as "Bring Flowers of the Fairest." The pioneers reminded their hearers that all congregational singing was not necessarily liturgical:

> Congregational singing may be taken to mean merely the collective singing of Catholic hymns that have been traditionally approved, or that ring with a true Catholic tone and spirit. It is then singing done in the vernacular by assembled congregations, whether in church or elsewhere. By congregational singing, however, some persons mean the collective singing of designated parts of the Mass in Latin and in Gregorian melody.[136]

Michel stated that the corporate singing of hymns was liturgical when it was in keeping with the "liturgical spirit." Congregational singing was liturgical when it contributed to the upbuilding of the Mystical Body of Christ as corporate worship. Congregational singing ran the risk of being anti-liturgical, however, when the chosen hymns had little to do with the liturgical act being celebrated, when the focus was on the individual and on his or her personal relationship with God, rather than on corporate membership in the body of Christ.[137]

As with other forms of art, liturgical music needed to be viewed in its proper role as a servant of the assembly's prayer, as a "handmaid of the liturgy." It was no easy task to convince organists and choir directors of this reality. Too often the result was a strong individualistic consciousness and a weak sense of the corporate dimension of liturgical singing. This issue brought significant tensions to the surface between musicians and liturgical reformers.[138] Archbishop John G. Murray of St. Paul, Minnesota, wrote a pastoral letter addressing those tensions:

> The purpose of the Church is to unite all her members in the liturgical action of the Mystical Body of Christ . . . Unison of prayer is facilitated . . . by ecclesiastical music which is a . . . support in united prayer. The

---

[135] Francis J. Guenther, "Handmaid of the Liturgy," *LA* 13 (1944–45) 85.

[136] Editor, "Editor's Corner," *OF* 3 (1929) 380.

[137] Ibid., 381.

[138] In fact, Ermin Vitry suggested that there was an evident lack of organic union between the liturgical movement and the musical restoration: "The liturgical movement has been musical-less as the musical restoration has been liturgy-less." Letter to Virgil Michel, 5 November 1935, SJAA: Z-28.

voices of all the congregation should be incorporated into this ennobled expression of praise so that the voice of the people becomes the voice of the Church . . . Any other conception of church music is in contradiction to the spirit and purpose of divine worship. The voice of the individual must be subordinated to the voice of the whole congregation, even as the instrument which sustains that voice must be subordinated to the vocal expression of adoration, thanksgiving and petition.[139]

Some suggested that one significant reason for the failure to inculcate the spirit of the liturgy in Church music was the loss of a sense of community, both within American society and within the Church. American Catholics had become overly concerned with their own personal needs—reciting their individual prayers—and lost sight of the group.[140] Archbishop John G. Glennon of St. Louis, was a great supporter of pioneers' efforts to restore the true liturgical spirit in the congregational singing of American parishes. Responding to those who claimed that the economic hardships of the 1930s left little to sing about, Glennon urged American Catholics to allow their liturgical singing to express their own lament as a corporate body:

In these days of depression a large percentage of people is dependent on the government for its daily bread. Everybody is poor now, so there is a tendency for humanity to become disconsolate, thinking that all is lost when money is gone. In the Christian ages of the past the people did not have banks, they did not have usury, they did not have millionaires and factories; but their voices, hearts, and souls were attuned to the service of God, and it is the songs of the poor, the humble, and the lowly that God hears. He is their Father. He is your Father, too, and He listens to your song when you sing His praises as you do . . . In your song let there be charity and peace, thus you will be able to promote by means of the Gregorian chant, the gospel, the peace, and the charity of Christ.[141]

The expression of lament through liturgical singing was also discussed vis-à-vis the Second World War,[142] and vis-à-vis the suffering experienced by the African-American community in the United States.[143]

---

[139] J. G. Murray, Pastoral Letter of 11 February 1935, quoted in "The Apostolate," *OF* 9 (1935) 230.

[140] See Marie Conti Oresti, "The Layman and the Liturgy," *The Caecilia* 71 (1943–44) 244.

[141] "Address by Most Rev. John J. Glennon, D.D., Archbishop of St. Louis, Mo., at Organists Guild Meeting," *The Caecilia* 62 (1935) 194.

[142] See "The Editor Writes," *The Caecilia* 69 (1941–42) 178–81.

[143] See Allan R. Crite, "The Meaning of Spirituals," *Catholic Art Quarterly* 17 (1953) 69; Theophilus Lewis, "The Negro Spirituals As Hymns of a People," *America* 61 (1939) 43–4.

Chicago pastor Fr. Bernard Laukemper wrote: "As the man without lungs cannot sing, so it is impossible for the man without the understanding of the liturgy to know, love, and use the chant of the Church." Liturgical music challenged the individualism of past centuries as it challenged the contemporary individualism of American society. When the liturgical assembly sang together it offered a profound statement of solidarity and union with one another in the Mystical Body of Christ. For that reason, pioneers argued that it was the assembly and not the choir who should sing the *Kyrie*, the *Gloria* and *Credo*, the acclamations of the Eucharistic Prayer, and the *Agnus Dei*.[144] Noting the significance of the Communion procession, liturgical leaders lamented the loss of congregational singing during the Communion and called for its restoration:

> . . . For it is still the rule that the faithful must proceed to the communion-table to receive the holy sacrament. It is but a feeble and inexpressive remnant of a splendid communal action. There is hardly any resemblance between a crowd of modern Christians milling around disorderly and the singing multitude of ages gone by, approaching the sacred banquet. The difference is in the presence or absence of the eucharistic singing.[145]

It was the presence or absence of congregational singing during the Communion procession that articulated the perception of what was taking place. The employment of liturgical music heightened the awareness of Communion as a corporate act, while its absence signaled the continuation of an individualistic piety operative in reception of the Sacrament. Benedictine Patrick Cummins wrote:

> Thanks to the reform of the communion-procession, which is reviving in many places, we begin to understand again one of the main aspects of the Communion: that it is the consummation of a corporate offering, and that the reception of the Sacrament is itself a corporate action . . . The liturgy uses for this, the communion-procession, no particular method, but the usual musical plan of all processions: an appropriate refrain, alternated with an appropriate psalm. The refrain, called an antiphon, is a text selected for its eucharistic meaning; it is sung again and again, so that its being repeated may help to reveal its spiritual implications.[146]

The priestly function of liturgical music was assisted most directly by liturgical musicians and choirs who were the servants of the assem-

---

[144] Laukemper, "What Does a Pastor Think of Chant?" *The Caecilia* 71 (1943–44) 13–4.

[145] Patrick Cummins, "Sacred Texts, Sacred Songs," *The Caecilia* 70 (1943) 186.

[146] Ibid.

bly's sung prayer. It is not surprising, then, that one discovers a great deal of literature on the vocation of the Church musician and the liturgical ministry of the choir in the 1930s and 1940s.

Liturgical pioneers and promoters encouraged Church musicians to view their own contribution as a ministry or vocation within the Church.[147] Such an awareness would only come about through proper education at musical institutes. While it was important to train Church professionals in a solid liturgical understanding and in chant methodology, those efforts would ultimately amount to nothing unless other American Catholics understood the role of liturgical music and appreciated chant as sung prayer.

Calling Gregorian chant the "language of devotion," editors of *The Caecilia* recommended that parishes form a core group of parishioners trained in chant to model such liturgical music for their co-parishioners. Liturgical pioneers and promoters consistently argued that the organization of choirs needed to include spiritual as well as musical formation. Parish music directors were encouraged to organize liturgical days of renewal and annual retreats for their choirs. In this way, choir members would grow in recognition that their function was not to engage in stage-performance, but rather to assist the sung prayer of the liturgical assembly.[148] A balance was needed. There was a place in the liturgy for choral motets and other musical texts that were better executed by the choir than by the whole assembly; such choral offerings, however, were to be incorporated according to solid liturgical norms.[149]

Since theirs was a liturgical ministry, choir members belonged in the front of the liturgical assembly along with the other ministers, and not in an upstairs gallery in the back of the church. Describing the arrangement at St. Aloysius Parish, Chicago, Bernard Laukemper wrote:

> We learned that the place of the schola is not in the balcony in the rear of the church, but near the sanctuary. This makes them more effective as leaders, places them organically where they belong in Divine Worship, and makes them conscious of their position in the holy work in Divine Worship. Our scholae are arranged in choir fashion in the place of three front pews, where you also find the organ console. The scholae are real

[147] See Francis X. Charnotta, "The Vocation of the Catholic Church Musician," *Christian Art Quarterly* 13 (1950) 129–32; Frater Climacus, "The Vocation of Church Music," *The Caecilia* 79 (1952) 96–7.

[148] See C. Lovell, "The Saint Rose Liturgical Choir of Men and Boys," *LA* 15 (1946) 74–5; J. Yonkman, "The Formation of a Liturgical Choir," *The Caecilia* 76 (1948) 6–8.

[149] H. A. Reinhold argued for what he called a "compromise" between choral and congregational singing. "Letter to the Editor" *The Caecilia* 82 (1954) 74–5.

leaders and they inspire the entire congregation to join them in chanting God's praise.[150]

Despite the placement of the choir, it was not always clear how best the choir might assist the assembly in its liturgical singing. Attempts to professionally train parishioners in the methodology of chant usually ended in frustration. Most American Catholics, at least initially, found chant a boring alternative to the more operatic music to which they were accustomed. Efforts at extrinsically imposing chant upon parishioners remained futile until that type of music could emerge as their prayer, and as a natural, musical expression of who they were as co-members of the Mystical Body of Christ. Many parish music directors in the United States failed to grasp this reality, and their frustration continued.

The goal was to present Gregorian chant in as uncomplicated and simple a manner as possible. A process of imitation was recommended, where parishioners would follow the example of their peers in the choir, imitating the breathing and chanting of the singers. For those parishioners who were interested in a more systematic study of chant, there were course offerings for adults on evenings and weekends throughout the year. Those courses took place in the diocesan centers of larger cities like New York and San Francisco,[151] and in dioceses known for their commitment to the restoration of chant.

Gregorian Chant as the Sung Prayer of the Mystical Body of Christ

John La Farge made the distinction between liturgical minimalism because of necessity and liturgical minimalism because of laziness or indifference. He used the example of Mass on the battlefield as a time when liturgical minimalism existed out of necessity and could be justified. The "rock Masses" cited in chapter two, celebrated quietly by

---

[150] "Editorial," *LA* 12 (1944) 27–8. As Archbishop of Saint Louis, John Glennon called for the placement of the choir in front of the assembly in his 1932 "Christmas Pastoral Letter." He did, however, recommend that the choir be separated by a screen "if the singers would otherwise be very conspicuous." "Christmas Pastoral Letter on Church Music" (Archdiocese of Saint Louis, 1932) SJAA: Z-25.

[151] One national leader in the promotion of chant was Reverend Edgar Boyle, Diocesan Music Director in San Francisco. Like Justine Ward, Boyle was trained at Solesmes. Consequently, one finds a great deal of attention to high musical quality within that archdiocese beginning in the late 1920s and continuing through the 1940s. In 1927, Boyle noted that there were 500 sisters in San Francisco trained in Gregorian chant, and that chant was being taught to students in six parish schools in the city. SJAA: Z-22.

Irish Catholics in times of persecution, offer another example. A typical Sunday morning in an American parish, however, was a different matter, and liturgical minimalism in those situations was often the result of lethargy or sheer indifference. La Farge argued that the normative Sunday liturgical experience in times of peace left no room for "speechless bystanders." The solution to the liturgical malaise within American parishes, according to La Farge, was the restoration of the "religious motive" for liturgical singing. No one found it strange that the presider would chant the Preface, the Lord's Prayer, and other parts of the Mass. The religious motive was self-evident. This was less the case, however, with the assembly's proper parts. La Farge discredited the common argument that chant was impracticable. If seven thousand railroad workers travelling to Lourdes in cattle cars were capable of singing "their Credo," why was it so impossible for American Catholics?[152]

On the other side of the issue, some musicians argued that the restoration of Gregorian chant would dissolve the relationship between the Church and "creative" music, arresting liturgical music in its sixteenth-century environment and prohibiting that music from its continued evolution in the twentieth.[153] Many American Catholics voiced their own protest against Gregorian chant as well. Its sobriety failed to please their senses. Some called it "ugly," preferring the more emotional, sentimental sacred music that liturgical reformers were attempting to eliminate.[154] One writer cautioned against such reactions: ". . . a great many who speak about Church music are concerned much more with the impression made upon themselves than with the expression of their sentiments to God." He argued that the point of liturgical music was not to make the assembly feel good, but rather to give praise and glory to God. Liturgical music was public prayer.[155] In

---

[152] La Farge, "Shall the People Sing at Mass?" *America* 49 (1933) 270–1.

[153] See Francis Guenther, "Church Music, a Neglected Liturgical Art," *LA* 13 (1944–45) 38–9.

[154] See Climacus, "Why We Are Prejudiced Against the Chant," *The Caecilia* 75 (1947) 39–40; and Editor, "Do You Like Liturgical Music?" *The Caecilia* 62 (1935) 186.

[155] J. Sellner, "Worship of God in Church Music," *The Christian Social Art Quarterly* 3 (1940) 6–7. Sellner's point in the article was not to attack the emotive response to liturgical singing, but to challenge an overly subjective response which gives greater priority to one's personal feelings than to the corporate act of praising God. He wrote: "A symphony is not conceived as an expression of divine worship, no matter how prayerful it may sound. An oratorio may be full of religious emotion, but it was not written for the Church. It is essentially imitative; the music for the Church must be real and actual. If the villain in a tragedy has carried out his part very well, you don't demand that he be hanged after the show is over. That's the

the estimation of the liturgical pioneers, American Catholics suffered from a deprived liturgical sense. This was at the root of their inability to understand the role of liturgical music and to appreciate Gregorian chant in that context.[156]

The pioneers and promoters of the liturgical movement remained insistent on the use of Gregorian chant as offering the best expression of sung liturgical prayer. Yes, Gregorian chant was "traditional," but the reasons for its continued use were not on the grounds of tradition, but rather on its suitability for the corporate worship of the Mystical Body. Jesuit musicologist C. J. McNaspy wrote:

> . . . Gregorian has become traditional because it perfectly fits the part destined for music in worship. Its melody, without the intricacy of part singing, expresses the prayer-text simply, directly, reverently. Its very rhythm has grown out of the Latin words . . . Its rise and fall are a perfect interpretation and adornment of the Church's prayer. It is, in a word, sung prayer.[157]

Chant specialist, Justine B. Ward, wrote that chant offered greater musical variation than modern music:

> Modern music has two scales, or modes. Chant has eight. It is evident that eight modes give greater variety of expression than two—an advantage for which even our modern indiscriminate use of the chromatic does not fully compensate.[158]

Ward made a further distinction regarding the suitability of chant in liturgical usage:

> Chant is joyful, but with the joy of the Cross, as distinguished from the joy of revel. Chant is fervent, but with the passion of asceticism, as distinguished from the passion of the world. Prayer-sorrow is never despair, nor is prayer-joy ever frivolous.[159]

---

transition from imitation to reality. So you can imitate the expression of divine worship in the theatre, but you worship in truth and reality in the Church." Ibid., 9.

[156] "To get over any remaining dislike of Gregorian chant, the way must be paved for it," wrote "Laicus Ignotus" to *The Commonweal* (XVII, 21). "That will be realized when there is a widespread and intimate knowledge of the Church's sacred liturgy on the part of her children. When they have caught its spirit, when they pray the Mass, when they live the liturgy, when they feel the liturgy . . . they can no more tolerate operatic music during the Holy Mysteries than a jazz band at a funeral." Editor, "The Apostolate," *OF* 7 (1933) 375.

[157] Clement J. McNaspy, "Singing with the Church," *The Caecilia* 71 (1943–44) 207.

[158] Justine Ward, "The Reform of Church Music," *The Atlantic Monthly* (April 1906) quoted in Ellard, *Men at Work and Worship*, 174.

[159] Ibid.

It must also be noted that the project of restoring the use of Gregorian chant in worship was not limited to Roman Catholics. While American Christians of other churches sang spirituals and hymns in their worship, the occasional use of Gregorian chant was not unheard of in some of those communities. In the Episcopal Church, for example, despite the strong tradition of Anglican chant, a number of Episcopal parishes also made use of Gregorian chant in worship. Episcopal priest Fr. Winfred Douglas studied chant theory at Solesmes and became known as a national authority on the subject, lecturing at such seminaries as Seabury-Western in Evanston, Illinois. Under Douglas's leadership as Director of Music, the Episcopal parish of St. Mary in Peekskill, New York, became known as a center for the restoration of Gregorian chant. Douglas also served as chief editor of the *Episcopal Hymnal 1940.*[160]

The chant research done at Solesmes, from which Justine Ward, Winfred Douglas, and so many others benefited, brought about a more refined understanding and interpretation of Gregorian chant, and the recovery of a pristine medieval musical notation. Such research called into question the authenticity of the nineteenth-century Ratisbon or Regensburg edition of chant, and recommended usage of the Solesmes edition in its place. The Ratisbon edition of chant had been developed by Franz Xavier Haberl and published by Frederick Pustet in 1870, as a response to the newfound interest in chant taking place in Germany and throughout Europe. Soon after its publication, that edition was approved by the Congregation of Sacred Rites as the official Church edition of chant. Its official status, however, was short-lived. Haberl was better trained in polyphony than in chant, and subsequent research at Solesmes revealed the flaw in Haberl's text: a heavily embellished musical notation that could not be found in the original medieval manuscripts. In France, the Ratisbon edition was used only in the Diocese of Cahors, and in the United States mainly among German-speaking Catholics, thanks to Ludwig Bonvin, S.J., and John Singerberger.

Solesmes monks Dom André Mocquéreau and Dom Joseph Pothier had studied those medieval manuscripts and through their investigations arrived at more authentic, sober versions of chant melodies. By 1899, Mocquéreau was certain enough to publish his results in *Paléographie Musicale,*[161] which presented documented evidence of the unity of the tradition within the chant manuscripts he had studied. Moreover, his work proved that the elaborate Ratisbon edition, with its many flourishes, contained too many musical notations that simply

---

[160] Westermeyer, 181–3.

[161] Mocquéreau, ed., *Paléogragphie Musicale* (Solesmes, 1889–1930).

were not present in original chant manuscripts. It was under the leadership of Pius X, at the beginning of the twentieth century, that the Solesmes version became the official Vatican edition. The shift in practice from the Ratisbon to the Solesmes editions took some time to arrive at parishes and monasteries within the United States. And as with all change, the new Solesmes chant was not always easily received.

In 1935, when monks involved in the liturgical movement at St. Vincent's Archabbey in Latrobe, Pennsylvania, introduced the new chant at the largely German monastery, there was a minor revolt. One day, annoyed at the intrusion of the Solesmes edition into their monastic liturgy, all the monks, in unison, threw the new books into the center of the choir and stormed out of the church. Rembert Weakland entered the monastery at Latrobe some years later and served as one of the monastery organists. Even then, he recalls with amusement, there continued to be resistance to what was still called the "new" chant. He intoned the Solesmes chant on the organ, knowing very well that the monks would consistently revert back to the Ratisbon version.[162]

The vernacular liturgy was another important factor regarding the use of chant. Liturgical realists suggested that Latin was difficult enough for American Catholics when spoken. Problems of pronunciation and comprehension only intensified when those texts were sung. Rather than teaching people to chant in Latin, there was some discussion within the liturgical movement about the greater feasibility of adapting Gregorian texts to English and creating worthy musical texts that American Catholics would then be capable of both singing and understanding.[163] This issue continued to surface in the late 1940s and early 1950s. Jesuit liturgist Herman Schmidt argued for the creation of a new chant that would be better accommodated to English. Schmidt's proposition, however, lacked consensus within the American liturgical movement.[164]

---

[162] Rembert G. Weakland, O.S.B., Interview by author, 10 December 1994.

[163] See Joel Gastineau, "Sure, the People Can Sing," *The Caecilia* 80 (1952–53) 56–7.

[164] Michael Mathis wrote: "Notwithstanding the fact that I for a long time was under the impression that Father Schmidt's suggestion was the correct thing, namely, that we have to develop a liturgical chant suitable to the English language, I am becoming very doubtful about that. I mean doubtful about just composing a new chant without reference to the development of chant in the Latin Rite. Fr. Vitry has made me doubtful in this matter, and I think he has a lot on his side, namely, our Gregorian Chant has been developed by people who first of all knew the true Latin liturgical language, and were dependent upon what preceded their work along this line in the Latin liturgical tradition." Letter to Godfrey Diekmann, 9 March 1954, SJAA: #1166.

Others argued for the simple adaptation of Gregorian chant to English. One of the leaders in such adaptation was Ermin Vitry, a monk of Maredsous in Belgium, who came to the United States around the time of the founding of the American liturgical movement in the mid 1920s, and collaborated extensively with the other liturgical pioneers, particularly in the instruction of Gregorian chant. In a letter to Godfrey Diekmann, Michael Mathis wrote: "I personally believe exactly with you that Fr. Vitry is the first man to insure that the melody and rhythm of the Gregorian chant cannot be destroyed by the adaptation of English or other vernacular words to the music."[165]

Numerous musical organizations helped to promote the proper usage of Gregorian chant in American parishes and religious communities. We shall now explore several of the more prominent groups who devoted their energies to such promotion.

Founded in Germany in 1868, The Caecilians were a group of composers and promoters of sacred music, especially the Ratisbon edition of chant. In 1874, the Caecilian movement was brought to the United States by Sir John Singenberger of Milwaukee. Their monthly journal, *The Caecilia,* was begun that same year. High musical standards were set for its composers. Among other interests, they were diligent in working to abolish eighteenth- and nineteenth-century rococo music in churches, while advocating a return to Palestrina and the polyphony of the sixteenth century. Initially, the Caecilians were located primarily in the middle west—Milwaukee, Chicago, and Minneapolis-St. Paul. Gradually, they spread to the dioceses of Covington, New Orleans, Charleston, several other dioceses in the south, then to San Francisco and Portland, Oregon. The east coast remained largely untouched by the Caecilian movement. Seen as an elitist group, they had their enemies on both sides of the Atlantic.

The Liturgical Arts Society made its own contribution to the promotion of chant. In 1934, a schola cantorum was formed within the Society. While the schola represented only a small number of the

---

[165] Letter of 6 January 1953, SJAA #1166. One year later, Mathis continued the discussion with Diekmann: "Certainly, with everybody making translations of the liturgical texts and translations which are being used in liturgical functions, it is about time that we had some general directions for those who are now engaged in this work. It would also be a good thing if we could have the same thing for the adaption of either Gregorian Chant to English words, or English words to Gregorian Chant. Fr. Vitry is coming here this month, and I am going to see if I can get out of him some seminars on that subject this summer." Letter of 9 March 1954, SJAA #1166.

Society's male members, they labored to demonstrate that chant was possible in American Catholic parishes. For a number of years, the "Quilisma Club," as they were called, sang at principal Sunday and festal Eucharists and Vespers in the major churches of New York City, wherever they might receive a positive reception. The schola existed "to praise God, [and] to give some example to the Catholic people as to how the chant could be performed, and to try to bring out some of the beauties which had been neglected."[166] On a number of occasions, they combined with the choir of the Pius X School of Liturgical Music for the common singing of Vespers and for larger Eucharists on solemn occasions. The Ninth Biennial Convention of the Catholic Alumni Federation was one such event. The choirs joined together in singing at that pontifical Mass on 26 October 1939 at St. Patrick's Cathedral, New York City.[167]

Organizations of Church musicians, however, failed to reach the average American Catholic population. More was necessary. American Catholics needed to be educated musically. The blame for disinterest in Gregorian chant and other forms of congregational singing was too often placed on the assembly, when, in reality, little was being done by clergy and parish music directors to help parishioners understand why congregational singing was an important value. Achille Bargers addressed some difficult questions to clergy and music directors at a Boston lecture given in 1945:

> Why do we deprive the Catholic people from the . . . experience of sa-
> cred singing, under the fallacious pretense that it is but a secondary mat-
> ter . . .? Are we to blame the faithful for their prejudices and their
> ignorance when clerical and educational leaders at large have done so
> far little or nothing to educate people . . .? Do you expect congrega-
> tional singing to grow in the midst of societies which are supposed to be
> the backbone of Catholicism and yet refuse to put sacred singing on the
> agenda . . .? Do you realize also that, because sacred singing is the force
> which leads people to take an active part in divine services, there will be
> no participation of the faithful unless singing is restored to the christian
> community?[168]

As baptized members of the body of Christ, American Catholics had the right to be informed about what they were being called to in their

---

[166] La Farge, *The Manner is Ordinary* (New York: Harcourt, Brace, and Company, 1954) 290.

[167] Ellard, *Men at Work and Worship*, 156.

[168] Achille Bragers, "Chant: The Handmaid of the Liturgy," *The Caecilia* 75 (1947–48) 181.

sung liturgical prayer. Referring to the *motu proprio,* one prominent Church musician stated this position firmly:

> Let it at once be said that success can only come when the congregation has received definite instruction as to what it all means, and what is expected from it by the powers that be, who have deliberately decided to issue a juridical code of music.[169]

If any success would be realized in the restoration and promotion of Gregorian chant on American soil, solid liturgical and musical education was needed. Pre-dating the founding of the liturgical movement by ten years, the most famous of the academic programs was the Pius X School of Liturgical Music.

The Pius X School of Liturgical Music

The hallmark of an American training in liturgical music was the Pius X School of Liturgical Music founded in 1916 by Mrs. Justine B. Ward and Mother Georgia Stevens, R.S.C.J. Inspired by the *Motu proprio,* these two women opened a school for the teaching of Gregorian chant at the College of the Sacred Heart, Manhattanville, New York.[170] Ward was an accomplished musician and a newcomer to Catholicism. Not lacking financial resources, she was a frequent visitor to the Benedictine monastery of Solesmes, France, then in exile on the Isle of Wight. Her own method of teaching Gregorian chant was greatly influenced by the study and execution of chant taking place at that monastery. Ward's association with Solesmes is well-known. But there were other influences on Justine Ward's method.

At The Catholic University in Washington, Ward was influenced by the philosophical and educational theories of Thomas Shields, dean of the Sisters' College at the time. While editing a series of texts for Catholic schools in 1910, Shields asked Ward to prepare the musical material. To assist her efforts, Ward consulted John Young, S.J., who had already earned a name for himself as a distinguished choirmaster at St. Francis Xavier Church on West Sixteenth Street in New York City. Young was a specialist in Church music and was known for his success in teaching chant to choir members at Xavier Parish. In addition, Young served as a member of the New York Music Commission and the Papal Commission for the revision of ritual music in the Catholic

---

[169] Becket Gibbs, "Letter to the Editor," *LA* 16 (1947) 62.

[170] See Catherine Carroll, *A History of the Pius X School of Liturgical Music: 1916–1969* (St. Louis: Society of the Sacred Heart, 1989); P. Combe, *Justine Ward and Solesmes* (Washington: The Catholic University of America Press, 1987).

Church. Young was responsible for producing chant recordings using the *Ward Method,* and for incorporating the exercises and drills from the *Chevé Manuals for Teaching Music* into the *Ward Method.*[171] By 1915, the first and second books of her *Ward Method* were published and used by a number of schools in the New York area.

Georgia Stevens and Justine Ward were friends. Herself a newcomer to Catholicism, Stevens was a professional violinist responsible for the improvement of liturgical singing in the Manhattanville chapel. Aware of Ward's success in teaching chant to children in Washington, Stevens invited her colleague to New York. Ward accepted the invitation and in the summer of 1916 brought her Washington choir to Manhattanville to demonstrate her method. That demonstration convinced Manhattanville administrators to begin the teaching of Gregorian chant at their academy. That was the beginning of the Pius X school. One year later, in 1917, Ward and Stevens instituted the first summer school in liturgical music at Manhattanville.

Justine Ward took the best of Shields' and Young's technique in the development of her own pedagogy, thus making the *Ward Method* distinctive. Shields contended that music was a language to be heard, read, and articulated creatively. Young recommended the inclusion of the number notation from the *Chevé Method.* Finger drills, ear tests, musical conversations, rhythmic drills, and melody writing were also included. Those elements were blended together by Ward. Books One and Two for educational use were supplemented with a service book, the *Ward Hymnal.*[172] The book was intended for older children as an encouragement to utilize their musical education in their liturgical participation. The first edition of the hymnal contained Latin and English hymns, and several English chants arranged by Young. The *Missa De Angelis, Credo III, Asperges,* and *Vidi Aquam* were also included. The hymnal was printed in the number notation for the students and in traditional musical notation for the organist.[173]

Justine Ward's correspondence with Virgil Michel at the beginning of the American liturgical movement reveals a strong liturgical awareness in her own understanding of chant.[174] Hearing of plans for the

---

[171] Known as the *Galin-Paris Chevé Method,* it was a popularized sight-reading manual used by schools in Belgium, France, and Holland in the late nineteenth century. The use of numbers and intonation exercises was borrowed by Ward in the development of her own method.

[172] *Ward Hymnal* (Washington: Catholic Education Press, 1919).

[173] Carroll, 11–7; 113–4.

[174] Writing enthusiastically of the emerging liturgical movement in the United States, Ward wrote: "I often think of what Rev. Dr. Shields said to me a few months

publishing of *Orate Fratres,* Ward urged Michel to use the pages of that periodical to pursue the important relationship between liturgy and chant.[175] Michel, in turn, invited Ward to serve as a member of the magazine's first editorial board. Ward, however, declined the offer.[176] With the founding of the liturgical movement in the United States, Ward expressed the desire that students at the Pius X school be properly informed about liturgical renewal and the movement's developments.[177] Michel joined the Pius X faculty in the summer of 1926.

The school had a powerful effect on the promotion of Gregorian chant in the United States and on the understanding of the role of music in the liturgy. By 1925, more than thirteen thousand teachers had studied Ward's method of chant. While teaching chant to children during the academic year, Ward and Stevens focused their efforts on adult education in summers. The summer musical faculty often included chant specialists such as André Mocquéreau, O.S.B., the choirmaster at Solesmes, and Abbot Paolo Ferretti, O.S.B., of Parma, Italy.[178]

---

before his death: 'We are all taking part in a movement that is much greater than any individual and is more far reaching than we imagine; it has all the characteristics of the great epoch making movements in the Church.' I wish he could have lived to have seen the realization of your plan." Letter to Virgil Michel, 10 May 1925, SJAA: Z-28.

[175] "It would be a beautiful thing if we could develop through this review the close connection between liturgy itself and its living voice—the Chant—and go more deeply into this than is possible in any review which exists at present. I think there is much unexplored ground here. In the Preface I touched on it very superficially and generally, but I think a closer study would reveal many facts of application of what we might call tone-symbolism in the melodies of that epoch—where all was symbolism." Ibid.

[176] "I feel doubtful whether I ought to accept your very kind invitation to be one of the *Editorial Collaborators* because I am so terribly pressed with other work that it would be impossible to make a definite promise to write 5 or 6 articles a year . . . Do you not think it would be better to let me be an occasional contributor? I am sure you realize, dear Father, that my reason for saying this is not lack of enthusiasm for the cause, but a desire not to disappoint you in the event that I could not fulfill the implied obligation." Letter to Virgil Michel, 7 February 1926, SJAA: Z-27.

[177] "I have not abandoned the idea of a series of conferences on the liturgy for our Summer School of 1926; indeed I have always felt that our school was incomplete because of its absence, and I should like to have this course a unit in our general training, that is a thirty hour course with an examination at the end, which would be obligatory on all pupils wishing a degree in Sacred Music." Letter of 10 May 1925.

[178] Under their direction, albums of Gregorian chant, sung by the Pius X choir were produced and widely acclaimed, as reported by Compton Pakenham in *The*

Summer participants included other teachers and clergy, Church musicians and lay parish leaders. Ward used her wealth to successfully promote the *motu proprio* on American soil. It was such wealth that sustained the school during periods of poor financial management and helped to increase its notoriety throughout the United States. Liturgical historian James White has rightly remarked that Ward and Georgia Stevens "may well be the most important women liturgical reformers of this century."[179] Their contribution was all the more significant in that women were not permitted to sing in Church choirs in those years.[180]

Ward encouraged Georgia Stevens to experiment with her method. When such experimentation was tried, however, Ward was less than pleased. In 1930, a rift developed between Ward and Stevens, and in 1931 Ward resigned from the Pius X School. Her departure had a much larger effect on the future of the school. The abbot of Solesmes supported Ward and refused to send monks to Manhattanville to teach in the summer session following Ward's departure. A reconciliation took place between Justine Ward and the Pius X School in 1958, although the relationship was never fully restored. Ward refused an honorary doctorate from Manhattanville. Further, she requested that her name be removed from the mailing lists of the college. A telegram informing Ward of the death of Georgia Stevens went unanswered, and her own obituary in *The New York Times* (28 November 1975) made no mention of her founding the Pius X School nor of her collaboration with Stevens in liturgical music.[181]

In the 1930s, course offerings in liturgy became a normative component in the Manhattanville summer schools. Other liturgical pioneers —Hellriegel, Hillenbrand, Reinhold, Ellard, and Diekmann—also joined the faculty.[182] Despite the presence of liturgical pioneers on the

---

New York Times: "Here in New York, we have a group of singers trained by Dom Mocquéreau himself, a choir which may be said to have established the tradition of Solesmes in this country." 28 May 1933, quoted in Editor, "The Apostolate," *OF* 7 (1933) 418.

[179] White, *Roman Catholic Worship: Trent to Today,* 89.

[180] The prohibition of Pius X, articulated in the *motu proprio,* was consistent with a defective Church policy which limited all liturgical ministries to males: ". . . singers in church have a real liturgical office, and . . . therefore women, being incapable of exercising such office, cannot be admitted to form part of the choir . . ." (No. 13).

[181] Carroll, 44–55, 121.

[182] Michel first offered the following course description for the 1936 summer program: "A synthesis of Christian solidarity as found in corporate worship: the place of worship in Catholic Action; of sacrifice in worship; and of social and individual

Pius X faculty, Mother Stevens was concerned that the school keep music rather than liturgy as its primary emphasis. Nonetheless, liturgical celebrations did constitute a normative part of the daily order at Pius X. One letter describes the students singing the full offices, including Mass and Vespers.[183] Writing to Stevens in 1935, Michel requested lodging at Manhattanville during the summer session that year, so that he could be more available to his students, allowing for more ample liturgical discussions.[184] Stevens responded: "we have already exceeded the number who can stay here among the Priests studying music and so we regret that we cannot offer you hospitality."[185]

Other Institutions of Education in Liturgical Music

In 1928, chant specialist Ermin Vitry, O.S.B., founded the St. Cloud Music Institute. While Vitry's summer program was less well-known than the Manhattanville school, it attended more thoroughly to liturgical interests.[186] In addition to three general courses that treated music and liturgical life, liturgical music in parishes, and organization of music in the parish,[187] there were listings under Gregorian chant, liturgy, and other optional courses. Under liturgy, courses considered

---

participation in sacrifice." He revised that description in the same letter to Mother Stevens: "A survey of the liturgy of the Church and its basic concepts and spirit; a general application of the latter to the entire sphere of Catholic life, culture, and civilization." Letter of 3 March 1936, SJAA: Z-27.

[183] Letter of Mother Stevens to Virgil Michel, 7 February 1926. SJAA: Z-27.

[184] Letter to Mother Stevens, 16 December 1935. SJAA: Z-27.

[185] The deeper issue, perhaps, was what followed in Stevens' response to Michel's request: "It would be quite impossible for the students to give any extra time as you suggest because they are here for the music and find it extremely difficult to get in the necessary assignments, so that we would not be able to have the extra conferences and talks, deeply as I regret this . . . We shall always hope to have lectures on the Liturgy but this School, as you know, is primarily for the Chant and people who come here come for that purpose. I have found it absolutely necessary, for the sake of the students, to concentrate on the musical side during the six weeks of the summer school." Letter to Virgil Michel, 27 December 1935, SJAA: Z-27.

[186] Vitry described his summer program: "The St. Cloud Music Institute was founded . . . with the special aim to become a center for the formation of musicians thoroughly trained in the requirements of Catholic church music, whether as organists, or as choir-masters and teachers. We are very glad to announce that the Institute has definitely made connection with the liturgical movement, so as to become in the future its official representative school." "The St. Cloud Music Institute" (1928) SJAA: Z-28.

[187] The St. Cloud Music Institute, "General Courses" (n.d.) SJAA: Z-28.

legislation regarding Church music, the relationship of liturgy to music, practical regulations.[188] Despite its liturgical emphasis and good intentions, Vitry's institute did not have the longevity of the Pius X School. By the early 1930s, the Institute was discontinued and Vitry moved to O'Fallon Missouri, where he collaborated with Martin Hellriegel as music director at the motherhouse of the Sisters of the Precious Blood.

In his 1935 letter on pastoral music, Archbishop John Murray of St. Paul, Minnesota, announced a liturgical summer school for choir directors. The program was held in July and August of that year at St. Thomas College in St. Paul. That same pastoral letter announced that choir directors would need to be certified by the Archdiocesan Commission of Sacred Music. The summer school in liturgical music would assist Church musicians in that task.[189]

In 1941, The Catholic Choirmasters' Correspondence Course was founded at Sacred Heart Church in Pittsburgh, Pennsylvania, by the parish music director, Clifford A. Bennett. Advised by Mother Georgia Stevens, Bennett devised a program that offered courses and accreditation for Church musicians throughout the United States.[190] Within a short time, the name was changed to the Gregorian Institute of Pittsburgh, bringing strong reaction from the Diocesan Music Commission. That commission published a strong condemnation of the Gregorian Institute's director, Clifford Bennett, in *The Priest*.[191] Entitled, "It's a Racket," Bennett was accused of jeopardizing the well-known musical standards of the diocese by calling himself director of the "Gregorian Institute of Pittsburgh," and stated that the group was not under the auspices of the local bishop. Further, Bennett was accused of sponsoring the sale of "non-authorized plainchant records among seminarians." A Sulpician on the faculty of St. Mary's Seminary, Baltimore, John C. Selver initiated a letter in support of Bennett, which was circulated in American liturgical circles. Godfrey Diekmann and Gerald Ellard were among those who signed. The Gregorian Institute of Pittsburgh

[188] Letter to Virgil Michel, 15 April 1928, SJAA: Z-28.

[189] Editor, "Liturgical School for Directors of Choirs Announced; Archbishop Urges Training of Young People for Congregational Singing; Requires Leaders to Obtain Certificates," *The Caecilia* 62 (1935) 182.

[190] "I had a long conference with Mother Stevens at the Pius X School and she was so enthusiastic about the whole plan and the good that it will accomplish that it was almost impossible to leave her for my next appointment. I am sure that this will be an encouragement to you, and to know also that she heartily approved of all the faculty." Letter of Clifford Bennett to Godfrey Diekmann, 6 November 1941, SJAA: #1163.

[191] (January 1945, 57).

soon became the Gregorian Institute of America, and re-located in Toledo.[192] Rather than focusing on one geographical area of the country, the Institute offered courses in different locations, usually centered at seminaries or monasteries. The faculty was varied and reflected both liturgical and musical concerns. Godfrey Diekmann and Gerald Ellard were early advisors and instructors in Bennett's program,[193] and the Institute later included an international faculty. British liturgist, Clifford Howell, S.J., was among those invited to teach in the 1951 summer session.

The summer of 1951 saw the expansion of course offerings in liturgical music around the United States. The Notre Dame Summer School of Liturgy expanded its program in 1951 to include a liturgical music division, under the direction of Ermin Vitry. The De Paul University School of Music in Chicago hosted a six-week summer session on the relationship between music and liturgy. St. Joseph's College in Collegeville, Indiana, announced their summer institute in Church music. The women of the Grail hosted a six-week seminar at their headquarters in Ohio, entitled "The Apostolate of Music." The Catholic University in Washington, D.C., offered a full summer program of liturgical music and musical theory. Newton College of the Sacred Heart in Massachusetts hosted a two-week course in chant for Church musicians from the Archdiocese of Boston. A similar course was offered at the College of St. Joseph in New Mexico.[194]

Liturgical Music in Praxis

By now, it should be clear that the liturgical pioneers emphasized Gregorian chant as normative for the sung prayer of the liturgical assembly. While ethnic parishes continued their tradition of hymnody in

---

[192] Letter of John C. Selver, S.S., to Godfrey Diekmann, 1 February 1945. SJAA: #1163.

[193] In inviting Diekmann's collaboration as an instructor, Bennett wrote: "Your task will be to present as clearly as possible the need for Vespers and Compline in the parish and try to give to the choirmaster an insight into the beauty and religious inspiration and great intelligence in the Psalms and Antiphons. Most country, and some city choirs have never heard the terms 'Vespers' and 'Compline' and so, the lessons will have to avoid all over-intellectualism and any speculation or too deep meditation which would be understood by those in religious life but would far over-shoot the mark as far as the NORMAL, EVERYDAY choirmaster is concerned." Letter of Clifford Bennett to Godfrey Diekmann, 6 November 1941. SJAA: #1163.

[194] Editor, "Summer Schools in Catholic Church Music," *The Caecilia* 79 (1952) 157–60.

diverse languages, there was little encouragement in the 1930s and 1940s to explore a peculiarly American form of liturgical music. It was not until the time of the Second Vatican Council that American Catholics began to make greater use of hymnody and incorporate American hymn tunes and African-American spirituals into the liturgy. Thus, parishes and religious communities were noted for their liturgical singing when they learned to sing chant well, which is to say, when they gathered to chant Sunday Vespers, and when they sang a Gregorian setting of the Mass in unison at the principal Sunday Eucharist.

Institutions like the Pius X School of Liturgical Music or the Gregorian Institute of America became centers of consultation for parishes, religious communities, Catholic Action groups, and others who were committed to improving the liturgical singing of their constituencies. In 1935, for example, members of the Catholic Worker Community in New York City sought the help of Mother Stevens at Pius X in beginning a liturgical choir, which would be formed to assist poorer parishes in learning how to sing Gregorian chant during the liturgy.[195] In 1941, Clifford Bennett wrote enthusiastically to Godfrey Diekmann that he had successfully introduced the singing of Credo III to the congregation at Sacred Heart Parish in Pittsburgh and recommended that other large city parishes attempt the same. In that letter, Bennett expressed the hope that this was only the beginning of fuller liturgical participation by the assembly.[196]

---

[195] Regarding the desire to begin a liturgical choir, the Co-Editor of the *CW* wrote to Mother Stevens: "That may seem a rather far cry from the work of the Catholic Worker, at first glance; but I'm sure I don't need to point out to you the fact that the entire Catholic social teaching is based, fundamentally, on liturgical doctrine. The group wishes to be able to open their evening meetings . . . with sung Compline. And they are especially anxious to learn a few of the simpler Gregorian Masses, in order to be able to offer their services free to poor parishes . . . What we hope you will be able to do, of course, is to send a teacher, or one of your students once a week, to assist in the training of the group." Letter of 5 June 1935, Dorothy Day-Catholic Worker Collection (W-6), Marquette University Archives, Milwaukee, Wisconsin.

[196] Bennett described his methodology for preparing the assembly for the new Credo: "For one month preceding the 'premier' singing of the Credo, an announcement was carried in the weekly mimeographed bulletin . . . that we would begin on a certain Sunday and that printed cards would be distributed to the congregation. For several Sundays the choir sang the Credo to be used. Every effort was made to get the word around to the members of all parish units, and on the appointed Sunday, the congregation was well represented by the children of the grade and high school departments who sat in scattered sections of the church. Father Coakley gave inspiring sermons at all the Masses and cards were distrib-

Paul Bentley wrote of his experience with the Catholic community at the military base of Fort Lewis, Washington in the mid-1940s. He described an active liturgical program with a choir that promoted congregational singing because it understood its own ministry. The choir had studied the *motu proprio* and held discussions on such topics as "the Liturgy, ecclesiastical architecture, religious art, vestments, appurtenances, the Divine Office, the place of the choir in the church and the sacred office of the choir singer." On the placement of the choir, Bentley wrote:

> Our choir sings from (the) loft because, of necessity, it is a mixed choir, but the console in the sanctuary is used when the congregation sings at low masses and devotions.[197]

Holy Cross Parish in St. Louis was a national leader in liturgical music throughout Martin Hellriegel's long pastorate. When Hellriegel arrived at the parish in June of 1940, there was virtually no music program. He began by introducing the singing of English hymns printed on mimeographed sheets, before and after Mass. Finally, a collection of over two hundred hymns were chosen and printed on colored cards to correspond with the different colors of the liturgical seasons. A hymn board was used to inform the congregation of the hymns for each day. The same method was followed with sung Mass responses. When Hellriegel arrived at Holy Cross, the people had not sung Gregorian chant, "which, in a way, was a blessing. It is easier to start from scratch than to re-build." With the help of recordings of Solesmes chant, Hellriegel personally taught the school children those same melodies. When parents heard their children singing those chants at the Sunday Eucharist, they expressed the desire to learn the same. Gradually, the entire congregation chanted the Mass. The choir sang in the choir stalls "between altar and people." Hellriegel recognized the importance of the choir's presence in the midst of the assembly:

> I am afraid that the "loft," "born out of due season," is not too conducive either to the spiritual life of singers or to the promotion of congregational

---

uted to all during the morning services. One of the assistant priests led the singing from the pulpit and the people alternated with the choir. Many of the parish returned from the earlier Masses and the reports gleaned from various members after the Mass were most encouraging. We shall use the director in the pulpit for one or two more Sundays and by then he will not be necessary . . . This is all very encouraging and we hope later to add more in the way of lay participation." Letter of 18 January 1941, SJAA: #1163.

[197] Paul Bentley, "Letter to the Editor," *LA* 14 (1945) 22.

singing. The choir should have its place *between* altar and congregation, to bring the two together; not *up* in the loft, nor *behind* altar where the singers can see nothing of the sacred functions "in which the divine Founder is present."[198]

During Lent, 1951, parishioners at Christ the King Parish, South Bend, Indiana, began singing the Mass together during the daily eucharistic celebration. Unlike Holy Cross in St. Louis where the music program originated with the pastor, here the idea came from the assembly itself:

> A few of us attending the weekday mass . . . decided that . . . we would sit near the organ, and would sing with the organist when the key was not too high. No one asked us to do this; we just exercised our right as members of Christ's Body, and did it. After Lent, of course, the size of the congregation diminished, but we kept on singing.[199]

The following summer, although the organist left the parish and was not immediately replaced, the parishioners continued to sing.[200] Unlike Hellriegel's approach, which relied on children to teach chant to the adults, parishioners at Christ the King suggested that adults would be better disposed to chant when learning from their peers rather than from children. "Children will follow adults, but adults will not follow children. Therefore the leadership in the singing should be in the hands of adults." Further, it was argued that members of the assembly learned best when they were not taught by a perfectionist or by a choir that sounded too professional.[201]

National Catholic movements and organizations like the Christian Family Movement (CFM) assisted their parishes in promoting congregational singing. In many cases, the national conventions of these

---

[198] Hellriegel, "Monsignor Hellriegel's Music Program," *The Caecilia* 83 (1955) 73–4.

[199] Willis Nutting, "Daily Sung Mass," *Amen* (1 July 1954) 12.

[200] "The absence of the organ is a positive help. It gives people confidence to use their voices, when the dominant sound around them is other voices rather than the sound of an instrument. It allows the people to reply immediately to the priest in the dialog, and in the same key, and thus does not break up the dialog into two separate musical pieces. It allows the words to stand out more clearly." Ibid.

[201] "People do not refuse to sing Gregorian if they are allowed to sing it as they sing anything else, that is, imperfectly. If it is presented to them by a perfectionist, of course they won't sing it, or anything else presented that way. And they won't sing it along with a choir they think is expert. They won't do anything in a be-careful-you-don't-spoil-it atmosphere; and that, unfortunately, is the atmosphere in which a lot of Gregorian is presented, both by teaching and by records." Ibid.

groups included a festive Eucharist sung by all participants. It was in such large gatherings where Catholic activists recognized the potential of congregational singing in their home parishes. CFM published its own service booklet *Sung Mass,* and encouraged its use both in CFM retreats and in the home parishes of CFM members. The text contained one full Mass, along with a number of English hymns.[202]

CONCLUSION

Like other themes promoted within the American liturgical movement, the liturgical pioneers addressed the theme of the arts in terms of their role in the Mystical Body of Christ—as a servant of the Church's worship. In response to some critics of the liturgical movement, who dismissed it as a movement of artists out of touch with the real experience of American Catholics, the liturgical pioneers attempted to prove otherwise, and promoted liturgical art grounded in its function as a servant of the Mystical Body of Christ. If the art itself was to be a servant of the liturgy, then so too were the artists. They had their own liturgical function to exercise. Thus, whether their ministry was direct, as in the case of a choir or musician, or indirect, as in the case of an architect, sculptor, or painter, all liturgical artists were called to be servants of the liturgy—servants of the corporate prayer of the Mystical Body of Christ, like the art they created.

Liturgical pioneers were given a dual challenge in their promotion of liturgical art, architecture, and music. First, they had to convince American Catholics of the importance of the arts; liturgical art, architecture, and music were not superfluous or unimportant, but had a crucial function to play. Liturgy was art. Second, the pioneers needed to convince their colleagues in artistic circles that the arts did not exist solely for themselves. Art that existed independent of the liturgy could not claim to be liturgical art. Church architecture was not necessarily liturgical even if it won awards for its unique design in the form of a fish. Music that was strictly performance and was not connected to the liturgical act of the assembly ceased to be liturgical music.

Another item on the agenda of the liturgical movement was the challenge of fostering collaboration among liturgical artists and the local church, particularly the local pastor. This was no easy task, as mutual suspicion and mistrust often dominated such relationships. Michel, Diekmann, Reinhold, La Farge, and others in the movement were well aware of the rift that had developed between the artistic community and the Church where artists often felt alienated. American

---

[202] Editor, "Parish Takes 1,000 of 'Sung Mass' Book," *ACT* 8 (September 1954) 1.

Catholics, in turn, accused artists and their artistic expression of being outside the circle of the normal, everyday life of their American peers. The lack of a good liturgical and artistic education was recognized as the root of many of the problems and tensions experienced both within the American church and the artistic community. Thus, the liturgical education of American Catholics, which promoted full and active participation in the Mystical Body of Christ, needed to include a serious treatment of the role of liturgical art within worship.

Despite the best efforts of Virgil Michel and his associates, it must be said that this item on the agenda of the liturgical movement was less successful than other themes which the movement adopted. The pioneers' passion for the movement's link with social justice, for example, was clear and effective. The liturgical pioneers' vision of the liturgical arts however, was less focused and not as easily implemented. Among those pioneers, H. A. Reinhold best understood the liturgical arts and their function from a professional perspective, but his contribution in that area did not begin until the late 1940s. Virgil Michel continued Herwegen's vision and spoke of liturgy as art and the liturgical participants as artists, but he failed to give clear direction to this aspect of the movement. On the level of leadership, the contribution of John La Farge is not to be underestimated, both in his role as chaplain of the Liturgical Arts Society and in his articles published in *America*. Nonetheless, Robert Rambusch's theory holds true that in many respects, the arts grew up outside of the American church in the 1930s, 1940s, and 1950s. This was not the case in Europe.

The fundamental call of the American liturgical pioneers was a call to artistic simplicity, rather than an overuse of artistic media which would be a distraction. Despite problems of implementation, the pioneers were unified in adhering to this age-old principle: "Less is more." Liturgical art, architecture, and music were not created as ends in themselves. When the church building was open and uncluttered, the colors and diversity of the members of the assembly were heightened. Then the liturgy truly became a work of art, and the gathered members of the Mystical Body of Christ, the artists.

Conclusion

The liturgical movement in the United States was not, as some had believed, concerned merely with new styles of liturgical vesture, but was a return to the very heart of the liturgy, to full and active participation as the source of Christian social consciousness. The movement was an organic part of twentieth-century American ecclesial renewal, closely related to the biblical, patristic, and neo-Thomistic movements which theologically supported the work of the liturgical pioneers. Together, these movements campaigned against individualism and materialism in the United States, offering a new vision of Church and human society.

That same liturgical movement gathered together American Catholics from all walks of life. Unlike the European movement that was centered in or around monasteries, the movement in the United States was more pluralistic, surfacing on college campuses and in Catholic bookstores, in social outreach centers and adult study groups. While many of the early liturgical leaders were ordained, the movement did not remain a clerical affair, but drew a diverse crowd. Among that crowd were a number of women: Patty Crowley, Dorothy Day, Catherine De Hueck, Jane Marie Murray, Sara Benedicta O'Neill, Mary Perkins, Nina Polcyn Moore, the women of the Grail Movement, Mother Georgia Stevens, Justine Ward, just to name a few. These women did not limit their liturgical efforts to other lay Catholics, but influenced bishops and priests, as well. This is extraordinary when one considers the American church of the 1930s and 1940s. In a word, this was a grassroots movement of the people, a microcosm of the Church in the United States.

Sociologists and liturgists have debated over to what extent this was a movement in the strict, sociological sense. Sociologist Andrew Greeley, for example, contends that the liturgical movement was not a movement at all,[1] while sociologist and liturgist, Virgil Funk argues

---

[1] "The nation seems to think that the liturgical movement was not a movement at all in the sociological sense. It was rather a very small and persistent elite group,

that the key to interpreting the liturgical movement is precisely in its sociological framework, because without that dynamic, "you only move from theological idea to theological idea."[2] Funk describes a social movement in this way:

> A gathering of people focused around a cause, often oriented toward change in the existing pattern of behavior in an organization, or society at large. This cause generates leaders with a commitment and, often, with charisma, and its sole criterion for its members is a general willingness to embrace the cause. A movement is distinguished from an organization, which is characterized by stated goals, an elaborate system of explicit rules and regulations, and a formal status structure with clearly marked lines of communication and authority. Movements follow a cycle beginning with issues, widening into a cause, coming to a climax or confrontation, and being absorbed into a new or existing organization.[3]

Recognizing the national impact of the liturgical movement in the United States, sociologist John Coleman, S.J., suggests that the movement might better be described as a network of relationships, contacts, and mutual concern.[4] Whether or not this was a movement in the strict sociological sense, it was clearly a movement to those who pioneered and promoted its agenda in the 1930s through the 1950s.

Another interesting aspect is that of ecumenical influences and convergences. Recent studies have been completed on the liturgical movement in other churches.[5] Were there common elements in the different liturgical movements of American Christian churches? Did the liturgical practice of Anglican or Lutheran churches, for example, have much

---

at least in the United States—Benedictines from St. John, Msgr. Hillenbrand, some occasional Jesuits, and dedicated lay people. Aside from Hillenbrand and Virgil Michel you have almost nothing in this country." Letter to author, 29 November 1994.

[2] Letter to author, 18 November 1993.

[3] "The Liturgical Movement," in Peter E. Fink, S.J., (ed.) *The New Dictionary of Sacramental Worship* (Collegeville: The Liturgical Press, 1990) 695–6. In this article, Funk analyzes the liturgical movement in its sociological framework. He argues that the one liturgical movement was really four: the Benedictine or monastic liturgical movement, the scholastic liturgical movement, the pastoral liturgical movement, and legislation.

[4] Interview by author, 14 March 1995, Rome, Italy.

[5] See, for example: Donald Gray, *Earth and Altar* (London: SPCK, 1988); Michael Moriarty, "The Associated Parishes for Liturgy and Mission, 1946–1991: The Liturgical Movement in the Episcopal Church," (Ph.D. diss., University of Notre Dame, 1993).

influence upon the liturgical movement in the Roman Catholic Church? Anglican liturgical pioneer A. Gabriel Hebert, in his classic work, *Liturgy and Society: The Function of the Church in the Modern World*,[6] attributed his own liturgical awareness to the Benedictine monks at Maria Laach. Methodist liturgist, James F. White, however, in his recent book, *Roman Catholic Worship: Trent to Today*, argues that the Catholic liturgical movement was strongly influenced by Protestantism since it adopted concerns for liturgical preaching, congregational singing, the vernacular, and other forms of participation, all of which had existed in Protestant churches for centuries. Further, White notes that the Catholic liturgical movement grew primarily in Protestant countries like Germany and England, for example, and wonders why the movement was less successful in more Catholic countries like Italy and Spain. He points to the successful founding of the movement in the United States in the largely Protestant state of Minnesota, and notes the slow growth of the movement on the heavily Catholic east and west coasts.

White's thesis is interesting and merits further exploration. My own research, however, points more to the ethnic significance than to the religious when evaluating the geographical areas of the movement's success. In Germany, for example, it would be difficult to prove Protestant influence upon the Benedictine monasteries of Beuron or Maria Laach, and yet, the central role which those monasteries played in the German movement cannot be denied. Further, in Catholic Bavaria, a strong tradition of German hymnody and congregational singing was already in existence for centuries, even prior to the Reformation. In the United States, the cultural factor was clearly the key to the movement's growth and success. St. John's Abbey, Collegeville, was a German monastery, so much so that German was the official language of the monastery until the early 1920s. Many of the monks who entered St. John's spoke only German at home and simply continued the practice in the monastic community when they were not obliged to speak Latin. Moreover, it was Germans and German-Americans who were the first to grasp the intrinsic connection between liturgy and social justice. The movement, then, was more successful in the middle west, than on the east or west coasts, not because that area was more Protestant, but because it was more German. New York, Boston, Washington, San Francisco, and Los Angeles were heavily Irish. If it were simply a matter of Catholic or Protestant, then it would be difficult to explain the tremendous success of the liturgical movement in Catholic Chicago, for example.

[6] (London: Faber and Faber, 1935).

The doctrine of the Mystical Body was at the heart of the liturgical movement. Godfrey Diekmann writes:

> It seems to me that at the *heart* of the entire liturgical movement in the U.S. was the doctrine of the mystical body of Christ. We had a Virgil Michel Symposium (national) here 2 or 3 years ago. *Every one* of the speakers had independently come to the same conclusion. The liturgical movement was a *spiritual,* life-shaping apostolate. They were heady, exciting days, because they meant an ever deepening and widening discovery of the dimensions of our life in Christ. The doctrine of the mystical body itself was a "new" discovery—more or less looked at with suspicion by the general stream of Catholic thinking, until Pius XII's encyclical in the early 40s gave it respectability! I'm not kidding. And it was the doctrine of the mystical body lived out in *pastoral liturgy,* esp. the *Missa recitata*, that largely occasioned the (I can only say) new (recovered) insights about *Christology* and *Ecclesiology,* which found expression in the liturgical document ("Mediator Dei") and then in subsequent ones.[7]

In 1930, Virgil Michel argued that there was a connection between the Church's lost consciousness as the Mystical Body of Christ and the loss of its liturgical awareness.[8] With the advent of the Second Vatican Council, the consciousness of the Church as the Mystical Body of Christ gave way to a new consciousness as "people of God." Despite great strides in liturgical participation since the Council, and despite the many positive aspects of the Church's consciousness as "people of God," something has been lost with this paradigmatic shift. "People of God" does not imply the same intrinsic union between members as is implied by "Mystical Body." The harmony is not necessarily implied, although it may be present. Members who share life in the same body, however, are radically linked to such an extent that attending to the needs of the weaker or sicker members cannot be avoided even if one might prefer to do so. "People of God" positively highlights diversity within the Church, but it also potentially highlights independence from others and individuation. Further, it lacks the transcendental sense of mystery that is inherent in Mystical Body theology.

Most liturgical leaders of the 1930s and 1940s were self-taught. Gerald Ellard was the scholar among that early group even though he had done no formal study of liturgy. Today, we have many professionally-trained liturgical scholars representing many different churches. Unfortunately, the discipline of liturgy has become strictly academic and the ecclesial and social justice dimensions have been lost. One of the

---

[7] Letter to author, 17 October 1994.
[8] "The True Christian Spirit," *Ecclesiastical Review* 82 (1930) 132, 135.

major critiques of the liturgical reforms following the Second Vatican Council is that the American church was not adequately prepared. Despite progress made in liturgical scholarship and the growing number of professionally-trained liturgists across the country, there remains a lack of adequate liturgical catechesis in many parishes. Thirty years after the Council, many American Catholics have yet to understand what they are doing when they gather for Sunday worship or why liturgical participation demands social responsibility.

American cultural influences such as individualism, consumerism, and the desire to be entertained, cannot be overlooked when considering tensions in American liturgical practice. These tensions are particularly present among young people where a serious gap between liturgy and spirituality is in evidence. Recent years have witnessed an increasing interest in New Age spirituality, incorporating various techniques of meditation and music, helping participants to relax or temporarily escape from the pressures and problems of life. While this trend may suggest a growing search for God among the young, the emphasis tends to be self-focused, individualistic, and disassociated from liturgy, for liturgy implies communion with others and social responsibility.

Mirroring the overall fragmentation within American life and culture, liturgy, in many cases, remains fragmented and divorced from life. We are in the midst of a liturgical malaise. Liturgical presiding, preaching, and music are in need of help. In many parts of the United States, liturgy has become a democratic, middle-class activity. Benedictine liturgical scholar Aidan Kavanagh remarks:

> The old discipline and its egalitarian sense of obligation is now replaced by local options often generated by committees made up of clergy and semiprofessional lay persons who represent largely middle-class values and techniques of short-term joining and therapy, which may often be problematic for the poorer classes and disdained by the upper classes. A kind of humorless symbol mongering often seems to result from this, buffering or even suffocating the fundamental sacramental reality at the core of the rite—the sacrifice of thanksgiving to God in Christ being transmuted into some kind of cultural high tea followed by seminars on social justice, world hunger, or how we are and are not permitted to speak of God in brave new ways. Such issues, no less than liturgical form and sacramental symbolism, are very important indeed. They are also *very* complex, require high discipline and competence, and are trivialized by simplistic reductionism when they fall into the hands of the undisciplined and incompetent.[9]

[9] Aidan Kavanagh, "Reflections on the Study from the Viewpoint of Liturgical History," in Lawrence J. Madden (ed.), *The Awakening Church: 25 Years of Liturgical Renewal* (Collegeville: The Liturgical Press, 1992) 93.

We have moved from a pre-conciliar time where the one presiding had too much control over the liturgy to the current situation where the presider often has very little say in what takes place because that is dictated by a liturgy committee. The situation is further complicated by some presiders and preachers who attempt to be relevant or entertaining, creating an artificial informality in the public, formal setting of the Sunday morning liturgical assembly. Unfortunately, those individuals reveal little more than an apparent insecurity with the role which the Church has designated them to fulfill.

The social, cultural, and religious climate in the United States has changed significantly since the days of Virgil Michel and his contemporaries. While immigration was a significant issue in the 1920s and 1930s, multicultural liturgical communities as a microcosm of American life are increasingly becoming a reality throughout the United States. A *New York Times* article notes that immigration is at its highest level since 1940.[10] From 1990 to 1994, 4.5 million immigrants came to the United States, almost as many as arrived during the whole decade of the 1970s. Unlike those early years of the liturgical movement when most immigrants came from Europe, today the largest number of immigrants come from Mexico, followed by the Philippines, Cuba, El Salvador, Canada, Germany, and China.[11] Liturgy will need to address these cultural differences.

Besides the continued ethnic diversity within the American church, parish life has changed significantly.[12] More and more parishes are staffed by non-ordained leaders, and this has implications for worship, especially when a priest is unavailable to preside at the Eucharist. Moreover, increasing numbers of American Catholics are finding a home in alternative or intentional Christian communities often with a liturgical life of their own. The multicultural liturgical communities of the 1990s are quite different from anything the American liturgical pioneers might have imagined, but the principles and goals advocated by those pioneers remain as valid and relevant today as they did in 1926: to find in our liturgical prayer the impetus for social action in the face of rising inflation, unemployment, and a growing problem of homelessness; to see the Eucharist as modeling a pattern of more just, more dignified human relationships.[13]

---

[10] Steven A. Holmes, "A Surge in Immigration Surprises Experts and Intensifies a Debate," *The New York Times* (August 30, 1995) A1.

[11] Ibid., A15.

[12] See: Mark Searle, "The Notre Dame Study of Catholic Parish Life," *Worship* 60 (1986) 312–33.

[13] Franklin, Spaeth, *Virgil Michel: American Catholic*, 94–5.

The social consciousness which motivated the pioneers and promoters in those early years of the liturgical movement has been lost and desperately needs to be rediscovered. Perhaps the liturgical movement needs to be re-founded, and a sense of the Church as the Mystical Body of Christ retrieved. What is clear is that the vision to which the liturgical pioneers gave their lives remains unread, unfulfilled. The higher dream of a united Mystical Body of Christ beckons, calling for the kind of liturgical participation that flows into humble service of those in need. "Redeem the unread vision in the higher dream."

Bibliography

This bibliography is divided into five (5) sections. The first section lists all Church documents used or referred to in this study. The second section lists manuscript sources and the location of those sources. The third section lists published sources, i.e., only material published by the liturgical pioneers and promoters in the United States in the period of study: 1926–1955. Thus, material published by European liturgical pioneers, even when written in the same historical period, appears in the next section. The fourth section, related works, in addition to listing published sources by the European pioneers, also lists all secondary sources on the liturgical movement in the United States and Europe. Articles and books on topics related to the liturgical movement, e.g., on The Catholic Worker, are also included. The final section of the bibliography lists supplementary works, i.e., background material to the European and American liturgical movements, e.g., on the origins of Jansenism, on the Great Depression in the United States, etc.

Full first names are provided in the bibliography where those names are available. In some cases, the authors cited used only first initials in their published works. This is particularly the case in various "Letters to the Editor." Likewise, the name of the publisher is given except for several cases where complete publishing information was unavailable.

1. Church Documents

Flannery, Austin, ed. *Vatican Council II: The Conciliar and Post Conciliar Documents*. Northport, N.Y.: Costello Publishers, 1975.

Mansi, J.D. *Sacrorum Conciliorum nova et amplissima collectio*. Arnheim, 1926.

Neuner, J., and J. Dupuis. *The Christian Faith in the Doctrinal Documents of the Catholic Church*. New York: Alba House, 1982.

Pius X. *Tra Le Sollecitudini*. Vatican City: ASS, 1903.

Pius XII. *Christ the Center of the Church's Liturgy, Address by His Holiness, Pope Pius XII, to the Delegates of the First International Congress of Pastoral Liturgy, assembled in Vatican City, 22 September 1956*. Translated by: Vatican Press Office. Clyde, Missouri: Benedictine Convent of Perpetual Adoration, 1957.

_____. *Mediator Dei*. Vatican City: AAS, 1947.

_____. *Mystici Corporis*. Vatican City: AAS, 1943.

Vatican II. *Sacrosanctum Concilium*. Vatican City: AAS, 1963.

2. Manuscript Sources

The Catholic Worker Collection (W-6). Marquette University Archives, Milwaukee, Wisconsin.

The Christian Family Movement (CFM) Papers. University of Notre Dame Archives, Notre Dame, Indiana.

The Godfrey Diekmann Papers (1160–1170). Saint John's Abbey Archives, Collegeville, Minnesota.

The Reynold Hillenbrand Papers (6/26; 8/2). University of Notre Dame Archives, Notre Dame, Indiana.

The Virgil Michel Papers (Z-20–Z-30). Saint John's Abbey Archives, Collegeville, Minnesota.

3. Published Sources

A.E.H. "Missal," *America* 64 (1941) 437.

Alfred, U. "The Liturgy and Catholic Education," *Journal of Religious Instruction* 16 (1945–46) 620–628.

Allen, Mary Lathrop. "Chant and the Lay Apostolate," *The Caecilia* 74 (1946–47) 192–194.

Arnaud, Leopold. "The Living Tradition of Christian Art," *LA* 9 (1941) 47–48.

Arnold, F. "Liturgy in the School," *The Catholic Educator* 24 (1953–54) 169–170.

B.A.B. "A Father Leads the Way," *OF* 7 (1933) 377–378.

Beauduin, Lambert. "Grief contre le movement Liturgique," *Questions Liturgiques* 2 (1912) 529–536.

"Belgian American Liturgy," *Placidian* 4 (1927) 103–123.

Benedictine Liturgical Conference, ed. *Proceedings: 1940 National Liturgical Week*. Newark: The Benedictine Liturgical Conference, 1941.

_____. *Proceedings: 1941 National Liturgical Week*. Newark: The Benedictine Liturgical Conference, 1942.

Bentley, Paul. "Letter to the Editor," *LA* 14 (1945) 22–23.

Bernarda, M. "The Liturgy Taught Through Formal Discussion," *The Catholic Educator* 18 (1947–48) 244–245.

Bethune, Adélaide de. "Common Sense," *The Catholic Digest* 1 (1937) 1–4.

_____. "This 'Here' Life," *The Christian Social Art Quarterly*, 3 (1940) 7–10.

Boisvert, Roland. "The Singing of Women During the Liturgical Functions of the Catholic Church," *The Caecilia* 61 (1934) 445–447.

Boswell, Peyton. "The Valiant Few," *Art Digest* 11 (1937) 3.

Bouwhuis, Caroline M. "Missals," *America* 62 (1939) 46.

Boyd, William. "Militants of Christ," *OF* 16 (1941) 338–347.

_____. "The Birth of the Catholic Action Cell," *OF* 16 (1941) 107–115.

Bragers, Achille. "Chant: The Handmaid of the Liturgy," *The Caecilia* 75 (1947–48) 178–184.

Brunner, Francis A. "Posing A Problem," *The Caecilia* 77 (1949) 47–48.

Busch, William. "An Apostle of Liturgical Life," *OF* 13 (1939) 101–106.

_____. "Equality in Christ," *Interracial Review* 9 (1936) 41–43.

_____. "The Liturgy: A School of Catholic Action," *OF* 7 (1933) 6–12.

_____. "Travel Notes on the Liturgical Movement," *OF* 1 (1927) 50–55.

_____. "Travel Notes on the Liturgical Movement II," *OF* 1 (1927) 177–181.

_____. "The Breviary for the Laity," *OF* 10 (1936) 102–107.

_____. "The Divine Office for All," *OF* 10 (1936) 526–530.

Bussard, Paul. "Merely Spectators," *OF* 8 (1934) 449–452.

C. "Missals," *America* 62 (1939) 102.

Casel, Odo. *Das christliche Kultmysterium*. Regensburg: Verlag Friedrich Pustet, 1960.

_____. *Die Liturgie als Mysterienfeier*. Freiburg: Herder and Co., 1922.

Cecilia, M. "School For Revolution In Chicago," *OF* 15 (1940) 352–359.

Charnotta, Francis X. "The Vocation of the Catholic Church Musician," *Catholic Art Quarterly* 13 (1950) 129–132.

Clifford, Henry. "Letter to the Editor," *LA* 11 (1942–43) 93.

Climacus, Frater. "The Vocation of Church Music," *The Caecilia* 79 (1952) 96–97.

_____. "Why We Are Prejudiced Against the Chant," *The Caecilia* 75 (1947) 39–40.

Columban, Richard. "Liturgical Spirituality in the Organist," *The Caecilia* 68 (1941) 215.

Confrey, Burton. "Reactions to Basing Catholic Action On The Liturgy," *OF* 7 (1933) 66–72.

_____. "Using *Orate Fratres* to Introduce the Liturgical Movement," *OF* 6 (1932) 175–181.

_____. "Using *Orate Fratres* to Motivate Catholic Action" *OF* 6 (1932) 226–229.

Conti Oresti, Marie. "The Layman and the Liturgy," *The Caecilia* 71 (1943–44) 234–244, 250.

Cort, John C. "O Come All Ye Faithful," *Amen* 6 (15 May 1951) 10.

_____. "The Labor Movement: Labor and the Liturgy," *The Commonweal* 51 (1949) 316–318.

Crite, Allan Rohan. "The Meaning of Spirituals," *Catholic Art Quarterly* 17 (1953) 69.

Cummins, Patrick. "Sacred Texts, Sacred Songs," *The Caecilia* 70 (1943) 186–187, 210.

Deutsch, Alcuin. "The Liturgical Movement," *OF* 1 (1927) 391–397.

Diekmann, Godfrey. "Lay Participation in the Liturgy of the Church." In *A Symposium on the Life and Work of Pope Pius X*. Washington: Confraternity of Christian Doctrine, 1946.

Donnelly, Francis B. "Our Catholic Liturgy in a Catholic Language: A rejoinder to 'English in Our Liturgy,'" *The Commonweal* 42 (1945) 89–92.

Donnelly, Gerard. "Let Us Glorify Him With Psalms: Reasons and a plan are added to exhortation," *America* 56 (1936) 268–269.

_____. "Laymen May Read the Breviary: If matrons sang matins and chauffeurs chanted," *America* 55 (1936) 318.

Doyle, Theresa Ann. "The Teaching Sister and the Liturgical Front," *Journal of Religious Instruction* 14 (1943–44) 211–219.

E.C.S. "A Convert's Plea," *Amen* 6 (15 May 1951) 2.

Editor. "A Bit of Vernacular History: 1946–1955," *Amen* 9 (1 July 1955) 3.

_____. "A Benedictine Monastery by Marcel Breuer," *Architectural Forum* 101 (1954) 148–156.

_____. "A Liturgical Retreat for Architects and Artists," *OF* 7 (1932) 86–87.

_____. "A Panel Discussion at the National Catholic Building Convention, Chicago, 1 July 1948," *LA* 17 (1948–49) 29–34.

_____. "A Program of Liturgical Study," *America* 51 (1934) 557.

_____. "Benet Library Founder Observes 80th Birthday," *New World* (25 March 1949).

_____. "'Black List' of Forbidden Music—Music That Is Contrary to the 'Motu Proprio' of Pope Pius X Because Unliturgical in Every Respect and Inartistic From A Musical Standpoint—Masses," *The Monitor* (San Francisco, 19 December 1925).

_____. "Can't Say Mass," *The Catholic Mind* 42 (1944) 100–101.

_____. "Church Leaders Guide Movement, States Lavanoux: Architect Says That Liturgy Rules Have Approval of Authorities," *The Michigan Catholic* (2 December 1937).

_____. "Church Music and Congregational Singing," *OF* 9 (1935) 230–231.

_____. "Comment," *America* 68 (1943) 368.

_____. "Comments on the Tenth Anniversary of *Orate Fratres*," *OF* 11 (1937) 137–138.

_____. "Communications," *OF* 5 (1931) 197.

_____. "Communications," *OF* 25 (1951) 474.

_____. "Correspondence," *LA* 8 (1939–40) 39.

_____. "Couples Sing Their Praises to God at Convention Mass," *ACT* 8 (July, 1954) 1.

_____. "Do You Like Liturgical Music?" *The Caecilia* 62 (1935) 186.

_____. "Editorial," *LA* 9 (1942) 67.

_____. "Editorial," *LA* 12 (1944) 27–28.

_____. "Editorial," *LA* 13 (1944) 2; 319.

_____. "Editorial," *LA* 14 (1946) 67; 128.

_____. "Editorial," *LA* 16 (1948) 66.

_____. "Editorial," *LA* 17 (1949) 77–79.

_____. "Editorial," *LA* 19 (1951) 53–54.

_____. "Editor's Corner," *OF* 1 (1927) 29; 32; 61–62; 90–91; 182.

_____. "Editor's Corner," *OF* 2 (1928) 93–94; 125; 220–223.

_____. "Editor's Corner," *OF* 3 (1929) 58–62; 157–158; 190; 380–381.

_____. "Editor's Note," *OF* 1 (1927) 182.

_____. "Foreword," *OF* 1 (1927) 1–2.

_____. "Gals Spur Action in Varied Fields: Reports on Best Use of the Liturgy," *ACT* (May, 1948) 3.

_____. "Historical and Liturgical Cycles," *The Caecilia* 79 (1951–52) 42–43.

_____. "Liturgical Enthusiasts and Violations of Rubrics," *HPR* 41 (1941) 1218–19.

_____. *Liturgy and the Liturgical Movement*. Collegeville: The Liturgical Press, 1926.

_____. "New Church Music Regulations: Archdiocese of New York, 1951," *The Caecilia* 78 (1951) 226–228.

_____. "Nine Years After," *OF* 10 (1936) 5–6.

_____. "Notes Along the Way," *The Chicago Catholic Worker* (February, 1941) 8.

_____. "Our Second Liturgical Day," *OF* 5 (1931) 36–40.

_____. "Parish Takes 1,000 of 'Sung Mass' Book," *ACT* 8 (September, 1954) 1.

_____. "Participation in the Mass," *The Ave Maria* 56 (1942) 678.

_____. "Prime and Compline," *The Chicago Catholic Worker* (November, 1940) 3.

_____. "Sara Benedicta O'Neill," *Amen* (1 July 1954) 20.

_____. "Society of Approved Workmen," *OF* 3 (1929) 62.

_____. "Substitution of Vernacular for Latin at Baptism," *ER* 79 (1928) 197–198.

_____. "Summer Schools in Catholic Church Music," *The Caecilia* 79 (1952) 157–160.

_____. "Summer Schools in Liturgical Music," *The Caecilia* 78 (1951) 142–143.

_____. "Teaching Chant in the Parish," *The Caecilia* 76 (1948–49) 126–128.

_____. "The Apostolate," *OF* 1 (1926) 253.

_____. "The Apostolate," *OF* 4 (1930) 424; 426; 558–562.

_____. "The Apostolate," *OF* 5 (1931) 561; 571–572.

_____. "The Apostolate," *OF* 7 (1933) 375; 418; 472.

_____. "The Apostolate," *OF* 8 (1934) 276–277; 280–281; 329; 420.

_____. "The Apostolate," *OF* 9 (1935) 34–36; 38; 132; 230–231; 332; 525.

_____. "The Apostolate," *OF* 11 (1937) 183; 229–230; 374; 518–519.

_____. "The Apostolate," *OF* 12 (1938) 272–275; 329; 523.

_____. "The Apostolate," *OF* 15 (1940) 32.

_____. "The Cisca Plan," *OF* 10 (1936) 68–77.

_____. "The Divine Office and the Christian Revolution," *Liturgy and Sociology* 1 (March, 1936) 2–3.

_____. "The Editor Writes," *The Caecilia* 69 (1941–42) 178–181.

_____. "The First National Liturgical Day in the United States," *OF* 3 (1929) 322–340.

_____. "The Liturgical Year and Adult Education," *The Catholic School Journal* 30 (1930) 290–291.

_____. "The Mystical Body at Prayer and Work in Summer Schools of Catholic Action, 1938," *OF* 12 (1938) 513–515.

_____. "What Is Wrong With Our Teaching of the Mass," *Journal of Religious Instruction* 13 (1942–43) 323–325.

Editors of the Catholic Worker. "Letter to the Editor," *OF* 8 (1934) 284.

Ellard, Gerald. "A Pilgrimage and a Vision," *America* 34 (1925) 201–203.

_____. *Christian Life and Worship*. Milwaukee: Bruce Publishing Co., 1950.

_____. "Evening Mass," *The Commonweal* 32 (1940) 37–39.

_____. *Men at Work and Worship*. New York: Longmans, Green and Co., 1940.

_____. "Open Up the Liturgy," *America* 33 (1925) 37.

_____. "Teaching the Mass in High School," *National Catholic Educational Association Proceedings* 38 (1941) 338–345.

_____. "The Dignity of a Christian," *The Catholic Digest* 1 (November, 1936) 41–42.

_____. "The Liturgical Movement: in and for America," *The Catholic Mind* 31 (1933) 61–76.

_____. "The Liturgy Course in College: A Proposed Outline," *Journal of Religious Instruction* 3 (1932–33) 783–791.

_____. "The Liturgy Course in College: Its Present Content," *Journal of Religious Instruction* 3 (1932–33) 689–695.

_____. *The Mass of the Future*. Milwaukee: Bruce Publishing Co., 1948.

_____. "What to Emphasize in Teaching the Mass," *Journal of Religious Instruction* 5 (1934–35) 11–16.

Ellis, Henry D. "Letter to the Editor," *LA* 17 (1948–49) 48.

Elms, David. "The Liturgical Movement," *The Commonweal* 12 (1930) 164.

England, John. *The Roman Missal Translated into the English Language for the Use of the Laity*. New York: William H. Creagh, 1822.

Falque, F. C. "A Liturgical Concept in Catholic Action," *OF* 9 (1935) 350–353.

Ferland, Auguste. "Priesthood of the Laity: The Foundation of Catholic Action," *OF* 15 (1940) 496–509.

Festugière, Maurice. *La liturgie catholique. Essai de synthèse suivi de quelques dèveloppements*. Maredsous 1913.

Ford, John C. "Teaching Liturgy in the Seminary," *National Catholic Educational Association Proceedings* 44 (1947) 119–130.

Gastineau, Joel. "Sure, The People Can Sing," *The Caecilia* 80 (1952–53) 56–57.

Gauchat, William. "Helping the Hobo to God," *OF* 15 (1940) 385–389.

Gibbs, Becket. "Letter to the Editor," *LA* 16 (1947) 62.

Gill, Eric. "Letter to the Editor," *LA* 8 (1939–40) 58.

Glennon, John J. "Address by Most Rev. John J. Glennon, D.D., Archbishop of St. Louis, Mo., at Organists Guild Meeting," *The Caecilia* 62 (1935) 193–194.

_____. "Christmas Pastoral Letter On Church Music," Archdiocese of Saint Louis, 1932.

Grace, Elizabeth. "The Lay Folk and the Liturgy," *OF* 4 (1930) 573.

Graf, Ernest. "A Vernacular Liturgy," *HPR* 45 (1945) 582–585.

Griffin, John H. "Letter to the Editor," *LA* 17 (1948–49) 71.

Griffin, John J. "Catholic Action and the Liturgical Life," *OF* 9 (1935) 360–371.

_____. "The Spiritual Foundation of Catholic Action," *OF* 9 (1935) 455–464.

Guardini, Romano. "A Letter from Romano Guardini," *Assembly* 12 (1986) 322–324.

_____. *The Church and the Catholic* and *The Spirit of the Liturgy*. Trans. Ada Lane. New York: Sheed and Ward, 1953.

_____. *The Lord*. Trans. Elinor Castendyk Briefs. Chicago: Henry Regnery Company, 1954.

_____. *Vom Geist der Liturgie*. Maria Laach, 1918.

Guenther, Francis J. "Church Music, a Neglected Liturgical Art," *LA* 13 (1944–45) 38–39.

_____. "Handmaid of the Liturgy," *LA* 13 (1944–45) 84–85.

Guéranger, Prosper. *Essai historique sur l'Abbaye de Solesmes*. Le Mans, 1846.

_____. *L'Année liturgique*. Paris: H. Oudin, 1841.

_____. *Le Monastere Saint-Pierre de Solesmes*. Solesmes, 1955.

Guinan, Alastair. "Modern Mass Music," *The Commonweal* 19 (1934) 353–354.

Harbrecht, John J. *The Lay Apostolate*. St. Louis: B. Herder Book Company, 1929.

Harrer, Philibert. "A Liturgical Parish," *OF* 7 (1933) 447–454.

Hayburn, Robert. "The Place of the Organist in Worship," *The Caecilia* 77 (1949) 33–34.

Hellriegel, Martin B. *How to Make the Church Year a Living Reality*. Notre Dame: University of Notre Dame Press, 1955.

_____. "Liturgy and the Minor Seminaries," *National Catholic Educational Association Proceedings* 33 (1937) 550–556.

_____. "Monsignor Hellriegel's Music Program," *The Caecilia* 83 (1955) 73–74.

_____. "The Spread of the Liturgical Movement," *Journal of Religious Instruction* 7 (1936–37) 208–214.

_____. *Vine and Branches*. St. Louis: Pio Decimo Press, 1948.

Hellriegel, Martin B., and A. J. Jasper. "Der Schluessel zur Loesung der sozial Frage." St. Louis: Central Blatt (July–August, 1925).

_____. *The True Basis of Christian Solidarity*. Trans. William Busch. St. Louis: Central Bureau of the Catholic Verein, 1947.

Herwegen, Ildefons. "Kirche und Mysterium," in *Mysterium, Gesammelte Arbeiten Laacher Monche*. Münster: Aschendorff, 1926.

_____. *The Art Principle of the Liturgy*. Trans. William Busch. Collegeville: The Liturgical Press, 1931.

Hillenbrand, Reynold. "The Priesthood and the World," *National Liturgical Week 1951: Proceedings*. Conception, Missouri: The Liturgical Conference, 1951, 162–170.

_____. "The Spirit of Sacrifice in Christian Society: Statement of Principle," *National Liturgical Week, 1943*. Ferdinand, Indiana: The Liturgical Conference, 1944, 100–108.

Howell, Clifford. "Language of the Liturgy," *The Commonweal* 52 (1950) 606.

Hurley, R. "Letter to the Editor," *LA* 21 (1952–53) 66–67.

Jaeger, L. "The Liturgical Movement in Relation to Catholic Action," *Catholic Mind* 33 (1935) 12.

J.I.S. "Theologian," *America* 64 (1941) 494.

Johnson, George. "The Liturgy as a Form of Educational Experience," *Catholic Educational Review* 24 (1926) 528–534.

Kelly, R. "Missal," *America* 64 (1941) 437.

Kelly, Thomas G. "Liturgical Academy at Esopus," *OF* 9 (1935) 426.

Kempf, Joseph G. "The Place of the Liturgy in the Teaching of Religion," *Journal of Religious Instruction* 1 (1931) 137–147.

Kerby, William J. "The Spiritual Quality of Social Work," *ER* 78 (1928) 376–390.

Knox, Ronald. "Understanded of the People," *The Clergy Review* 23 (1947) 534–537.

Kreuter, Joseph. "Catholic Action And The Liturgy," *OF* 3 (1929) 165–170.

La Farge, John. "Catholic Religious Art." In Thurston N. Davis, ed. *A John LaFarge Reader*. New York: The America Press, 1956, 38–46.

_____. "Catholic Religious Art," *LA* 16 (1947–48) 119–123.

_____. "Further Thought on Christian Art and Artists," *America* 59 (1938) 42–43.

_____. "Religious Problems of the Catholic Artist," *America* 58 (1938) 547–548.

_____. "Shall the People Sing at Mass?" *America* 49 (1933) 270–271.

_____. *The Manner is Ordinary*. New York: Harcourt, Brace, and Co., 1954.

_____. "With Scrip and Staff: The Layman's Great Action," *America* 58 (1937) 275.

Laukemper, Bernard. "What Does A Pastor Think of Chant?" *The Caecilia* 71 (1943–44) 13–14.

Lavanoux, Maurice. "Because It Is the House of God," *LA* 8 (1940) 62–63.

_____. "Catholics and Religious Art." In *Catholicism in America: A Series of Articles from* The Commonweal. New York: Harcourt, Brace, and Co., 1953, 201–207.

_____. "Collegeville Revisited," *LA* 22 (1954) 44–47.

_____. "Saint Mark's Church, Burlington, Vermont," *LA* 11 (1942) 82.

_____. "The Liturgy, Art, and Common Sense," *LA* 13 (1944–45) 54–55.

_____. "Two Broadcasts and a Commentary," *LA* 17 (1948–49) 14–21.

Lewis, Theophilus. "The Negro Spirituals as Hymns of a People," *America* 60 (1939) 43–44.

L.J.H. "Begins to Understand the Mass," *OF* 7 (1933) 475.

Lord, Daniel. *Our Part in the Mystical Body*. St. Louis: The Queen's Work, 1935.

Lovell, Charles Linde. "The Saint Rose Liturgical Choir of Men and Boys," *LA* 15 (1946) 74.

Maginnis, Charles D. "The Artistic Debate," *LA* 12 (1944) 81–82; 85.

Martindale, C. C. "My Sacrifice and Yours," *The Month* 161 (1933) 140–149.

Matt, Alphonse J. "Father Virgil and the Social Institute," *OF* 13 (1939) 135–138.

McDonald, Joseph. "A Liturgical Apostolate," *OF* 12 (1938) 272–273.

McLaughlin, Mary. "Evening Mass," *The Commonweal* 32 (1940) 127.

McMahon, John T. "Suggested Liturgical Program for Schools I: Stemming the Leakage," *Catholic Educational Review* 29 (1931) 449–457.

_____. "Suggested Liturgical Program for Schools II: The Mass is the Center," *Catholic Educational Review* 29 (1931) 513–526.

McNaspy, Clement J. "Singing with the Church," *The Caecilia* 71 (1943–44) 205–208.

McSorley, J. "The Mystical Body," *Catholic World* 81 (1905) 307–314.

McSweeney, Eugene. "Laypraises," *America* 55 (1936) 378.

_____. "Liturgical Life," *America* 55 (1936) 117.

Michel, Virgil. "Adequate Preparation for Teaching the Mass," *Journal of Religious Instruction* 8 (1937–38) 594–598.

_____. "Announcing Baptisms," *OF* 2 (1928) 404–407.

_____. "Architecture and the Liturgy," *LA* 5 (1936) 13–18.

_____. "Are We One in Christ?," *ER* 81 (1934) 395–401.

_____. "Art and the Christ-Life," *Catholic Art Quarterly* 5 (1941) 2–5.

_____. "Back To The Liturgy," *OF* 11 (1937) 9–14.

_____. "Baptismal Consciousness," *OF* 1 (1927) 309–313.

_____. "Catholic Workers and Apostles," *OF* 13 (1939) 28–30.

_____. "City or Farm," *OF* 12 (1938) 367–369.

_____. "Communion at Mass: V. Effect of Communion," *OF* 4 (1930) 311–315.

_____. "Defining Social Justice," *The Commonweal* 23 (1936) 425–426.

_____. "Liturgical Summer School for Directors of Choirs Announced; Archbishop Urges Training of Young People for Congregational Singing; Requires Leaders to Obtain Certificates," *The Caecilia* 62 (1935) 182.

_____. "Liturgy and Art," *Catholic Art Quarterly* 19 (1955–56) 24–28.

_____. "Liturgy, True Remedy," *Social Forum* (December, 1938).

_____. "Natural and Supernatural Society," *OF* 10 (1936) 243–247; 293–296; 338–342; 394–398; 434–438.

_____. *Our Life in Christ*. Collegeville: The Liturgical Press, 1939.

_____. "Our Social Environment," *OF* 12 (1938) 318–320.

_____. "Significance of the Liturgical Movement," *NCWC* Bulletin 10 (1929) 6; 8; 26.

_____. "Social Aspects of the Liturgy," *Catholic Action* 16 (1934) 9–11.

_____. "Social Injustices," *OF* 11 (1937) 78–80.

_____. "Social Justice," *OF* 12 (1938) 129–132.

_____. "Summer Schools in Catholic Church Music," *The Caecilia* 79 (1952) 157–160.

_____. "Summer Schools in Liturgical Music," *The Caecilia* 78 (1951) 142.

_____. "The Catholic Spirit In Church Architecture: An Address to the Gargoyle Club of the Twin Cities" (unpublished manuscript) (5 April 1927).

_____. "The Family and the Mystical Body," *OF* 11 (1937) 295–299.

_____. "The Liturgical Apostolate," *The Catholic Educational Review* 25 (1927) 3–5.

_____. "The Liturgical Movement," *ER* 78 (1928) 135–145.

_____. "The Liturgical Movement and the Catholic Woman," Central Catholic Verein of America: *Annual Report, 1929*, 57–62.

_____. "The Liturgical Movement and the Future," *America* 54 (1935) 6–7.

_____. "The Liturgy and the Liturgical Movement: Some Corrections and Suggestions," *ER* 4 (1936) 225–236.

_____. *The Liturgy of the Church*. New York: Macmillan Co., 1938.

_____. "The Liturgy the Basis of Social Regeneration," *OF* 9 (1935) 536–545.

_____. *The Mystical Body and Social Justice*. Collegeville: Saint John's Abbey, 1938.

_____. "The Parish, Cell of Christian Life," *OF* 11 (1937) 433–440.

_____. "The Significance of the Liturgical Movement," *NCWC Bulletin* 10 (1929) 26–28.

_____. *The Social Question: Essays on Capitalism and Christianity by Father Virgil Michel, OSB*, Collegeville: Office of Academic Affairs, Saint John's University, 1987.

_____. "The True Christian Spirit," *ER* 82 (1930) 128–142.

_____. "Unless the Lord Build the House," *LA* 6 (1937–38) 65–68.

_____. "With Our Readers," *OF* 5 (1931) 430–431.

Mocquéreau, André, ed. *Paléographie Musicale*. Solesmes, 1889–1930.

Morrison, Joseph P. "The Spirit of Sacrifice in Christian Society: The Racial Problem," *The National Liturgical Week, 1943*. Ferdinand, Indiana, 1944.

Mueller, Franz. "Heretical Concepts of Religious Art," *The Christian Social Art Quarterly* 1 (1938) 4–6.

Munier, Joseph D. "The Catholic High-School Student and the Mass," *The Catholic Educator* 19 (1948–49) 107–109.

Murphy, John P. "Parishioners and the Liturgy," *The Clergy Review* 24 (1944) 481–486.

Musser, Benjamin, "Letter to the Editor," *LA* 1 (1932) 78.

Mutch, F. Joseph. "Question of Terms," *America* 65 (1941) 130.

Nicolas, Joep. "The Credo of An Artist," *LA* 9 (1941) 50–52.

Nuesse, C. J. "English in the Liturgy," *The Commonweal* 41 (1945) 648.

Nutting, Willis. "Daily Sung Mass," *Amen* (1 July 1954) 12.

Ohligslager, Maurus. "An Investigation of the Teaching of Liturgy in Catholic High Schools," *Catholic School Interests* 8 (1929) 187–189.

Parishioner. "What to Do?," *OF* 4 (1930) 45–46.

Parsch, Pius. *Study the Mass*. Trans. William Busch. Collegeville: The Liturgical Press, 1941.

_____. *The Liturgy of the Mass*. Translated by Frederic C. Eckhoff. St. Louis: Herder, 1936.

Perkins Ryan, Mary. "I'm Going to Like More Vernacular," *Amen* 9 (1 July 1955) 5–7; 12.

Phelan, Gerald B. "Aestheticism and the Liturgy," *LA* 4 (1935) 87–90.

Pilgrimage, Polly. "Notes on Missals," *America* 63 (1940) 213.

Puetter, William H. *Missa Recitata*. St. Louis: The Queen's Work, 1928.

Reed, Henry Hope Jr. "Toward a New Architecture?" *LA* 24 (1956) 53–56.

Reinhold, Hans A. "About English in Our Liturgy: What its advocates ask for and why," *The Commonweal* 41 (1945) 537–538.

_____. "ACTU and Liturgy," *OF* 14 (1939) 32–34.

_____. Address in *National Liturgical Week: Proceedings*. Washington: The Liturgical Conference, 1947, 11.

_____. "A Radical Social Transformation Is Inevitable," *OF* 19 (1944) 362–368.

_____. "A Revolution in Church Architecture," *LA* 6 (1937–38) 123–126.

_____. "A Social Leaven?," *OF* 25 (1951) 515–519.

_____. "Collective Ownership is Collectivism," *OF* 15 (1941) 225–227.

_____. "Denver and Maria Laach," *The Commonweal* 45 (1946) 86–88.

_____. "Depersonalized Property," *OF* 15 (1940) 273–275.

_____. "Dom Odo Casel," *OF* 22 (1948) 366–372.

_____. "Dom Virgil Michel's Columns," *OF* 13 (1939) 223–225.

_____. "Freedom of Worship," *OF* 17 (1943) 130–132.

_____. *H.A.R., The Autobiography of Father Reinhold*. New York: Herder and Herder, 1968.

_____. "House of God and House of Hospitality," *OF* 14 (1939) 77–78.

_____. "Let Us Give Thanks for Our Colored Brethren," *OF* 17 (1942) 172–174.

_____. "Letter to the Editor," *LA* 8 (1939–40) 39.

_____. "Letter to the Editor," *LA* 12 (1943) 22.

_____. "Letter to the Editor," *The Caecilia* 82 (1954) 74–75.

_____. "Liturgical Arts at Notre Dame," *LA* 17 (1948) 13–14.

_____. "Liturgical Fascism," *OF* 16 (1941) 217–221.

_____. *Liturgy and Art*. New York: Harper and Row, 1966.

_____. "Liturgy and the 'New Order,'" *OF* 15 (1940) 77–79.

_____. "More Confidence Needed," *Amen* 6 (15 May 1951) 2.

_____. "Popular Christianity," *OF* 15 (1940) 169–172.

_____. *Speaking of Liturgical Architecture*. Notre Dame: Liturgical Programs of the University of Notre Dame, 1952.

_____. "The Architecture of Rudolf Schwarz," *Architectural Forum* (January, 1939) 24–26.

_____. *The Dynamics of Liturgy*. New York: Macmillan Company, 1961.

_____. "The Vernacular Problem in 1909," *The Clergy Review* 27 (1947) 361–372.

Resch, Peter A. "On Teaching How To 'Pray the Mass,'" *Journal of Religious Instruction* 2 (1931–32) 12–18.

Ritter, Joseph E. "Toward a Living Climate of Religious Art," *LA* 23 (1954–55) 3–4.

Ross-Duggan, John K. "Letter to the Vernacular Society," *Amen* 9 (1 July 1955) 4.

Rossini, Carlo. "Women in Church Choirs," *The Caecilia* 62 (1935) 162–164.

Ryan, Edwin. "Social Action and the Liturgy," *Liturgy and Sociology* 1 (Summer, 1936) 5–7.

Ryan, George A. "Art in the Liturgy," *The Christian Social Art Quarterly* 2 (1939) 4–7.

Schaefer, Wellington J. A. "Letter to the Editor," *LA* 16 (1947–48) 136.

Schlarman, Joseph H. "The Liturgy and the Parish," *OF* 9 (1935) 10–13.

Schmitt, Kathleen W. "Offeramus," *America* 65 (1941) 186.

Schoenbechler, Roger. "Liturgy In Our Seminaries: Some Practical Suggestions," *National Catholic Educational Association Proceedings* 35 (1938) 577–592.

_____. "Pius X and Frequent Communion," *OF* 10 (1936) 59–63.

Sciocchetti, Luigi. "Letter to the Editor," *LA* 19 (1950–51) 79–80.

Sellner, John. "Worship of God in Church Music," *The Christian Social Art Quarterly* 3 (1940) 6–10.

Sheehan, John. "Catholic Action at Manhattan College," *OF* 11 (1937) 512–515.

Sheen, Fulton J. *The Mystical Body of Christ.* New York: Sheed and Ward, 1935.

_____. "The Mystical Body and the Eucharist," *The Sign* 15 (1935) 201–203.

Sheppard, Lancelot C. "The Liturgy and Language," *OF* 11 (1937) 62–68.

_____. "The Divine Office and the Laity: The Right of the Laity to the Divine Office," *OF* 11 (1937) 169–173.

Stegmann, Basil. "Christ in His Church," *OF* 7 (1933) 108–115.

_____. "Importance to Seminarians of the Present Liturgical Movement," *National Catholic Educational Association Proceedings* 29 (1932) 609–619.

Steinfels, Melville. "Modern Religious Art," *Catholic Art Quarterly* 7 (1944) 3–7.

Stoll, Vitus. "Our Present Situation?," *OF* 4 (1930) 141–142.

Sturges, Walter Knight. "Brick and Mortar Grace," *LA* 17 (1948) 12–13.

Tennien, William A. "Letter to the Editor," *LA* 12 (1943) 50.

Timmins, Anthony. "Missa Dialogata," *The Catholic World* 140 (1935) 614–615.

Ward, Justine. *Ward Hymnal.* Washington: Catholic Education Press, 1919.

Weller, Philip T. "Early Church Music in the United States," *LA* 7 (1938–39) 6–8.

Werner, G. B. "Church Goods," *America* 63 (1940) 718.

Wilson, Gladstone O. "The Mass and Interracial Justice," *Interracial Justice* 13 (1940) 28–29.

Wines, James N. "Letter to the Editor," *LA* 22 (1953–54) 130.

Winnen, J. A. "Teachers and the Liturgical Movement," *Journal of Religious Instruction* 11 (1940–41) 792–799.

Winzen, Damasus. "The Liturgical Movement and the Confraternity of Christian Doctrine," *Journal of Religious Instruction* 12 (1941–42) 566–569.

Worker, The Catholic. "From the Catholic Worker," *OF* 8 (1934) 284.

Yonkman, John. "The Formation of a Liturgical Choir," *The Caecilia* 76 (1948) 6–8.

4. Related Works

Ariovaldo Da Silva, José. *O Movimento Litúrgico No Brasil: Estudo Histórico.* Petrópolis: Editora Vozes Ltda., 1983.

Attwater, Donald. "In the Beginning was the Word: A Plea for English Words," *The Dublin Review* 429 (1944) 125–137.

Aubert, Roger. *La Chiesa negli stati moderni e i movimenti sociali, 1878–1914.* Milan: Jaca, 1993.

_____. "La géographie ecclésiologique au XIXe siècle." In *L'ecclésiologie au XIXe siècle.* Paris, 1960, 11–55.

_____. "L'ecclesiologie au concile du Vatican." In *Le Concile et les Conciles.* Paris, 1960, 245–284.

_____. "Un homme d'Eglise, Dom Lambert Beauduin," *Revue Nouvelle* 31 (1960) 225–249.

Avella, Steven M. *This Confident Church: Catholic Leadership and Life in Chicago, 1940–1965.* Notre Dame: University of Notre Dame Press, 1992.

Barrett, Noel Hackmann. "The Contribution of Martin B. Hellriegel to the American Catholic Liturgical Movement." Ph.D. diss., St. Louis University, 1976.

Barry, Colman J. *Worship and Work.* Collegeville: The Liturgical Press, 1993.

Becquet, Th. "La figure et l'oeuvre de Dom Lambert Beauduin," *Revue Général Belge* 96 (1960) 109–117.

Bluette, John. "The Mystical Body of Christ, 1890–1940, A Bibliography," *Theological Studies* 3 (1942) 261–289.

Bolger, Theodor. *Benedikt und Ignatius. Maria Laach als Collegium maximum der Gesellschaft Jesu, 1863–1872–1892.* Maria Laach, 1963.

_____. *Beten und Arbeiten, Aus Geschichte und Gegenwart Benediktinischen Lebens.* Maria Laach, 1961.

Botte, Bernard. *Le mouvement liturgique. Témoignages et souvenirs.* Paris: Desclée, 1973. English translation by John Sullivan. *From Silence to Participation: An Insider's View of Liturgical Participation.* Washington: The Pastoral Press, 1988.

Bouyer, Louis. *Dom Lambert Beauduin, Un homme d'Eglise.* Tournai: Casterman, 1964.

_____. *Liturgical Piety.* Notre Dame: University of Notre Dame Press, 1954.

Broderick, Frederick. *The Right Reverend New Dealer: John A Ryan.* New York: Sheed and Ward, 1962.

Brovelli, Franco. ed. *Ritorno alla liturgia: Saggi di studio sul movimento liturgico.* Rome: Edizioni Liturgiche, 1989.

Brown, Alden V. *The Grail Movement and American Catholicism, 1940–1975.* Notre Dame: University of Notre Dame Press, 1989.

Cardijn, Joseph. *Challenge to Action*. Ed. Eugene Langdale. Chicago: Fides, 1955.

Carey, Patrick. "Lay Catholic Leadership in the United States," *U.S. Catholic Historian* 9 (1990) 223–246.

Carroll, Catherine A. *A History of the Pius X School of Liturgical Music, 1916–1969*. St. Louis: Society of the Sacred Heart, 1989.

Chinnici, Joseph P. *Living Stones: The History and Structure of Catholic Spiritual Life in the United States*. New York: MacMillan, 1989.

_____. "Virgil Michel and the Tradition of Affective Prayer," *Worship* 62 (1988) 225–236.

Chupungco, Anscar J. *Liturgical Inculturation: Sacramentals, Religiosity, and Catechesis*. Collegeville: The Liturgical Press, 1992.

Coles, Robert. *Dorothy Day: A Radical Devotion*. Reading, Massachusetts: Addison-Wesley Publishers, 1987.

Combe, Pierre. *Justine Ward and Solesmes*. Washington: The Catholic University of America Press, 1987.

Cooke, Bernard. *The Distancing of God: The Ambiguity of Symbol in History and Theology*. Minneapolis: Fortress Press, 1990.

Davis, Florence Henderson. "Lay Movements in New York City During the Thirties and Forties," *U.S. Catholic Historian* 9 (1990) 401–418.

Davis, Thurston N., ed. *A John LaFarge Reader*. New York: The America Press, 1956.

Day, Dorothy. *Loaves and Fishes*. New York: Harper and Row, 1963.

_____. *The Long Loneliness*. New York: Harper and Row, 1952.

_____. *The Mystical Body of Christ*. East Orange, New Jersey: Thomas Barry, 1936.

Dehne, Carl. "Roman Catholic Popular Devotions." In *Christians at Prayer*, by John Gallen, ed. Notre Dame: University of Notre Dame Press, 1977, 83–99.

De Hueck, Catherine. *Friendship House*. New York: Sheed and Ward, 1946.

_____. "I Saw Christ Today," *OF* 12 (1938) 305–310.

Delfeld, Paula. *The Indian Priest: Father Philip B. Gordon, 1885–1948*. Chicago: Franciscan Herald Press, 1977.

Delloff, Linda Marie, et. al. *A Century of The CENTURY*. Grand Rapids: Eerdmans, 1984.

De Meyer, A. *Les premières controverses jansénistes en France*. Louvain: Université catholique de Louvain, 1917.

De Moreau, H. *Dom Hildebrand de Hemptinne*. Maredsous, 1930.

Diviney, Charles E. "The Mystical Body of Christ and the Negro," *Interracial Justice* 8 (1935) 86–88.

Dolan, Jay P., et al. *Transforming Parish Ministry: The Changing Roles of Catholic Clergy, Laity, and Women Religious*. New York: Crossroad Publishing Co., 1989

Dowling, Austin. "The National Catholic Welfare Conference," *ER* 9 (1928) 337–354.

Ducey, Michael. "Maria Laach and the Liturgy," *OF* 9 (1935) 108–113.

Editor. "A Papal Warning About Liturgical Excesses," *HPR* 48 (1948) 289–291.

_____. "Boston Church Music Regulations," *The Caecilia* 80 (1952) 133–136.

_____. *Bulletin of the University of Notre Dame: Religious Survey of Undergraduates, 1935–36*. Notre Dame: University of Notre Dame, 1936.

_____. *Bulletin of the University of Notre Dame: Religious Survey of Undergraduates, 1937–38*. Notre Dame: University of Notre Dame, 1940.

_____. *Christian Family Movement Annual Inquiry Program, 1953–54*. Chicago: The Christian Family Movement, 1954.

_____. "Church Music Regulations: Archdiocese of Detroit," *The Caecilia* 79 (1951) 6–7.

_____. "Church Music Regulations for Cleveland," *The Caecilia* 79 (1951) 44–45.

_____. "France: The Vernacular in the Liturgy," *The Tablet* 191 (1948) 104.

_____. *Rapports au Congrès de Malines, 23–26 September 1909*, Brussels, 1909 216–22.

_____. "Sacred Music in the Archdiocese of Chicago," *The Caecilia* 81 (1953) 93–95.

_____. "Shall Artists Run to Europe?" *Literary Digest* 100 (1929) 23–24.

_____. "Shiel School Opens Doors," *New World* (22 January 1943).

Egan, John J. "Liturgy And Justice: An Unfinished Agenda," a paper delivered at the Liturgical Symposium, Boston College, 21 June 1983, later published in *Origins* 13 (1983) 399–411.

Engelmann, Ursmar. *Beuron, die Benediktinerabtei im Donautal*. Munich: Herder, 1957.

Fallon, G. "Les Aumôniers du Travail," *Revue Sociale Catholique* 2 (1897) 372–377.

Fenwick, R. K., and Brian D. Spinks. *Worship in Transition: Highlights of the Liturgical Movement*. Edinburgh: T. and T. Clark, 1995.

Finn, Seamus P. "Virgil Michel's Contribution to Linking the Liturgical and Social Apostolates in the American Catholic Church: A 50 Year Perspective." Ph.D. diss., Boston University, 1991.

Florence, Mary. *The Sodality Movement in the United States, 1926–1936*. St. Louis: The Queen's Work, 1939.

Franklin, R. William. "Guéranger and Pastoral Liturgy: A Nineteenth Century View," *Worship* 50 (1976) 146–152.

_____. "Guéranger and Variety in Unity," *Worship* 51 (1977) 378–389.

_____. "Guéranger: A View on the Centenary of his Death," *Worship* 49 (1975) 318–328.

_____. "Johann Adam Möhler and Worship in a Totalitarian Society," *Worship* 67 (1993) 2–17.

_____. "Response: Humanism and Transcendence in the Nineteenth Century Liturgical Movement," *Worship* 59 (1985) 326–353.

_____. "The Nineteenth Century Liturgical Movement," *Worship* 53 (1979) 12–39.

Franklin, R. William, and Robert L. Spaeth. *Virgil Michel: American Catholic*. Collegeville: The Liturgical Press, 1988.

Funk, Virgil. "The Liturgical Movement, 1830–1969." In *The New Dictionary of Sacramental Worship*. Edited by Peter Fink. Collegeville: The Liturgical Press, 1990, 695–715.

Galven, Jean. "Living the Liturgy: Keystone of the Grail Vision," *U.S. Catholic Historian* 11 (1993) 22–35.

Garner, Joel Patrick. "The Vision of Liturgical Reformer: Hans Ansgar Reinhold, American Catholic Educator." Ph.D. diss., Columbia University, 1972.

Gleason, Philip. *Keeping the Faith: American Catholicism Past and Present*. Notre Dame: University of Notre Dame Press, 1987.

Glenstal Abbey, Monks of. *More About Dom Marmion*. Westminster: Newman Press, 1948.

Gray, Donald. *Earth and Altar*. Norwich: Alcuin Club Collections, No. 68, 1986.

Guilday, Peter. *The Life and Times of John Carroll*. 2 vols. New York: Encyclopedia Press, 1922.

_____. *The Life and Times of John England*. New York: America Press, 1927.

Guiton, Jacques. *The Ideas of Le Corbusier*. New York: George Braziller, 1981.

Gy, Pierre-Marie. "Dom Bernard Botte (1893–1980)," *La Maison-Dieu* 141 (1980) 167–169.

Hall, Jeremy. *The Full Stature of Christ: The Ecclesiology of Virgil Michel, OSB*. Collegeville: The Liturgical Press, 1976.

Haquin, André. *Histoire du renouveau liturgique belge, 1882–1914*. Louvain: Université catholique de Louvain, 1966.

_____. *Recherches et Syntheses: Dom Lambert Beauduin et le Renoveau Liturgique*. Grembloux: J. Ducolot, 1970.

Hammond, Peter. *Liturgy and Architecture*. New York: Columbia University Press, 1961.

Häußling, Angelus. "Briefe den Laacher Abt Ildefons Herwegen Aus Den Jahren 1917 bis 1934," *Archiv für Liturgiewissenschaft* 27 (1985) 205–262.

_____. "Um Das Jahrbuch Für Wissenschaft 'Breife an Odo Casel, O.S.B. 1920–1921,'" *Archiv für Liturgiewissenschaft* 28 (1986) 184–192.

Hayburn, Robert F. *Papal Legislation on Sacred Music, 95 A.D. to 1977 A.D.* Collegeville: The Liturgical Press, 1979.

Hilpisch, Stephanus. *Klosterleben Mönschleben.* Maria Laach: Abtei Maria Laach, 1953.

Himes, Kenneth R. "Eucharist and Justice: Assessing the Legacy of Virgil Michel," *Worship* 62 (1988) 201–224.

Hughes, Kathleen. *How Firm a Foundation: Voices of the Early Liturgical Movement.* Chicago: Liturgy Training Publications, 1990.

_____. *The Monk's Tale: A Biography of Godfrey Diekmann, O.S.B.* Collegeville: The Liturgical Press, 1991.

Huneke, Anne. "Monsignor Hellriegel and the Church Year: lent, holy week and easter," *The Priest* 39 (1983) 20–33.

Husslein, Joseph. *Social Wellsprings.* vol. 2. Milwaukee: Bruce Publishers, 1943.

Janssens, L. *L'Arte della scuola benedettina di Beuron.* Milan, 1913.

Johnson, Cuthbert. *Prosper Guéranger, 1805–1875, A Liturgical Theologian: An Introduction to his Liturgical Writings and Work.* Rome: Pontificio Ateneo S. Anselmo, 1984.

Jurgensmeier, Friedrich. *The Mystical Body of Christ As the Basic Principle of Spiritual Life.* Trans. Harriet G. Strauss. New York: Sheed and Ward, 1954.

Kauffman, Christopher J. "W. Howard Bishop, President of the National Catholic Rural Life Conference, 1928–1934," *U.S. Catholic Historian* 8 (1989) 131–140.

Kavanagh, O.S.B., Aidan. "Reflections on the Study from the Viewpoint of Liturgical History." In *The Awakening Church: 25 Years of Liturgical Renewal,* Lawrence J. Madden, S.J., ed. Collegeville: The Liturgical Press, 1992, 83–97.

Kennedy, Robert J. *Michael Mathis: American Liturgical Pioneer.* Washington: The Pastoral Press, 1987.

Klein, John Leo. "The Role of Gerald Ellard (1894–1963) in the Development of the Contemporary American Catholic Liturgical Movement." Ph.D. diss., Fordham University, 1971.

Koenker, Ernest Benjamin. *The Liturgical Renaissance in the Roman Catholic Church.* Chicago: The University of Chicago Press, 1954.

Krawczyk, Boleslaw. *Liturgia e laici nel'attivita e negli scritti di Pius Parsch.* Rome: Pontificio Ateneo S. Anselmo, 1990.

Kreitmaier, Josef. *Beuroner Kunst: eine ausdrucksform der christlichen Mystik.* Freiburg: Herder, 1914.

Kwatera, Michael. "Marian Feasts in the Roman, Troyes and Paris Missals and Breviaries and the Critique of Dom Prosper Guéranger," Ph.D. diss., University of Notre Dame, 1993.

Lenz, Desiderius. *Zur Asthetik der Beuroner Schule.* Vienna, 1912.

Leonard, William J. *The Letter Carrier,* Kansas City: Sheed and Ward, 1993.

_____. "The Liturgical Movement in the United States." In William Baruana. *The Liturgy of Vatican II: A Symposium in Two Volumes,* vol. 1. Chicago: Franciscan Herald Press, 1966, 293–331.

Lindsey, Sandra L. "Accents of Candor and Courage: H. A. Reinhold in the American Liturgical Movement," M.A. Thesis: Theology, University of Portland, 1992.

Maas-Ewerd, Th. *Die Krise der Liturgischen Bewegung in Deutschland u Österreich. Zu den Auseinandersetzungen um die "liturgische Frage" in den Jahren 1939–1944.* Freiburg: Herder, 1981.

Madden, Lawrence J. "The Liturgical Conference of the U.S.A. Its Origin and Development: 1940–1968." S.T.D. diss., University of Trier, 1969.

Maritain, Jacques. *Art and Scholasticism.* New York: Charles Scribner's Sons, 1930.

_____. "Reflections on Sacred Art," *LA* 4 (1935) 131–133.

Marx, Paul. *Virgil Michel and the Liturgical Movement.* Collegeville: The Liturgical Press, 1957.

Maurin, Peter. "The Dynamite of the Church," *Easy Essays.* New York: Sheed and Ward, 1936, 15.

Mayer, Suso. *Beuroner Bibliographie. Schriftsteller uns künstlerwährend der ersten hundert jahre der Benediktinerklosters Beuron, 1863–1963.* Beuron: Beuroner Kunstverlag, 1963.

_____. *Benediktinisches Ordensrecht in der Beuroner Kongregation.* (4 vols.) Beuron, 1929–1936.

McGreevy, John T. *Parish Boundaries: The Catholic Encounter With Race in the Twentieth–Century Urban North.* Chicago: The University of Chicago Press, 1996.

McManus, Frederick R. "American Liturgical Pioneers." In *Catholics in America, 1776–1976.* Robert Trisco, ed. Washington: NCCB Committee for the Bicentennial, 1976, 155–158.

McShane, Joseph M. *"Sufficiently Radical," Catholicism, Progressivism, and The Bishops' Program of 1919.* Washington, D.C.: The Catholic University of America Press, 1986.

_____. "'The Church Is Not For The Cells And The Caves,' The Working Class Spirituality of the Jesuit Labor Priests," *U.S. Catholic Historian* 9 (1990) 289–304.

Merkle, Coelestin. *Das hunderste Jahr; Zur hundertjahrfeier der Benediktiner in Beuron 1963*. Beuron: Beuroner Kunstverlag, 1963.

Mersch, Emile. *The Whole Christ, the Historical Development of the Doctrine of the Mystical Body in Scripture and Tradition*. Translated by John R. Kelly. Milwaukee: Bruce Publishing Company, 1938.

Michel, Virgil. "Brownson, A Man of Men," *Catholic World* 125 (1927) 755–762.

_____. Introduction to *Catholic Social Action*, by John F. Cronin. Milwaukee: Bruce Publishers, 1948, vii–viii.

_____. *Critique of Capitalism*. St. Paul: Wanderer Publishing Co., 1936.

_____. *The Nature of Capitalism,* St. Paul: Wanderer Publishing Co., 1936.

_____. "What is Capitalism?," *The Commonweal* 28 (1938) 6–9.

Michels, Thomas. "Abbot Ildefons Herwegen," *OF* 21 (1946) 2–7.

Miller, David W. "Irish Catholicism and the Great Famine," *Journal of Social History* 9 (1975) 81–98.

Mitchell, Nathan. *Cult and Controversy: The Worship of the Eucharist Outside Mass*. New York: Pueblo Publishing Company, 1982.

_____. "The Amen Corner: A Mansion for the Rat," *Worship* 68 (1994) 64–72.

Mize, Sandra Yocum. "Lay Participation in Parish Life: Little Flower Parish, South Bend, Indiana," *U.S. Catholic Historian* 9 (1990) 419–425.

Möhler, Johann A. *Die Einheit in der Kirche*. Cologne: J. Henger, 1957.

Möhler, Johann A. *Symbolik*. Cologne: J. Henger, 1958.

Moriarty, Michael. "The Associated Parishes for Liturgy and Mission, 1946–1991: The Liturgical Movement in the Episcopal Church." Ph.D. diss., University of Notre Dame, 1993.

Murphy, J. J. "A Call for Irish-American Honest Self-Appraisal," *HPR* 54 (1954) 510–516.

Neunheuser, Burkhard. "Il movimento liturgico: panorama storico e linamenti teologici." In *Anamnesis* 1, Milan: Marietti, 1991, 3–11.

_____. "Maria Laach Abbey: A Double Jubilee, 1093–1993; 1892–1992," *Ecclesia Orans* 10 (1993) 163–178.

_____. "Odo Casel in Retrospect and Prospect," *Worship* 50 (1976) 500–501.

_____. "Biographie," *La Maison-Dieu* 14 (1948) 11–14.

Ogudo, Donatus Emeka. *The Liturgical Movement in Nigeria. An Historical Study of the Liturgical Movement in the Igbo-Speaking Area of Eastern Nigeria*. Rome: Pontificio Ateneo S. Anselmo, 1987.

O'Meara, Thomas F. "The Origins of the Liturgical Movement and German Romanticism," *Worship* 59 (1985) 326–353.

Orsi, Robert Anthony. *The Madonna of 115th Street*. New Haven: Yale University Press, 1985.

O'Shea, William. "Liturgy in the United States 1889–1964," *American Ecclesiastical Review* 150 (1964) 176–196.

Piehl, Mel. *Breaking Bread: The Catholic Worker and the Origin of Catholic Radicalism in America*. Philadelphia: Temple University Press, 1982.

Piré, Abbé. *Histoire de la Congrégation des Aumôniers du Travail*. Charleroi: Castelman, 1942.

Poellmann, A. *Vom Wesen der hieratischen Kunst*. Beuron, 1905.

Priest, Canadian. "A Voice from Western Canada," *OF* 8 (1934) 42–43.

Putz, Louis J. "The Need for Developing In the Pupil an Awareness of His Role In the Mystical Body," *National Catholic Educational Association Proceedings* 51 (1954) 426–431.

Quitslund, Sonya A. *Beauduin: A Prophet Vindicated*. New York: Newman Press, 1973.

Rousseau, O. *In memoriam, Dom Lambert Beauduin, 1873–1960*. Chevetogne, 1960.

Ryan, John K. "Bishop England and the Missal in English," *ER* 95 (1936) 28–36.

Saint John's Abbey, Monks of. "The Liturgical Press," (unpublished manuscript, n.d.).

Santagada, O. "Dom Odo Casel," *Archiv für Liturgiewissenschaft* 10 (1967) 7–9.

Schilson, Arno. *Erneuerung der Kirche aus dem Geist der Liturgie*. Maria Laach: Abtei Maria Laach, 1992.

Searle, Mark. "The Notre Dame Study of Catholic Parish Life," *Worship* 60 (1986) 312–333.

Slawson, Douglas J. *The Foundation and First Decade of the National Catholic Welfare Council*. Washington: The Catholic University of America Press, 1992.

Stoughton, Judith. *Proud Donkey of Schaerbeek: Adé Bethune, Catholic Worker Artist*. St. Cloud: North Star Press, 1988.

Taft, Robert F. *The Byzantine Rite: A Short History*. Collegeville: The Liturgical Press, 1992.

_____. *The Liturgy of the Hours in East and West*. Collegeville: The Liturgical Press, 1986.

Taves, Ann. *The Household of Faith: Roman Catholic Devotions in Mid-Nineteenth Century America*. Notre Dame: University of Notre Dame Press, 1986.

Taylor, S.J., Michael J. *The Protestant Liturgical Renewal*. Westminster, Maryland: The Newman Press, 1963.

Tentler, Leslie Woodcock. *Seasons of Grace: A History of the Catholic Archdiocese of Detroit*. Detroit: Wayne State University Press, 1990.

Trapp, W. *Vorgeschichte und Ursprung der liturgischen Bewegung*. Regensburg: Verlag Friedrich Pustet, 1940.

Tuzik, Robert L. *How Firm a Foundation: Leaders of the Liturgical Movement*. Chicago: Liturgy Training Publications, 1990.

_____. "The Contribution of Msgr. Reynold Hillenbrand (1905–1979) To The Liturgical Movement In The United States: Influences and Development." Ph.D. diss., University of Notre Dame, 1989.

Verheul, A. "Hommage à Dom Bernard Botte, O.S.B., 1893–1980," *Questions liturgiques* 61 (1980) 83–92.

Verkade, Willibrord. *Yesterdays of an Artist-Monk*. New York: Kenedy and Sons, 1929.

Vishnewski, Stanley. *Wings of the Dawn*. New York: Catholic Worker Books, 1984.

Von Edwards, H. *Enkainia, Gesammelte Arbeiten zu, 800 jähringen weihegedächtnis der Abteikirche Maria Laach am 24 August 1956*. Dusseldorf: J. Henger, 1956.

Ward, Leo R. *Catholic Life, USA: Contemporary Lay Movements*. St. Louis: Herder Book Co., 1959.

Warren, Donald. *Radio Priest: Charles Coughlin, the Father of Hate Radio*. New York: The Free Press, 1996.

Weaver, F. Ellen. "The Neo-Gallican Liturgies Revisited," *Studia Liturgica* 16 (1986–87) 62–65.

Weber, Joanna. "The Sacred in Art: Introducing Father Marie-Alain Couturier's Aesthetic," *Worship* 69 (1995) 243–262.

Westermeyer, Paul. "Twentieth-Century American Hymnody and Church Music." In *New Dimensions in American Religious History*, Jay P. Dolan, ed. Grand Rapids: Eerdmans Publishing Co., 1993.

Weyland, F. "The Value of Retreats to Home Life, to Social, Business and Personal Contact," *Proceedings of the First National Conference of the Laymen's Retreat Movement in the United States of America*. Philadelphia: Laymens' Weekend Retreat League, 1928.

White, James F. *Roman Catholic Worship: Trent to Today*. New York: Paulist Press, 1995.

White, Susan J. *Art, Architecture, and Liturgical Reform: The Liturgical Arts Society, 1928–1972*. New York: Pueblo Publishing Company, 1990.

Wiethoff, William Edward. "Popular Rhetorical Strategy in the American Catholic Debate Over Vernacular Reform," Ph.D. diss., University of Michigan, 1974.

Wills, Garry. *Bare Ruined Choirs: Doubt, Prophecy, and Radical Religion*. Garden City: Doubleday and Company, Inc., 1972.

Winzen, Damasus. "Progress and Tradition at Maria Laach," *LA* 10 (1941) 19–22.

Zielinski, Martin A. "Working for Interracial Justice: The Catholic Interracial Council of New York, 1934–1964," *U.S. Catholic Historian* 7 (1988) 233–260.

Zotti, Mary Irene. *A Time of Awakening: The Young Christian Worker Story in the United States, 1938–1970*. Chicago: Loyola University Press, 1991.

5. Supplementary Material

Abercrombie, Nigel. *The Origins of Jansenism*. London: The Clarendon Press, 1966.

Adam, Adolf. *Les Jansénistes au XVII siècle*. Paris: Casterman, 1968.

Aubert, Roger. "La géographie ecclésiologique au XIXe siècle." In *L'ecclésiologie au XIXe siècle*. Paris: Editions de l'Orante, 1960, 5–11.

Barry, Colman J. *The Catholic Church and German Americans*. Milwaukee: Bruce Publishers, 1953.

Bishop, John P. "The Arts," in *The 1940s: Profile of a Nation in Crisis*, by Charles Eisinger. Garden City, New York: Doubleday and Co., 1969.

Brown, Burchard and Bush Brown. *Architecture of America*. Cambridge, Massachusetts: The M.I.T. Press, 1969.

Cashman, Sean Dennis. *America in the Twenties and Thirties: The Olympian Age of Franklin Delano Roosevelt*. New York: New York University Press, 1988.

Chandler, Lester W. *Economics of Money and Banking*. New York: Harper, 1953.

Congar, Yves. "My Path-Findings in the Theology of Laity and Ministries," *The Jurist* 32 (1972) 169–188.

Davis, Cyprian. *The History of Black Catholics in the United States*. New York: Crossroad Publishing Co., 1993.

De Meyer, A. *Les premières controverses jansénistes en France*. Louvain: Université Catholique de Louvain, 1917.

De Percin De Montgaillard, J. F. *Du droit et du pouvoir des évêques de régler les offices divins dans leurs diocèses*. Paris, 1686.

Dolan, Jay P. "Religion and Social Change in the American Catholic Community," in Lotz, David W., *Altered Landscapes: Christianity in America, 1935–1985*. Grand Rapids: Eerdmans Publishing Co., 1989, 42–60.

_____. *The American Catholic Experience: A History from Colonial Times to the Present*. Notre Dame: University of Notre Dame Press, 1992.

_____., ed. *The American Catholic Parish: A History from 1850 to the Present. Volume 1, The Northeast, Southeast and South Central States*. New York: Paulist Press, 1987.

_____., ed. *The American Catholic Parish: A History from 1850 to the Present. Volume 2, The Pacific, Intermountain West and Midwest States*. New York: Paulist Press, 1987.

_____. *The Immigrant Church: New York's Irish and German Catholics, 1815–1865* Baltimore: The John's Hopkins University Press, 1975.

Enochs, Ross Alexander. "Lakota Mission: Jesuit Mission Method and the Lakota Sioux, 1886–1945." Ph.D. diss., University of Virginia, 1994.

Faherty, William Barnaby. *American Catholic Heritage: Stories of Growth*. Kansas City: Sheed and Ward, 1991.

Fisher, James Terence. *The Catholic Counterculture in America, 1933–1962*, Chapel Hill: The University of North Carolina Press, 1989.

Flynn, George Q. *American Catholics and the Roosevelt Presidency*. New York, 1968.

_____. *Roosevelt and Romanticism: Catholics and American Diplomacy, 1937–1945*. Westport, Connecticut: Greenwood Press, 1976.

Fogarty, Gerald. "Public Patriotism and Private Politics: The Tradition of American Catholicism," *U.S. Catholic Historian* 4 (1984–85) 1–48.

Giedion, Stephen. *Space, Time and Architecture*. Cambridge, Massachusetts: Harvard University Press, 1956.

Gill, Eric. *Art Nonsense and Other Essays*. London: Cassell and Co., 1929.

_____. *Beauty Looks After Herself*. New York: Sheed and Ward, 1933.

_____. *Art and a Changing Civilization*. London: John Lane, 1934.

Gleason, Philip. *Catholicism in America*. New York: Harper and Row, 1970.

Gray, James Henry, and Loren Baritz. *The Culture of the Twenties*. Indianapolis: Bobbs-Merrill, 1970.

Gray, James Henry, and Charles Angoff. *The Tone of the Twenties, and Other Essays*. South Brunswick, New Jersey: A.S. Barnes, 1966.

Gray, James Henry, and Edmund Wilson. *The Twenties: From Notebooks and Diaries of the Period*. New York: Farrar, Straus, and Giroux, 1975.

Halsey, William M. *The Survival of American Innocence: Catholicism in an Era of Disillusionment, 1920–1940*. Notre Dame: University of Notre Dame Press, 1980.

Haughey, John. "The Eucharist and Intentional Communities." In *Alternative Futures for Worship* 3, Bernard Lee, ed. Collegeville: The Liturgical Press, 1987, 49–84.

Hennesey, James. *American Catholics: A History of the Roman Catholic Community in the United States*. New York: Oxford University Press, 1981.

Hitchcock, Henry-Russell. *Architecture, Nineteenth and Twentieth Centuries*. New York: Penguin Books, 1958.

Holmes, Steven A. "A Surge in Immigration Surprises Experts and Intensifies a Debate," *The New York Times*, (August 30, 1995) A1, A15.

Kantowicz, Edward R. *Modern American Catholicism, 1900–1965: Selected Historical Essays*. New York: Garland Publishing, Inc., 1988.

Kincheloe, Samuel C. *Research Memorandum on Religion in the Depression*, No. 33. New York: Social Science Research Council, 1937.

LaFollette, Suzanne. "The Artist and the Depression," *The Nation* 137 (1933) 264.

_____. "The Government Recognizes Art," *Scribner's Magazine* 95 (1934) 132.

Le Corbusier. Trans. Frederick Etchells. *Towards a New Architecture*. London: Architectural Press, 1927.

Liptak, Dolores. *Immigrants and Their Church*. New York: Macmillan Publishing Co., 1989.

Lynd, Helen M. and Robert S. Lynd. *Middletown: A Study in American Culture*. New York: Harcourt, Brace, and World, 1929.

Marty, Martin. *An Invitation to American Catholic History*. Chicago: St. Thomas More Press, 1986.

_____. *Modern American Religion: The Noise of Conflict, 1919–1941*. Chicago: The University of Chicago Press, 1991.

McElvaine, Robert S. *Down & Out In The Great Depression: Letters from the "Forgotten Man."* Chapel Hill: University of North Carolina Press, 1983.

McGreevy, John T. "American Catholics and the African-American Migration, 1919–1970." Ph.D. diss. Stanford University, 1992.

McNally, Michael J. "A Peculiar Institution: Catholic Parish Life and the Pastoral Mission to the Blacks in the Southeast, 1850–1980," *U.S. Catholic Historian* 5 (1986) 67–80.

Mumford, Lewis. *Sticks and Stones*. New York: Dover Publishers, 1955.

O'Brien, David. *American Catholics and Social Reform*. New York: Oxford University Press, 1968.

_____. *Public Catholicism*. New York: Macmillan Publishing Co, 1989.

Perrett, Geoffrey. *America in the Twenties: A History*. New York: Simon and Schuster, 1982.

Raboteau, Albert J. "Black Catholics: A Capsule History," *Catholic Digest* (June, 1983) 32–33.

Recken, Stephen L. "Fitting In: The Redefinition of Success in the 1930s," *Journal of Popular Culture* 27 (1993) 205–222.

Richards, J. M. *An Introduction to Modern Architecture*. New York: Penguin Books, 1953.

Rodnitzky, Jerome L. *Essays on Radicalism in Contemporary America*. Arlington: University of Texas Press, 1972.

Roth, Leland. *America Builds: Source Documents in American Architecture and Planning.* New York: Harper and Row, 1983.

Ryan, John A. *Distributive Justice: The Right and Wrong of Our Present Distribution of Wealth.* New York: The Paulist Press, 1916.

_____. "New Deal and Social Justice," *The Commonweal* 19 (1934) 657–659.

_____. *Organized Social Justice: An Economic Program for the United States Applying Pius XI's Great Encyclical on Social Life.* New York: Paulist Press, n.d.

Segers, M. "Equality and Christian Anarchism: The Political and Social Ideas of the Catholic Worker Movement." In *Modern American Catholicism, 1900–1965,* Edward Kantowicz, ed. New York: Garland Publishing Co., 167–230.

Strakosch, Avery. "I Married An Artist," *Saturday Evening Post* (3 October 1936) 27–28.

Susman, Warren. *Culture and Commitment, 1929–1945.* New York: George Braziller, 1973.

Tafuri, Manfredo. *Design and Capitalist Development.* Cambridge, Massachusetts: The M.I.T. Press, 1976.

_____. *Theories and History of Architecture.* New York: Harper and Row, 1976.

U.S. Department of Commerce, Bureau of the Census. *Abstract of the Fourteenth Census of the United States.* Washington: Government Printing Office, 1923.

_____. *Abstract of the Fifteenth Census of the United States.* Washington: Government Printing Office, 1933.

Vicchio, Stephen J., and Virginia Geiger, eds. *Perspectives on the American Catholic Church: 1789–1989.* Westminster, Maryland: Christian Classics, 1989.

Whiffen, Marcus. *American Architecture Since 1780.* Cambridge, Massachusetts: The M.I.T. Press, 1969.

Yox, Andrew P. "An American Renaissance: Art and Community in the 1930s," *Mid-America* 72 (1990) 107–118.

Yuhaus, Cassian. *The Catholic Church and American Culture: Reciprocity and Challenge.* New York: Paulist Press, 1990.

Subject Index

Index of Names